Contemporary
International Law

SECOND EDITION

Contemporary International Law

A Concise Introduction

Werner Levi

Westview Press
BOULDER • SAN FRANCISCO • OXFORD

Copyright © 1979, 1991 by Westview Press, Inc.

Published in 1991 in the United States of America by Westview Press, Inc., 5500 Central Avenue, Boulder, Colorado 80301, and in the United Kingdom by Westview Press, 36 Lonsdale Road, Summertown, Oxford OX2 7EW

Library of Congress Cataloging-in-Publication Data
Levi, Werner, 1912–
  Contemporary international law : a concise introduction / Werner Levi. — 2nd ed.
    p.   cm.
  Includes bibliographical references and index.
  ISBN 0-8133-1094-6.   ISBN 0-8133-1095-4 (pbk.)
  1. International law.   I. Title.
JX3091.L48   1991
341—dc20   90-41677
                                                                                CIP

Printed and bound in the United States of America

The paper used in this publication meets the requirements
of the American National Standard for Permanence of Paper
for Printed Library Materials Z39.48-1984.

10   9   8   7   6   5   4   3   2   1

CONTENTS

ABBREVIATIONS

ADIRC	Académie de Droit International, *Recueil des Cours.* The Hague.
AJIL	*American Journal of International Law*
Ann. Dig.	*Annual Digest of Public International Law Cases* (covering cases to 1945; continued thereafter as *ILR*)
AV	*Archiv des Völkerrechts*
BYIL	*British Yearbook of International Law*
F. Supp.	*Federal Supplement* (decisions of the U.S. District Courts)
F. 2d.	Federal Reporter 2nd series (decisions of the U.S. District Courts)
ICJ	*Reports of Judgments, Advisory Opinions and Orders* of the International Court of Justice
ILM	*International Legal Materials* (published by the American Society of International Law, Washington, D.C.)
ILR	*International Law Reports* (continuation of *Ann. Dig.*, covering cases after 1945)
Int. & Comp. L. Q.	*International and Comparative Law Quarterly*
JDI (Clunet)	*Journal du Droit International* (from 1915; founded by Edouard Clunet 1874)
PCIJ	*Judgment, Orders and Advisory Opinions* of the Permanent Court of International Justice
RGDIP	*Revue Générale de Droit International Public*, 3rd series
UN Reports	United Nations *Reports of International Arbitral Awards*
US Reports	*United States Supreme Court Reports* (including reports by reporters Dallas, Cranch, Wheaton, Peters, Howard, Black, Wallace)
Z	*Zeitschrift für ausländisches öffentliches Recht und Völkerrecht*

Contemporary
International Law

PART 1
THE NATURE
AND FUNCTION
OF INTERNATIONAL LAW

Law is an instrument for creating, maintaining, and changing a society. Law prescribes the behavior of the society's members so that social order—that is, regularity and predictability of social behavior—prevails, the survival of the society becomes possible, and the members can live in peaceful coexistence. When law addresses itself to natural and juridic persons (corporations and associations, for instance) in national societies, it is called municipal law. When law addresses itself mainly to states in international society, it is called international public law. The function of law is the same in both cases.

What the prescribed behavior of individuals or states is to be, hence what law is needed to produce an orderly society, is neither predetermined nor can be stated in the abstract. The members can to a very large extent choose the character of their society and then formulate their laws accordingly. In other words, law is made by people and reflects the type of society they have chosen. Only a very few fundamental and indispensable elements are beyond choice for there to be a society (for example, the life of some members must be preserved) or a legal system (for example, agreements must be kept [*pacta sunt servanda*]). Beyond those minimal requirements human choices determine the content, functioning, and efficacy of the law. The quality of the law depends therefore upon how well people have formulated their laws in the light of the goals they pursue with the help of law. Law is "living" when it parallels the social goals of the society.

When a law is found to be inadequate or ineffective, it is usually because the prescribed behavior or goal of that law is valued less than some other behavior or goal. The remedy then is either to adjust the law (bring it up to date) or to change the values to fit the law. If, for instance, the veto right in the Security Council of the United Nations is found to hamper the peace-preserving function of the organization, the inadequacy does not lie in the law because no state *has* to use the veto.

1

Most particulars of a legal system are neither ordained nor immutable. Although law has a conserving quality, how well it responds to social change depends largely upon the degree of flexibility built into the system. Many great differences between national and international legal systems exist because of the values and corresponding choices of people regarding their national society and the international society.

This relationship between people and their law makes clear two very important factors in the origin of law. The first is that a law must be preceded by a choice regarding the desired behavior or, more broadly, the desired character of the society. The second is that there must be some people who make the choice and the corresponding laws.

The function of choosing the character and details of the society belongs to politics, which determines, to use Harold D. Lasswell's definition, "who gets what, when and how." Politics is an ongoing process in which social issues are evaluated and decided. Once an issue is decided, it is embedded, firmed, and conserved in the law. The result is that every law is preceded by a political decision in, for instance, a parliament, a government council, or an international conference. To understand the meaning and significance of a law fully, as well as its efficacy, it is necessary to consider the political context from which it originated.

The function of making the choice and the corresponding law is performed by those in a society who possess, organize, and exercise power and those whom they represent (or who give them the power) in the political system (a major determinant of the society's character). In national societies, this group can be the aristocracy, the capitalists, the proletariat, the majority party; in international society, this group can be the states sufficiently influential to make and enforce individual decisions.

The different distribution and uses of power largely account for differences in legal systems. The unique formal organization of power in modern international society endows the international legal system with a character different from all municipal legal systems.

Within states, power is organized vertically from bottom to top. The eventually decisive power potential—the potential enabling enforcement of political decisions and the law—is located at the top, normally in a central government. In international society, power is organized horizontally. Each state is an independent power center, with neither any one state nor an organization of states having a decisive power potential to control the entire international society.

Such diffusion of a power potential affects the quality of international law. Diffusion aggravates agreement on the creation, interpretation, and enforcement of the law. There is usually no authoritative backing of international law other than by every state, the interested party itself. Each state assumes the right to fulfill these tasks itself and in its own interest. It does so, most of the time, with the use of its power potential, which generates the urge to enhance this potential and thus becomes a major cause of the eternal struggle for power.

Possession of a power potential by each state enables it sometimes to impose, reject, or escape the law. The unequal magnitude of the power potential among states, its changing dimensions over time, and the impossibility of measuring it with reliability make a prediction of whose power will prevail (who the lawmaker will be and how existing law will be interpreted) very difficult in any given case. A state's acceptance of a legal norm will depend upon its effect upon the state's national interest. Rejection of a norm may endanger the very existence of international society. In the most extreme cases, such rejection may lead to war. This is a basic, qualitatively different situation from national societies, where individual disobedience of the law by a citizen can have no such consequences, except perhaps in the case of civil war.

With the national interest as the most powerful motor of a state's behavior toward international law, there must be constant awareness that states are using international law as an instrument to further their own ends. Two great difficulties result. One is that the attitude of a state toward international norms is, with very few exceptions, unpredictable because the national interest is nothing more than what the government of the day says it is. The law, instead of supporting order and social stability, tends to become a tool to reach the political goals of states. Nevertheless, the growing interaction among states is making the fulfillment of national interests dependent upon the welfare of other states. As a result, the prospect for an orderly society is improved, as is the efficiency of international law.

The other difficulty is that states will not readily admit such selfish use of the law. They will affirm that their use of the law is determined "objectively," not by their particular interests. They will attempt to endow their use of legal norms with universal validity and justice. If they succeed, they will remove the stigma of selfishness and possibly even attract supporting states. The norm's legitimacy will be enhanced. To strengthen this result, lawgivers, national and international, like to invoke a higher authority than themselves as the source of the law. God, the will of the people, nature, and right reason have all been used for this purpose. What started as a utilitarian principle serving some state's interest is thus metamorphosed into a moral principle. The alleged universality of the norm obliterates its lowly origin. The higher source invoked by the lawgiver obscures the norm's mundane function of protecting some state's interest. The fact remains that no matter whom or what the lawgiver claims as the originator of the law, it is always mediated by a person and thus becomes human, reflecting the strength and weaknesses of human beings.

With no formal, central legislature, complete judiciary, or disinterested enforcer, the genesis of laws, their interpretation, and their application must be found in the interests of states. In national societies, the common and foremost interest of citizens in the maintenance of their states (nationalism) serves as a major basis and partial explanation of the municipal legal system, especially its hierarchical order. Such an overwhelming, comprehensive common interest in the international society is absent among states, and an equally strong foundation of the law is missing. There is no common referent for the making or interpretation of legal norms, except, for instance, when national interests coincide. The same international norm can be and remains interpreted in quite different ways by states according to their individual interests. If these interests deviate from each other, the effectiveness of international law becomes greatly weakened if not nullified. Even unanimity in accepting a treaty may not improve the situation if the signatories interpret it in their own ways. When on June 13, 1989, President Mikhail Gorbachev and Chancellor Helmut Kohl made a joint declaration that the internal and external policy of states must be based on the preeminence of international law, they may not have agreed on the same thing!

There is little incentive for states to sacrifice their national interests to an international interest. Therefore, they have no incentive to create an effective international law, except insofar as this may serve their purposes. Many of the interests states are pursuing are heterogeneous and conflictive. Once these interests are designated "vital," they become nonnegotiable. The changing conditions and volume of international intercourse, which affect national interests differently, can create limited common, similar, or coinciding interests. Law then serves useful purposes. The conditions of international intercourse can also create conflicts. Then, with no common higher interest, each side will expediently use law to support the state's claim. Within states, such conflicts among citizens are limited by subordination to the common interest in the welfare of the state. But with each state being interested more in its own than in any common international welfare, there is no such touchstone by which an individual norm can be judged.

Yet, there is international law and states claim to obey it, although they often do so according to their idiosyncratic interpretation. As will be seen, they do so for a great number of reasons, virtually all selfish. For example, the increasing cost of war, or perhaps the unfeasibility of a major war, makes a legal settlement of conflicting interests more attractive. At any rate, war costs diminish the types of interests over which states are willing to fight a war.

How much states adjust the rule of law to their national interests is well illustrated by the reluctance or refusal of many new states* or Communist states to accept the entire body of international law and

---

*New states become old. Some problems of the international legal system are specifically connected to the age of states, just as some are connected to a state's state of development. In this book *new states* is a shorthand reference to all states of the Third and Fourth Worlds.

details of the legal system. These states argue that they do not necessarily share the interests that gave rise to this body of law, which was created mostly before their arrival on the international scene, or that they are opposed to some of these interests.

An even more impressive illustration of the state-interest argument is the evolution of international law. It has developed as a response to the needs of states. In the Middle Ages there was no international law; in the late twentieth century, there is a vast body of customary and treaty law resulting from interactions in international society. Even when international law was the law regulating relations mainly between Western states, it was not static; it reflected the dynamic patterns of politics. Most judges, arbitrators, and writers dealing with international law, just as those dealing with municipal law, are quite aware that law is a living force. They pay their respects to it in the various forms: judgments, awards, treaties, and interpretations in which legal norms find expression. "Old" law does not prevail because of its age but because it benefits someone with the power to maintain it. "New" law arises not because of its novelty but because someone who will benefit from a legal innovation has the power to create it.

International law, like any other, has always depended upon its sociopolitical environment and origin. These characteristics of the international legal system require that in the study of international law, its sources and origins be analyzed as indicators of its purpose; that it be examined in the context of the international system past and present, especially in the context of international politics as the major generator of international law; and that its relation to municipal law receive attention. With some clarity on these points, the rationale of individual legal principles and norms and the attitude of states toward them—which limit their effectiveness—become more intelligible.

1
THE DEVELOPMENT
OF INTERNATIONAL LAW

Some roots of modern international law go back to several ancient civilizations and canon law. The Romans, Greeks, Jews, Indians, and Chinese in their external relations had rules about treaties, the exchange of ambassadors, trade, the treatment of aliens, and war. Traces of those rules can be found in contemporary international law, but the disappearance of those states from an international society dominated by the Western states (or their insignificance in that society) has practically turned contemporary international law into a creature of Western states.

The law was designed to serve the purposes of the ancient cultures. The historic details of the growth of law evidence its continual response to needs at successive stages in the development of international society—at that time European political and economic life. These needs eventually included norms to assure the predominant position of the Western states in the world. Thus, new and Communist states often found at their birth that international law was unsuitable or outright opposed to their interests, so those states accepted international law only selectively. As was to be expected, they are insisting now as full members of international society that modern international law reflect their interests as well as those of the older Western states. Their success in achieving the inclusion of their interests is extremely limited. This is partly due to their insistence upon sovereignty, which has certain inevitable legal and political consequences not to their liking. In principle sovereignty prevents special treatment for these states, it maintains the heavy politicization of international society, and it supports the foremost role of power. Nevertheless, to some extent, as the needs of newer states are joined to those of older states, the "new" international law is influenced, as it has always been, by the requirements of an enlarged international society.

The Middle Ages

Before the rise of nation-states in the fifteenth and sixteenth centuries, there was neither room nor need for a comprehensive body of rules regulating relations between existing political entities. Only a few subjects (mainly relating to warfare) were controlled by legal norms. The Holy Roman emperor and the pope reigned over the Western world. Under their overall rule, extraordinarily complex sets of feudalistic relationships of dominance and subjection crisscrossed an equally complex, politically fractionated Europe.

Relations among lords, seigniors, and other possessors of power were of a personal nature. Their rights and duties referred to specific, limited subjects within a given geographic area, so that several lords could have different jurisdictions and competences in the same territory. Exclusivity or monopoly of political power within a territorially defined area was unknown. Only exceptionally was a ruler able to amass sufficient power to control a given territory without its being split up into different jurisdictions of several rulers. In such cases, the ruler was able to prevent the exercise of power by others in his or her territory; to lay claims to the coastline or even the high seas contiguous to the ruler's territory (as, for example, Venice did to the Adriatic Sea or England did to the North Sea); and eventually to claim territories the ruler conquered overseas.

Mainly as a result of new economic forces, the Holy Roman Empire broke down, which brought about the collapse of the at least nominally centralized order of Europe and foreshadowed the need for a different legal system. The reality of a unified Christian community with one law and order for all humankind faded away. Enough of the idea survived, however, to affect international law for several centuries to come. The influence of Christian values was particularly important. For eventually, the Peace of Westphalia in 1648 confirmed the existence of independent states, with mastery over their territories. Kings and princes eagerly furthered this development, correctly calculating that future new states would be considered their personal dominion, granting them what came to be called sovereignty toward other states as well as toward their own people.

The Fifteenth and Sixteenth Centuries

As new centers of independent power arose, laws regulating their coexistence and relations were needed, although until the age of absolutism had passed, these laws had to refer to the person of the rulers more than to political entities. Gradually, the relationships of subordination and superordination under the universalist reign of one emperor and pope were replaced by a system of coordination among sovereign rulers. The feudalistic entities with their relatively uncertain borders gave way to states based upon sharply defined territory. In this territory, kings and princes had exclusive personal power over people and things. By analogy to the norms of Roman law regarding private property, the dominion of rulers over their territory, including acquisition and transfer, was largely defined by those norms. The preeminent role of territory in international law began.

Laws were needed to safeguard the individuality and inviolability of the new states, the power of their rulers, and the orderliness of their relations with each other. Some of these laws were taken over in adjusted form from the ancient Jewish, Greek, and Roman worlds. Others were gradually generated as need and practice demanded.

Of equal importance was the spirit in which statesmen and writers conceived the development of international law. It was inspired by Roman law, Christianity, and the classic (mainly Renaissance) tradition. This inspiration perpetuated religious and moral values and a sense of (Christian) community. These values restrained the use of power by considerations of a "divine" or "natural" social order and humanitarianism. This restraint was limited, however, to relations among the members of the Christian community.

The surviving sense of community did not prevent or even mitigate hostilities among European states. As a group, however, these states felt superior to peoples outside their select circle. They all felt justified, when the occasion arose, to exclude these peoples from the realm of international law. Imperialism and colonialism with virtually unlimited means were legitimate in this legal system. It tried to regulate these activities only as they affected the European states among themselves. Not until the middle of the nineteenth century were some "non-Christian" states fully admitted to the select circle, and not until the middle of the twentieth century were most traces of this superiority complex eradicated, at least formally. Not surprisingly, the newer states of the twentieth century approach international law gingerly and are choosy regarding the parts they will accept or reject.

The Seventeenth and Eighteenth Centuries

The consciousness and the generally weak reality of the international Christian community continued into the seventeenth and eighteenth centuries. This sense of community may have contributed to states taking their subjection to international law for granted and monarchs softening their absolutism by considerations of human dignity. At any rate, the danger that relations between independent, territorially defined states under sovereign rulers would be chaotic was avoided. Practicality and probably family relations among Europe's rulers, as well as class considerations (noblesse oblige!), permitted coexistence under the legal rule of custom and treaties even before legal writers justified the binding force of international law upon sovereign rulers by natural law and the demands of the Christian community.

As disputes between sovereign rulers arose, diplomacy and war were substituted for the former authoritative settlement by emperor or pope. Nevertheless, during the seventeenth and part of the eighteenth centuries the idea of just wars (*bellum justum*) as the only legal wars remained influential. Monarchs claimed to fight wars only to right wrongs, even though the benefits the victors reaped sometimes seemed disproportionate to the alleged wrong. The more humane conduct of war during the eighteenth century and after was probably due more to the rise of professional and disciplined armies than to high moral considerations.

Once the multitude of specific limited jurisdictions of various rulers within the same geographic area came to an end and was replaced by the principle of territoriality with one sovereign ruler as the basis of the state, a number of legal consequences followed. One was the absolute power and exclusive jurisdiction of one ruler in his or her territory. The second was the prohibition of interference by other monarchs in a state's internal affairs. The third was the rise of immunity. The fourth was the gradual elaboration of equality among states in diplomatic practice and of the principles regulating this practice.

The territoriality principle led to the creation of religious and other minorities within states whose protection was laid down in treaties. And so the first very modest rules to protect human rights (as applied to groups) made their appearance.

The new conditions and the multiplying relationships between independent rulers resulting from these developments needed regulation before practice had time to develop into customary law. Therefore, the body of law regarding treaties expanded significantly.

Many of the principles and norms developed during this time, especially those fortifying sovereignty, are still accepted today, with states replacing rulers as subjects of the law. But initially, the law was not applicable to peoples and territories outside Western society (except the United States when it became independent). This restriction of application was a matter of general principle, and it was sometimes expressly stipulated in treaties between European states. As discoveries and exploration expanded possessions and special privileges of European states, peoples overseas could be subjected to European rule and their territories annexed through effective occupation by the conquering state. (Sometimes occupation took only symbolic form, such as raising the flag.) The territory then became subject to treatment or mistreatment without protection of international law or, indeed, with its approval. Rules legitimizing imperialism and its means, which eventually included agreement among the seafaring states that the high seas would be free and common to all, endured well into the twentieth century, until most colonies became independent.

Early Writers on International Law

During these first centuries in the development of international law, legal and political writers had considerable influence upon its formulation. Their contribution to international law was twofold. They collected existing norms and suggested new ones. And they provided the theoretical and philosophical foundations, justifications, and guidelines for the international legal system, always keeping in mind the interests of their countries.

Initially, these writers devoted themselves to selected topics, often of particular relevance to their own states—war, reprisals, and diplomacy. The Spaniard Francisco Vitoria (1480–1546) argued that Spain was obliged to treat the conquered Indians in the Americas humanely, and he even granted these Indians a limited right to conduct "just wars" against their cruel conquerors. But he defended Spain's right in principle to create overseas dependencies and to exploit them. Another Spaniard, Francisco Suárez (1548–1617), dealt with the by then obvious interactions of states and how to regulate them. Like all writers of the era he was particularly concerned with the nature of just war and rules for its conduct. The Italian Alberico Gentili (1552–1608)—in contrast to his Spanish colleagues, who were both professors of theology—emphasized the secular nature of international law. He therefore deduced the rules of the law not from some metaphysical source but from the practice of states and the writings of historians. He was thus the first representative of the "positivists," who argue that law is created by humans for definite conditions and purposes rather than by some supreme being for all eternity.

The limited treatment of specific topics by these writers soon became inadequate for the needs of the growing interaction among states. The requirement was for treatises about a comprehensive, unified, and generally valid body of laws to cover these extensive relationships. These treatises were forthcoming.

Outstanding was Hugo de Groot's (Grotius, 1583–1645) *De iure belli ac pacis* (On the Law of War and Peace), which brought him the sobriquet "father of international law." He became equally influential in writing on the laws of treaties, extraterritoriality, and the sea while focusing on the law of war and on the theoretical foundation of international law. Grotius believed that there was a law of nature (not necessarily divine) that could be implemented, not counteracted, by people using right reason. The combination of these two sources was, to Grotius, the foundation of international law. By this argument he avoided commitment to a particular religion and deliberately so, for he felt that to be effective, international law had to be acceptable to all, conceivably even "infidels." Even though many of the laws he formulated were influenced by a tradition now discarded, others retain their validity to this day. Three doctrines in the latter category are the applicability of laws of war to all parties regardless of the justness of the war, freedom of the seas (argued in his book *Mare liberum* and a particularly important concept for a Dutchman to undo the claims of England and other states to dominion over the seas), and extraterritoriality of ambassadors. Philosophically, Grotius was the first representative of the eclectic school, which believes that the foundation of international law is a combination of natural and positive law.

In spite of Grotius's influence, writers continued to argue in their treatment of international law either the naturalist or the positivist view, although they did so with varying degrees. The Germans Samuel Pufendorf (1632–1694) and Christian Wolff (1676–1756) and the Swiss Emmerich de Vattel (1714–1767) could generally be classified as naturalists. The Englishman Richard Zouche (1590–1660) represented the positivist school. But few of these writers were extremists, and most took account of state practice. The contributions of these writers to the development of a body of international law continue to have some effect upon contemporary international law. Their works are still cited in the decisions of national and international courts and tribunals.

The Nineteenth Century

International law during the nineteenth century retained most of its major eighteenth-century features. At the same time, important details and refinements were added in response to intensifying and multiplying international relations. When the French Revolution and others ended the age of absolutism, the state became identified with its people rather than with the person of its monarch. This change required adjustments in the law. A state's territory or people could no longer be treated as appendixes of the ruler. The state itself became the subject of international law. The state's form or government personnel no longer affected the state's rights or obligations. The separation of the ruler's person from the objective legal existence of the state fulfilled the political need of including non-Christian states (Turkey, Japan, China) into the international community of states.

In increasing measure, treaties, especially multilateral treaties, implemented and eventually surpassed in volume custom as a source of international norms. The growing importance and numbers of treaties also meant a simplification of their conclusion, the routinization of what used to be prestige matters, and, most important to the new and Communist states today, a greater effectiveness of the rule that states cannot be bound against their will or that they should participate in the making of rules binding them.

The material covered by treaties was greatly augmented, reflecting both the growing volume of interaction among states and the multiplication of state interests. Agreements were reached on rules of state conduct. Communications, trade and commerce, financial matters, scientific and health subjects, and humanitarian concerns surpassed politics in volume, not importance, as topics of international conferences, thereby inaugurating a trend that continues in the contemporary era. Treaties establishing international organizations, mainly in the "noncontroversial" field of communications, made their appearance.

The rise of positivism and the simultaneous decline of the naturalist theory of law—or, in other words, the ostensible elimination of value judgments about legal norms so as to facilitate the growth of law in a multicultural world—legitimized the conduct of wars for the enforcement of political demands even without a legal basis or "just cause." At the same time, the prospect of increasing numbers of wars, with their growing destructiveness and cost, led to the popularization of peaceful methods for settling international disputes, attempts to establish international courts, and pressure for the humanization of warfare. The great conferences at the Hague in 1899 and 1907 highlighted this development.

At the beginning of the twentieth century, a comprehensive body of international law existed. The methods and institutions for the creation of new norms were fairly well established. This body of law reflected the state of international politics and the character of international society at that time. International law had impressively progressed step by step from its modest beginnings in the fifteenth century and already showed many of the trends that characterized its further development in the twentieth century.

But it was still true (and remains true today) that the making of the law and its execution were in the hands of individual states. No supranational institutions truly comparable to a legislature and an executive were created. The League of Nations, charged with forming an international court, completed this task by 1921 when the Permanent Court of International Justice was established. So much discussion before World War I about such a court had taken place that its creation was taken for granted. Some disagreements among states related only to details of the statute upon which the Court was founded. This unanimity was not surprising. First, a court presumably only interprets the law, thus, the basic obligations of a party before the court were agreed upon when the law was made. Second, submission of cases to the Court was voluntary. The statute stipulated that "the jurisdiction of the Court comprises all cases which the parties refer to it" (Article 36). Third, the statute provided no effective means for the enforcement of a judgment by the Court. In 1946, the Permanent Court was succeeded by the International Court of Justice (ICJ), an integral part of the United Nations. The statute defining this court's structure and functions was virtually the same as the statute that created the Permanent Court of Justice. Again, submission of cases to the Court by states is voluntary, and enforcement of a judgment is practically impossible.

Even this cursory summary of the history of international law permits some important conclusions. The nature and status of international law are closely related to the nature and status of international politics. International law is a real and indispensable instrument in the relations between states. International law is dynamic, even in the absence of formal institutions for its creation and adjustment, and it corresponds to the dynamism of the society that it regulates. International law grows as the interactions between states increase, as the number of participants in international society rises, and as the violent means states use toward each other become more destructive and costly. But more interaction and a growing volume of mostly nonpolitical international law do not necessarily mean an approach to "one world." Interaction and interdependence, especially when the parties are unequal, may also serve pressure and coercion. Thus, the dominance of politics endures and is reflected in the norms and practice of international law.

2
THE BASIS AND PURPOSE
OF INTERNATIONAL LAW

The Need for Law

Humankind has become a global society. In all societies, the co-existence and continuing survival of the members require regular and predictable behavior—that is, social order. This order is threatened by several sources. One is that no member of the society has an adequate overview of the social results of his or her own behavior or that of others. Guidance is needed to render social behavior harmless—and, if possible, useful—to the social order. In general, this guidance is provided in the process of socializing the member into the society.

A second threat comes from the scarcity of resources. To avoid destructive competitive strife, the allocation of resources should be arranged by consensual social decisions. This is normally achieved by the political process, which tries to enforce the allocation if consensus cannot be reached.

The multitude of political systems indicates that there are many ways in which behavioral guidance and resource allocation can be undertaken. Whichever is chosen, in every system the law represents the firming and perpetuation of the political decisions by which the requisite behavior is guided and enforced and resources are allocated. Law translates political decisions into binding instructions to the society's members about how to behave. This dependent relationship of law to politics has important consequences for the nature of international society and the efficacy of international law.

Law and Politics

One consequence is the contamination of the dependent legal system with the political system's inadequacy to maintain social order reliably. Insistence of states upon sovereignty—that is, upon each state's ultimate authority in determining its behavior—disables the law's ability to perform its ordering function efficaciously. Sovereignty as the fundamental organizational principle of international society means the diffused horizontal distribution of power among all states. There can be no central government, legislature, executive, or fully developed judiciary. The institutions that maintain an effective legal system in national societies are absent. Their unpredictable and unreliable substitute is the consent of states.

A second consequence is that international law represents the prevailing power constellation in international society. The same is true, of course, of law in national societies. The difference is that normally, at least in democratic societies, the acquisition and use of power are regulated and enforced by the political and legal systems. In international society, however, this process is quite chaotic. Only will and capability set limits to the acquisition of a power potential by individual states. Thus, in a given case political decisions and the dependent legal norms most often reflect the ad hoc power relationship.

This applies to the creation of norms as well as to their interpretation and application. International law, instead of performing law's usual function of safeguarding the requisite behavior patterns of the society's members, is subject to the ever-changing shifts of power between states, their varying interests, and the diverse methods they employ in international relations. Even common agreement on a particular norm (in a treaty, for instance) may not mean much. Its idiosyncratic interpretation to serve the state's interests may undo the benefits of unanimity on the abstract rule. When a similar situation arises between citizens of a state, they submit their disagreement to a judge whose verdict they are obliged to accept. Under the conditions of the international society, international law tends to become a political instrument of states to reach their goals. Law, instead of regulating the struggle for power, becomes one of its tools.

A third consequence is the possibility of discrepancy between politics and law in international society. Compared to the rapid shifting of politics, the relatively slow process of remaking the law, either through authoritative reinterpretation or creation, is more likely to make a "dead letter" of the law in the international arena sooner than in national societies. The always existing tension between politics and law is enhanced by the absence of effective institutions through which the two can be continually reconciled.

Although this utter politicization of the international legal system greatly reduces the efficacy of the law, it does not entirely rob the law of its usefulness. Politicization only minimally affects the law as a means of social communication. The prevailing law still reflects the essential features of the international society. International norms supply some orientation as to what behavior is expected of states and what they may expect of others. Governments may discover what interests they can legitimately pursue, in what manner, and what reactions they may expect to their own actions. The system establishes some framework within which states can act without always having to anticipate completely negative responses.

The politicization is softened somewhat by the growing mutual needs and complementary interests of states, a situation that is initiating a very slowly developing tendency toward what C. Wilfred Jenks anticipated as "the Common Law of Mankind" (in his book of the same title). This trend is not due to a change of heart among peoples, whose nationalism, if anything, appears to be growing stronger. It is mostly due to the force of circumstances antagonistic to the divisive effects of sovereignty. All states share an interest in subjecting some extrasovereign matters (such as the environment, epidemics, migrating fish, the atmosphere, outer space, and even certain human rights) to legal controls. The existence of these issues highlights the anachronism of sovereignty and the international lawmaking process. Sovereignty and its legal effects are being slowly overcome by conclusion of treaties incompatible in subject matter with traditional concepts of sovereignty (for instance, the value of a national currency); by innovative court judgments reinterpreting the old rules of sovereignty (*Filartiga v. Peña-Irala* [1980], for instance); and by innumerable international declarations and resolutions. These declarations are creating, in Lord Arnold McNair's words, "soft law": a gray area between law and politics located in political understandings that lack the binding force of law but that exert a quasi-obligatory influence, such as the Helsinki Accords and the Strategic Arms Limitation Talks [SALT] agreements. Not infrequently, the United States and the Soviet Union accuse each other of breaking the SALT agreement, which lacks legally binding force but has nevertheless created an expectation in each state, as well as in others, that neither party to the agreement will act contrary to it.

Is International Law Real Law?

The deleterious effects of overpoliticization on the nature of international law have raised the question whether international law is "real" law at all. Several arguments have been made in favor of a negative answer. There is no international legislature. Law is made by state lawgivers, interpreters, and executors who are themselves subject to the law. There is no agency that states must use to obtain a disinterested, objective definition of law violations or a settlement of their conflicts. There are no effective sanctions for violators of the law. The arbitrary use of force continues, thereby testifying to the absence of effective legal controls.

The general response to these arguments is that they rest upon a possible, but not the only, definition of law. All can be answered specifically. For instance, much "primitive" law originates in tradition. Common law develops independently of a legislature. In many (mostly totalitarian) states the legislator, lawgiver, and executor are identical, yet there is law. Legislators are themselves subject to the laws they make. There are national laws (such as refusal to pay gambling debts) whose

similar action by the other state). Reciprocity is a major motor behind international political and legal action. Charity begins and stays at home.

State behavior demonstrates that states obey law because they find it in their interest to do so. But they never admit disobedience. They strain to legitimate their evasive action—itself an indication of their wish to consider law binding. Whatever the reason states find international law binding, the evidence indicates that they consider it so. This suffices for the legal system. The ultimate reason cannot be found in the legal system itself. It lies beyond, in the realm of faith or philosophy.

3
INTERNATIONAL LAW
AND OTHER LAW

Types of Law

In the *Lotus* case (1927, p. 18), the Permanent Court of International Justice said that "international law governs relations between independent States." This application of law only to states is distinct from municipal law, which applies to private individuals in one country, or from international private law (or conflict of laws), which applies to individuals of different citizenship residing in different countries or, more generally, to cases involving two or more municipal legal systems.

Practice usually precludes any clear delineation between these types of law, however. In many situations, international law and municipal law are mutually relevant. For example, whether U.S. activities in Vietnam in the 1960s legally amounted to war was an international law question that was also relevant for the rights and duties of U.S. citizens under U.S. law. Likewise, the municipal law question of an individual's nationality also affects the right of states to protect their citizens abroad under international law.

Even an apparently more feasible delineation between the law to be applied in a municipal court and the law to be applied in an international court is problematic. A judge in either court would not be relieved where necessary of having to apply aspects of both legal systems in his or her judgment. Even to determine that a legal point in one system can be introduced as a fact in the other requires a judge to look at both systems. The problem of the relationship between international law and municipal law has become the subject of much debate, with the protagonists of various views being much influenced by a desire to strengthen either international law or a state's sovereignty or a world community.

The Monist and Dualist Views

The main parties in the debate are the monists and the dualists (or pluralists). In the monist view, there is only one legal system in the world. International law and municipal law are its parts. The question is merely whether one is superior to the other. To the dualists, international law and municipal law are two separate legal systems, although each may incorporate parts of the other.

Dualists argue that municipal law originates in customs and laws within states, whereas international law originates in customs and treaties between states. Therefore, the subjects of municipal law are individuals; of international law, states. The subject matter and functioning of each system also differ from those of the other. Municipal law is a command from a sovereign to the citizens. International laws prevail among equals.

The monists argue that conceptually law is one for all legal systems. All law ultimately addresses itself to individuals. In the end, all relations are between individuals, regardless of the social entity in which they may be organized. Some monists add that because international law defines the jurisdiction of municipal law (such as its jurisdiction over which persons and what territory), it is the higher law, thereby proving that the legal order is one. Other monists place municipal law above international law because international law is the external branch of municipal law under which all state organs operate.

State Practice Regarding Different Types of Law

State practice, although not uniform, tends to follow the monist view. This is more the result of inevitability than of theoretical considerations. A decision occasionally must refer to municipal law and international law. If they belong to two different systems, contradictory adjudications of the same case can result.

In principle, municipal courts must use municipal law. The Scottish Court of Judiciary in *Mortensen v. Peters* (1906, p. 67) stated, "For us an Act of Parliament . . . is supreme, and we are bound to follow its terms." Similarly, a U.S. federal court stated in *Over the Top* (1925, p. 843), "International practice is law only in so far as we adopt it, and like all common or statute law it bends to the will of Congress." International courts must apply international law, although when the statute of the ICJ in Article 38 instructs the Court to apply "the general principles of law recognized by civilized nations," municipal law may enter.

More generally, in order to avoid clashes between legal systems in a given case or, for that matter, obligations of states to their citizens as well as to international society, many states have constitutional provisions or practices that in some form make international law part of municipal law. The U.S. Constitution allows Congress to punish violators of international law, and the Supreme Court has many times stated that international law is part of the law of the land. Similar practices obtain in most Commonwealth states, Israel, the German Federal Republic, India, the Netherlands, Austria, and Japan. Ireland's constitution imposes certain restrictions on making international law ipso facto part of the law of the land, whereas Norwegian law requires legislation to make treaties effective municipally. The Soviet Union in a letter to the U.N. secretary general in 1989 wrote that international legal norms and obligations take precedence over national statutes and that international order requires the primacy of law in politics.

Some states apply different rules to customary and treaty law, with the first more readily acknowledged as binding upon municipal law than the second. If, however, a municipal law should be contrary to a rule of international law, a state may not apply the rule internally but remains bound externally to the international norm. The Declaration of Rights and Duties of States, adopted by the International Law Commission in 1949, stated in Article 13, in confirmation of frequent international court decisions, that a state "may not invoke provisions in its constitution or its laws as an excuse for failure to perform" its duties under international law.

Contradictions between municipal law and international law are unlikely to be frequent for three reasons. First, international customary law develops from the customs of states, making a contradiction unlikely. Lord Chief Justice Alverston of England decided in *West Rand Central Gold Mining Co. v. the King* (1905, p. 302), "Whatever has received the common consent of civilized nations must have received the assent of our country, and that to which we have assented along with other nations in general may properly be called international law, and as such will be acknowledged and applied by our municipal tribunals."

Second, treaties become the law of the land in accordance with prescribed procedures. In some states they are even superior to municipal law. In the United States, only self-executing treaties—that is, treaties forming part of the law of the land without any enabling action by Congress—become directly binding upon U.S. courts. Non-self-executing treaties first require such action by Congress. The U.S. Court of Appeals, District of Columbia, in *Diggs v. Schultz* (1972, pp. 466–467) decided that Congress could denounce treaties.

Third, the practice of courts in many countries is to reconcile the norms of the two legal systems as much as possible through interpretation. The court in *Over the Top* (1925, p. 842) stated, "Unless it unmistakably appears that a congressional act was intended to be in disregard of a principle of international comity, the presumption is that it was in conformity with it," so that an act of Congress had to be interpreted, if at all possible, not to violate international law. This practice has remained intact (see, for example, *United States v. Palestine Liberation Organization* [1988], p. 1073). Under the consent theory of international law it must be assumed that a state, having consented to a norm of international law, would not deny such consent in its internal legal system.

In principle, international tribunals have to apply international law. But on many occasions such tribunals have to apply, expose, or interpret municipal law in order to reach a decision. Examples include the nationality of an individual or a corporation according to municipal law, damage done to a foreigner by municipal legislation in his or her country of residence, and the rights and duties of foreign individuals or corporations under aid and assistance treaties. In the case of a successor state, the court must decide to what extent the successor state is bound in its municipal legislation by obligations entered into by the predecessor state. Many prominent cases grew out of the treaties after World War I protecting minorities in Eastern Europe and their complaints that municipal legislation interfered with their protection.

In *German Interests in Polish Upper Silesia (Merits)* (1926, p. 19), the Permanent Court of International Justice said that from the standpoint of international law "municipal laws are merely facts which express the will and constitute the activities of states." But then the Court could not escape the necessity of going more deeply into municipal legislation. In the *Payment in Gold of the Brazilian Federal Loans Issued in France* case (1929, pp. 19, 41), the Court stated it was "bound to apply municipal law when circumstances so require." Once it had decided which municipal law must be applied, that law must be applied "as it would be applied in that country" by the national courts. If the jurisprudence of the national courts was uncertain, the International Court would have to make its own interpretation. This practice by international tribunals makes municipal law an integral part of international law to the extent that the circumstances of the case require.

The mutual influence of both types of law has been going on since international law was born. Growing interaction between states is bound to increase the interweaving of the two laws. In the European Community (EC) this process has already advanced considerably. This advance supports Myres McDougal's rejection of the monist and dualist theories on the ground that they fail to recognize how authoritative decisions are made in different social contexts.

In the United States the interweaving of international law and municipal law has received additional impetus from a desire to punish violations of human rights. U.S. courts have rediscovered the Alien Tort Claims Statute, 28 U.S.C. § 1350, which has been in existence and unused for two hundred years. It grants federal district courts original jurisdiction over any civil action by an alien anywhere for torts committed against anyone "in violation of the law of nations." The statute therefore allows an alien who suffered damage from a violation of human rights committed as an official act in his or her own country to bring a lawsuit in U.S. courts, provided that the right is recognized as international law. The U.S. Court of Appeals, Second Circuit, decided in *Filartiga v. Peña-Irala* (1980, p. 876) that torture had become a crime under international law, thereby making the torturer an enemy of all humankind (*hostis humanis generis*), as the pirate or slave trader was. The court therefore permitted the plaintiffs, Paraguayan citizens, to bring an action against a Paraguayan official temporarily in the United States who tortured their son and brother to death in Paraguay. Terrorism, however, was found not to be a crime under international law by the U.S. Court of Appeal, District of Columbia Circuit, in *Tel-Oren [Hanoch] v. Libyan Arab Republic* (1984). In several comparable cases in the 1980s, other U.S. courts did not reach uniform decisions for several reasons. Nor is there agreement among writers on the subject.

The Act of State Doctrine

Questions arise whether a state's legislative, judicial, or executive acts performed within that state's jurisdiction should have validity in another state's jurisprudence. Specifically, does international law obligate the second state to recognize without question such acts? For instance, must a U.S. court recognize as valid the expropriation by a country's government of a U.S. citizen's property in that foreign country? In particular, must the U.S. court do so even if the expropriation is contrary to international law or contrary to the public policy (the *ordre public*) of the United States?

Part of the answer relates to the sovereign immunity of states. Sovereign immunity holds that a state's domestic affairs must not be interfered with by other states and therefore that a state's internal official acts must be recognized by other states.

Another part of the answer relates to the act of state doctrine, developed mainly in the United States. An early case initiating the doctrine was before the Supreme Court in 1897. In *Underhill v. Hernandez*, Underhill, a U.S. citizen, claimed unlawful assault, coercion, and detention in Venezuela by Hernandez, a revolutionary commander whose government was later recognized by the United States. Underhill demanded compensation for damages against Hernandez in a U.S. court. Chief Justice Fuller, in rejecting the claim, stated, "Every sovereign state is bound to respect the independence of every other sovereign State, and the courts of one country will not sit in judgment on the acts of the government of another done within its territory." He suggested such cases should be settled through "means open to be availed of by sovereign powers as between themselves" (p. 252).

Later cases followed this decision, arguing that various legal principles required its application. The Supreme Court eventually denied this contention, however. Still later cases gradually clarified that the doctrine was used to avoid court judgments in the United States of governmental acts performed in other countries. In 1959, for instance, the Cuban government nationalized property owned by U.S. citizens, who claimed that they were inadequately compensated. The Supreme Court in *Banco Nacional de Cuba v. Sabbatino* (1964, p. 422) reconfirmed the act of state doctrine, stating that the doctrine protected foreign acts of state from being challenged in U.S. courts even if the other state by its act violated international law or U.S. public policy. The Court added that the doctrine must reflect "the proper distribution of functions between the judicial and political branches of the Government on matters bearing on foreign affairs." The Court felt, in other words, that the judicial branch should not interfere in the conduct of foreign policy.

The essence of this decision was supported subsequently by Supreme Court decisions in *First National City Bank v. Banco Nacional de Cuba* (1972) and *Alfred Dunhill of London v. Republic of Cuba* (1976) and by U.S. Court of Appeals, Second Circuit, decisions in *Banco Nacional de Cuba v. Chase Manhattan Bank* (1981) and *Hunt v. Mobil Oil* (1977).

Congress was sufficiently upset by the opinion in the *Sabbatino* case to enact provisions to the Foreign Assistance Act of 1964 that undid to some extent the *Sabbatino* judgment. Even more radical was the Hickenlooper amendment to the Foreign Assistance Act. It forbids courts to "decline on the ground of the federal act of state doctrine to make a determination on the merits giving effect to the principles of international law" in certain cases involving the taking of property, such as confiscation by an act of state, contrary to international law. The amendment also gives the president the right to order the application of the act of state doctrine in the courts (that is, recognize the foreign official act) if U.S. foreign interests so require.

This exception follows the Supreme Court's statement in the *Sabbatino* case that there are situations in which application or nonapplication of the doctrine may lead to conflict with the executive or legislative branches in the field of foreign relations—for instance, by embarrassing a president who wants friendly relations with a particular government so that its acts should not be found unacceptable to the United States. The practice has therefore developed that before deciding upon the application of the doctrine, the courts will ask the State Department if doing so or not doing so would be contrary to U.S. diplomatic interests. If, for instance, in cases dealing with Cuba, the State Department has no objection to the courts finding Cuban expropriations illegal because such a finding would not interfere with U.S. relations with Cuba, it will tell the courts that they need not apply the act of state doctrine.

Politics enters the act of state doctrine in at least two ways. First, by depending on State Department decisions regarding the political feasibility of applying the act of state doctrine, the judiciary, according to some critics, has surrendered its nonpolitical function to the political executive and has breached the separation of powers between the branches. Although the courts have denied this, it is nevertheless true that politics intrudes on their deliberations. Second, if foreign powers that are defendants in a case cannot claim immunity, they have on occasion attempted to get protection under the doctrine (for example, *Letelier v. Republic of Chile* [1980, pp. 673–674]). In such cases the courts apply the same procedure they always apply in regard to the doctrine: They consult the State Department.

Political Matters and the Judiciary

There are other situations in which the judiciary defers to decisions by the executive in international matters if a court finds an issue outside the reach of judicial competence and therefore nonjusticiable—that is, political—as the Supreme Court decided in the case *Baker v. Carr* (1962, p. 186). Courts have left to the executive such sensitive decisions as whether a state of war exists, whether a state exists, which is the proper government of a state, and whether a given territory is within the bounds of a foreign state.

This approach of the judiciary is to some extent another testimony to the political nature of international law, which the courts do not deny. In many decisions in the United States and abroad, the precedence of political over legal action is acknowledged. Supreme Court Justice Felix Frankfurter in the *Republic of Mexico et al. v. Hoffman* case (1945, p. 42) stated that courts should disclaim jurisdiction in cases involving a foreign government when the Department of State or Congress explicitly asserts that the proper conduct of foreign affairs calls for judicial abstention. "Thereby responsibility for the conduct of our foreign relations will be placed where power lies." In the *Republic of Peru* (1943, p. 589) case, a Cuban corporation filed a libel in district court against a Peruvian government-owned freighter. The Peruvian government asked for release of the freighter on grounds of immunity. The State Department allowed the claim of immunity and the Supreme Court ordered release of the vessel, arguing that the certification of the vessel as immune "must be accepted by the courts as a conclusive determination by the political arm of the Government that the continued retention of the vessel interferes with the proper conduct of our foreign relations." The Supreme Court of Pennsylvania in *F. W. Stone Engineering Co. v. Petroleos Mexicanos* (1945, p. 390) expanded the judicial abstention to "political matters growing out of or incidental to our Government's relations with a friendly foreign state."

In addition to the oft-repeated argument that the judiciary should not "embarrass" the executive in the conduct of foreign relations, the argument has been made by the House of Lords in the *Arantzazu Mendi* case (1939, p. 18) that "our State cannot speak with two voices . . . the judiciary saying one thing, the executive another" and by the *Sabbatino* case that for purely practical reasons, some matters are more successfully handled by political (diplomatic) than by legal processes. Nevertheless, indications are that some courts are not very happy with this relationship between the executive and the judiciary. The U.S. District Court, Southern District New York, in *New York & Cuba Mail v. Republic of Korea* (1955, p. 686) asserted, "This course entails no abrogation of judicial power;

it is a self-imposed restraint to avoid embarrassment of the executive in the conduct of foreign affairs." In *Bank of China v. Wells Fargo Bank & Union Trust Co.* (1952, p. 63), the State Department had determined which of the two Chinese governments was entitled to act on behalf of China and had expected that the courts would have nothing more to say. In its ruling, the U.S. District Court, Northern District California, said that on the contrary, the courts could evaluate the acts of both governments on their legal significance: "To permit this expression of executive policy to usurp entirely the judicial judgment would relieve the court of a burdensome duty, but it is doubtful that the ends of justice would thus be met. It has been argued that such is the accepted practice. But the authorities do not support this view."

Because international society is based upon the sovereignty of its members, one should expect that everything will be done to strengthen that sovereignty, even if this means subordinating one branch of government to another, especially if that branch is likely to be more objective and less political than the others, and using international law as a political instrument.

4
METHODS AND PRINCIPLES FOR CREATING INTERNATIONAL LAW

The Origin

Where does international law come from? The question is answerable from various perspectives. Institutions and actions have been considered generators of law; so have God and nature. Rudolf von Jhering asserted that law's purposes create law. These purposes derive from society's culture, which could thus be called the ultimate creator of law. Because all cultures have some similar purposes (for example, preserving lives and keeping agreements), the same basic norms can be found in all societies. In addition, every society has norms corresponding to its specific culture.

But no matter who or what creates law, persons are always involved, either as original actors, as interpreters, or as intermediaries. Empirically, persons determine what the law is, and if one assumes some rationality, the ends they pursue with the law can be considered the sources of law. "The law is not a metaphysical creation, a consequence of cold and abstract reasoning of the human mind, which has no regard for social reality," said Judge Moreno Quintana in the *Application of the Convention of 1902 Governing the Guardianship of Infants (the (Boll Case) (Netherlands v. Sweden)* (1958, p. 109) before the International Court of Justice. All law therefore bears the imprint of human characteristics.

International society's culture is reflected in its legal system. Among the system's earliest purposes were the preservation of states in sovereign independence and the maintenance of social order. The first gave rise to the entire structure of the international political and legal system, particularly the rules obliging states to preserve each other's identity. The second produced the fundamental rule *pacta sunt servanda* and the legal rules needed to cope with the growing complexity of international society.

These two purposes have hardly changed in the course of time. But their realization has. Many results of technology have made sovereignty anachronistic, have complicated maintenance of social order, and have created a dichotomy between the two. Separating states is contrary to their needs, which require cooperation. Yet the basic framework of international law is still defined by that earlier goal when self-sufficiency was more feasible. Present-day interaction calls for socialization rather than individualization of states. Hence, the number of international resolutions and treaties calling for cooperation is growing, and new interpretations of old norms have the effect of overcoming the separative intent of traditional international law. In deference to the emotional adherence to sovereignty, the transition of the law is sometimes covert, subtle, or sudden, but it is inevitable for contemporary social existence. This makes it impossible, as Judge Alvarez wrote in his dissenting opinion in *Reservations to the Convention on the Prevention and Punishment of the Crime of Genocide* (1951, p. 51), "to define exactly where the development of this law ends and its creation begins." International law is in flux, said the judge, and "must always reflect the international life of which it is born, if it is not to be discredited."

Public Policy or *Ordre Public*

The substance of legal norms is largely determined by the needs or desires of the society as they emerge from the society's culture. This foundation of the law leads to the concept of public policy or to the somewhat broader French concept of *ordre public*. Both concepts serve as a signpost and guide in the evolution of a legal system.

Public policy is neither a binding norm nor a concrete policy. It is a concept expressing a people's sense of morality, decency, justice, and fairness, all of which affect legal norms and their interpretation. Public policy represents the spirit imbuing the legal system, the general basic principles on which the specific legal order is founded. In speaking of national public policies in *Payment in Gold of the Brazilian Federal Loans Issued in France* case (1929, p. 46), the Permanent Court of International Justice pointed out that the substance of such policies "in any particular country is largely dependent on the opinion prevailing at any given time in such country itself."

Occasionally, judges may rely upon public policy when it becomes necessary to support a decision by the spirit of the law. The question is whether in view of so many national *ordres publics* there is a public policy in the international society from which the creation or meaning of a norm can be derived. Judge P. Nervo in the *Legal Consequences for States of the Continued Presence of South Africa in Namibia* case (1971, p. 123) gave a description of public policy in international society when he said of the League Covenant that its

noble ideas, principles and concepts . . . were not born to have a precarious or temporary existence, linked to the mortal fate of a particular forum or to an international organization which would not be immune to change. They were intended to survive and prevail to guide the political conduct of governments and the moral behaviour of men. They were meant to persist and endure no matter what new social structures of juridical forms might evolve and change through the passage of time in this ever-changing world.

This enduring character is the controlling factor in adapting a society's basic goals and values, and especially its implementing institutions, to social change. But the notion of *ordre public* is "elastic" and "comprehensive"; it is "variable, indefinite and occasionally productive of arbitrariness and abuse," in the words of Judge Lauterpacht in the *Boll Case* (1958, pp. 94, 96).

The very vagueness and flexibility of the concept are either a great annoyance or a welcome refuge to lawyers. The concept's usefulness as a possible broad foundation for the birth or denial of legal norms or their interpretation and further development cannot be denied. So far, the concept has been used mainly in the sphere of conflict of laws (international private law) when national courts have been confronted with the question of recognizing a foreign public law, decision, or act contrary to the public policy of the forum.

In international law, the concept of an international public policy has been shunned by courts and lawyers alike. Nevertheless, there are coinciding or similar elements of public policies in many national societies. Like so-called world public opinion, they may make possible a summary of parallel national elements of public policy without, however, merging into a homogeneous international public policy. This situation is now changing.

The need for international cooperative law has produced agencies in which a truly international—rather than merely coinciding national—public policy can be formulated and expressed. Examples abound. The preamble and principles of the United Nations Charter represent public policy. The "common heritage of mankind" regarding "public" or "collective" goods, the general commitment to international cooperation, and the subscription to human rights are other examples. Few of these are legal norms. They are part of the sum of comprehensive values and goals the international society as such is (allegedly) aspiring to and from which specific obligations can be derived.

The International Court of Justice in the *Fisheries Jurisdiction (United Kingdom . . . v. Iceland) (Merits, Judgment)* case (1974, p. 31) declared:

> It is one of the advances in maritime international law . . . that the former *laissez-faire* treatment of the living resources of the sea in the high seas has been replaced by a recognition of a duty to have due regard to the rights of other States and the needs of conservation for the benefit of all.

Sir Humphrey Waldock, as rapporteur of the International Law Commission in its 1963 session, reported:

> Imperfect though the international legal order may be, the view that in the last analysis there is no international public order . . . has become increasingly difficult to sustain. The law of the Charter concerning the use of force and the development—however tentative—of international criminal law presupposes the existence of an international public order (p. 52).

In the *Oscar Chinn* case heard before the Permanent Court of International Justice (1934, p. 150), the question arose whether a treaty was null and void because of immoral terms. In a dissenting opinion, Judge Schücking remarked that the Court would never apply a convention whose terms were contrary to "public morality." When a convention was null and void because of a flaw in its origin, the attitude of the Court should be governed "by considerations of international public policy." (The Treaty of Rome creating the European Economic Community [Article 48, §3] specifically permits a state to withdraw from an obligation if it is against the public policy of that state.)

Parties to an international dispute, courts, and arbitrators have invoked the idea of public policy. Nevertheless, the concept is still vague in its influence. In the end, every case must rest on concrete legal norms. Until such time as international public policy achieves substantial legal status, it will continue to affect discussions dealing with the creation of international legal norms and help the growth of an orderly international community.

Treaties

A treaty (or covenant, agreement, pact) is an international agreement between two or more subjects of international law, is governed by international law, and, presumably, is intended to create rights and obligations for the parties (see Vienna Convention on the Law of Treaties, 1969, Article [1][a]). The judges of the International Court of Justice are directed by Article 38 of the statute to apply "international conventions, whether general or particular, establishing rules expressly recognized by the contesting parties." This directive confirms treaties as rules establishing rights and obligations for those international legal subjects having conclusively recognized a treaty. If law is defined as a rule enjoining a certain behavior, a treaty is law for those parties. The controversial question is avoided whether treaties are international law (the majority opinion) or whether, for instance, the law is *pacta sunt servanda*, whereas treaties create obligations based on that rule.

The Court statute's reference to "general or particular" conventions is ambiguous. The terms could refer to the number of parties to the treaty. In that case, the archetype of a particular convention would be a bilateral treaty. The archetype of a general convention would be a multilateral treaty, such as the U.N. Charter. The reference could also be to the contents of the treaty, which raises the question of "international legislation" because a treaty between two or among a very limited number of subjects having a contents of interest mainly to them is probably not intended to bind (be law for) other subjects.

"Lawmaking" treaties are cherished by those eager to see the creation of an international legislature. Their argument is that treaties establishing commitments that can be generalized (such as the U.N. Charter) are lawmaking, whereas those that cannot (for example, treaties on landing rights) are not. This argument is based on misleading terminology.

All treaties make "law" for the parties. The designation "lawmaking" treaties is usually reserved for those treaties that codify what was previously customary law or that produce new law for the parties but of such a kind and for so many subjects that it is virtually law for every subject. A lawmaking treaty, in other words, would have a binding force that went beyond the signatories. Yet states not parties or not consenting to the treaty are not bound, however much the treaty may affect them. For this reason, for instance, Article 6 (6) of the U.N. Charter says that the organization "shall ensure that states not Members of the United Nations act in accordance with these Principles so far as may be necessary for the maintenance of international peace and security." Soviet jurisprudence claims that third states affected by a treaty may protest its conclusion.

The most such lawmaking treaties can do for third parties is to serve as evidence of customary law. This is especially likely in two cases: when the preambles of the treaties refer to their character as declarative of customary law or when the treaties regulate interests so widespread and intense among numerous states, including those not parties to the treaties, that all states are willing to forego the presumption that they cannot be bound without their agreement and consider them- selves bound by the norms of such treaties. An example is the prohibition of the use of force in international relations; this prohibition is now embedded in so many treaties that the few states not having signed a treaty calling for it would still be bound by the rule as customary law.

The International Court of Justice in the *North Sea Continental Shelf* cases (1969, p. 41) confirmed that a treaty provision may pass into the general body of international law as customary law binding even states not parties to the treaty. There is no doubt, the Court said, that this process "constitutes indeed one of the recognized methods by which new rules of customary law may be formed," provided that other conditions for creating customary law are fulfilled, particularly that the provision has a "fundamentally norm-creating character."

In the same case (p. 26), the Court hinted at another process, much narrower in scope and not falling into the category of established formal lawmaking, through which a state could become bound to a treaty between two other states. By "a very definite, very consistent course of conduct," by showing "a real intention to manifest acceptance or recognition of the applicability" of a conventional regime, declared the

Court, a state may by such unilateral actions assume the obligations of that treaty. Clearly, however, binding a state to a treaty by such conclusive action and not through the usual formalities of signing, ratifying, and so on would require overwhelming evidence.

The attitudes of Third World states and some Communist states may slow down these processes. Being mistrustful of the overwhelming influence of the First World upon international law, these states may be reluctant to recognize as binding any treaty to which they are not partners. Their insistence that participation in the making of multilateral treaties is a right because generally binding law may emerge from them points in the direction of such a development.

Custom

The statute of the International Court directs the Court to apply customary law after conventional law. This should be distinguished from comity, which is the application of politeness in relations among states, the respect they show each other's polities, and the treatment they expect from each other. The statute prescribes that the Court apply "international custom, as evidence of a general practice accepted as law." The directive clarifies at least that there must be objectively a custom and subjectively a sense that the custom is accepted as law (*opinio juris sive necessitatis*).

A custom is a habitual behavior. The U.S. Supreme Court in the *Paquete Habana* and the *Lola* cases (1900, p. 696) spoke of "ancient usage." The same Court in the *North Sea Continental Shelf* cases (1969, p. 43) spoke of "extensive and virtually uniform" state practice. This criterion can be discovered by examining a state's laws, treaties, statements, and behavior, as well as the repetition, volume, and consistency of state practice.

The term *custom* implies a time element. There was agreement in the past that to become customary law a habit had to exist for a certain period of time, although no fixed length was ever established. In the less leisurely contemporary era, with greater numbers of states behaving in similar ways within a relatively short period, the opinion is increasingly expressed that a customary rule can develop quickly. After the launching of *Sputnik*, Soviet lawyers claimed that instant customary law was created that artificial earth satellites could fly unimpeded over any state's territory in outer space. No state raised any objection.

Any agreement on the time factor still leaves open the questions, first, how often the behavior has to be engaged in by how many states and, second, whether it matters what types of states are engaging in it. The International Court of Justice in the *North Sea Continental Shelf* cases (1969, p. 43) expressed the opinion that "the passage of only a short period of time" is no bar to the formation of a new rule of customary law, providing that "within the period in question, short though it may be, state practice, including that of states whose interests are specifically affected, should have been extensive and virtually uniform in the sense of the provision invoked." In short, length of time or occasional deviation is less weighty than volume of practice and the interests of states affected in establishing a customary norm.

If a state engages in behavior previously never engaged in by any state, this behavior could be either illegal or the beginning of a new customary rule, especially if no state objects to the new behavior. The decisive factor is the presence or absence of *opinio iuris*.

In view of the small number of states in the world and the relatively rare repetition of comparable situations, expectations regarding frequency should be modest. But to argue that one precedent may be sufficient is overly modest. In the end, as is so often the case, the court will have to decide what amounts to "general practice."

Frequency and the time element are both affected by technology. News now travels fast. Knowledge of state practice spreads rapidly and can be imitated quickly. Massive interaction among states leads to more frequent occurrence of analogous situations. Both factors could favor more rapid development of customary law as well as more rapid growth of treaty law.

But a customary norm may bind only those states engaging in the custom (for example, regional customary law in Latin America or Western Europe) or only one state (Norway's coastal baseline). Moreover, customary law cannot always be applied to roughly comparable situations. The practice of states and courts indicates flexibility in application and some individualization of even universal customary norms. For example, the decision of the International Court of Justice in the *Norwegian Fisheries* (*United Kingdom v. Norway*) case (1951, p. 116) allowed Norway as a custom to measure its territorial sea from a straight baseline following the general contours of the Norwegian coast and ignoring the identations because the coastline is so heavily indented.

Opposition to customary law in favor of treaty law has been growing as Communist and Third World states have gained influence. They argue that much customary law was established by the most influential states and imposed on the international society by "bourgeois" and "imperialist" states. The nonparticipation of the Communist and newer states in creating that law yet their being bound by it is contrary to the legal equality of states and is sheer "power politics." These states admit only that a new or any other state entering into relations with other states without reservation thereby signifies its acceptance of the prevailing body of international law. They admit that even treaty law in whose creation they did have a part may still result from very uneven power relationships among the parties. But the increasing numbers of these states make them more inclined to accept customary law. Nevertheless, having had their say, they feel more comfortable with it, although they continue to prefer treaty law.

Even more difficult than discovering the objective facts of practice is discovering the subjective opinion that a state follows a custom because it thinks it is obliged to do so (*opinio iuris*). There is no hard and fast rule for such a discovery. The general attitude of states has to be taken into consideration. The International Court of Justice in the *Nicaragua* (*Merits, Judgment*) case (1986, p. 109) confirmed that a state breaking a customary norm, as was mentioned earlier, may not act illegally but may be aiming at a modification of customary law when it has the acquiescence of other states. Custom, after all, implies change. If the possibility of such a change were totally excluded, customary law would have died long ago of anachronism. A consideration of all the circumstances is necessary to decide whether a new norm is in the making or an old one is being illegally broken. Among these circumstances, the behavior of other states—approving or disapproving—must be a foremost consideration. A Chamber of the International Court of Justice stated in the *Delimitation of the Maritime Boundary in the Gulf of Maine Area* (*Canada/United States of America*) (1984, p. 299) that the presence of *opinio iuris* of states "can be tested by induction based on the analysis of a sufficiently extensive and convincing practice, and not be deduction from preconceived ideas." But in any case, changing behavior alone cannot be conclusive as to whether an old law is being broken or a new one is being created. *Opinio iuris* is crucial.

In this connection, nonaction by a state represents 'an additional difficulty. There had been general agreement, until it was challenged by Communist and newer states, that only a few states—those most powerful and most concerned—had to engage in the required behavior to create a universally valid norm. That, in turn, raised the question whether consistent abstention or continuous silence by states is tantamount to passive assent to a rule of customary law. One answer is that in some cases the situation of "passivity" so clearly implies assent that acceptance by the state of the customary rule is obvious. But once the norm exists, abstention cannot easily be interpreted as tacit consent to its validity. Absent assent may imply nonrecognition of the norm, or it may simply be a politically motivated stance with no implication intended for or against a norm.

Thus, nonaction may still mean tacit consent to a rule of customary law. Or it may mean adherence to a rule prescribing nonaction. The Permanent Court of International Law in the *Lotus* case (1927, p. 28) stated that abstention (inaction) implies a customary rule only if a state is conscious of a duty to abstain. Inaction, finally, may also mean nothing at all if a state has no need to act or not to act. One thing is certain: No matter what lip service a state may pay publicly to norms (such as human rights), if it does not apply them at home, there is no *opinio iuris*.

The advantages and disadvantages of treaties versus customary law as sources of law have been much debated. Each has advantages and disadvantages regarding differing specificity, dynamism in adapting to changing conditions, universal validity, and binding force. The objections of Communist and newer states to aspects of customary law have introduced a political and emotional element into the discussions. But it may be said, first, that treaties have become more important generators of law than custom; second, that almost all states act as if they accept customary law, at least in principle; and third, that the tendency is to codify well-established and generally recognized norms of customary law, thereby turning them into treaty law. Whether a "persistent objector" to a customary rule is no longer bound by an established (as distinct from an evolving) rule remains uncertain. The International Court of Justice in the *Nicaragua (Merits, Judgment)* case (1986, p. 94) reached the conclusion that customary law and treaty law can coexist. But this can be the case only if the custom supplements the treaty because treaty law has precedence.

Ius Cogens

Ius cogens is defined in Article 53 of the Vienna Convention on the Law of Treaties (1969) as follows:

> A peremptory norm of general international law is a norm accepted and recognised by the international community of States as a whole as a norm from which no derogation is permitted and which can be modified only by a subsequent norm of general international law having the same character.

Quite apart from the fact that the second part of the definition undoes the first, doubt has been expressed whether such a norm exists at all. Adherents to the naturalist school would have no difficulty recognizing one because they would argue that certain norms are given by nature and are untouchable by humans. But when more specificity is demanded and examples are provided of *ius cogens* norms, every example is contested by some states as inappropriate. Moreover, if consent is accepted as the basis for the binding nature of international legal norms, *ius cogens* becomes incompatible with that assumption. In practice, the substance of *ius cogens* is politically determined by individual states. Even if the existence of *ius cogens* is admitted, it is unsuitable as a source of law. First, there is no agreement at all on its substance. Second, its norms would have to be universally accepted before they could become peremptory—that is, the existence of the norms would precede their becoming peremptory. *Ius cogens* does not create norms; it gives existing norms a peremptory character. Thus, for instance, in the *Nicaragua (Merits, Judgment)* case (1986, p. 101), the United States, Nicaragua, and the International Court of Justice agreed that the prohibition of the use of force had become *ius cogens*.

General Principles of Law

The statute of the International Court of Justice authorizes the Court to apply "the general principles of law recognized by civilized nations." The multitude of doubts, concerns, and questions bedeviling the authors of this clause is reflected in its ambiguity. One certain thing is that it rejects the positivist school of international law because in the absence of a positive norm, a case may nevertheless be decided by the application of general principles of law. Whether the clause inclines toward the natural law school by permitting specific norms to be derived from universally valid general principles of law is possible but doubtful. The history of the clause permits the conclusion that its authors wanted to avoid *non liquet* (a gap in the law). But the clause caused much controversy.

One controversial issue is what the meaning of "general" is, especially given the numerous legal systems existing in the modern world. In how many states must the principles be found to be "general," and can any be found at all? Another issue is the meaning of the phrase "civilized nations." No nation considers itself uncivilized. The ex-colonial states in particular are unpleasantly reminded of their former assigned inferior status. Some Communist states or writers deny altogether that principles from the municipal system can be relevant; others do not. Those who deny relevance fear that the application of such principles would enable the "capitalist" and "bourgeois" states to foist them on states that totally opposed them. These writers insist that only those general principles found in the international system are applicable.

Another issue is whether a general principle is to be applied directly or whether a specific norm to be derived from a general principle is to be applied. Lord McNair addressed this and part of the other issues in the *International Status of South-West Africa* case (1950, p. 148): "The duty of international tribunals in this matter is to regard any features or terminology which are reminiscent of the rules and institutions of private law as an indication of policy and principles rather than directly importing these rules and institutions."

International tribunals, conscious of their need to rely on states' voluntary compliance with their verdicts, and conscious of their need to stimulate respect for international law, have not abused the law-creating discretion granted them in this clause of the statute. The principles they have chosen as sources of applicable international law have usually been well established everywhere.

In the *Factory at Chorzów (Jurisdiction)*, the Permanent Court of International Justice (1927, p. 29) stated that every violation of an obligation involves a corresponding duty to make reparation. In the *Corfu Channel* case heard before the International Court of Justice (1949, p. 18), the verdict held that indirect evidence is admitted in all legal systems and international decisions. Other examples of general principles are (1) no party can be a judge in its own case, (2) a party cannot deny the truth of a statement and the existence of a fact that it had earlier led other parties to accept (estoppel), and (3) the municipal law concept of a limited company can be applied to an international law case (as in the *Barcelona Traction, Light, and Power Co. Ltd. (Judgment)* case [1970], p. 37).

The importance of these controversies should not be exaggerated. The idea of creating norms in one legal system by analogy to norms in another is not new. Much of universally recognized international law stems from Roman law. Arbitration tribunals have used analogy from one system to another frequently and successfully for a long time. In addition, international contacts requiring legal decisions are dominated by universal nationalism, sovereignty and its many consequences, and economic needs; these act as the foundation of international norms. Culturally conditioned differences between municipal legal systems are therefore likely to be much less relevant in most international cases than system similarities are. In other words, states are more likely to conflict on national interests, which are essentially alike, than on cultural issues, which are not, so that generally accepted general principles protecting national interests are not too difficult to discover.

Equity

Equity is the principle of fairness and justice and possibly of good faith. In contrast to its technical concept in English law, equity in international law is not a separate body of legal norms—although some lawyers argue that it is. Decisions *ex aequo et bono* are based upon "just and good" considerations rather than upon the letter of the law. By general agreement, however, these decisions must remain compatible with basic legal principles. Equity expresses a spirit or an attitude pervading all law (as well as all international tribunals) and aligning it with a sense of justice. Because equity does not create new legal norms but rather affects the meaning of existing norms, its role as a generator of law has been in doubt.

Depending on a given case, there are three ways that equity may function as a quasi-source of law. One way is through the power granted to the ICJ by its statute (Article 38, paragraph 2) to "decide a case *ex aequo et bono,* if the parties agree thereto." (Note that the *Cayuga Indians Arbitration [Great Britain v. United States]* [1926, p. 307] and the International Court of Justice in *United Kingdom & France Merits Arbitration on the Delimitation of the Continental Shelf* [1977] differentiated between *ex aequo et bono* and equity.) No party has ever agreed to let the Court decide *ex aequo et bono,* however. Arbitration tribunals have frequently been instructed by the parties to decide *ex aequo et bono* or *ex aequo et bono* plus the law. If the International Court were to decide a case under the second paragraph of Article 38, specific legal norms would have been set aside and the case would have been decided according to what the judges found to be just. Equity created law only for the parties to the case because equity was based on the unique facts of the case. Equity lacks universally applicable concrete contents.

A second way is through the assumption that the judiciary must use its competence in a just and fair manner. In fact, decisions of international courts have occasionally made reference to the judge's obligation to interpret treaties and other legal norms in a fair, just manner. Article 31 of the Vienna Convention on the Law of Treaties (1969) stipulates that treaties shall be interpreted in "good faith," and the convention's preamble proposes that disputes concerning treaties be settled "in conformity with principles of justice and international law." Article 59 of the Law of the Sea Convention (1982) refers to equity as a basis for the resolution of conflicts or the reaching of an agreement. When equity is applied in this sense alone and exclusively or in connection with legal norms as their generally valid and enduring clarification, definition, and interpretation, it becomes a source of law.

A third way is as one of the "general principles of law recognized by civilized nations" because every legal system at least claims to achieve justice and fairness for its subjects. Manley O. Hudson, as judge of the Permanent Court of International Justice, declared in the *Diversion of Water from the Meuse (Judgment)* case (1937, p. 77), after affirming that "the principles of equity" have an established place in the legal system of many nations, "Under Article 38 of the Statute, if not independently of that Article, the Court has some freedom to consider principles of equity as part of the international law which it must apply." This still leaves open the question whether a principle can be applied directly or can be used merely as a generator of norms.

International courts have used this freedom quite often, although they have not always labeled references to equity as such. In the *Diversion of Water from the Meuse* case, for instance, the Court declared that a state cannot complain about the action of another state contrary to a treaty when the complaining state previously engaged in the same action. In the *Factory at Chorzów (Jurisdiction)* case (1927, p. 31), the Court decided that a state cannot rely on the fact that another state has not fulfilled its obligations if the first state is itself responsible for the inability of the other state to fulfill these obligations.

The International Court of Justice insists on a distinction between equity and equitableness. But on many occasions, especially in several decisions on the delimitation of the maritime boundary or continental shelf between two or more states, the Court itself failed to uphold clearly the distinction. Nevertheless, the Court argued in the *Continental Shelf (Tunisia/Libyan Arab Jamahiriya)* case (1982, p. 60) that equitable principles have to be distinguished from decisions *ex aequo et bono*. The Court added that equitable principles are part of international law; to give them contents, the Court would have "to balance up the various considerations which it regards as relevant in order to produce an equitable result."

The Court stated in the *Continental Shelf (Libyan Arab Jamahiriya/Malta)* case (1982, p. 38) that the dictum "The result of the application of equitable principles must be equitable" was not satisfactory because the term *equitable* was employed to describe the result to be achieved and the means to be applied to achieve this result. "It is, however, the result which is predominant; the principles are subordinate to the goal." A principle may become equitable if its application leads to an equitable result. This consideration led the Court to conclude that "equitable principles" cannot be interpreted in the abstract. Such rules and principles must be applied in the process of achieving a particular equitable result. In international law, the Court argued, the legal concept of "equity" is a general principle (it did not say a norm) directly applicable as law. When the Court applies positive international law, it may choose those norms that are closest to the requirements of justice in the given case. In the arbitration in the *Dispute Concerning the Delimitation of the Maritime Boundary Between Guinea and Guinea-Bissau* (1985, pp. 209, 302), the tribunal pointed out that the method to be used for the determination of the maritime border would depend upon the equitable result. Although, said the Court, it could not compensate for the inequalities between states, it should in reaching the result not "completely lose sight" of the economic and security conditions of the two parties.

In the *Delimitation of the Maritime Boundary in the Gulf of Maine Area* case, which was heard before a chamber of the International Court of Justice (1984, p. 300), the Court stated that the delimitation of a maritime boundary "is to be effected by the application of equitable criteria" to ensure "an equitable result." The Court then went on to elaborate on the relation between customary law and equitability, saying, "Customary law merely contains a general requirement of the application of equitable criteria and the utilization of practical methods capable of implementing them." Criteria are, of course, not identical with legal norms, but the effect of solving a dispute by choosing norms fulfilling equitable criteria amounts to the same thing as applying the criteria as legal norms.

Because equitableness as applied to a given case can usually be defined only in light of the circumstances of the case, states find the principles of equity and equitability nebulous. For that reason, states are traditionally reluctant to appeal to them, especially when political issues are involved, because the outcome is often quite uncertain. These principles give the court considerable discretionary power—the last thing states are normally willing to grant. Even though the law-creating character of equity cannot always be denied, in most cases the principle merely modifies, rectifies, or softens existing legal norms to achieve a just and fair result.

The flexibility of the meaning of equity agitates for as well as against its usefulness. No state can publicly disavow its devotion to justice. But the substance of justice in a given situation may be contrary to the national interest and, in any case, differs from state to state because the concept is culture-bound. Nevertheless, equity can contribute significantly to the severe problem of peaceful change. Equity can obviate the felt need of a state to be released from an onerous commitment by the use of force or some illegal means. And equity can achieve a mutually satisfactory solution by adjusting legal commitments on the basis of fairness and justice and by replacing the possibly uncertain satisfaction of only one of the parties through the arbitrament of power in a political contest. This of course assumes that justice is a primary concern of states in international society, which it is not when their major interests are at stake.

The newer African and Asian states, allegedly distrusting the settlement of conflicts on a legal basis and preferring settlement by consensus, may prefer equity to a strictly legal settlement on the basis of a positive law, much of which they consider unjust, because equity comes closer to a negotiated settlement. In any case, these states should welcome the International Court's emphasis on the justice of the result rather than on any rigid application of positive law.

The problem is very acute for the many states insisting upon rectification of past injustices done to them. Their present method of demanding a broad and unspecified equality in law and substance has not been well received by the older and more developed states. A more compelling, albeit more modest, case could be made on the basis of equity. The mellowing influence of equity could dissolve confrontations into adjustments acceptable to both sides and could assuage some of the frustrations of the smaller, newer, and weaker states stemming from the inequalities between states. The Chinese are in fact, although not expressly, relying on equity in their argument that formally equal treaties are not in substance equal—and hence invalid—if the use of rights and duties is not reciprocal and equally beneficial to all parties.

Similarly, most of the former colonies are now trying not only to wipe out norms that make colonialism possible but also to introduce norms compensating them for damage suffered in the past. Equity could perform this function particularly well—although in a politically risky fashion—if equity were used for the nonapplication of unjust laws.

The abuse of rights principle could be useful here, too, if there were an objective agency to determine when an abuse had taken place and if the very existence of the principle were not so controversial. Equity would certainly be among the criteria in such a determination. An abuse of rights is present when a state uses a right in an arbitrary manner, thereby inflicting an injury upon another state that cannot legitimately be justified by the needs of the abusing state. In practice, this principle would simply be used as another political tool by states. On a broader base, writers from the newer states deny that these principles can be introduced as customary law because they deny that customary law can be created by powerful states when it is contrary to the basic principles of contemporary international law based on the sovereign equality of states, their right to self-determination, and the restoration of justice (that is, of equity denied them in the past).

As law transmutes from coexistence to cooperative law and as increasing emphasis is given to an obligation and need by states to consider international community interests in the exercise of their sovereignty, international courts will, and actually do, use equity in balancing competing interests of states. This practice is becoming increasingly fashionable and very useful in situations for which no positive norms previously existed.

5
INSTITUTIONS AND PERSONS AS CREATORS OF INTERNATIONAL LAW

States

States have a monopoly on deciding what international law shall be. This privilege is a consequence of sovereignty and nationalism. States may or may not be a source of law, depending upon how this term is understood. Other institutions and even individuals could promote international law. They could initiate a chain of events leading to the creation of law by an act of states—for instance, by suggesting, inspiring, proposing, furthering, or recommending legal norms. Or they could advance the law by discovering, clarifying, interpreting, or confirming legal norms already accepted by states. In either case, they may be credited as sources of law in a broader sense; yet only states can make law for states.

States are always reluctant to commit themselves. They are especially intolerant of anyone else committing them. They eagerly attempt to prevent the rise of competing lawmakers, be they international public or private agencies (multilateral corporations, for instance). States are still the only actors in the international system in which ultimately relevant legal powers reside. States may delegate lawmaking powers, to international organizations, for instance, but they can abolish the organizations.

International Organizations

The monopolistic position of states was not in doubt until international organizations were considered to possess some legal personality. International organizations compete with states as lawmakers in three different ways. But their authority to do so is always derived from states.

First, international organizations have a right to arrange for their own internal structure and functioning. They can make legally binding arrangements for their "housekeeping," including administrative tribunals for the protection of their own staffs (for example, the United Nations and the International Labor Organization).

Second, international organizations can conclude treaties with each other as well as with states. They are entitled to do so by the 1986 Vienna Convention on the Law of Treaties Between the States and International Organizations, or Between International Organizations, but they are limited to treaties that are "necessary for the exercise of their functions and the fulfillment of their purposes" (preamble of the convention; also see Article 6). Even before this convention, the United Nations and other organizations could conclude treaties to determine their status in the host country (regarding, for example, immunities), to create an international armed force (Article 43), to set up trusteeships (Articles 75, 79, 83, 85), and to elaborate interorganization relations (Articles 57, 63).

Third, the agreements reached in the general organs (plenary assemblies, for instance) of international organizations can arguably be considered international legislation. Final conference statements (resolutions, agreements, recommendations, declarations) containing normative regulations of a general character have been held to be international law. Other types of rules and regulations possessing norm-creating characteristics, especially those by specialized agencies of the United Nations, have similarly been said to have legal character, especially when a state does not object.

There is virtual unanimity among states that such agreements of organizations are not legally binding. Occasional announcements by a state that it will act in accordance with a resolution if other states do make clear at the same time that the state does so voluntarily.

The issue of international organizations as lawmakers beyond their right to make certain treaties is unresolved. Two facts create much uncertainty. First, with few exceptions, agreements reached at international conferences require formal agreement by states in accordance with their constitutional requirements (such as ratification) to become legally binding. Second, international organizations are not autonomous entities; they are creatures of states. Their status is derived from the will of states. They are associations of sovereign states acting together within the organizational framework of an international agency, and these states are acting autonomously in their sovereign capacity. It makes no difference whether they are so acting within or without an organization. They remain individually the final arbiters of what is to be a legal norm binding them, and they have nowhere surrendered that capacity. Nevertheless, this principle leaves open the possibility that by implication or otherwise states have agreed to be bound by certain procedures and agreements of international organizations and, much more important, that these organizations as a collective of states may play a participatory role in the creation of international law.

This opportunity has been pushed hard by writers cherishing the thought of an international legislature. It has also been much advanced by newer and Third World states wishing to exploit their majority positions. Both groups have been responsible (at best) for starting a trend in this direction, which has received further impetus from several opinions by the International Court of Justice. But it is essential to distinguish two different areas of "legislative" power. One relates to "legislation" dealing with the status of the organization itself: its rights, duties, powers qua organization. The other relates to legislation dealing with the subject matter of the organization.

In regard to the first kind of legislative power, the ICJ in *Reparation for Injuries Suffered in the Service of the United Nations* (1949, pp. 178, 180) addressed itself in an advisory opinion to the status of the United Nations. The Court stated that the United Nations is "an international person" but that this is not equivalent to being a state and therefore does not establish the same rights and duties for the United Nations as for a state. "What it does mean is that it is a subject of international law and capable of possessing international rights and duties" of a limited kind. The United Nations "must be deemed to have those powers, which, though not expressly provided in the Charter, are conferred upon it by necessary implication as being essential to the performance of its duties." The Court then applied this principle to other organizations by saying that "the rights and duties of an entity such as the Organization must depend upon its purposes and functions." This opinion is essentially embodied now in the Convention on Treaties Concluded Between States and International Organizations (1986).

In regard to the second kind of legislative power, particularly resolutions (as distinct from treaties) passed within the organization, the ICJ addressed itself to resolutions on aggression, genocide, and racism (among others) made in the United Nations and elsewhere. The International Court in *Barcelona Traction, Light and Power Co. Ltd. Judgment* (1970) referred to the outlawing of acts of aggression and genocide and the protection of basic human rights, including protection from slavery and racial discrimination, as obligations by every state *erga omnes*, although not every state had ratified the relevant conventions. The Court in *Legal Consequences for States of the Continued Presence of South Africa in Namibia* (1971, p. 50) held that it would be incorrect to assume that "because the General Assembly is in principle vested with recommendatory powers, it is debarred from adopting, in specific areas within the framework of its competence, resolutions which make determinations or have operative designs." In the *Fisheries Jurisdiction (Merits, Judgment)* case (1974, p. 24), the Court referred to the resolutions of the states at the Fishery and the Law of the Sea Conferences (1958 and 1960) to support its opinion, while pointing out that views and opinions of states expressed at such conferences are "vehicles of their aspirations, rather than . . . expressing principles of existing law."

States, which are less careful than courts, exploit this borderline between political propaganda and law-creating measures. They often find it expedient to refer to resolutions as legally binding. States of Asia and Africa are frequent practitioners of this method. Innumerable resolutions relating to racism, colonialism, and liberation movements are passed by these states with the help of assured majorities, presumably in the hope that repetition will create the impression of practice and the existence of *opinio iuris* and will lead to the conversion of their aspirations into customary law. This is one way of using legal methods for political ends. That these states have not been totally unsuccessful is demonstrated by the *Filartiga v. Peña-Irala* case (1980) in which U.S. Court of Appeals Judge Irving R. Kaufman declared torture a crime against international law, basing his judgment largely upon the various declarations and resolutions passed in international organizations.

These states would like to provide these resolutions with some normative influence in order to locate them somewhere between mere recommendations and legislative command. Hence these resolutions have been called quasi-law or prelaw. Lord Arnold McNair spoke of "soft" law, a concept that has lately come back into fashion. But it is a dangerous concept because it blurs the clear-cut division between *lex lata* and *lex ferenda*. It might be better to consider these resolutions as aspects of an international *ordre public*.

Depending upon their character—recommendations, declarations, clarifications, directives, standards—these resolutions may gradually set boundaries for the discussion of future legal norms. They may narrow and guide the legislative process. They may be persuasive for governments and courts, which might find it difficult to maintain legal positions opposing the high principles embodied in these resolutions. They may affect the relations between states without binding them (gentlemen's agreements!) They may make it difficult for a state voting for a resolution to act contrary to it at a later date.

These resolutions reflect a majority consensus about (but not necessarily consent to) expectations of future state behavior and may eventually become law. But the nonlegal character of these resolutions is shown, for instance, when states disagreeing with them prophylactically object to them to make sure they will not later be considered as conventional law, as evidence of customary law, or as an interpretation of existing law. Nevertheless, these resolutions have some effect upon the behavior of states, for instance, as soft law or as a means of social communication.

In examining the practice of states, one can assume that in any case two conditions must be fulfilled for these resolutions to approximate the making of law. First, they must refer to principles and norms suitable for generalization. Second, they must be credible—that is, they must be more than obvious propaganda moves by some majority passing them, and the majority passing these resolutions must contain most or many of those states needed to make them operative. This second condition—obviously obnoxious to many smaller or weaker states—results from the fact that states are politically unequal and that a resolution, even as prelaw, cannot be effective if it lacks adequate political support because a political decision must precede a norm.

In sum, international organizations can contribute to the growth of law. They do not make law. Giving them the character of a legislature is anticipating possibly desirable developments rather than stating facts. In creating international organizations, states had no intention of divesting themselves of their monopoly on the making of international law. That the General Assembly was to be specifically denied the right to make binding law was made quite clear during the San Francisco Conference of the United Nations. Notwithstanding the occasional insistence, particularly by smaller states, that General Assembly resolutions be considered legally binding, as long as nationalism is as rampant as it is, most states will not want to endow the United Nations (or even lesser agencies with smaller memberships) with law-creating capacity for the vast areas of its concerns. Only insofar as international organizations make treaties with states do they create international law in the usual manner in which treaties create law.

Legal Agencies

Several agencies, public and private, are devoted to the furthering of international law without themselves having any formal law-creating power. The most prestigious is the International Law Commission, an agency of the U.N. General Assembly, which appoints its members as private experts in international law. The commission's task is to codify existing international law and to develop progressively new international law. It has been fulfilling its assignment in a slow, thorough, and fairly successful manner (especially in its youth) during frequent meetings in which major topics of international law are debated but in which absenteeism is rampant. Occasionally, when consensus can be achieved, the results of the commission's labor are presented in draft form to the parent body, where agreement has been reached on such important but rather noncontroversial matters as the Vienna Conventions on Diplomatic Relations (1961) and the law of Treaties (1969). The commission has for years also worked on such topics as the law of the sea and responsibility of states without having been able to achieve a draft proposal or have one accepted.

The Legal (Sixth) Committee of the U.N. General Assembly could play an important part in furthering the progress of international law but hardly does so. The committee is large and slow moving, it hesitates to create "new" international law, it changes membership annually, and on most of the important subjects it is undermined by specially created committees.

Unofficial agencies dealing with the codification and development of international law are the International Law Association, the Institut de Droit International, the Harvard Research in International Law, the American Law Institute, and the Asian African Law Commission (which devotes itself to considering legal topics from the perspective of the states of Asia and Africa). Courts, to fortify their decisions, occasionally refer to the findings of these agencies.

Courts

The jurisprudence of international tribunals and municipal courts has special significance as a source of international law. In theory, courts interpret law; they do not make it. Indeed, judges are usually eager to reject the notion that they play a norm-creating role. In practice, the situation is different. The somewhat extreme argument could even be made that a law is complete only after the judge defines what it means, so that the judge is, in fact, part of the legislative process. It is also a fact that makers of decisions prefer to rely on precedents and to proceed incrementally rather than radically. Cumulatively, therefore, a chain of decisions in comparable cases establishes a meaning of the law that may itself be an act of judicial lawmaking! The claim of courts that they interpret but do not create law must be accepted with a grain of salt, especially now that the International Court has become increasingly inclined to follow the sociological and policy-oriented school of jurisprudence, if not in its final judgments, at least in its dissenting opinions. To some extent, this is due to the greater influence of Third World states on the choice of judges through the General Assembly. So far, however, these states have failed to exploit this new possibility of adding "new law" because of their continuing reluctance to submit disputes to the International Court.

The International Court is specifically instructed in Article 59 of the statute not to apply precedent or the doctrine of stare decisis. Its decisions, according to Article 38, may serve only as evidence for the existence of international law. But the fact is that all courts and tribunals—international courts, arbitration tribunals, military international courts, municipal courts—rely upon and cite each other abundantly in their verdicts. Decisions, especially repetitive, similar decisions, acquire an authority affecting the formulation of judgments and legal norms in subsequent cases. Decisions are not merely evidence of existing law. They often become the creators of law, especially customary law, by becoming part of international practice.

Individuals

Article 38 of the statute of the International Court of Justice authorizes the Court to apply "the teachings of the most highly qualified publicists of the various nations, as a subsidiary means for the determination of the rules of law." It is clear from this unclear statement that the teachings themselves are not legally binding. Beyond this, courts have used these teachings mainly as a labor-saving device: The courts use what the publicists have found rather than themselves digging up whatever evidence is needed to prove the existence or nonexistence of a legal norm.

In the *Paquete Habana* and *Lola* case (1900, p. 700), the U.S. Supreme Court said that "the works of jurists and commentators, who by years of labor, research and experience, have made themselves peculiarly well acquainted with the subjects of which they treat" should be used "not for the speculations of their authors concerning what the law ought to be, but for trustworthy evidence of what the law really is." Chief Justice Cockburn of the English Court of Crown Cases Reserved confirmed that writers cannot make the law; they can only elucidate and ascertain it. The judge must still look for the assent of states as the only decisive criterion for the existence of international law. And Judge Marriott in the English High Court of Admiralty, very sceptical of writers altogether, asked, "Who shall decide, when the doctors disagree?"

Legal advisers in foreign offices may have considerable influence upon legal state practice by interpreting, defining, or creating laws and treaties. The appointment of such officers is for most states a relatively recent phenomenon indicative of the growing importance of legal questions in international relations. In political questions, the role of these advisers remains subsidiary. They rarely play an active part in the formulation of political policies. Rather, if they participate at all, they formulate accepted policies in legal terms or criticize the policies of other states on legal grounds. Their role is more active when foreign offices have to deal specifically with legal questions. In any case, the role of these advisers as sources of international law may be quite significant, especially when states face new situations.

Private individuals—for instance, as claimants against a foreign government—or corporations engaged in foreign transactions may become sources of international law indirectly when they try to support their interests by legal arguments accepted by their states or to reject those of their opponents. In the constantly growing number of situations involving economic transactions between public and private agencies, private interests have considerable influence upon the formulation of legal principles and the legal practice of states.

REFERENCES AND READINGS FOR PART 1

Sociology of Law

Blenk-Nocke, Edda. *Zu den soziologischen Bedingungen völkerrechtlicher Normenbefolgung*. Ebelsbach, West Germany: R. Gremer, 1979.

Collins, Hugh. *Marxism and Law*. Oxford: Clarendon, 1982.

Cotterell, Roger. *The Sociology of Law: An Introduction*. London: Butterworth, 1984.

Dupuy, René-Jean, ed. *The Future of International Law in a Multinational World: ADIRC Workshop*. The Hague: Martinus Nijhoff, 1984.

Ehrlich, Eugen. *Fundamental Principles of the Sociology of Law*, vol. 5. Cambridge, MA: Harvard University Press, 1936.

Geiger, Theodor. *Vorstudien zu einer Soziologie des Rechts*. Neuwied am Rhein, West Germany: Hermann Luchterhand, 1964.

Gould, Wesley, and Michael Barkun. *International Law and the Social Sciences*. Princeton, NJ: Princeton University Press, 1970.

Gurvitch, George. *Sociology of Law*. London: Routledge and Kegan Paul, 1953.

Huber, Max. "Beiträge zur Kenntnis der soziologischen Grundlagen des Völkerrechts und der Staatengesellschaft." *Jahrbuch des öffentlichen Rechts der Gegenwart* 4 (1910):56–134.

Jenks, C. Wilfred. *The Common Law of Mankind*. London: London Institute of World Affairs, 1958.

Landheer, B. "Contemporary sociological theories of international law." *ADIRC* 91 (1957 I):7–103.

Merle, Marcel. *The Sociology of International Relations*. New York: St. Martin's, 1987.

Weber, Max. *Rechssoziologie*. Neuwied am Rhein, West Germany: Hermann Luchterhand, 1960.

New States

Agrawala, S. K., T. S. Rao, and J. N. Saxena, eds. *New Horizons of International Law and Developing Countries*, Bombay: N. M. Tripathi, 1983.

Anand, R. P. *New States and International Law*. Delhi: Vikas, 1972.

———— . *Confrontation or Cooperation? International Law and the Developing Countries.* Dordrecht: Martinus Nijhoff, 1987.

Bokor-Szegö, H. *New States and International Law.* Budapest: Akadémiai Kiadó, 1970.

Buirette-Maurau, Patricia. *La participation du tiers-monde à l'élaboration du droit international.* Paris: Bibliothèque de Droit International, 1983.

Crawford, James. *The Creation of New States in International Law.* Oxford: Clarendon, 1979.

Falk, Richard A. "The new states and the international legal order." *ADIRC* 118 (1966 II):7–103.

Franck, Thomas M. "Legitimacy in the international system." *AJIL* 82 (October 1988):705–759.

Malekian, Farhad. *The System of International Law: Formation, Treaties, Responsibility.* Uppsala: n.p., 1987.

Menon, P. K. "An enquiry into the sources of modern international law." *Revue de Droit International de Sciences Diplomatiques et Politiques* 64 (July 1986):181–214.

O'Brien, William V., ed. *The New Nations in International Law and Diplomacy: The Yearbook of World Policy,* vol. 3. New York: Praeger, 1965.

Okoye, Felix C. *International Law and the New African States.* London: Sweet and Maxwell, 1972.

Rudolf, Walter. "Neue Staaten und das Völkerrecht." *AV* 17 (1976 I):1–45.

Schröder, D. *Die dritte Welt und das Völkerrecht.* Hamburg: Forschungsstelle für Völkerrecht und ausländisches öffentliches Recht der Universität Hamburg, 1970.

Snyder, Frederick E., and Surakiarat Sathirathai, eds. *Third World Attitudes Toward International Law.* Dordrecht: Martinus Nijhoff, 1987.

Société Française pour le Droit International. *Pays en voie de développement et transformation du droit international.* Paris: A. Pédone, 1974.

Syatauw, J.J.G. "Old and new states: A misleading distinction for future international law and international relations." *Indian Journal of International Law* 15 (1975 II):153–172.

Thomas, Caroline. *New States, Sovereignty and Intervention.* New York: St. Martin's, 1985.

Udokang, O. N. "The role of new states in international law." *AV* 15 (1971 II):147–196.

Changing International Society

Elias, Tashin O. "Modern Sources of International Law." In *Transnational Law in a Changing Society,* edited by Wolfgang Friedman, Louis Henkin, and Oliver Lissitzyn, pp. 34–69. New York: Columbia University Press, 1972.

Falk, Richard A. *Revitalizing International Law.* Ames: Iowa State University Press, 1989.

Fatouros, A. A. "The participation of the 'new states' in the international legal order." In *The Future of the International Legal Order,* edited by Richard A.

Falk and Cyril F. Black, vol. 1, pp. 317–371. Princeton, NJ: Princeton University Press, 1969.

Friedman, Wolfgang. *The Changing Structure of International Law.* New York: Columbia University Press, 1964.

———. *Law in a Changing Society.* New York: Columbia University Press, 1972.

Ginther, K., and W. Benedek, eds. *New Perspectives and Conceptions of International Law: An Afro-European Dialogue.* Vienna: Springer, 1985.

Jenks, C. Wilfred. *Law in a World Community.* New York: David McKay, 1967.

Kunz, Josef L. *The Changing Law of Nations.* Columbus: Ohio State University Press, 1968.

Lissitzyn, Oliver J. *International Law Today and Tomorrow.* Dobbs Ferry, NY: Oceana, 1965.

Röling, B.V.A. *International Law in an Expanded World.* Amsterdam: Djambatan, 1960.

Politics, Power, and Law

Barker, Charles A., ed. *Power and Law American Dilemma in World Affairs.* Baltimore, MD: Johns Hopkins University Press, 1971.

Fain, Haskell, *Normative Politics in the Community of Nations.* Philadelphia: Temple University Press, 1987.

Falk, Richard A. "The relevance of political context to the nature and functioning of international law: An immediate view." In *The Relevance of International Law,* edited by Karl W. Deutsch and Stanley Hoffmann, pp. 177–202. Garden City, NY: Doubleday, 1971.

Goldmann, Kjell. *International Norms and War Between States: Three Studies in International Politics.* Stockholm: Utrikespolitiska Institutet, Läromedelsförlagen, 1972.

Kaplan, Morton, and N. deB. Katzenbach. *The Political Foundation of International Law.* New York: Wiley, 1961.

Keeton, George W., and Georg Schwarzenberger. *Making International Law Work.* New York: Garland, 1972.

Levi, Werner. *Law and Politics in the International Society.* Beverly Hills, CA: Sage, 1976.

McWhinney, Edward. *International Law and World Revolution.* Leiden, A. W. Sijthoff, 1967.

Rosenstiel, Francis. *Le principe de "supranationalite": Essai sur les rapports de la politique et du droit.* Paris: A Pédone, 1962.

Tsoutros, Athos G. *Politique et droit dans les relations internationales: Etudes sur l'évaluation de l'ordre juridique international.* Paris: Librairie Générale de Droit et de Jurisprudence, 1967.

Visscher, Charles de. *Theory and Reality in Public International Law.* Princeton, NJ: Princeton University Press, 1968.

Theories of Law

Carty, Anthony. *The Decay of International Law? A Reappraisal of the Limits of Legal Imagination in International Affairs.* Manchester: Manchester University Press, 1986.

Cassirer, Erich. *Natur- und Völkerrecht im Lichte der Geschichte und der systematischen Philosophie.* Aalen, West Germany: Scientia, 1963 (reprint).

D'Amato, Anthony A. "The neo-positivist concept of international law." *AJIL* 59 (April 1956):321–324.

―――. *International Law: Process and Prospect.* Dobbs Ferry, NY: Transnational, 1987.

Fried, John H. E. "International law—neither orphan nor harlot, neither jailer nor never-never land." In *The Relevance of International Law*, edited by Karl W. Deutsch and Stanley Hoffmann, pp. 124–176. Garden City, NY: Doubleday, 1971.

Gottlieb, Gideon. "The nature of international law: Toward a second concept of law." In *The Future of the International Legal Order*, edited by Cyril F. Black and Richard A. Falk, vol. 4, pp. 331–383. Princeton, NJ: Princeton University Press, 1972.

Krasner, Stephen D. "Structural causes and regime consequences: regimes as intervening variables." *International Organization* 36 (1982 II):1–21.

―――, ed. *International Régimes.* Ithaca, NY: Cornell University Press, 1986.

Kratochwil, Friedrich V. *Rules, Norms and Decisions on the Conditions of Practical and Legal Reasoning in International Relations and Domestic Affairs.* Cambridge: Cambridge University Press, 1989.

Lupis, Ingrid Detter de. *International Law and the Independent State*, 2nd ed. Brookfield, VT: Gower, 1987.

MacDonald, Ronald St.J, and Douglas M. Johnston, eds. *The Structure and Process of International Law.* The Hague: Martinus Nijhoff, 1983.

McDougal, Myres S. "Some basic theoretical concepts about international law: A policy-oriented framework of enquiry." *Journal of Conflict Resolution* 4 (September 1960):337–354.

Midgley, E.B.F. *The Natural Law Tradition and the Theory of International Relations.* New York: Barnes and Noble, 1975.

Nardin, Terry. *Law, Morality and the Relations of States.* Princeton, NJ: Princeton University Press, 1983.

Nussbaum, Arthur. *A Concise History of the Law of Nations.* New York: Macmillan, 1954.

Tunkin, G. I. *Theory of International Law.* Cambridge, MA: Harvard University Press, 1974.

Binding Force of Law

Fisher, Roger. *Improving Compliance with International Law.* Charlottesville: University Press of Virginia, 1981.

Simma, Bruno. *Das Reziprozitätselement in der Entstehung des Völkergewohnheits-rechts.* Munich: W. Fink, 1970.

Sinha, S. P. "Perspectives of the newly independent states on the binding quality of international law." *Int. & Comp. L. Q.* 14 (January 1965):121–131.

Relations Between International and Municipal Law

Bayzler, Michael. "Litigating the international law of human rights: A 'how to' approach." *Whitter Law Review* 7 (1985 III):713–740.

Blum, Jeffrey M., and Ralph G. Steinhardt. "Federal jurisdiction over international human rights claims: The Alien Tort Claims Act after *Filartiga v. Peña-Irala.*" *Harvard International Law Journal* 22 (1981 I):53–113.

Lillich, B. Richard. *Invoking Human Rights Law in Domestic Courts.* Washington, DC: Division of Public Services, American Bar Association, 1985.

Marek, K., ed. *Droit international et droit interne.* Geneva: Droz, 1961.

Papadimitriu, Georgios. *Die Stellung der allgemeinen Regeln des Völkerrechts im innerstaatlichen Recht.* Berlin: Duncker und Humblot, 1972.

Paust, Jordan S. "Federal jurisdiction over extraterritorial violators of international law under the FSIA and the act of state doctrine." *Virginia Journal of International Law* 23 (Fall-Summer 1982–1983):191–249.

Verzijl, J.H.W. *International Law in Historical Perspective,* vol. 1, pp. 90–183. Leiden: A. W. Sijthoff, 1968.

Conflict Between International and Municipal Law

Combacau, Jean. "La doctrine 'l'act of state' aux Etats Unies: Développements récents." *RGDIP* 77 (1973):35–91.

Delson, Robert. "The act of state doctrine—judicial defense or abstention?" *AJIL* 66 (January 1972):82–93.

Falk, Richard A. *The Role of Domestic Courts in the International Legal Order.* Syracuse NY: Syracuse University Press, 1964.

Folz, Hans-Ernst. *Geltungskraft fremder Hoheitsäusserungen: Eine Untersuchung über die anglo-amerikanische Act of State Doctrine.* Baden-Baden, West Germany: Nomos, 1975.

Hollrah, David C. "Notes: Act of state." *Harvard International Law Journal* 14 (Winter 1973):131–144.

Lardy, Pierre. *La force obligatoire du droit international en droit interne.* Paris: Librairie Générale de Droit et de Jurisprudence, 1966.

Lowenfeld, Andreas F. "Act of state and Department of State: First National City Bank v. Banco Nacional." *AJIL* 66 (October 1972):795–814.

Mann, F. A. "Conflict of laws and public law." *ADIRC* 132 (1971 I):107–197.

Meuwissen, D.H.M. "The relationship between international and municipal law and fundamental rights." *Netherlands International Law Review* 24 (special issue 1972):189–204.

Sources of International Law: General

Boos, Maarten. *A Methodology of International Law.* Amsterdam: Elsevier Science, 1984, pp. 48–104.

Bos, A., and H. Siblesz, eds. *Realism in International Law Making.* Dordrecht: Martinus Nijhoff, 1986.

Cassese, Antonio, and Joseph H.H. Weiler. *Change and Stability in International Law Making.* Berlin: Walter de Gruyter, 1988.

Hoof, G.J.H. van. *Rethinking the Sources of International Law.* Deventer, the Netherlands: Kluwer Law and Taxation, 1983.

McDougal, Myres S., and Harold D. Lasswell. "The identification and appraisal of diverse systems of Public Order." In *International Law: A Contemporary Perspective,* edited by Richard Falk et al., pp. 163–168. Boulder, CO: Westview, 1985.

McWhinney, Edward. *United Nations Law Making,* New York: Holmes and Meier, 1984.

Menon, K. P. "An enquiry into the sources of modern international law." *Revue de Droit International de Sciences Diplomatiques et Politiques* 64 (July-September 1986):181–214.

Parry, C. *The Sources and Evidences of International Law.* Dobbs Ferry, NY: Oceana, 1965.

Schwarzenberger, Georg. "The problem of international public policy." *Current Legal Problems* 18 (1965):191–214.

Walbeck, N. V. "Global public political culture." *Peace Research Review* 5 (November 1973):1–128.

Sources of International Law: Treaties

Baxter, Richard R. "Multilateral treaties as evidence of customary international law." *BYIL* 41 (1965–1966):275–300.

Schweisfurth, Theodor. *Der internationale Vertrag in der modernen sowjetischen Völkerrechtstheorie.* Cologne: Wissenschaft und Politik, 1968.

Verdross, Alfred. *Quellen universalen Völkerrechts: Eine Einführung.* Freiburg im Breisgau, West Germany: Rombach, 1973.

Villiger, Mark E. *Customary International Law and Treaties.* Dordrecht: Martinus Nijhoff, 1985.

Sources of International Law: Custom

Bravo, Luigi F. "Méthodes de recherche de la coutume internationale dans la pratique des états." *ADIRC* 192 (1985 III):233–329.

Charney, Jonathan I. "The persistent objector rule and the development of customary international law." *BYIL* 56 (1985):1–24.

D'Amato, A. A. *The Concept of Custom in International Law.* Ithaca, NY: Cornell University Press, 1971.

Dupuy, René-Jean. "Coutume sage et coutume sauvage." In *Mélanges offerts à Charles Rousseau: La communauté internationale,* pp. 75–87. Paris: A. Pédone, 1974.

Günther, Herbert. *Zur Entstehung von Völkergewohnheitsrecht.* Berlin: Duncker and Humblot, 1970.

Schweisfurth, Theodor. "Das Völkergewohnheitsrecht—verstärkt im Blickfeld der sowjetischen Völkerrechtslehre." *German Yearbook of International Law* 30 (1987):36–77.

Thirlway, H.W.A. *International Customary Law and Codification.* Leiden: A. W. Sijthoff, 1972.

Villiger, Mark E. *Customary International Law and Treaties.* Dordrecht: Martinus Nijhoff, 1985.

Sources of International Law: General Principles

Cheng, Bin. *General Principles of Law as Applied by International Courts and Tribunals.* Cambridge: Grotius, 1987.

Friedmann, Wolfgang. "The uses of 'general principles' in the development of international law." *AJIL* 57 (April 1963):279–299.

Jenks, C. Wilfred. *The Prospects of International Adjudication.* London: Stevens, 1964.

McNair, Arnold D. "The general principles of law recognized by civilized nations." *BYIL* 33 (1957):1–19.

Sinha, S. Prasad. "Identifying a principle of international law today." *Canadian Yearbook of International Law* 11 (1973):106–122.

Sources of International Law: Equity

Akehurst, Michael. "Equity and general principles of law." *Int. & Comp. L. Q.* 25 (October 1976):801–825.

Cheng, Bin. "Justice and equity in international law." *Current Legal Problems* 8 (1955):185–211.

Degan, V. D. *L'équité et le droit international.* The Hague: Martinus Nijhoff, 1970.

Jenks, C. Wilfred. *The Prospects of International Adjudication.* London: Stevens, 1964.

Lukashuk, I. I. "Morality and international law." *Indian Journal of International Law* 15 (January-March 1975):47–62.

Luper-Foy, Steven, ed. *Problems of International Justice.* Boulder, CO: Westview, 1988.

Schwarzenberger, Georg. *The Dynamics of International Law*. South Hackensack, NJ: Fred B. Rothman, 1976.

Stone, Julius. *Human Law and Human Justice*. London: Stevens, 1965.

Visscher, Charles de. *De l'équité dans le règlement arbitral ou judiciaire des litiges de droit international public*. Paris: A Pédone, 1972.

Zoller, Elizabeth. *La bonne foi en droit international public*. Paris: A. Pédone, 1978.

Sources of International Law: International Organizations

Briggs, Herbert W. *The International Law Commission*. Ithaca, NY: Cornell University Press, 1965.

Butler, W. E., ed. *International Law and the International System*. Dordrecht: Martinus Nijhoff, 1987, pp. 5–65.

Chiu, Hungdah. *The Capacity of International Organizations to Conclude Treaties and the Special Legal Aspects of Treaties so Concluded*. The Hague: Martinus Nijhoff, 1966.

Detter, Ingrid. *Law Making by International Organizations*. Stockholm: P. A. Norstedt, 1964.

Dupuy, René-Jean, ed. *A Handbook on International Organizations*. Dordrecht: Martinus Nijhoff, 1988.

Falk, Richard A. "On the quasi-legal competence of the General Assembly." *AJIL* 60 (October 1966):782–791.

Frowein, Jochen A. "Der Beitrag der internationalen Organisationen zur Entwicklung des Völkerrechts." *Z* 36 (1976 I–III):147–167.

Gaja, Giorgio. "A 'new' Vienna convention on treaties between international organisations or states and between international organisations: A critical commentary." *BYIL* 58 (1987):253–269.

Higgins, Rosalyn. *The Development of International Law Through the Political Organs of the United Nations*. London: Oxford University Press, 1963.

McWhinney, Edward. *United Nations Law Making*. New York: Holmes and Meier, 1984.

Monaco, Riccardo. "Le caractère constitutionnel des actes institutifs d'organisations internationales." In *Mélanges offerts à Charles Rousseau: La communauté internationale*, pp. 153–172. Paris: A. Pédone, 1974.

Pernice, Ingolf. "Völkerrechtliche Verträge internationaler Organisationen." *Z* (1988 II):229–250. The Hague: Martinus Nijhoff, 1977.

Schwelb, Egon. "Neue Etappen der Fortentwicklung des Völkerrechts durch die Vereinten Nationen." *AV* 13 (1966-1967) I):1–52.

Sinclair, Ian. *The International Law Commission*. Cambridge: Grotius, 1987.

Sloan, Blaine. "General Assembly resolutions revisited (twenty years later)." *BYIL* 58 (1987):39–150.

Thürer, Daniel. " 'Soft Law'—eine neue Form von Völkerrecht?" *Neue Zürcher Zeitung* 21-22 (July 1989), p. 31.

Verdross, Alfred. "Kann die Generalversammlung der Vereinten Nationen das Völkerrecht weiterbilden?" Z 26 (1966 III–IV):690–697.
Visscher, Paul de. "Cours général de droit international public." ADIRC 136 (1972 II):9–202.
Weissberg, Guenter. "United Nations movement toward world law." Int. & Comp. L. Q. 24 (July 1975):460–524.
Yemin, Edward. Legislative Powers in the United Nations and Specialized Agencies. Leiden: A. W. Sijthoff, 1969.
Zemanek, K., ed. Agreements of International Organisations and Vienna Convention on the Law of Treaties. New York: Springer, 1971.

Sources of International Law: Individuals

François, J.-P.-A. L'influence de la doctrine des publicistes sur le développement de droit international." In Mélanges en l'honneur de Gilbert Gidel, pp. 275–281. Paris: Sirey, 1961.
Merillat, Herbert C.L., ed. Legal Advisers and Foreign Affairs. Dobbs Ferry, NY: Oceana, 1964.
Sørensen, Max. Les sources du droit international. Copenhagen: Munksgaard, 1961, pp. 177–190.

Sources of International Law: Courts and Tribunals

Friedmann, Wolfgang. "International Court of Justice and the evolution of international law." AV 14 (1970 III–IV):305–320.
Jenks, C. Wilfred. The Prospects of International Adjudication. London: Stevens, 1964.
Lauterpacht, Hersch. The Development of International Law by the International Court of Justice. New York: Praeger, 1958.
Rosenne, Shabtai. The Law and Practice of the International Court, 2 vols. Leiden: A. W. Sijthoff, 1965.

PART 2
INTERNATIONAL
LEGAL CAPACITY

Subjects of law are individuals (natural persons) or groups of individuals (collectivities, juridic persons) directly recognized by law as capable of having rights and duties and of acting with legal consequences. But ultimately law always addresses itself to individuals in their different qualities. Strictly speaking, juridic persons, whether a corporation or a state, are anthropomorphized fictions assuming reality only in the persons composing them. Nevertheless, legal systems and norms deal with persons in their various capacities: as individuals (automobile drivers, criminals, shareholders, ministers) or as nameless members of a collectivity (a union, a corporation, a government, a state). Yet legal consequences are always experienced by individuals.

On the basis of such considerations, some international lawyers argue that only individuals can be subjects of international law. These lawyers are correct in the sense that nothing inherent in the nature of international law would give states the monopoly of legal subjectivity or in the sense that states work through individuals. Indeed, the modern trend is to agitate for expanding international legal subjectivity to persons and entities other than states or even to claim that they already possess it. But as long as humankind remains organized in the collectivity of sovereign states and nationalism remains strong, states will retain their monopoly and insist that any subjectivity acquired by other entities is their grant and derived from their subjectivity.

State practice in this respect is obvious, although it becomes increasingly difficult to maintain the monopoly on subjectivity. Occasionally, states find it even politically expedient to endow other entities with legal subjectivity—for instance, when they wish to grant a rebel group or a liberation movement legal personality. Recognition by some states of the Palestine Liberation Front as a state is a most recent illustration.

In principle, states remain the only entities having the fullest measure of rights and duties and the capacity to act legally on the international scene. The International Court of Justice in the *Reparation for Injuries Suffered in the Service of the United Nations* (1949, p. 178) asserted that "the subjects of law in any legal system are not necessarily identical in their nature or in the extent of their rights, and their nature depends

61

upon the needs of the community." The point is, however, that states determine the nature of the community and directly or indirectly determine its needs.

Both can differ greatly, a fact states exploit for political purposes. States have full rights and duties as well as full capacity to act. But there are quasi-states, divided states, federal and unitary states, confederated states, and several other kinds of states. The legal capacity of each is often uncertain and much debated. International organizations have been granted some capacity to act with legal consequences, some rights, and some duties. Revolutionary and insurgent groups may have some rights and duties directly under international law. Individuals, either singly (such as under human rights conventions) or as members of special groups (such as minorities), may have limited rights and certainly many duties under international law. In the European Community, for instance, individuals can turn directly to an international agency, claiming violation of their human rights by their own state. In Scandinavia, individuals can accuse their state of illegal environmental practices. The Convention on the Settlement of Investment Disputes of the International Bank of Reconstruction and Development (1965) allows individuals to participate in the arbitration process (although in some instances they need their state's permission to do so).

There is no way of generalizing for all subjects of international law. In every case, an examination must determine the extent to which states have endowed such entities with legal personality. This situation makes it highly unlikely that there are entities other than states with an original legal personality of their own. These possess "borrowed" personality, lent by states and revocable by them. If in exceptional cases such entities can obligate states, this is due to an "autolimitation" by states of their own personality in favor of the entity.

6
SUBJECTS OF
INTERNATIONAL LAW

States

States are the foundation of the international political system. They agree that international law shall be their tool, not their master. They achieve this goal by maintaining themselves as the mainspring of the creation and use of law.

International law was originally fashioned into one of the instruments for safeguarding the "personality" and existence of states. To be effective, this instrument had to offer a fairly comprehensive regulation for the identification and survival of states. It had to specify the manner in which states would arise, exist, and demise and in which, while in existence, they should behave toward each other. Although these ends remain constant, reaching them in a dynamic world requires dynamism in the law as well; perhaps in the future the law will no longer have the capacity to undergo the necessary changes (or these ends will have to be abandoned). In the meantime, some norms of international law have become an anachronism or a dead letter, while others have been adapted or added to (especially in the form of treaties) to serve the major purposes of maintaining states intact under modern conditions.

Despite the long-standing importance of states, there is no authoritative definition for them in international law; this greatly expands the space in which existing states can maneuver politically. Yet the consequences of this lack can be serious. There is a significant difference in law and politics whether an act is performed on behalf of a state or some other entity (a freedom movement, revolutionaries, insurgents, terrorists). The rights and duties of entities other than states are very much inferior to those of states. The members of such entities may be aliens and poorly protected; their property may be insecure; their participation in international conferences and the making of treaties is severely restricted—to name just a few disadvantages.

There is far-reaching agreement only on a few minimum conditions that must exist before a group is entitled to be a state. There must be a territory, although it need not be contiguous. There must be a population, although its size is irrelevant. There must be a government in control of territory and population, although the government's character is inconsequential.

Beyond these conditions, disagreements begin either in regard to some qualifications of these minimum conditions ("effective" government, "permanent" population, "defined" territory) or in regard to additional conditions ("peace loving," "full" independence, ability and willingness to carry out international relations effectively and legally). Nevertheless, these seemingly legal conditions are essentially political. The existence of a state is independent of actions by other states. Other states qualify minimum conditions for political purposes of their own to deal or not to deal with the state. The treatment by Arab states of the Palestine Liberation Organization (PLO) as a state and the refusal of the United States to do so fully are good illustrations of this situation.

The question of whether there is a state is further complicated by the existence of various forms in which a state can exist. They are of significance, although internal arrangements of a state are not relevant to international law. Of importance is mainly—if the minimum conditions are fulfilled—whether the entity to be a state can act responsibly in international society under the terms of international law. Who would make such a determination is extremely dubious. In a unitary state, no special problems arise. In federal states a problem may be whether the federation acts for all units or whether the component units (states, cantons, provinces) have legal subjectivity of their own. Australian and German states, for instance, have trade representatives abroad; some Soviet Union republics are members of the United Nations. In a personal union (with two states having the same head of state), in a confederation, or even in a union of states sharing some governing organs, the compact creating the entities will usually define the location of the legal personality. The same is true of states in various stages of integration, such as the European Community and the Organization of African Unity. The legal personality of such creations must be examined in regard to their own members and outside states (which would in any case have to recognize the legal personality if it is to be valid toward them).

Neutralized and guaranteed states have problems of their own. Dependent states normally have no legal personality, unless by internal arrangements or treaties with third states they acquire some limited personality. Independent states (for example, Liechtenstein) may have some of their international affairs taken care of by other states, thereby raising questions about their legal personality.

No matter how a state is defined, there is always room for debate on whether the agreed criteria are fulfilled. Even ostensibly objective conditions can usually be fully defined only with the help of some subjective judgment. Is, for instance, a given government indeed a government? Whether a state (or a government) exists and is peace loving involves an ambiguity cherished by states as providing them with room for political maneuvering. They can call an entity a state or not a state according to their political preferences. For the entity, at least in regard to those states, the resulting uncertainty can be politically unfavorable. This issue assumed some importance with the rise of so many ministates in the 1960s and 1970s and divided states applying for membership in the United Nations. Some of these states were probably unable to fulfill some obligations of statehood or membership, which was used by some members as a reason for denying statehood to some applicants. The question was politically sensitive, and the United Nations itself failed to produce a recommendation. The chance for garnering a few more votes proved sufficiently tempting, however, for certain members to plead successfully for the admission of all applicants into the United Nations.

The importance of the entire situation is in the political more than the legal realm. U.S. municipal courts testify to that fact when they often leave the determination of statehood and U.S. recognition of such to the executive. The courts concern themselves mainly with forms or legal consequences of recognition. Substantively, recognition is primarily a political measure with far-reaching political and legal consequences.

Recognition

Recognition is a state's acknowledgment of an internationally relevant fact and its legal consequences. Recognition can be express, conditional, or implied by action. It is not limited to recognizing states or governments, although it is applied most often to them. Recognition can refer to all kinds of international facts. The United States, for instance, developed the "nonrecognition" doctrine as a means of applying political pressure to Japan when it represented its Twenty-One Demands (1915) to China and invaded Manchuria (1932). The doctrine stated that the U.S. government would not recognize "the legality of a situation de facto" or any treaty or agreement between Japan and China impairing treaty rights of the United States; nor would it recognize any situation, treaty, or agreement brought about by means contrary to the (Peace) Pact of Paris of August 27, 1928.

In relation to states (and governments), recognition can be de facto. It is used when a territory is no longer under the control of its former government and the recognizing state has to deal with the group in control in order to preserve the state's interests in the territory. Such recognition is limited in scope for the conduct of minimally necessary, factual relations. The state recognized de facto has, in regard to the recognizing state, at most a limited and possibly temporary legal subjectivity.

When a state (or government) is recognized as existing de iure, it possesses in regard to the recognizing state full legal personality (or, in the case of a government, the right to speak and act for the state). It has all the rights, duties, and capacity to act under international law.

Disputes have arisen over a number of legal characteristics of recognition. Do states have a right to be recognized, and do they have an obligation to recognize an entity fulfilling the conditions of being a state? Majority opinion is "no." Is recognition declaratory (a means for a state to declare that there is a new state in existence), or is it constitutive (the entity becomes a new state through being recognized)? Majority opinion favors the declaratory nature of recognition. This opinion follows and expands the Montevideo Convention on Rights and Duties of States, Article 3 (1933): "The political existence of the state is independent of recognition by the other states." This interpretation is also in agreement with the understanding of Communist states, which have maintained that legal interpretations of recognition in "bourgeois" states were merely a disguise to use recognition as an "imperialist" political device. The anomalies this interpretation can produce—some states recognize a state while others do not, or some members of the United Nations are not recognized as states by other members—do not trouble states.

Recognition of a new state normally implies recognition of its government. Recognition of a new government in an old state is an even more subjective act and hence more subject to political considerations. For such recognition requires a judgment not only whether the government is in effective control of the state but also whether the government is "new." It is "new" not when its personnel changes but when it has come into power by irregular means according to the state's internal arrangements (such as through revolution).

Legal problems connected with recognition of states (or governments) have been dealt with mainly by domestic courts. They have to decide whether acts of a state or government not recognized by their own government have legal consequences for the purposes of the domestic court. Cases involving such questions arise most frequently in regard to governments, not states, when nationals of the foreign country want to sue a nonrecognized government in domestic courts of their residence. A great number of such cases developed when the Soviet Union succeeded tsarist Russia, when China became Communist, when Germany acquired a National Socialist government. Very often, nationals or former nationals of such countries had their property confiscated or nationalized without compensation and wished to obtain damages in the form of some property the particular state had abroad.

U.S. courts have been inconsistent in their decisions. Generally, U.S. courts and those of several other states do not allow unrecognized states or governments to sue or be sued in domestic courts. Sovereign acts by such states or governments are sometimes recognized as legally valid, sometimes not. But the courts have distinguished between allowing the agent of an existing state to appear before a domestic court and disallowing the agent of a nonrecognized government to appear (for example, *Lehigh*

Valley Railroad Company v. State of Russia [1927]). The decisions are seemingly based upon careful discussion of each situation and various legal theories, such as the weight to be given to a determination by the executive of the political implications of a case; the legal system— national or international—to be applied; or the legitimacy of applying analogies from private law. It appears, however, that the climate of the relationships between the countries involved has some effect upon the decisions. Courts are not immune to the effects of international politics.

Public International Organizations

Public international organizations are subjects of international law, a fact expressed with certainty since the Vienna Convention on the Law of Treaties Concluded Between States and International Organizations (1986). But this subjectivity was generally acknowledged, even by the Soviet Union, before this convention. Public international organizations can operate on the international plane. But their legal personality is far from matching that of states, although some states are worried that the convention may eliminate all differences between states and international organizations. The International Court of Justice pointed this out in the *Reparations for Injuries* case (1949, p. 185) when it said that the rights and duties of the United Nations are not the same as those of states. But the possible rights and duties and acting capacities of international organizations are still uncertain.

There is also the question whether an international organization has legal personality toward states not parties to the treaty creating the organization. In the same case, the International Court expressed the opinion (not shared by all international lawyers) that in regard to the United Nations, "fifty States, representing the vast majority of the members of the international community, had the power, in conformity with international law, to bring into being an entity possessing objective international personality, and not merely personality recognized by them alone." General international law had no rules for international organizations, mainly because they came into existence after the general rules. The new convention of 1986 seems to answer the question positively.

International organizations are creatures of states. The legal foundation of an organization's personality is the treaty establishing the organization and serving as its constitution. In most cases, this treaty defines the legal status and personality of the organization. The U.S. International Organizations Immunities Act of 1975 took cognizance of this fact in § 288a by granting certain immunities "to the extent consistent with the instrument creating them." This instrument of the organization has always stipulated its legal competence, which includes treaty-making competence and scope, immunity, exchange of representatives with states, expulsion of member states, creation of other international organizations, ability to sue states, and responsibility for international torts. The instrument defines the organs and individuals entitled to represent the organization and the international status of its personnel. Most important, the instrument defines the purpose and function of the organization, setting the broad boundaries for the exercise of its legal personality.

These boundaries are necessarily ill-defined (where, for instance, are the boundaries of U.N. peace-preserving activities?), and so states, depending upon their goals, tend to define these boundaries according to expedience. When the International Court of Justice in *Reparations for Injuries* (1949), *Certain Expenses of the United Nations,* and *Effects of Awards of Compensation Made by the U.N. Administrative Tribunal* (1962) argued for a doctrine of "implied powers," it expanded what was already hinted at in Articles 104 and 105 of the U.N. Charter. They mention such legal capacity of the organization in each member's territory "as may be necessary for the exercise of its functions and the fulfillment of its purposes" and of "such privileges and immunities . . . as are necessary for the fulfillment of its purposes." This formulation can now be found in the preamble to the convention but is obviously subject to diverse interpretations.

In the course of their activities, international organizations inevitably have exercised rights, assumed obligations, or engaged in actions not specifically anticipated in their constituent treaties, thereby provoking accusations of illegal activities. But they have also generated theories legitimizing these expanded activities: customary law developing within organizations or tacit agreement among treaty partners to enlarge the purposes of the organization (in application of Article 31[3] of the Vienna Convention on the Law of Treaties, 1969). The organizations are responsible for wrongful acts of their agents (the United Nations has paid damages caused by its peacekeeping forces in the Congo). A largely unanswered question is to what extent the member states may be liable for activities of their organization. One precedent occurred when the Soviet Union ignored the legal personality of the European Community and held the Federal Republic of Germany liable for some EC action in West Berlin. It could be argued, however, that once an organization has acquired its own personality, it is abstracted from its constituent members, who are no longer responsible for the organization's actions.

When the present situation is compared with that prevailing at the birth of international organizations, the trend toward their legal personality becomes clear. The Vienna Convention on the Law of Treaties Between the States and International Organizations, or Between International Organizations (1986) says in Article 6, "The capacity of an international organization to conclude treaties is governed by the rules of that organization." But it should be remembered that sovereignty remains the exclusive prerogative of states and that in the power structure of the international society, states stand far above organizations. Theoretically, by dissolving the constituent treaty, states could wipe out an organization with a stroke of the pen. Organizations have no more than a "derived" or "borrowed" personality. They are subject to the political interests of their members. The United States demonstrated this approach by leaving the United Nations Educational, Scientific, and Cultural Organization (UNESCO) when it was dissatisfied with the organization's administration.

Insurgents and Liberation Movements

The activities of rebels and revolutionaries may generate problems of subjectivity. If their goal is secession, a new state may be born. If it is to replace the existing government, a new government may be born. The political situation is very sensitive for third states. Their support of either side will be branded hostile by the other and possibly an illegal interference in domestic affairs to boot.

Third states may recognize insurgents as a new government or as creators of a new state once they have stable success and maintain an organization controlling territory and population therein. Such recognition provides a more dignified status to insurgents and may help give them legal subjectivity.

As long as insurgents are recognized only as such, they have at most limited international rights and duties in the territory under their control. If they are recognized by third states or their own as belligerents, the territory is close to being treated as a state and they as a government. Many rights, duties, and capacities to act apply, as do the laws of war and neutrality.

Liberation movements have given these legal problems international prominence. But their discussion so far has done little more than highlight problems and disagreements because the legal terminology employed is essentially a disguise for passionate political conflicts that have expanded far beyond the parties directly involved in the liberation movements. Or, to put the matter another way, because the issue is rarely settled politically, it cannot be settled legally.

The difficulty of agreeing on the legal subjectivity of liberation movements is not only that in each concrete case states have differing political interests and therefore make different responses to the liberation movement in question. The difficulty is also that defining the legal status of such movements involves defining other practically indefinable concepts, such as self-determination, colonialism, and equality. Subjective (political) judgments dominate the entire complex, and politics goes wild at the expense of legal clarity and objectivity and international order.

In principle, the older Western states maintain that the goal of liberation movements is to become independent states but that this goal has not yet been reached. These Western states do not limit liberation movements to struggles against colonialism or neocolonialism. They include struggles against suppression or oppression of many kinds, including opposition to "satellite" status.

The Soviets (but not under Mikhail Gorbachev) have argued that "oppressed peoples fighting for liberation" are subjects of international law. The Chinese Communists have so far not taken such a clear-cut position. They seem to consider liberation movements domestic affairs, unless outsiders interfere. Yet they have also granted such movements rights and privileges normally reserved for states (such as maintaining "missions" in Beijing). They also, like many newer states, occupy an ambivalent position. While agitating in global international organizations for the admission of liberation movements as the legitimate, governmental representatives of their peoples, nearer home the Chinese Communists' position is different. The Tibetan liberation movement, headquartered in India, is considered a conspiracy. Until 1973, the Organization of African Unity admitted African liberation movements only as petitioners and thereafter only as observers in the liberation committee.

Those who wish to grant liberation movements legal subjectivity distinguish them from insurgents by pointing out that these movements are well organized, have a constitution, send representatives to other countries, and sign treaties. In short, they very closely resemble states and are a new species of international legal subject.

In the United Nations, especially since 1972, liberation movements have received increasingly favorable treatment. Many have obtained observer status, mainly in the suborgans of the General Assembly and some specialized agencies. Their participation is usually limited to subjects relating to their countries. The most favorable treatment so far has been received by the PLO, which is allowed to address the Security Council directly (not through the intermediary of a member) as "Palestine."

The basis for the role of the liberation movements are numerous resolutions in the General Assembly. Those of particular importance are the Declaration on Principles of International Law Concerning Friendly Relations (Resolution 2625 [XXV]) and Resolutions 2105 (XX), 2918 (XXVII), 3115 (XXVIII), 3111 (XXVIII), 3294 (XXIX), and 3237 (XXIX). Nevertheless, none of these roles can be said to give international legal subjectivity to the liberation movements.

Because the whole issue remains so fully in the political arena, the legal situation can at best be said to be in the process of formation. The current situation allows states to take almost any position they please and to find legal justification or legal condemnation for any action.

Corporations

Because many states participate in economic activities, certain corporations may become subjects of international law. A prerequisite is their involvement in some way with a government: A government may own the corporation, or a private corporation may conclude an agreement with a government under rules of international law. In addition, the corporation's activities are relevant. This was pointed out by the U.S. Court of Appeals in *Isbrandtsen Tankers Inc. v. President of India* (1971) and *Victory Transport Inc. v. Comisaria de Abastecimientos y Transportes* (1964).

A distinction has to be made between acts *iure imperii* (of a public, policy nature) and *iure gestionis* (of a private, commercial nature). As described in a May 19, 1952, letter written by the acting legal adviser to the State Department, Jack B. Tate, the U.S. government denies immunity to acts of a private nature, even when performed by a government, so that any corporation involved in such acts cannot be a subject of international law. The political background of this U.S. policy is clear. With the growing number of states engaged in state trading, granting all their acts sovereign immunity would place private U.S. traders at a great disadvantage. The practical difficulty in applying this doctrine lies, however, in drawing the line between the two types of acts. The court in the *Victory Transport* case enumerated official acts as internal administrative acts, acts concerning the armed forces, acts concerning diplomatic activity, and public loans. Other courts have tried to define the difference by arguing that public acts are those that private individuals cannot perform. The Foreign Sovereign Immunities Act of 1976 exempts "commercial activity" by a foreign state from jurisdictional immunity, a view needing reconsideration because state interference in domestic and foreign economics has become commonplace. An Italian Cassation's Court in 1977 (*ILR* 77 [1988]:603) denied immunity to an interpreter acting for a research institute of an international organization but granted a foreign embassy interpreter immunity as a performer of the state's public function. The idea has generally not been accepted that a private company contracting with a state may by virtue of that fact acquire subjectivity vis-à-vis that state and that the contract be considered a treaty. But the Arbitral Tribunal in the *Texaco v. Libyan Republic* case (1977, p. 459) maintained that such a contract confers "certain capacities" enabling a private person to act internationally.

A number of states pursue the same policy as the United States does. State-trading states oppose it, although they are often willing to conclude contracts specifically acknowledging the jurisdiction of the courts of the other party's state. Non-state-trading states have been willing to grant immunity to state-trading states if these reciprocate by giving foreign private companies immunity in their countries (see *Aldona S. v. United Kingdom* [1948]). In all these cases, the corporation does not have legal subjectivity. But if a contract of a private corporation represents an act *iure imperii*, the contract may be said to have the quality of a treaty and the corporation to be, in a very narrow sense, a subject of international law. The point is very controversial, and courts have decided in different ways.

Multinational Corporations

Multinational corporations have provoked much discussion in recent years, partly as a result of emotional, mainly nationalistic reactions against them and partly because they may indeed possess novel features requiring political and legal management. One reason these corporations have generated many questions and few answers is failure to reach agreement on their character or on their consequences. They may be little more than old-fashioned corporations with investments abroad in enterprises, each of which is strictly separated from the others. In this case, few new problems would arise either politically or legally. If they are enterprises with many branches or subsidiaries abroad, controlled from a center, with assets, resources, and personnel moving freely among the branches, they may be akin to a supranational organization on a private basis. Their political, economic, and social importance could be in and certainly affect the international realm.

In recognition of this fact, a number of international agencies have devoted themselves to developing a code of conduct for these multinational corporations, considering obligations of governments to control the corporations, or creating international legal norms directly regulating them. Although the desire to affect the multinational corporations directly by some international device has been strong, no comprehensive agreement had been reached except that they should not be granted international subjectivity and that their subservience to the state should be guaranteed.

The likelihood is that, as in the European Community, limited and specific, rather than all-encompassing, agreements will be reached in treaties between states establishing rights and duties of states regarding these corporations. Such treaties will be enforced through their national legislation. The surprise of the International Court of Justice, expressed in *Barcelona Traction, Light and Power Co. Ltd. (New Application: 1962)* (1970, §89), "that the evolution of law has not gone further and that no generally accepted rules in the matter have crystallized on the international plane" remains justified. The nearest to subjectivity—if one wants to stretch the point—is in the direct right, occasionally granted to the corporation, to defend its interests against states through prescribed procedures (such as the International Centre for Settlement of Investment Disputes, which does have international legal personality). Quite distinct from private multinational corporations are the public supranational corporations (for example, the International Bank for Reconstruction and Development and the International Monetary Fund) that have not been granted international legal subjectivity.

Individuals

The position of the individual as a subject of international law is extremely controversial. The issue has obtained great prominence from worldwide agitation for the advancement of human rights and, perhaps even more, from their worldwide violation. On the one hand, those yearning for "one world" are eagerly exploiting every opportunity to give individuals standing before international law in their own right, not mediated by states. On the other hand, governments are defending their sovereignty and are most reluctant to weaken their absolute jurisdiction over their nationals or to allow infringements of the exclusive legal personality they claim for themselves because granting individuals legal subjectivity would limit a state's freedom of action. So far, governments have lost a few skirmishes but have won the war. But, say the optimists, a change could not be expected overnight from the individual as the "forgotten person" to a subject in international law.

The plethora of resolutions by global and regional international organs in support of a great variety of human rights has greatly encouraged the defenders of legal subjectivity for individuals and exposed the hypocrisy of numerous governments, which have generally refused to go beyond exhortatory declarations in granting individuals standing under international law. Among the precedents usually considered to have given individuals some legal personality are Central American Court of Justice judgments from 1907 to 1917; some mixed arbitral tribunals of 1918; peace treaties after World War I giving minorities certain rights; several U.N. declarations during World War II; peace treaties after World War II to protect minorities; certain rights of peoples in the trusteeships; the many declarations and some covenants of the United Nations and some of its organs on comprehensive human rights; and various regional declarations on human rights (and those mentioned earlier).

The key question regarding all these instruments is whether the individual has rights and duties directly under international law (against his or her own government) and can deal with international agencies directly or whether the individual's rights and duties can be enforced only through the intermediary of states and between states on the individual's behalf. An examination of the instruments shows that the individual has standing directly under international law in only a very few cases, and in most of those he or she can obtain legal satisfaction only in national courts. In principle, the situation is still as described by the Permanent Court of International Justice in the *Mavrommatis Palestine Concession (Jurisdiction)* case (1924, p. 12): "By taking up the case of one of its subjects and by resorting to diplomatic action or international judicial proceedings on his behalf, a state is in reality asserting its own rights—its right to ensure, in the person of its subjects, respect for the rules of international law."

The best hope of the individual is the conclusion of treaties obliging his or her state to give him or her rights under municipal law. There is no doubt, said the Permanent Court of International Justice in the *Jurisdiction of the Courts of Danzig* (1928, p. 18), "that the very object of an international agreement . . . may be the adoption by the parties of some definite rules creating individual rights and obligations and enforceable by the national courts."

There are exceptions, however; some are of long and some are of very recent standing. Pirates, blockade runners, slave traders, official torturers, genocists, war criminals, and officials practicing apartheid are committing crimes *erga omnes*, against humankind, directly under international law and can be punished by any state that can get a hold of them and is willing to do so. Diplomats have some standing directly under international law. In a very few cases an individual may sue a state in an international court or tribunal (for example, the European Court of Human Rights or the International Centre for Investment Disputes).

Indirectly, individuals may influence the creation of legal norms through their position as, for example, multinationals or legal advisers to foreign offices. Nevertheless, these obligations and rights of individuals under international law are still few and far between, even though change is occurring. To conclude, however, that the individual now has international legal subjectivity is premature.

REFERENCES AND READINGS FOR PART 2

States

Arango-Ruiz, Gaetano. *L'état dans le sens du droit des gens et la notion de droit international*. Bologna: Cooperativa Libraria Universitaria, 1975.

Barberis, Julio A. "Nouvelles questions concernant la personalité juridique internationale." *ADIRC* 179 (1983 I):145–212.

Bernier, Ivan. *International Legal Aspects of Federalism*. Hamden, CT: Archon Books, 1973.

Boutros-Ghali, B. "Ligue des états Arabes." *ADIRC* 137 (1972 III):1–81.

Dugard, John, ed. *The South West Africa/Namibia Dispute: Documents and Scholarly Writings on the Controversy Between South Africa and the United Nations*. Berkeley: University of California Press, 1973.

Falk, Richard A. *The Vietnam War and International Law*. Princeton, NJ: Princeton University Press, 1968.

Feldman, David. "International personality." *ADIRC* 191 (1985 II):343–413.

Hall, H. Duncan. *A History of the British Commonwealth of Nations*. New York: Van Nostrand Reinhold, 1971.

Pescatore, Pierre. *Droit de l'intégration*. Leiden: A. W. Sijthoff, 1972.

Seidl-Hohenveldern, Ignaz von. "International economic law." *ADIRC* 198 (1986 III):9–264.

Slonim, Solomon. *South West Africa and the United Nations: An International Mandate in Dispute*. Baltimore, MD: Johns Hopkins University Press, 1973.

Small States

Blair, Patricia W. *The Ministate Dilemma*. Occasional Paper #6. New York: Carnegie Endowment for International Peace, 1967.

Fisher, Roger. "The participation of microstates in international affairs." In *Proceedings*, pp. 164–170. Washington, DC: American Society of International Law, 1968.

Gunter, Michael M. "What happened to the United Nations ministate problem?" *AJIL* 71 (January 1977):110–124.

Mendelsohn, Maurice. "Diminutive states in the United Nations." *Int. & Comp. L. Q.* 21 (October 1972):609–630.
Rapaport, Jacques et al., eds. *Small States and Territories: Status and Problems.* New York: UNITAR, 1971.
Saint-Girons, B. "L'organisation des Nations Unies et les micro-états." *RGDIP* 76 (1972):445–474.
Schwebel, S. M. "Mini-states and a more effective United Nations." *AJIL* 67 (January 1973):108–116.

Recognition

Blix, H. M. "Contemporary aspects of recognition." *ADIRC* 130 (1970 II):587–703.
Brownlie, Ian. "Recognition in theory and practice." *BYIL* 53 (1982):197–211.
Czerwinski, Günter. *Das Universalitätsprinzip und die Mitgliedschaft in internationalen universalen Verträgen und Organisationen.* Berlin: Duncker und Humblot, 1974.
Dugard, J. *Recognition and the United Nations.* Cambridge: Grotius, 1987.

International Organizations

Ahluwalia, Kuljit. *The Legal Status, Privileges, and Immunities of the Specialized Agencies of the United Nations and Certain Other International Organizations.* The Hague: Martinus Nijhoff, 1964.
Bowett, D. W. *The Law of International Institutions,* 2nd ed. London: Stevens, 1970.
"Coloqium 1971: Legal aspects of economic integration." *ADIRC* (1971).
Ducezio, Vittorio. "La personalità giuridica internazionale del Comecon." *Revue de Droit International de Sciences Diplomatiques et Politiques* 52 (July-September 1975):161–172.
Gaya, Giorgio. "A 'new' Vienna Convention on treaties between states and international organizations and international organizations: A critical commentary." *BYIL* 58 (1987):253–270.
Leopold, Patricia M. "External relations power of EEC in theory and practice." *Int. & Comp. L. Q.* 26 (January 1977):54–80.
McRae, D. M. "Legal obligations and international organizations." *Canadian Yearbook of International Law* 11 (1973):87–105.
Meessen, Karl M. "The application of rules of public international law within Community law." *Common Market Law Review* 13 (November 1976):485–501.
Mosler, Hermann. "Die Erweiterung des Kreises der Völkerrechtssubjekte." *Z* 22 (1962 I–II):1–48.
Osakwe, Chris. "Contemporary Soviet doctrine on the judicial nature of universal international organizations." *AJIL* 65 (July 1971):502–521.

Pescatore, Pierre. "International law and Community law—a comparative analysis." *Common Market Law Review* 7 (May 1970):167–183.

Schermers, H. G. "Community law and international law." *Common Market Law Review* 12 (February 1975):77–90.

Seidl-Hohenveldern, Ignaz von. *Recht der Internationalen Organisationen, einschliesslich der supranationalen Gemeinschaften.* Cologne: C. Heyman, 1971.

_____. "International economic law." *ADIRC* 198 (1986 III):9–264.

Yasseen, Mustafa K. "Setting up and legal personality of international organisations." *A Handbook on International Organisations*, edited by René-Jean Dupuy, pp. 33–55. Dordrecht: Martinus Nijhoff, 1988.

Insurgents and Liberation Movements

Barberis, Julio A. "Nouvelles questions concernant la personalité juridique internationale." *ADIRC* 179 (1983 I):145–304.

Bertelsen, Judy S., ed. *Nonstate Nations in International Politics: Comparative System Analysis.* New York: Praeger, 1977.

Kulski, W. W. "Present trends in Soviet international law." *Proceedings*, pp. 59–75. Washington, DC: American Society of International Law, 1953.

McWhinney, Edward. " 'Peaceful Co-Existence' and Soviet-Western international law." *AJIL* 56 (October 1962):951–972.

Corporations

Bertin, Gilles Y. *Les sociétés multinationales.* Paris: Presses Universitaires de France, 1975.

Fatouros, A. A. "Problèmes et méthodes d'une règlementation des entreprises multinationales." *JDI* 101 (July-September 1974):495–521.

_____. "International law and the internationalized contract." *AJIL* 74 (January 1980):134–141.

Feld, Werner J. *Multinational Corporations and U.N. Politics: The Quest for Codes of Conduct.* New York: Pergamon, 1980.

Jenks, C. Wilfred. "Multinational entities in the law of nations." In *Transnational Law in a Changing Society*, edited by Wolfgang Friedmann, Louis Henkin, and Oliver Lissitzyn, pp. 70–83. New York: Columbia University Press, 1972.

Menchaca, Andrés A.A. "Multinational firms and the process of regional economic integration." *ADIRC* 150 (1976 II):337–479.

Rubin, Seymour J. "The multinational enterprises at bay." *AJIL* 68 (July 1974):457–488.

_____. "Reflections concerning the United Nations Commission on Transnational Corporations." *AJIL* 70 (January 1976):73–91.

Wallace, Don. *International Regulation of Multinational Corporations.* New York: Praeger, 1976.

Individuals

Barberis, Julio A. "Nouvelles questions concernant la personalité juridique internationale." *ADIRC* 179 (1983 I):145–304.

Ford, W. J. "Members of resistance movements." *Netherlands International Law Review* 24 (special issue 1977):92–108.

Gormley, W. Paul. *The Procedural Status of the Individual Before International and Supranational Tribunals.* The Hague: Martinus Nijhoff, 1966.

Leigh, Guy I.F. "Nationality and diplomatic protection." *Int. & Comp. L. Q.* 20 (July 1971):453–475.

Obilade, A. O. "The individual as a subject of international law." *Indian Journal of International Law* 14 (January-March 1974):90–99.

PART 3
INHERENT LEGAL QUALITIES OF SUBJECTS

At least until the end of the nineteenth century, international lawyers, and very rarely states, struggled with the doctrine of fundamental rights as the basis of the international legal system. This doctrine was to explain the binding nature of international law or, more narrowly, the basic rights and duties with which every state as a member of the international society was endowed. Depending upon a lawyer's philosophic outlook, the fundamental norm binding states (the *Grundnorm*) was believed to be (1) *pacta sunt servanda*, (2) states ought to behave as states have always felt they ought to behave (customary law), or (3) states should act according to the law of nature, or some similar nonhuman rule. There was, however, wide agreement that these rights—independence, self-preservation, equality, respect, and intercourse—must result from the fundamental norm.

These rights reflect a historical stage in the development of international society. They did not exist at an earlier time, and some are difficult to maintain at the present. Thus, they are subject to change both in principle and meaning. The attempt to fix these fundamental rights for all eternity presumably aimed at organizing the emerging international society by at least defining the political status of its members and by guaranteeing the stability of that society on the basis of rights and corresponding obligations. The purpose of these rights was to safeguard the existence of states as separate, independent entities, a condition still anchored in the U.N. Charter but barely feasible in the present age of mutual needs and intense international interaction. The doctrine has therefore lost most of its popularity with theorists. But its legacy is still highly visible in the form of sovereignty and all its consequences in law, politics, and economics.

Many writers prefer to concentrate on the specific rights and duties of states and to discard the overall concept of sovereignty as undefinable and anachronistic in the modern world—which may be one reason state practice remains attached to it. But because one state's sovereignty ends where another's begins, legal norms and their interpretation must balance the sovereignties to allow each state a maximum but not unrestricted freedom of action—an increasingly difficult task as the growth of "cooperative" and the decline of "separative" norms indicate.

7
THE STATUS OF STATES

Sovereignty

In the international system, sovereignty is a quality of states. It is the operationalization of nationalism and the translation of the supreme value people attach to their state into international behavior. Centuries ago, kings and princes sought release from the pope's control. Nationalists seeking absolute independence for their cherished state seized upon and corrupted to their ends Jean Bodin's formulations of sovereignty in 1576 as "the absolute and perpetual power within the state, that is, the greatest power to command" and of the sovereign as one "who, after God, acknowledges no one greater than himself."

Theoreticians of the Western world have since struggled to clarify the concept and make it functional. They agree that sovereignty means exclusive state control over citizens and territory, the use of international collective goods (high seas, outer space), and the capacity to relate with other states in a manner regulated by international law. But there has been much disagreement on details, with some vexing questions remaining incompletely answered. How can sovereignty be reconciled with obedience to international law? Is it divisible—can states be sovereign in some matters but not in others? Growing interaction and interdependence among states have made the answers more difficult but also less important because these interactions have led to more "cooperative" law and diminished the substance of sovereignty. Sovereignty means nonrecognition of a higher authority above the state, but it no longer means, if it ever did, absolute freedom of action. Nevertheless, these changes have hardly affected the essentiality of the principle as the basis for the organization of international society.

Governments continue to rely heavily upon the concept. It serves their legal, political, and propagandistic ends. Powerful states rely on it to perpetuate their predominance, weak states to protect their personality and even to weaken the powerful states' predominance. The Communist states, and some of their writers, expediently exempted socialist internationalism (the Brezhnev Doctrine) until President Gorbachev abolished it; otherwise, they are strongly attached to sovereignty. Within the Soviet Union, when the president uses the term *sovereignty*, particularly regarding the demands of the Baltic states, the meaning of sovereignty becomes at most synonymous with autonomy. The Soviet government has no intention of giving any part of the Soviet Union sovereignty in the international law sense of the word. In the vocabulary of the Chinese Communist government, the term *proletarian internationalism* has altogether disappeared.

The Chinese Communists have emphasized as strongly as the Soviet Communists did that they consider sovereignty to be the central point of all international legal principles and norms. They are not alone in this view. All states are unanimous in their praise of sovereignty, whose ambiguous meaning permits them to interpret the concept expediently to serve their various purposes while simultaneously catering to their publics' nationalism. And the Communists are quite correct in pointing out that sovereignty is the organizing device for the entire international system, including international law. Differences among states relate mostly to the degree of strictness or looseness with which they interpret or use the concept, especially its consequences.

In the practice of states, sovereignty means freedom of a state from control by other states. Max Huber, the arbitrator in the *Island of Palmas* (1928), defined sovereignty as independence. This particular understanding makes clear at least that the sovereignty of a state and that state's subjection to international law are compatible because international legal control is not control by another state. Beyond this limitation upon their behavior, states are legally free to behave as they see fit and, in actual practice, as their political and economic capabilities permit them to behave.

Courts and lawyers have tried to define this independence. Either they have detailed the rights and obligations of states within the legal scope of independence, or they have interpreted the meaning of independence when used synonymously with sovereignty. Judge Anzilotti and others in the Permanent Court of International Justice's decision on the *Customs Regime Between Germany and Austria* case (1931, pp. 57, 77) argued that independence can best be understood by comparing it to dependence. Dependent states are

> subject to the authority of one or more States. The idea of dependence therefore necessarily implies a relation between a superior State . . . and an inferior or subject State; the relation between the State which can legally impose its will and the State which is legally compelled to submit to that will. Where there is no such relation of superiority and subordination, it is impossible to speak of dependence within the meaning of international law.

Other dissenting judges in the case elaborated further that a state would lose its independence "if it ceased to exercise within its own territory the *summa potestas* or sovereignty, i.e. if it lost the right to exercise its own judgment in coming to the decisions which the government of its territory entails." In line with many preceding and succeeding decisions, Judge Anzilotti confirmed that "restrictions upon a State's liberty, whether arising out of ordinary international law or contractual engagements do not as such in the least affect its independence." Indeed, international courts have consistently held that the conclusion of treaties is the exercise of an attribute of sovereignty, not a limitation of it.

This possibility raises the question, How many rights can a state contract away or how many obligations can it contractually assume before it has contracted its sovereignty away? This question became acute, for instance, when France conducted Morocco's international affairs, when Switzerland took care of Liechtenstein's defense, and when Germany and Austria arranged a customs union. Although the recent development of highly integrated regional unions has indicated that states can contract away what used to be significant attributes of statehood without losing their independence, the question is still relevant. In the Canadian elections of November 1988, for instance, some parties argued that a treaty with the United States eliminating all customs duties would deprive Canada of its sovereignty.

A neat separation between legal and other freedoms has been rejected by the newer states, with support from most Communist states. They reason that in the face of enormous political and economic inequalities among states, sovereign or formal legal independence is a sham because the economic dependence of the newer states on developed states in fact cancels their right to exercise their judgment freely to decide on matters involving the government of their territories. These states insist that to make sovereignty and independence substantive, the legal, political, and economic consequences of sovereignty must be redefined to make sovereignty genuine. In fact, the newer states are trying to use this redefinition as a legal tool to improve their general position, especially by the grant of special, favorable, or preferential (unequal) treatment.

Apart from the wishes of any particular group of states, new international conditions constantly require new definitions. As these conditions affect states differently, the difficulty of reaching agreement on concrete consequences of sovereignty other than generalities remains. The main legal consequences flowing from sovereignty are the legal equality of states, the protection of a state's internal affairs from outside intervention, and the right of a state to have its sovereign acts recognized by other states (sovereign immunity).

Equality

The principle of equality is of long standing. Chief Justice Marshall in the *Antelope* case (1825, p. 122) stated, "No principle of general law is more universally acknowledged than the perfect equality of nations." Article 2 of the U.N. Charter bases the organization upon the principle of the "sovereign equality" among states, although nobody is certain about the meaning of the principle, particularly in its legislative applications. The term's ambiguity is a guarantee of popularity with governments of disadvantaged states, which make demands in sovereignty's name, and with theorists, who debate its meaning. The commonsense interpretation that in the face of inequalities among states, equality could mean only equality before the law or equal application of the law is unacceptable to those lawyers and states that insist that it means equal rights and duties for states. Their opinions have not been generally accepted.

In practice, states have a few agreements. In principle, each state has one vote in voting procedures. States are entitled to the equal legal protection of those rights that they do possess. Equality, they agreed until recently, relates only to legal equality. And no state can claim jurisdiction over another; therefore, each must recognize the acts of a state in its own territory as long as these are not in conflict with international legal norms.

This limited scope of agreement is due to the nature of international society with its greatly unequal member states. The powerful states, creating much international reality in the first place, make the law to protect that reality. The smaller, weaker states, having few other means, are trying to adjust reality with the help of law, but with little success.

Attempts by international society to even out inequalities have much of the time ended up confirming rather than abolishing them. Inequalities have been legalized by making peace treaties foisted upon a defeated state legal, by treating unequal nineteenth-century treaties with China as legal, and by giving the five major states permanent seats and the veto power in the Security Council. Distributive justice has helped powerful states by giving them greater influence through weighted voting according to use of or contribution to an organization and more privileges in some functional, mainly economic, international organizations. Moreover, equal voting rights as a last step in a political process have relatively little significance when the situation in which the vote eventually takes place has been created largely by the major powers.

Many newer states demand, although rarely define, substantive equality in the name of legal equality and argue that for legal equality to become genuine, it must include substantive equality. Hence their continual requests for favorable but unequal economic treatment as an obligation of the "have" states to make the new states' equality real. To them, sovereign equality includes equal opportunity (the presumed purpose of which is to create comparable standards of living among states, including, perhaps, an obligation for retroactive redistribution of wealth). To the older states, however, inequality in living standards is not a legal consideration.

Also in the name of equality, Communist states give moral support to the claims of the newer states and very material support to the demand of these states for the right to participate, and not merely accede to, multilateral treaties that concern general norms of international law, deal with matters of interest to the entire international society, or are likely to produce eventually general norms of international law. The Soviet Union has argued that sovereign equality of states entitles them, on the one hand, to choose their partners for the conclusion of a treaty but, on the other hand, to do so only if the treaty does not affect the rights and legitimate interests of many states. But the USSR has qualified this right with so many ambiguous conditions that in concrete cases, its position hardly differs from that of older, Western states, which is that sovereignty entitles states to choose their treaty partners. Indeed, the Soviet Union allegedly accepted the "unequal" veto power in the Security Council in order to protect small states against "imperialist aggressors."

Conceivably, the internationalization of social life may move international law in the direction allegedly desired by the newer and Communist states. A state would no longer be responsible to another state, as is the case under traditional law, but would be responsible to the international society as a community. Natural law doctrine has made this proposal for centuries. Vattel wrote more than two hundred years ago that "the first general law" was "that each nation ought to contribute all in its power to the happiness and perfection of others."

Nonintervention

Respect for a state's sovereignty requires that other states do not interfere in its internal affairs, including the internal aspects of foreign policymaking. The U.N. Charter acknowledges this very old principle by forbidding the United Nations to intervene "in matters which are essentially within the domestic jurisdiction of any state." Unfortunately, the longevity of the principle has not contributed to its clarity. On the contrary, increasing interaction and the rise of new international regimes have also increased the means of intervention while at the same time making it more difficult to draw the line between illegitimate intervention and legitimate politics. The charter aggravates this difficulty by designating such matters "essentially" within domestic jurisdiction. There remains the major problem of defining what action is to be called intervention.

In general, the principle was more in accord with former international relations than contemporary ones. It accorded, and still does, with nationalist sentiments. But it no longer is so easily reconcilable with voluminous international interaction, growing internationalization of formerly domestic affairs, and the ability of a state to intervene while remaining in its own territory (for instance, through media or through currency manipulations). Sentiments against intervention have largely persisted. Nevertheless, it continues directly or indirectly as in the past but often assumes new forms because conditions have changed. The satisfaction of mutual needs has augmented contacts that some states may consider intervention; technology has improved, necessitated, and facilitated means and types of intervention. Some progress in the national enforcement of some human rights as an international right and duty has further increased possibilities of intervention. For insofar as the violation of certain human rights has become an international crime, neither the sovereignty nor the domestic affairs principles protect the violating state.

Such expansion of licit and illicit intervention has heightened sensitivity to interventionist activity, and the nebulous concept of intervention has been further politicized. The Permanent Court of International Justice in the *Nationality Decrees Issued in Tunis and Morocco* case (1923, p. 24) stated convincingly that "the question whether a certain matter is or is not solely within the jurisdiction of a state is an essentially relative question; it depends upon the development of international relations." Equally relative has been the nature of the action involved, even though for a while there was agreement that it meant "dictatorial interference." But this definition is now out of date because, for instance, subversion can well be intervention. In the *Nicaragua Merits* case (1986, p. 1078), the International Court decided that support of subversion or terrorist activities in another state is wrongful intervention. In view of this increasing relativization of the meaning of intervention, mainly the newer and Communist states sponsored a number of resolutions in the United Nations designed to eliminate all conceivable kinds of intervention. Typical was Resolution 2131 (XX) of the General Assembly (December 21, 1965).

1. No State has the right to intervene, directly or indirectly, for any reason whatever, in the internal or external affairs of any other State. Consequently, armed intervention and all other forms of interference or attempted threats against the personality of the State or against its political, economic or cultural elements, are condemned.
2. No State may use or encourage the use of economic, political or any other type of measures to coerce another State in order to obtain from it the subordination of the exercise of its sovereign rights, or to secure from it advantages of any kind.

This formulation, which is found in many resolutions and treaties of regional organizations, if taken at face value would eliminate all international politics because by their nature they always involve a measure of pressure or influence. This is a vain attempt to dissolve a dilemma by denying the social facts of international life—or all life, for that matter. By now, a catalogue of actions branded intervention would probably contain nearly every action a state has ever engaged in.

The highly political significance of intervention—actual, potential, or alleged—renders futile any refinements either in the concept or in the distinction between domestic or international affairs. Little is to be gained—mainly because states do not want to gain—by limiting intervention to an intentional influence upon a state's affairs or the use of illegal means or to a distinction among illegal intervention by force, interference by economic, cultural, and social means, or intercession by influence. Nor is it any more useful to make intervention dependent upon how it affects a state's freedom of decision. The nature of any society always prevents such freedom to certain, undefinable degrees. With the great variety of means available to affect another state's behavior, some of which may be normal bargaining items in a political process and some of which may be legal nonaction, the concept of intervention has lost legal usefulness in most instances. But note, for instance, the incongruity between these two situations: The cessation of U.S. aid to the Sandinista regime in Nicaragua was called intervention in the *Nicaragua (Merits, Judgment)* case (1986); the 1973–1974 Organization of Petroleum Exporting Countries oil boycott, which presumably was economic coercion for political ends not in conformity with U.N. resolutions, received no such label.

Nevertheless, although intervention generally remains illegal, distinctions continue to be made because intervention does exist and cannot be wished away. If one follows von Glahn's classification scheme, three kinds of intervention can be distinguished: intervention by right, permissible intervention, and subversive intervention.

Intervention by right can happen on various grounds. A treaty may ask or allow the other party to help if one of the parties is attacked (as the United States claimed in the *Nicaragua* case). If a state does not obey restrictions imposed upon it by treaty, outside states may intervene to enforce them. Other states may intervene if a state seriously violates norms of international law (for example, when Germany violated Belgium's neutrality in World War II). Intervention is permissible if a state mistreats the citizens of another state (the U.S. invasion of Grenada in 1983 and of Panama in 1989 was allegedly to save U.S. citizens); if an international organization collectively intervenes in a country to enforce norms of international law; if a threatened state invites another to help in its defense; or if the other state invites itself. As virtually all such cases involve a small, weak state inviting a more powerful state, the invitation is probably politically motivated (and may itself involve an intervention).

Outstanding examples of such situations were the Truman and Brezhnev doctrines. In 1947 President Truman announced that the United States would help free peoples to maintain their free institutions against aggressive movements seeking to impose totalitarian regimes. The United States would assist those countries "at their request" by sending civilian and military experts. The Brezhnev Doctrine claimed the right of socialist-state intervention in other socialist countries if their socialism was threatened.

But President Gorbachev canceled the Brezhnev Doctrine when he told the U.N. General Assembly on December 7, 1988, that processes of social change within countries cannot achieve their ends by following "parallel courses" that ignore their own circumstances. Intervention in such processes is dangerous to peace. He added that "deideologization" of interstate relations is a requirement of the new world politics. The use or threat of force is no longer a viable instrument of foreign policy (but in January 1990, he threatened to use force within the Soviet Union if necessary to avoid civil war). Contrarily, however, President Reagan stated on October 19, 1983, that covert CIA actions in other countries is part of the government's responsibilities if it believes this to be in the best interests of the country. The Bush administration reconfirmed this opinion when a policy for CIA activities was publicized in November 1989.

Permissible intervention is mostly justified as self-defense, especially "anticipatory" self-defense, and is often difficult to distinguish from aggression. Permissible intervention played a role in the *Nicaragua (Merits, Judgment)* case (1986) and was one of the U.S. excuses for the invasion of Panama in 1989 (to be discussed under self-defense).

Subversive intervention does not involve dictatorial interference but is nevertheless designed to bring about major changes in the government or social order of another state. This is also one of the few means that smaller and weaker states have to intervene in more powerful states.

The definition of this type of intervention is particularly difficult because ideological considerations enter. What the BBC considered an objective news broadcast, the Soviet Union considered an attempt to undermine its government. In order to maintain credibility, Radio Free Europe and Radio Liberty made great efforts to broadcast true facts to formerly Communist Eastern Europe but were accused by governments there of subversive intervention. Government statements accepted as information or policy announcements in free countries may be interpreted as intervention in totalitarian countries. Foreign aid to a party at election time has been branded as subversive intervention. The United Nations passed several resolutions forbidding seditious propaganda threatening peace or inciting armed aggression within or without states without making a distinction between freedom of expression and subversive action. Appeals by U.S. administrations to foreign peoples to overthrow their government (for example, to overthrow Noriega in Panama in 1989) or to change their political regimes, often combined with economic sanctions, can be considered subversive intervention.

A related and equally difficult issue is whether foreign aid to rebels or liberation movements is illegal intervention. Such a determination depends to some extent upon the status granted to these groups. The local government will consider them enemies and aid to them as unfriendly, if not illegal. On the contrary, the U.N. Charter establishes a legal obligation for its members to realize the self-determination of peoples. The Declaration on Principles of International Law Concerning Friendly Relations (1970) provides a nonsolution of the problem by stating that no State shall organize, assist, foment, finance, incite or tolerate subversive, terrorist or armed activities directed towards the overthrow of the régime of another State, or interfere in the civil strife in another State. . . . [A state must not aim at] the partial or total disruption of the national unity and territorial integrity of a State or country. . . . [At the same time, every state is obliged] to refrain from any forcible action which deprives peoples . . . of their right to self-determination and freedom and independence, which might empower other states to support such right in the name of enforcing general international law.

(Soviet activities in Afghanistan during the 1980s and U.S. activities in Nicaragua during the same period clearly contravened this admonition.)

The ambiguities in these statements allow states to legitimize a variety of contradictory actions. The newer and Communist states have claimed that intervention in support of national liberation movements, decolonization, and the suppression of racist regimes is a duty. (This could be called a modern version of the Holy Alliance's and Concert of Europe's claim that it was their duty to maintain monarchical regimes and the territorial arrangements of European states.) This claim would be more convincing if it were not applied exclusively to Western colonialism and to liberation and antiracist movements directed exclusively at white suppression of blacks. This is presumably among the reasons changes advocated by Third World states, often supported by majorities in U.N. resolutions, have been adopted only very selectively by many major older states. Instead, where intervention has in fact taken place, the older states, adhering to traditional law, have disguised it in terms of existing rules (such as self-defense) rather than justified it by new norms. Only to a very limited extent do they admit the legal character of some of these concepts. The International Convention on the Elimination of All Forms of Racial Discrimination (1965), although not ratified by the United States and other major states, has by now become international law under general customary law, even for those states not a party to the convention. The Australian High Court, in *Koowarta v Bjelke-Petersen* (1982) considered it so even before Australia ratified the convention. The sanctions imposed by the U.S. Congress against South Africa in 1986 can therefore be considered a justified "intervention" in support of antiracism as a legal obligation.

One can conclude that in principle states oppose intervention, that the newer and Communist states are widening the concept beyond traditional law, and that the concept primarily serves political purposes. In practice, power, not law, usually determines who intervenes and where. The Permanent Court of Justice in the *Corfu Channel* case (1949, p. 35) stated outright that "the alleged right of intervention" is "the manifestation of a policy of force," a contention proved correct by U.S. actions in Panama in 1989.

Sovereign Immunity of States

Sovereignty expresses the right of a state to independence, territorial integrity, equality, and noninterference and the right not to be subject to a higher authority. Sovereignty limits the right of a state to prescribe and enforce a rule of law to the point where the same right of another state begins. In their respective areas of jurisdiction, states have the right to have other states recognize their sovereign acts. This mutual relationship is called sovereign immunity. It includes the inadmissibility of bringing one state before the judicial authorities of another. States as sovereign equals cannot enforce their laws against each other, except by consent. A state cannot perform a sovereign act inside another state without that state's permission. The United States may have done this by seizing Manuel Noriega in 1989. The new Panamanian Endara government was "informed of" and "welcomed" the invasion when it was sworn in forty minutes before the U.S. invasion. But as U.S. courts seem to consider the manner in which the accused has been brought before them irrelevant, a plea by Noriega that he was brought into the United States illegally would in any case be insufficient to contest the drug trafficking charges against him. On this point the case is complicated, however, by the findings of U.S. courts that if the accused was brought before the court by means involving violence, brutality, or inhuman treatment, he or she could not be tried. The question of sovereign immunity is acute also in relation to the ownership, possession, or control by a state of property or another material interest in the territorial jurisdiction of another state.

Sovereign immunity can apply to the state as an entity, to a person (persona) officially representing the state, or to the object of a state's material interest (res). Chief Justice Marshall confirmed in *Schooner Exchange v. M'Faddon* (1812, p. 136) the principle of "complete exclusive territorial jurisdiction." Sovereign immunity is also responsible in part for the development, mainly in U.S. courts, of the act of state doctrine.

The principle of equality (*par in parem non habet imperium*) led courts to maintain that a sovereign state was not entitled to question the sovereign acts of another state but had to accept them as facts even if those acts were contrary to the public policy of the United States or international law. The U.S. Supreme Court found, however, that international law did not require such a doctrine, a finding confirmed by different practices in other states. England has a similar, but less extensive doctrine. In states of Continental Europe and Japan, courts are free to reject foreign acts of state if they are found to be illegal under international law or contrary to the state's own public policy. In the course of time, the scope of sovereign immunity has become increasingly restricted. Chief Justice Marshall in the *Schooner* decision already favored a restricted immunity when he said, "A prince, by acquiring private property in a foreign country, may possibly be considered as subjecting that property to the territorial jurisdiction; he may be considered as laying down the prince, and assuming the character of a private individual."

Such a view follows from the capitalist-state practice of separating private property from public property and treating each differently. Nevertheless, until 1952 U.S. courts considered sovereign immunity absolute, and so did several other countries. The growing direct participation of states in communications, commerce, shipping, and other economic ("nonsovereign") activities led to the adoption by most non-Communist countries of the principles of restricted immunity. In the Tate letter of May 19, 1952, the State Department announced that it would follow "the restrictive theory of sovereign immunity in the consideration of requests of foreign governments for a grant of sovereign immunity." On May 16, 1972, the Council of Europe agreed on a convention stipulating the restrictive principle, and most members ratified it. The U.S. Congress further detailed the practice regarding sovereign immunity by passing the Foreign Sovereign Immunities Act of 1976.

The difference between absolute immunity and restricted immunity is that under the former, all actions and interests of states are treated as immune. Under the latter, only sovereign actions and interests, not private (mainly commercial) activities, are granted immunity. (The difference between sovereign actions and private activities is determined by their nature, not their purpose.) This distinction corresponds to acts *iure imperii* and *iure gestionis*.

A further qualification of absolute immunity is in the process of development regarding the violation of crimes directly under international law. There is nothing new regarding older crimes such as piracy or slave trade. Their prosecution by any state raised no problems because they were committed by private persons. But because human rights have tended to become legally binding on governments under international law, their violation anywhere by an official act of government would become a crime directly under international law and could be prosecuted in accordance with municipal legislation by any state within its jurisdiction. In the United States, 28 U.S.C.A. §1350 of the Alien Tort Claims Act gives the courts material jurisdiction: "The district courts shall have original jurisdiction of any civil action by an alien for a tort only, committed in violation of the law of nations or a treaty of the United States." A number of cases have appeared in civil action before U.S. courts. But judges are not unanimous in their views and decisions. They disagree on the nature of the international legal norms as a ground for action without further implementation by national legislation (self-executing or non-self-executing) or whether §1350 itself is a sufficient ground for action. They also disagree about whether a given act has become an international crime. In the *Filartiga v. Peña-Irala* case (1980), for instance, torture when committed by an official was so considered. In the *Tel-Oren [Hanoch] v. Libyan Arab Republic* case (1984), terrorism was not (in addition to the fact that the terrorism was committed by the PLO, a nonofficial agency in U.S. eyes).

Communist states hold to the principle of absolute immunity because, they argue, it is not a variable of international law but an attribute of sovereignty. The protection of their (state-)economic activities by immunity would be as advantageous to them as it would be disadvantageous to their capitalist trading partners. Because they desire to continue economic activities with the capitalist world, they either agree in particular contracts to waive immunity or to apply reciprocity (give foreigners and their enterprises immunity).

The Chinese Communists have made very clear that the national handling of human rights is always a national affair because the many U.N. declarations are not self-executing. The Chinese consider the thesis that human rights know no national boundaries "utterly unjustified."

The Trend Regarding Sovereignty

Notwithstanding universal realization of sovereignty's drawbacks for the fulfillment of some national interests and its opportunistic interpretation by many, states cherish the concept as politically useful and as a protection against unwanted legal obligations. Nevertheless, modern conditions are producing changes in sovereignty's character. It is gradually failing to preserve a state's freedom of action. The isolated existence of states is becoming impossible. The Permanent Court of International Justice in the *Wimbledon* case (1923, p. 25) asserted that "the right of entering into international agreements is an attribute of state sovereignty." It also admitted that "any convention creating an obligation . . . places a restriction upon the exercise of the sovereign rights of the State."

With thousands of treaties in force, the volume of sovereignty restricted by them is considerable. The rise of international regimes requiring collective action to solve collective problems (ecology, currency, natural resources, for instance) has a similar effect. International developments resulting from technology are affecting sovereignty in two opposite directions. One result strengthens it. The assumption of increasing economic roles by states provides a more material, substantial foundation for popular emotional and political support of sovereignty. In socialist countries the state is the directing economic actor; in developing states it is the central agency for modernization. In capitalist states "social welfare" as well as subsidies and protection from foreign competition are expected from the state. Virtually all demands by newer states for a "new" international law directly or indirectly emphasize orthodox sovereignty, usually by making sovereignty more genuine for them. The U.N. declaration concerning sovereignty over the natural resources of a state, the catalogue of the Five Principles of Peaceful Coexistence, and aspects of the New International Economic Order (NIEO) are leading to a stagnant international law rather than to a progressive law.

The other result of technological developments is to erode sovereignty. Even purely national interests can be satisfied in many cases only by joint international action, so that the welfare of other states is in the self-interest of a state. Sovereignty is virtually inapplicable to outer space (although new international organizations can make binding decisions by weighted majority votes) and difficult to realize in the oceans. Multinational corporations overshadow sovereignty and force arrangements ignoring international borders. Communications cannot be restrained by the "sovereign independence" of states. Regional organizations are often a response to the restrictive influence of sovereignty. The prohibition of the use of force as well as its counterproductivity limits a state's freedom of sovereign action.

All states, old and new, are adjusting reluctantly to the vanishing substance of sovereignty. The truly new or innovative international law proposed by jurists, such as the creation of new subjects of international law or a direct international protection of human rights by an effective international institution (the European Court of Human Rights!), has been opposed more by new and Communist states than by some of the older states as an infringement upon sovereignty. President Gorbachev's Soviet Union stresses sovereignty even for (formerly) satellite Communist states. But while extolling human rights, Gorbachev has not advocated that individuals be able to go to an international agency to enforce their rights against their own governments. Current trends in the rise and decline of sovereignty indicate that it will survive in the foreseeable future but with reduced effectiveness.

8
THE ORGANS OF SUBJECTS AND THEIR PROTECTION

The Problem of Juridic Persons

The legal status of a state or of an international organization becomes real and relevant mainly through human behavior. For some purposes (such as aspects of sovereign immunity of states as entities), treating these social entities as juridic persons is adequate; for other purposes, it is not. Situations arise in which the will, consent, and/or actions of entities must be expressed and discovered in the behavior of natural persons as organs of these entities. For such situations, international law imputes the behavior of these persons to the juridic person and thus answers the question, Who is acting on behalf of the state?

This point was of importance in the *Nicaragua (Merits, Judgment)* case (1986). The International Court of Justice found that the mining of Nicaraguan harbors and attacks on ports and oil installations were undertaken either by U.S. personnel or by Latin Americans paid by and acting on the direct instructions of U.S. military or intelligence personnel, with the permission of the president. On the basis of these findings, the International Court considered these attacks imputable to the United States.

In general, it follows that in their official acts these persons must receive the treatment international law prescribes for states or international organizations. In the vast majority of cases, the persons acting on behalf of a state or an international organization are officially recognized by the entity and are then accorded the treatment prescribed by law to that entity so that they can perform their functions adequately. This treatment may also have to be extended to their private acts.

International law must first determine who the legitimate organs are. Or, more weighty in consequences, it must determine which organs third parties may legitimately consider to act for an entity. When this is established, the law must determine when the occasion arises how these organs are to be treated by third parties (mainly concerning their inviolability and immunity). This second task is clearly one for international law because it involves relations between its subjects. The first task may not appear to be so clearly within the bailiwick of international law because it is a matter of a state's or an organization's internal jurisdiction to establish what its organs are. But that municipal law and international law in combination determine the appropriate organ is accepted doctrine.

International law recognizes individuals specifically entitled by the law of states or organizations to act as organs. It also normally permits third parties to recognize as organs with certain competences the occupant of an office assumed to exist in every state (such as the head of a state or a foreign minister), even if the internal law of an entity does not endow such an occupant with the right to act as an organ. Thus, the possibility of conflict between international law and an internal system exists. Usually there is coincidence between the two, especially in view of the general principle that the norms of the two systems should be made as compatible as possible. But if an organ recognized as such by international law but not by the internal law of the entity acts on behalf of the entity, the solution of this problem is subject to controversy. There is a widespread opinion that if the internal limitations upon the competence of an organ are well known, the acts of the organ that go beyond the limitations are invalid under international law.

The chance of discrepancies is reduced by the state practice of certifying some organs. Foreign governments are usually notified of the institution of a new head of state or foreign minister. Diplomats carry letters of credence and withdrawal upon their official arrival and departure. Consuls get an exequatur from the receiving state that permits them to begin their functions. In contrast to this practice, the Vienna Convention on the Representation of States in Their Relations with International Organizations of a Universal Character (1975) enables members of delegations and missions to arrive and depart without the host country's knowledge; yet the host must grant inviolability and immunity to these organs.

A special situation developed when the United Nations invited Yasir Arafat, chair of the Palestine Liberation Organization, to address the General Assembly in New York in 1988. Under the U.N.-U.S.A. Headquarters Agreement of 1947, U.S. authorities cannot impose any impediments to the transit to or from the headquarters to persons invited by the United Nations on official business. Yet Arafat was denied entry into the United States on the debatable ground that the U.S. government can deny entry to anyone considered a threat to its security.

Organs of States

International law considers that heads of state are empowered by virtue of their office to commit their states, probably even if they exceed their constitutional power in doing so, because sovereignty protects the state against judgment of its domestic affairs by international law. There is agreement that the actual, not the nominal, holder of the office is the head of state (*qui actu regit*), even though it may be difficult—for instance, in a civil war situation—to determine who the actual holder is. Ambassadors are the personal representatives of the head of state. When President Eisenhower once spoke of "his" ambassador (to which some people objected), he was quite correct.

The government or cabinet as such has no standing as an organ of the state. Individual ministers may have. Normally the foreign minister speaks on behalf of the state. The Vienna Convention on Diplomatic Relations (1961) channels official international business through the Ministry of Foreign Affairs. The Permanent Court of International Justice decided in the *Eastern Greenland* case (1933, p. 71) that "beyond all dispute" an oral reply "given by the Minister for Foreign Affairs on behalf of his Government in response to a request by the diplomatic representative of a foreign Power, in regard to a question falling within his province, is binding upon the country to which the Minister belongs." Other ministers of the government may act as organs after they have been certified as such, usually by the Foreign Ministry.

Diplomats are organs of the state representing it to another state or an international organization. Customary law regulates in great detail the classes, character, status, function, rights, and obligations of diplomats. Much of customary law has been codified in the Vienna Convention on Diplomatic Relations (1961), which was concluded with relative ease not only because customary law was well developed but because diplomatic relations rest on reciprocity, a most effective principle of international law.

Consuls as organs of state are a class distinct from diplomats. Their activities used to be related mainly to commercial matters and the affairs of nationals of their state in the receiving country. Their duties have in recent times been expanded to include cultural, scientific, and other "nonpolitical" matters. They do not represent their state as comprehensively as diplomats do and each consul usually functions within limited regions inside the receiving country. Consuls' privileged status is therefore not as comprehensive as that of diplomats. It is regulated in the Vienna Convention on Consular Relations (1963), in customary law, and in numerous bilateral treaties.

The armed forces are considered organs of the state in peace and in war. They are distinguished from a police force because they also deal with the external defense of the state and from guerillas and organized liberation or resistance forces because they are under the control of the legitimate government. The entry of armed forces upon the territory of another state in peacetime or wartime and their status while there are well regulated by international law, with special rules applying to warships and war planes. Additional rules regulate the conditions for members of the armed forces while on leave on foreign territory.

The growing volume and subject matter of international relations have given rise to the sending of many types of officials, from ministers to technical experts, from state to state for limited durations and special purposes. They are certified in their capacities in letters given to them by their head of state or foreign minister. The United Nations Convention on Special Missions (1969) suggests that states should grant to them for the duration of their missions privileges similar to those granted diplomats. In addition, their status is usually regulated by mutual agreement between the states concerned.

Members of agencies or other agents who are not diplomats, consuls, or other types of envoys may differ in international character depending upon their functions. If they are staff members of official agencies (tourist, information, railways) run by governments as nonsovereign enterprises (*iure gestionis*), they are usually not considered organs of their state, although their status may be as dubious as that of some trade agents or similar officials. Official agency staffs may enjoy privileges as state organs if they perform "acts of state."

Organs of International Organizations

International organizations are so young that customary law has little to say about them. Fundamentally, the constitutive instruments of each organization determine their structure and their organs. Additionally, the practice of these organizations and international bi- or multilateral agreements produce norms for them.

There is a great variety in the nature and competence of these organs. They can be collective (for example, the U.N. General Assembly) or individual (for example, the U.N. general secretary). They may perform various functions, either permanently or from time to time. National constitutions determine the arrangement for each. But, a Swiss court decided, the immunity of officials lasts only as long as they perform duties, which means that immunity can be intermittent. On March 14, 1975, a U.N. conference at Vienna adopted the Convention on the Representation of States in Their Relations with International Organizations of a Universal Character. The conference split early into two groups, one mainly representing states sending delegations, the other mainly representing receiving delegations. The first group attempted to expand the status of delegations to equal or better that of diplomats. The second group felt no need for the convention because most international organizations contained in their charters seemingly adequate rules protecting their personnel as well as delegations and missions. Because the first group commanded a majority, the convention was adopted.

Types of Protection

The mutual respect among states for their sovereignty implies respectful treatment. This duty applies to states as entities, their symbols (flag, uniform, national anthem), and their organs. The long-developed practice of states works well because their interests are mutual and retaliation against improper treatment is fairly easy. At the same time, because the practice is well developed in all details, slight variations, short of insult or hostility, can convey political changes in relationships.

This mutual treatment is expressed in three categories of behavior. One is courtesy or comity, such as an honor guard for a visiting dignitary or ships greeting each other on the high seas. This category is outside the legal framework but could be a step toward customary law. Much behavior in the other two categories, both legally regulated, has developed in this manner.

The second category is inviolability of the state. Every state has the duty to protect the material interests and organs of other states within its territorial jurisdiction against illegal or unfriendly acts. This duty involves a greater protection from injury than citizens or aliens enjoy. And it makes actions against a foreign state (for instance, violation of its dignity) illegal that are not illegal when undertaken against other entities. Many states have municipal legislation for the punishment of crimes against organs of states or international organizations.

Nevertheless, in the early 1970s, in view of increasing terroristic acts against diplomats, some special convention was considered desirable. But its formulation met with some difficulty because the definition of a terrorist is clearly a political matter. So the United Nations Convention on the Prevention and Punishment of Crimes Against Internationally Protected Persons, Including Diplomatic Agents (1973) is permanently attached to Resolution 3166 (XXVII). Whereas the convention spells out the special measures states should take to guarantee such prevention and punishments, the resolution emphasizes that the convention cannot in any way prejudice "the exercise of the right of legitimate self-determination and independence." The primacy of self-determination over terrorism, insisted upon by the newer states, combined with the interpretation these states give to self-determination opens the door to greater protection for terrorists than for "internationally protected persons" (diplomats). Although the United States and Iran did not employ this terminology, Iran implied that it held U.S. diplomatic staff hostage in 1979 in reprisal for U.S. denial of Iranian self-determination during the preceding years.

The third, and most important, category is immunity, formerly known as extraterritoriality. This last term has largely been discarded for two reasons. First, it has disagreeable connotations because in the past it referred to unilaterally favorable treatment of citizens from Western states in parts of Asia and Africa. Second, it suggests that territory is the reference when in law and in fact the reference is to the treatment of foreign states, foreign organs, and foreign possessions in the territory.

Immunity means exemption from a state's civil, criminal, and administrative jurisdiction. It does not mean exemption from the state's laws. Who or what is immune from which jurisdiction varies and is regulated by customary or conventional law as well as by the comprehensive regulations in the Vienna Convention on Diplomatic Relations (1961), the Vienna Convention on Consular Relations (1963), and the New York Convention on Special Missions (1969).

There are no generally accepted rules for dealing with a protected person who abuses immunity, although there are precedents. Entry of a local official into the protected building without permission is forbidden. When a Soviet Union Embassy building was on fire, the firefighters were not allowed into the building. In 1973, Pakistani police entered the Iraq Embassy and found many weapons, whereupon the ambassador and an attaché were sent out of the country as *personae non gratae*. In 1984, during a demonstration that took place outside the Libyan Embassy in London, a shot from the embassy killed a policewoman. The Libyans left the building. It was searched in the presence of a Saudi Arabian diplomat, and weapons were found. The United Kingdom argued that the building was no longer inviolable but was entitled merely to respect and protection. The leaving personnel were searched for weapons so as to protect the police surrounding the building. The Soviet textbook *International Law* affirms that the activity of Soviet representatives abroad "must be subordinated to the noble aims of the Soviet socialist State— peace and international friendship."

The Protected Entities

The head of a diplomatic mission (ambassador, envoy, minister) and the members of his or her family and household are absolutely immune, with some specified exceptions (mainly when acting in a private, commercial capacity). The mission's diplomatic, administrative, and technical staffs (counselors, attachés, secretaries) and families are also immune, except for acts performed outside their duty. Members of the service staff are immune in respect to acts performed in the course of their duty, and they are also exempt from some taxes and dues. Private servants of the mission are exempt mainly from income tax and immune in such respects as the receiving state may determine. In any case, the receiving state must not exercise jurisdiction in such a way as to interfere with the performance of the mission's functions. The immunity of the mission includes all forms of communications (electronic, mail, bags, luggage) in all quarters of the mission and in the diplomatic agent's official residence. This immunity prevails also in relation to any other state acting within the receiving state. The treatment of the Cuban ambassador by the U.S. invasion forces in Panama in 1989 was therefore illegal.

Because the diplomatic agent is an organ of the state, his or her immunity is based upon the sovereign equality of states. Therefore, only the state can waive the immunity. The envoy and the staff also enjoy immunity when traveling through countries to reach their final destination.

Many questions of detail can arise regarding immunity and the conditions of its application, especially when immunity is not absolute. Courts have reached contradictory conclusions. The Austrian Supreme Court (1961) rejected a U.S. plea of immunity for an embassy car transporting embassy mail from the post office as a "sovereign act" when it became involved in an accident. The court argued that only the act itself—driving the car—not its purpose, had to be considered. A fine imposed on a secretary of the British Embassy in Washington, D.C., by a police magistrate for dangerous driving was canceled because of the secretary's diplomatic status. In 1964, a New York court dismissed a paternity suit against a U.N. ambassador because of immunity. The search of luggage, bags, boxes, and even trucks belonging to diplomatic agents or states has been treated in different ways by different countries, especially after these items have been found to be used for the transportation of weapons, drugs, even kidnapped humans. There is a trend, in view of the ostensibly greater international respect for human rights, for courts to decide in favor of humans if there is a conflict between human life and immunity. More generally, however, courts are inclined to apply the principle of "functional necessity." Immunities must be granted and states must exercise their jurisdiction when they have it in such a manner that the mission can perform its functions adequately.

Consular officers enjoy a more limited inviolability and immunity as compared to those of diplomats. These limits correspond to consular functions. But because these are expanding, and because diplomatic activities once performed by ambassadors are now the province of consuls, the distinction between the two tends to become blurred. The Vienna conventions are therefore frequently implemented by bilateral treaties to keep them in line with modern developments.

In principle, consular officers are immune only for their official activities. Their private actions are subject to the civil and criminal jurisdiction of the receiving state. Offices, archives, and documents are (with some exceptions) immune. Consular officers can be arrested and detained for grave crimes. Any other restrictions upon their freedom (such as imprisonment) require a final judicial decision.

The position of a head of state in a foreign country is uncertain but also not very important, as it is unlikely that such a person would not be treated with great respect. Nevertheless, the U.S. refusal to grant a visa to the chair of the Palestine Liberation Organization in 1988 raised questions about the statehood of the organization and Yasir Arafat's status as head of state (among other legal questions). President Marcos of the Philippines was subject to U.S. and Swiss court proceedings for acts committed during his tenure of office but after he was ousted—an arguable procedure as he was immune when he performed these acts.

The same issue could arise in the case of Manuel Noriega. The drug trafficking involving the United States for which he was indicted took place while he was president of Panama. The United States did not recognize his presidency. But this fact is irrelevant because the declarative theory of recognition has been generally accepted and U.S. courts have considered acts of unrecognized governments as legally valid and have granted such governments certain immunities. (Nor do U.S. courts consider how an accused person is brought before them.) Nevertheless, U.S. courts have also argued that immunity should depend upon the act in question rather than upon recognition. On that basis, Noriega is subject to the jurisdiction of U.S. courts regarding the charges of drug trafficking, a crime under U.S. law and international law.

The receiving state has a special obligation to protect the inviolability of a head of state. To what extent the official is immune has been debated. One argument is that the head of state cannot enjoy an immunity greater than the state. Another is that his or her immunity must be at least as great as that of a diplomat (with the same exceptions as apply to diplomats). Agreement is therefore that a head of state is immune from criminal jurisdiction and likely to be treated as immune for private actions.

The Convention on Special Missions adopted by the General Assembly in 1969 grants the head of state who is leading a special mission the same immunities as international law grants to a head of state on an official visit (a meaningless grant because international law is uncertain on this point). The same convention has a similar (and equally meaningless) formulation for other persons of high rank as leaders of special missions. The convention is clear, however, regarding the inviolability of the persons of these missions and their abode.

The status of armed forces in foreign territory with the permission of the government is usually regulated by treaty. General international law merely prescribes that the members of the armed forces remain under the jurisdiction of their own state, at least in regard to official acts. Customary norms regulating warships in foreign waters are codified in the United Nations Convention on the Law of the Sea (1982) when it comes into force as well as in the Convention on the Territorial Sea and the Contiguous Zone (1958). Warships are immune to the jurisdiction of a foreign state. But because immunity does not mean exemption from the laws, warships must obey the laws of the port and may be required to leave port if they disobey. Very similar regulations apply to military planes under the territorial jurisdiction of a foreign state as agreed in the Paris Convention on Aerial Navigation (1919). National practice varies regarding immunities of off-duty crew members in the territory of the foreign state.

International organizations and their organs have no special status under international law. Their inviolabilities and immunities are regulated in conventions, either those creating the organization or those implementing the constituent instruments. Nevertheless, the Convention on the Privileges and Immunities of the United Nations (1946), the Convention on the Privileges and Immunities of the Specialized Agencies (1947), and the Headquarters Agreement Between the United Nations and the United States (1947) are comprehensive and precedential for most international organizations.

REFERENCES AND READINGS FOR PART 3

Sovereignty

Alan, James. *Sovereign Statehood: The Basis of International Society.* London: Allen and Unwin, 1986.

Bedjaoui, Mohammed. "Non-alignment et droit international." *ADIRC* 151 (1976 III):336–456.

Bleckmann, Albert. "Das Souveränitätsprinzip im Völkerrecht." *AV* 23 (1985 IV):450–477.

Delupis, Ingrid D. *International Law and the Independent State.* London: Gower, 1986.

Duchacek, Ivo D. et al. *Perforated Sovereignties and International Relations.* Westport, CT: Greenwood, 1988.

Farley, Lawrence T. *Plebiscites and Sovereignty: The Crisis of Political Illegitimacy.* Boulder, CO: Westview, 1986.

Hossain, Kamal, and Subrata R. Chowdry. *Permanent Sovereignty over Natural Resources in International Law.* New York: St. Martin's, 1984.

Riphagen, W. "Some reflections on 'functional sovereignty.' " *Netherlands Yearbook of International Law* 6 (1975):121–165.

Salcedo, Juan A.C. *Soberanía del Estado y Derecho Internacional,* 2nd ed. Madrid: Editorial Tecnos, 1976.

Tenekides, Georges. "Souveraineté et hégémonie: Securité égalitaire et securité extensive." *Revue Belge de Droit International* (1974 I):117–141.

Ushakov, N. A. "International law and sovereignty." In *Contemporary International Law,* edited by Grigori Tunkin. Moscow: Progressive Publishers, 1969.

Equality

Anand, R. P. "Sovereign equality of states in the U.N." *Eastern Journal of International Law* 2 (April 1970):34–50.

Fleiner, Thomas. *Die Kleinstaaten in den Staatenverbindungen des zwanzigsten Jahrhunderts.* Zurich: Polygraphischer Verlag, 1966.

Gardner, Richard N. "United Nations procedures and power realities: The international apportionment problem." *Proceedings*, pp. 232–245. Washington, DC: American Society of International Law, 1965.

Klein, Robert A. *Sovereign Equality Among States: The History of an Idea*. Toronto: University of Toronto Press, 1974.

Lacharrière, Guy, Ladroit de. "L'influence de l'inégalité de développement des états sur le droit international." *ADIRC* 139 (1973 II):227–269.

Levi, Werner. "Are developing states more equal than others?" *Yearbook of World Affairs* (1978):286–302.

Rothstein, Robert L. "Inequality, exploitation, and justice in the international system: Reconciling divergent expectations." *International Studies Quarterly* 21 (June 1977):319–358.

Tucker, Robert W. *The Inequality of Nations*. New York: Basic Books, 1977.

Nonintervention

Bull, Hedley, ed. *Intervention in World Politics*. Oxford: Clarendon, 1984.

Damrosch, Lori Fisler. "Politics across borders: Nonintervention and nonforcible influence on domestic affairs." *AJIL* 83 (January 1989):1–50.

Falk, Richard A. "Revolutionary nations and the quality of international legal order." In *The Revolution in World Politics*, edited by Morton A. Kaplan, pp. 310–331. New York: Wiley, 1962.

Franck, Thomas M., and Nigel S. Rodley. "After Bangladesh: The law of humanitarian intervention by military force." *AJIL* 67 (April 1973):275–305.

Higgins, Rosalyn. "International law and civil conflict." In *The International Regulation of Civil Wars*, edited by Evan Luard, pp. 169–186. New York: New York University Press, 1972.

Jacquet, Louis G.M., ed. *Intervention in International Politics*. The Hague: Martinus Nijhoff, 1971.

Leurijk, N. H. "Civil war and intervention in international law." *Netherlands International Law Review* 24 (special issue 1977):143–159.

Lillich, Richard B., ed. *Humanitarian Intervention and the United Nations*. Charlottesville: University Press of Virginia, 1973.

Little, Richard B. *Intervention, External Involvement in Civil War*. Charlottesville: University Press of Virginia, 1973.

Moore, John N., ed. *Law and Civil War in the Modern World*. Baltimore, MD: Johns Hopkins University Press, 1974.

Moore, John N., and Robert F. Turner. *International Law and the Brezhnev Doctrine*. Lanham, MD: University Press of America, 1987.

Pimont, Yves. "La subversion dans les relations internationales contemporaines." *RGDIP* 76 (1972):768–799.

Stowell, Ellery C. *Intervention in International Law*. Littleton, CO: Fred B. Rothman, 1983.

Tesón, Fernando R. *Intervention: An Inquiry into Law and Morality*. Dobbs Ferry, NY: Transnational, 1988.

Vincent, R. J. *Non-Intervention and International Order.* Princeton, NJ: Princeton University Press, 1974.
White, Nigel D. "The legality of intervention following the Nicaragua case." *International Relations* (London) 9 (1989 VI):535–551.

Sovereign Immunity

Badr, Gamal Moursi. *State Immunity: An Analytical and Prognostic View.* Dordrecht: Martinus Nijhoff, 1984.
Bazyler, Michael. "Litigating the international law of human rights: A 'how to' approach." *Whittier Law Review* 7 (1985 III):713–740.
Damian, Helmut. *Staatsimmunität und Gerichtszwang.* New York: Springer, 1985.
Lewis, Charles I. *State and Diplomatic Immunity,* 2nd ed. London: Lloyds of London Press, 1985.
Schreuer, Christoph H. *State Immunity: Some Recent Developments.* Cambridge: Grotius, 1988.
Trooboff, Peter D. "Foreign state immunity: Emerging consensus on principles." *ADIRC* 200 (1986 V):235–431.

Organs of States

Ahmad, M. A. *L'institution consulaire et le droit international.* Paris: Librairie Général de Droit et de Jurisprudence, 1973.
Ciobanu, Dan. "Credentials of delegations and representation of member states at the United Nations." *Int. & Comp. L. Q.* 25 (April 1976):351–381.
Dembinski, Ludwik. *The Modern Law of Diplomacy: External Missions and International Organizations.* Dordrecht: Martinus Nijhoff, 1988.
Denza, Eileen. *Diplomatic Law: Commentary on the Vienna Convention on Diplomatic Relations.* Dobbs Ferry, NY: Oceana, 1976.
Hevener, Natalie, ed. *Diplomacy in a Dangerous World and Protection for Diplomats Under International Law.* Boulder, CO: Westview, 1986.
Higgins, Rosalyn. "The abuse of diplomatic privileges and immunities: Recent United Kingdom experience." *AJIL* 79 (July 1979):641–651.
Kohlhase, Norbert et al. *Les missions permanentes auprès des organisations internationales.* Brussels: Emile Bruylaut, 1973.
Lang, Winfred. "Das Wiener Übereinkommen über die Vertretung von Staaten in ihren Beziehungen zu internationalen Organisationen universellen Charakters." *Z* 37 (1977 I):43–86.
Langrod, Jerzy S. *International Civil Service: Its Origins, Its Nature, Its Evaluation.* Dobbs Ferry, NY: Oceana, 1963.
Lewis, Charles J. *State and Diplomatic Immunity,* 2nd ed. London: Lloyds of London Press, 1985.
Maresca, Adolfo. "Les relations consulaires et les fonctions de consul en matière de droit privé." *ADIRC* 134 (1971 III):105–161.

O'Keefe, Patrick J. "Privileges and immunities of the diplomatic family." *Int. &
Comp. L. Q.* 25 (April 1976):329–350.
Sen, B. *A Diplomatic Handbook of International Law and Practice*, 3rd ed. Dordrecht:
Martinus Nijhoff, 1988.
Silva, G. E. do Nascimento e. *Diplomacy in International Law*. Leiden: A. W.
Sijthoff, 1972.
Wilson, Clifton E. *Diplomatic Privileges and Immunities*. Tucson: University of
Arizona Press, 1967.
Zehetner, Franz. "Staatliche Aussenvertretungsbefugniss im Völkerrecht." Z 37
(1977 II):244–275.

Organs of International Organizations

Bloomfield, Louis M., and Gerald F. FitzGerald. *Crimes Against Internationally
Protected Persons: Prevention and Punishment. An Analysis of the UN Con-
vention.* New York: Praeger, 1975.
Dominicé, Christian. "L'immunité de juridiction et d'exécution des organisations
internationales." *ADIRC* 187 (1984 IV):144–238.
Jenks, C. Wilfred. *International Immunities*. Dobbs Ferry, NY: Oceana, 1961.
Michaels, David B. *International Privileges and Immunities*. The Hague: Martinus
Nijhoff, 1971.
Tillinghast, David R. "Sovereign immunity from the tax collector: United States
income taxation of foreign governments and international organizations."
Law and Policy in International Business 19 (1978 II):495–543.

PART 4
THE JURISDICTION OF STATES

Social order and the coexistence of states necessitate boundaries between their sovereignties and jurisdictions. Because a contraction of every state's power is inevitably involved, states endeavor to widen their own and narrow every other state's jurisdiction. Nevertheless, they have agreed through international law to allot to each state in principle exclusive jurisdiction in given spheres of its interests and activities and to transfer certain jurisdictions to international law, either exclusively or in conjunction with municipal law, for the regulation of their relations.

Jurisdiction means the delimitation by international law of a national legal order's validity. The American Law Institute's Restatement Second (1965) defines jurisdiction as "the capacity of a state under international law to prescribe or enforce a rule of law." This focus upon the legal power of states may explain why agreement on the arrangement has been relatively easy. For, apart from the obvious need for it, the arrangement does not seriously interfere with a state's extension beyond its jurisdiction of its political power to prescribe and enforce another state's behavior even by legitimate political means.

The institute's definition draws attention to the distinction between a state's jurisdiction to prescribe and to enforce law. A state cannot enforce a law it has no right to prescribe. But a state may prescribe a law it may be unable to enforce (as when a criminal escapes into another state's jurisdiction). Nevertheless, that situation represents only one type of difficulty related to jurisdiction. Several bases of jurisdiction have to be considered: the temporal, spatial, personal, and material. International law deals with each. They may overlap and the rules affect each other. Yet in their totality, these rules define the spheres of legal autonomy of states and thereby to a large extent those of international law.

Temporal jurisdiction concerns the existence of states in time and defines when states begin and cease to be of legal consequence. Spatial jurisdiction relates to the physical areas (territory, sea, air, and outer space) in which a state may exercise legal power. Spatial jurisdiction may refer either to the areas for which a state may define legal situations or the areas for which a state may enforce a law. Strictly speaking, spatial jurisdiction should refer only to the physical-geographic areas, but the term is often used also to refer to persons, things, and events located within the areas. Personal jurisdiction refers to the natural or juridic persons under a state's legal autonomy. Material jurisdiction refers to subject matter with which a state may deal.

Jurisdiction flows from sovereignty. Although in practice they mostly coincide, conceptually they are distinct. The exercise of jurisdiction over no-man's-land may lead to the establishment of title to (hence sovereignty over) that land. In the Canal Zone of Panama, Panama is sovereign, but the United States has jurisdiction. The Permanent Court of International Justice in the *Lighthouses in Crete and Samos* case (1937, p. 103) decided that although the island of Crete had far-reaching autonomy under the Ottoman Empire and the sultan had accepted important restrictions on the exercise of his sovereign rights, "sovereignty had not ceased to belong to him, however it might be qualified from a juridical point of view." The International Court of Justice in the *International Status of South West-Africa* case (1950 p. 132) confirmed that the creation of mandates after World War I implied transfer of neither territory nor sovereignty to the mandatory power, although it exercised jurisdiction in the mandate.

There are several other possibilities for the exercise of sovereignty and of jurisdiction by two different subjects in the same location. Most such cases originate in an agreement between the two or in the belligerent occupation by one state of another's territory. One way of explaining this division is to maintain a clear juridical distinction between sovereignty and jurisdiction (as the Vienna school of international lawyers and Alfred Verdross do). Sovereignty is conceived as endowing the state with rights, including various jurisdictions, that the state may transfer to another state while still keeping its sovereignty intact. How many of such jurisdictions a state can transfer before its sovereignty is extinguished, if ever, remains an unanswered question. The more accepted way of explaining the division between the two concepts is to consider the exercise of jurisdiction by one state within the area of another a restriction of the state's sovereignty. When a state exercises jurisdiction in a no-man's-land, no state's sovereignty is involved (which shows that one can exist without the other). States may have jurisdiction, but not sovereignty, over zones in oceans contiguous to their territorial waters.

Commonly, legal terminology uses territorial jurisdiction to refer to all physical-geographic areas under a state's jurisdiction: land, sea, air, and outer space. The practice is imprecise and indicative of the importance of land as the basis for the spatial delimitation of jurisdiction. All other spatial areas are traditionally measured and relevant as they relate geographically to a state's land.

Territorial jurisdiction is, also imprecisely, often identified with territorial sovereignty, although the two are distinct and territorial jurisdiction is only one of the rights flowing from sovereignty. But, again, the practice indicates that territory is so important an element in international politics and law that a state's exercise of legal authority over it is readily considered synonymous with its sovereignty over it.

The great emphasis on territorial jurisdiction more than on other types of jurisdiction and the association of sovereignty with territory are fundamental to modern international politics and law. These emphases originated in European feudalism, where personal duties (hence personal rights) became connected to landownership. The continuing existence and importance of this association derive from several factors. First, the earth's division into delimited geographic areas is neat, orderly, and stable. Second, until modern technology changed conditions, land was relatively easy to protect. Third, territory is a major source of wealth and, sometimes, a major source of a state's prestige. Finally, Roman law relating to real property was highly developed; by analogy, it could be applied to the land of states (thereby creating the erroneous identification of sovereignty over territory with ownership of land).

This origin and regulation of territorial sovereignty can help explain the near-identification of territorial jurisdiction with it and the contemporary uncertainties regarding jurisdiction in areas other than land. Roman law had little to say about sovereignty in these other areas. In fact, the traditional law of the newly independent African states is concerned almost exclusively with land; other areas have been irrelevant to their interests.

The new conditions of the contemporary era require greater precision. Territory should be used in the stricter sense of land (terra firma), including the relatively narrow strip of ocean bordering on coastal lands known as territorial waters (as a firmly established concept), if only for the practical reason that other areas have assumed a much greater importance and can no longer be treated as mere appendixes or extensions of a state's land. Legal problems in regard to these areas have arisen that did not even exist in earlier times and that require regulation in their own right (for example, outer space, the continental shelf, seabed resources). The solution of international law whose primary concern, as exemplified by jurisdiction, is the separation of states and the maintenance of their independence in sovereign equality.

Territorial jurisdiction was originally developed to implement sovereignty and keep states apart. Yet new developments are making sovereign independence increasingly anachronistic because too many of these developments (pollution, rockets, communications, terrorism) are no respecters of territory or national frontiers. Many "domestic" affairs can be protected only by international cooperation, allowing an at best nominal sovereignty through the fiction that cooperative treaties are concluded voluntarily by states. This is the approach states are taking to deal with the onslaught of modern developments upon the continued existence of sovereignty. Where possible, states use the traditional method of expanding their sovereignty and their jurisdiction (for example, the creeping "territorialization" of the oceans through an extension of the territorial waters, the establishment of the continental shelf, the creation of an economic exploitation zone), or else they conclude, because they have to, bi- or multilateral treaties regulating matters (such as outer space, Antarctica, the environment, international crimes) that cannot be handled by national jurisdictions.

9
TEMPORAL JURISDICTION

The Birth of States

The point at which a state's existence begins and ends has important legal consequences for such matters as ownership of assets abroad, responsibility for public debts, and the nationality of individuals. But birth and death are not always points in time; they are processes. The question then is when in the process a birth or death has occurred.

For instance, when Irish volunteers tried to create the independent Irish Republic in 1919 and after, they did not succeed in creating an organization with the usual appurtenances of a state (postal service, tax collections, currency, foreign representation). Consequently, the New York Supreme Court in the *Irish Republic Funds* case (1927, p. 752) decided that there was no government and, by implication, no state called the Irish Republic. But the Irish Free State Court argued that even without complete independence and international recognition and with a de facto government controlling all the claimed territory, the republic "had advanced to such a stage of self-realization as made it something more than a mere association for the promotion of a political ideal." The court also held that the republic had acquired enough sovereignty to enter into a treaty with Great Britain (resulting in the creation of the Irish Free State). U.N. General Assembly Resolution 3061 (XXVIII) of November 2, 1973, welcomed "the recent accession to independence of the people of Guinea-Bissau thereby creating the sovereign state of the Republic of Guinea-Bissau." Portugal, claiming complete control, objected to the recognition of this "ghost" republic. Palestine proclaimed itself a state in November 1988, as Czechoslovakia and Poland had done earlier. Such proclamations help mark the date of the birth of a state.

Even though the existence or nonexistence of a state could be articulated as a factual issue, doing so would rob other states of the opportunity to use this issue for political purposes. And so, international law provides no rules for an objective determination of the fact, although international law attaches considerable consequences to the fact's existence. General agreement that territory, people, and government make a state is insufficient because there is disagreement about what additional components may be required and how their existence is to be determined.

Nor is the principle of recognition of much help in this regard because recognition can be retroactive and a state can be a member of an international organization or a multinational conference without having been recognized by all participants. If a state can have legal relevance as such without having been recognized by some states, it must have relevance without having been recognized by any other state. Indeed, the Pan American Convention on Rights and Duties of States (Montevideo, 1933) declares in Article 3 that "the political existence of a state is independent of recognition by the other states." When North Korea seized the U.S. ship *Pueblo*, the United States asked North Korea to adhere to international law.

In the absence of clear international norms on the point, national jurisprudence makes its own determination about the existence of a state. Usually, states do not deny sovereignty to other states that they have not recognized. They often accept the proclamation of the leadership of a new state that there is a new state (especially when it is politically expedient to do so). They also insist that unrecognized states have rights and duties under international law—an obvious adherence to the declarative theory of recognition.

The Identity or Continuity of States

Once a state exists, the dynamics of its own internal life or of international society do not affect its character as an international person. But they may affect its legal situation.

A change in the personnel or form of government, however produced, does not affect the identity of the state. The U.S. Supreme Court in the *Sapphire* case (1871, p. 168) stated the principle, which has only lately been questioned (mostly by the Communist states): "The reigning sovereign represents the national sovereignty, and that sovereignty is continuous and perpetual, residing in the proper successor of the sovereign for the time being."

Soviet international lawyers have blurred this principle for the transparent political purpose of enabling the Soviet Union to be selective in what it keeps from the past. They agree that a state emerging from a social revolution, although a new "historical type," still has continuity with the territory and property of the "old" state. But in regard to commitments under "old" treaties, the "qualitatively new" subject of international law may decide whether it wants to keep them.

The arbitrator in the *Tinoco Claims Arbitration* (1923, p. 36) found that a state remains identical and responsible when it has only a de facto government recognized by no other state. When there is no central government at all, as, for instance, during a civil war, general opinion is that the state continues because and perhaps only so long as the "greater part of governmental machinery in a modern country is not affected by the changes in the higher administrative officers" (General

Claims Commission in the case *United States [Hopkins] v. Mexico [1923, p. 161])*. Perhaps a better, although more uncertain, criterion for continuity would be the essential preservation of the people as the real carriers of the state.

Governments in exile are considered the de iure governments as long as they are trying to return to their countries under belligerent occupation and their exile is presumably temporary. The Southern District Federal Court of New York in *State of the Netherlands v. Federal Reserve Bank* (1951, p. 461) decided that "military occupation by a belligerent enemy does not transfer sovereignty over the territory to that enemy." The exiled government's legal powers are limited only by the very restricted powers international law gives to the occupation authority for the regulation of affairs in the occupied area.

A change in a state's territory—as long as the state claims any territory at all—is not considered by most national courts to affect the continuity of the state. The same would have to be the case in changes of areas other than territory—for instance, a substantial extension of territorial waters. Yugoslavia is considered to be the same state as Serbia, although the territory has greatly increased, whereas Turkey is considered the same as the Ottoman Empire, although the territory is greatly diminished. Russia and the United States in the nineteenth century maintained their identities throughout their expansions.

The question of the rise of new states remained acute even after post–World War II decolonization. Divided states such as Germany, Korea, and Vietnam arose for which international law supplied no reliable rules. Conflicts developed in many ex-colonies about their statehood, either in regard to the ex-colony as a whole or to its parts. Each case has to be decided pragmatically, which usually means politically, according to general rules. In some cases (Germany, Vietnam), the contending parties solved the problem themselves. In other cases (Korea and several African ex-colonies), it remains unsolved.

How uncertain, hence contradictory, the situation can be was shown in two cases heard before English authorities. In the *Harshaw Chemical Co.'s Patent* case (1964, p. 19), the comptroller of patents held that Britain was not at war with North Korea because it was never recognized by the United Kingdom and because there was only one Korean people, who were divided by a civil, not an international, war. In *Al-Fin Corporation's Patent* (1969, p. 761), the chancery division came to the opposite conclusion on the ground that North Korea was a "sufficiently defined area of territory over which a foreign government has effective control."

The Death of States and Succession

A state becomes extinct with the disappearance of one constituent element. Extinction occurs as a result of voluntary or forcible action. A state can merge into another, can be annexed by another, can break up into several states, or can be broken up into parts, each of which may be annexed by another state. When any one of these events occurs, the fate of particular international rights and obligations related to the old state or its area must be settled. That jurisdiction disappears with the state is beyond discussion.

The extinction of a state is dealt with in international law under the heading of succession. But the analogy between the death of a person and of a state is incomplete and therefore misleading, particularly as general international law can regulate only that part of the problem dealing with the rights and obligations of states toward each other, not with the fate of individual ex-citizens of the dead state. Their condition is a matter of "domestic affairs" and is in principle beyond the reach of international law, unless they become the object of an international commitment in a treaty between the extinct and the successor state (as in the case of minorities). Nevertheless, the law of succession, as largely developed during the nineteenth century, evidences much concern with the protection of private rights, especially acquired rights. This concern typifies, according to Communist legal doctrine, the class character of international law.

The need to regulate state succession stems also from the requirement for continuity as one aspect of social order. The sudden disappearance of one party to international interactions could prove disruptive. States therefore aim at finding a legal surrogate for the extinct state to deal with its assets, liabilities, and various commitments. The prevention of discontinuities should be a guiding principle in the making and interpretation of legal norms. Nevertheless, the desire for continuity diminishes among states in proportion to the price to be paid for it in the form of taking over the dead state's liabilities and obligations—either all of them when the state disappears altogether or parts of them when an area is transferred from one state to another.

This selectively selfish approach of states to succession has led to so many contradictory practices and legal theories that almost any position a state wants to take in a given case for political reasons can be supported by a legal argument. The norms and principles of general international law in relation to territory have at best a tenuous existence and the support of only a limited number of states and international lawyers.

The nineteenth-century conditions that gave rise to the norms regulating state succession were greatly changed by the arrival of the new states in Asia and Africa. They were loath to begin their new life carrying the burden of advantages acquired by foreigners in colonial times, or, sometimes, to accept previous conditions governing relations with each other. Moreover, in many instances the colonizing country had concluded treaties or had made other arrangements with third states relating only to the colonies or had made treaties applying only to itself but not to its colonies. Thus, the new states were in a dilemma. Eager to establish their credibility and trustworthiness, they did not want to reject out of hand any responsibility for obligations incurred for them by their metropolitan powers. They therefore favored a limited succession and in many cases entered into treaties with third states regulating the succession problem by mutual agreement.

Before two conventions regulating succession were agreed upon, some international lawyers distinguished among three types of treaties on which succession would depend: (1) "personal" treaties closely identified with the individuality of a particular state (such as an alliance); (2) impersonal treaties (such as multilateral and so-called lawmaking treaties) in which the state is more important as a political entity than as an individual "personality"; and (3) dispositive or localized treaties in which a legal situation is inherent in a given piece of territory on locally related matters (such as a customs zone, military base, or port facility). According to this reasoning, in the case of new states whether these treaties were "local" would have to be determined, and if so, they would have to be kept.

In practice, and in regard to all states, old and new, successor states tend to determine their commitments according to political, ideological, and other reasons. They agree, therefore, that automatic, complete succession is unfeasible and unacceptable. Relying upon their sovereignty, they decide which rights and obligations they are willing to take over. This freedom is limited, however, by general agreement that devolution agreements between a metropolitan power and its former colony or a unilateral declaration by a new state cannot affect the third state without that state's assent. Freedom is further limited by agreement that treaties affecting borders are unaffected by succession. When a newly independent state belonged formerly to a state that was a party to a multilateral treaty, the newly independent state may opt to become a party to that treaty, unless such an option is incompatible with the nature of the treaty.

In 1978, the Vienna Convention on Succession of States in Respect to Treaties was concluded; the Vienna Convention on Succession of States in Respect to State Property, Archives, and Debts was concluded in 1983. Taken together, the two conventions cover virtually all possibilities of the birth and death of states and their consequences. But as an insufficient number of states have ratified these conventions, the situation remains as it was before they were signed; that is to say, either specific treaties or customary law prevails.

Types of Succession of States

When part of a state's area is transferred to another state, treaties between both states and third states in principle remain unaffected because treaties are concluded with states regardless of their area. The piece of area involved in the transfer exits from the treaty system of the one state and enters that of the other. If there is also a dispositive or localized treaty relating to the transferred area, the successor state is bound to honor it in any case. The state property located in the area becomes the property of the successor state. The successor state is not obligated to take over the public or administrative debts (for example, civil servant pensions) of the transferred area, unless special circumstances make the taking over of a proportionate part of the debts equitable. Individuals living in the transferred area are subject to the laws of the successor state, which, thanks to its sovereignty, may introduce its legal order.

When an entire state becomes extinct and another state comes into possession of its area and people, treaties (except possibly for dispositive treaties) die with the state. So does membership of the dead state in international organizations, except that conventions signed under their aegis or with them remain in force. (Organizations such as the World Bank take the precaution of making the predecessor state responsible for default on debts if only a part of that state's area is transferred.) The public property of the extinct state, wherever it is located, belongs to the successor state. The successor state must also take over public debts, except those incurred for political or war-making purposes. This rule can apply only to foreign creditors whose state can act in their behalf because the claims of nationals who are creditors of the extinct state must be handled by the municipal law of the successor state whose citizens they have become.

Succession to contractual liabilities (such as public works) of the extinct state toward private parties is undecided. State practice varies from complete to no succession. A foreign contractor may have a claim under the doctrine of unjust enrichment for work already completed that benefits the successor state. Private rights of aliens originally established under the legal order of the extinct state are to be honored by the successor state under the principle of acquired rights, at least to the extent that they cannot simply be terminated.

When a state becomes extinct through dismemberment and the succession of several states, the public property and the public debt of the extinct state are divided proportionately among the successor states. But only equity can determine the proportionality. The successor states either have to agree on this point or submit to arbitration. Third states in possession of some of the property may await a final settlement before handing the property back to the successor states or use their own judgment if no agreement is reached or award made.

There is general agreement that torts committed by a state are of a "personal" nature. Successor states are not responsible for them. The same applies to claims the extinct state had for torts committed against it. Once a claim has been adjudged and the material compensation determined, it may be possible to succeed to the right for compensation as a debt.

The regulation of succession in general international law is inadequate. Political considerations prominently affect the solution of specific problems. States are not likely to abandon these considerations in favor of subscribing to the regulations proposed by the two conventions. The political and utilitarian interests of all states, greatly conditioned by the circumstances of each individual case, can explain why states wish to retain utmost freedom of decision and why so little agreement has been reached on even a few general legal principles of succession. These interests can also explain the popularity of bilateral treaties in settling these problems; these treaties can overcome the uncertainties of temporal jurisdiction and its consequences.

10
SPATIAL JURISDICTION

Content of Spatial Jurisdiction

Sovereignty may be said to be a negative concept, its role being to keep states free from control by other states by instructing them in what not to do to each other. Jurisdiction is positive, allowing states to make and enforce laws.

Chief Justice Marshall in *Schooner Exchange v. M'Faddon* (1812, p. 135) asserted, "The jurisdiction of the nation within its own territory is necessarily exclusive and absolute. It is susceptible of no limitation not imposed by itself." Arbitrator Max Huber said in the *Island of Palmas* case (1928, p. 91) that sovereignty "in regard to a portion of the globe is the right to exercise therein, to the exclusion of any other State, the functions of a State" and that territorial sovereignty is "the exclusive right to display the activities of a state." In the *Lotus* case (1927, p. 18), the Permanent Court of International Justice declared that a state "may not exercise its power in any form in the territory of another state. In this sense jurisdiction is certainly territorial."

These decisions clarify that in addition to the content, the boundaries of jurisdiction are of great importance. Jurisdiction and national boundaries are related because at a minimum a state has jurisdiction within its boundaries. But this does not exhaust all possibilities because sovereignty and jurisdiction do not coincide.

The concern of states with spatial jurisdiction—content and boundary—is shifting, conflicting, and increasingly intensive. States often aim to expand their jurisdiction into as much space as possible in regions contiguous to their territory without necessarily expanding their national frontiers or sovereignty. Examples are the creation of special zones, such as a security zone, a contiguous zone, or the continental shelf, where coastal states have "sovereign rights" (conventions of 1958) but not sovereignty.

Two major problems have become acute. One is drawing boundaries of jurisdiction. The other is regulating the content of jurisdiction, especially in international spaces. Neither problem is adequately soluble with traditional norms because new political and economic possibilities and demands are changing the values states bring to international spaces. Under contemporary conditions, international law's traditional approach—that international spaces are under no state's jurisdiction and that a state's jurisdiction goes with its flag—is likely to lead to conflicting jurisdictions and disorder.

Recognizing this danger, states have mainly chosen two ways of avoiding it. One way is to conclude treaties designed to safeguard the social order in international spaces. States have done so, for instance, in regard to the high seas, the Antarctic, and outer space. The other way is to act unilaterally, for instance, in expanding territorial waters or creating rights in continental shelves. The drawn-out negotiations over the United Nations Convention on the Law of the Sea (1982) are indicative of the states' reluctance to specify and finalize their interests (especially in view of rapidly developing new technologies), to adjust their conflicting interests, and even to reach internal agreement among competing interest groups. States often prefer to be pragmatic about the matter, accepting the risks always involved in such a solution. In the process, land as a fixed point for neatly defining geographic limits of sovereignty and jurisdiction is becoming increasingly unproductive.

Jurisdiction in Airspace

The airspace over a state, including over its territorial waters, is technically part of its territory. A state therefore has sovereignty and jurisdiction over its airspace. But in this situation, possession of independence and exclusive rights is of limited value because a state that does not wish to be cut off from international air traffic cannot exist in sovereign independence in its airspace. Thus, compromise and reciprocity among states are necessary.

Many legal problems, such as the conditions for the right of innocent passage of airplanes, normal and emergency landing rights, passenger and freight traffic have been settled in some multilateral treaties, such as the Paris Convention for the Regulation of Aerial Navigation (1919), the Chicago Convention on International Civil Aviation (1944), and the Warsaw Convention for the Unification of Certain Rules Relating to International Carriage by Air (1955). These conventions have been implemented by amendments, numerous bilateral treaties relating to air traffic, and several multilateral agreements relating to criminal acts in and against airplanes. But none of them affects the basic principle of a state's jurisdiction over its airspace, which does not include the airspace of special zones such as the continental shelf or the exclusive economic zone (EEZ).

The special problem of the unauthorized penetration of a state's airspace by an airplane remains to be solved authoritatively. The several incidents that have occurred have been treated in various ways, although weapons were used only exceptionally when the intruder was a civil aircraft. The most important question, of course, is how a state whose airspace is being violated may protect itself. One school of thought (as represented by Oliver Lissitzyn) advocates that a state's measures be proportionate to the reasonably expected harmfulness of the intrusion. Another school suggests that a state must refrain from using weapons in all cases of intrusion by civil aircraft. The likelihood is that a state's action will depend upon its evaluation of the cause and harmfulness of the intrusion and the available choice of effective responses.

Jurisdiction in Outer Space

For obvious reasons, general international law has no norms for outer space. A U.N. committee suggested that the charter should be applied because it had no terrestrial limits. But it was soon discovered that such a measure would be insufficient to deal with the special problems created in that area. Instead, a number of multilateral agreements were developed that addressed general as well as specific matters.

The inability of any one state to control outer space combined with vast ignorance about the potential of outer space for national interests generated an obvious international agreement: Because states were unsure of any benefits for themselves, all agreed that no state should be allowed to claim any benefit. "The exploration and use of outer space, including the moon and other celestial bodies, shall be carried out for the benefit and in the interests of all countries, irrespective of their degree of economic or scientific development, and shall be the province of all mankind" was established as the fundamental jurisdictional principle in outer space by the Treaty on Principles Governing the Activities of States in the Exploration and Use of Outer Space, Including the Moon and Other Celestial Bodies (1967). As soon as exploitation becomes feasible, the treaty partners are obliged to establish an international regime for the development and management of these resources and the equitable sharing of the benefits. In the meantime, a 1977 resolution guarantees the developing countries equitable access to the geostatic orbit (where space devices and the earth move at equal speed).

In the 1976 Declaration of Bogotá, Colombia argued that the geostationary orbit is not included in the moon treaty because the orbit is a natural resource and an "integral part" of the territory over which it had sovereignty; several other states whose territory crosses the equator amplified this argument in a 1987 protocol. Athough they did not object to satellites transiting that orbit, they insisted that placement of stationary satellites in that orbit required their permission; some even asked for monetary compensation for giving that permission.

A number of treaties on various activities related to outer space and their possible consequences implemented the 1976 treaty without affecting the absence of any one state's sovereignty or jurisdiction. The Agreement Governing the Activities of States on the Moon and Other Celestial Bodies (1979) (not yet ratified by the United States) reemphasizes demilitarization of these bodies and the resources of the moon as the common heritage of humankind. According to all these agreements, jurisdiction is maintained only over objects launched into outer space and any personnel in them.

The question of a state's sovereignty as it relates to the unwanted reception of radio and television broadcasts from satellites in space remains to be answered. Marxist and Third World countries insist that their sovereignty requires foreign broadcasts to their countries to secure prior consent (especially because "overspill" of such broadcasts can be prevented). Other countries refer to Article 19 of the Universal Declaration of Human Rights and many other documents granting everyone the right "to seek, receive and impart information and ideas through any media and regardless of frontiers." A related, unresolved issue involves sovereignty and jurisdiction vis-à-vis spacecraft carrying remote sensors and surveillance.

Clearly the entire complex of the legal regulation of outer space is highly undeveloped. An improvement of the situation, except for some relatively insignificant problems, is hardly to be expected in the light of great political differences and the unpredictability of future conditions.

Jurisdiction over Contiguous and Similar Special Zones

Beyond territorial waters, the sovereignty of states ends, but not necessarily their jurisdiction. Customary law establishes a contiguous zone for limited purposes, usually relating to protective or preventive control beyond territorial waters. The United Nations Convention on the Law of the Sea, Article 33 (1982), essentially reaffirms a similar clause, Article 24, from the Convention on the Territorial Sea and Contiguous Zone (1958), when it says, "1. In a zone contiguous to its territorial sea, described as the contiguous zone, the coastal state may exercise the control necessary to: (a) prevent infringement of its customs, fiscal, immigration or sanitary laws and regulations within its territory or territorial sea; (b) punish infringement of the above laws and regulations committed within its territory or territorial sea."

As early as 1804, Chief Justice Marshall asserted in *Church v. Hubbard* that a nation's power to secure itself from injury could be exercised beyond the limits of its territory. This position was reaffirmed in *United States v. Baker* (1980) and became law for the United States when it ratified the 1958 convention.

Since 1950, the United States has established air defense identification zones reaching several hundred miles into the Atlantic and Pacific oceans. Foreign aircraft intending to enter the United States must identify themselves and report on their flight as soon as they enter this zone.

Jurisdiction in the Exclusive
Economic Zone

Since 1960, a large number of bi- and multilateral treaties and declarations have been signed, the *Fisheries Jurisdiction (United Kingdom . . . v. Iceland) (Merits, Judgment)* (1974) was decided by the International Court of Justice, and the "codfish war" was conducted by the United Kingdom and Iceland. All of these events led to the creation of fishing zones for many coastal states and eventually to the creation of the EEZ. The impetus came from interest in fishing, especially of those states declaring fishing zones beyond their territorial waters. But the zone ended up including all resources in and below the water and represented a compromise between expanding the territorial waters to 200 miles and retaining a more narrow, traditional territorial sea. The establishment of this zone is an excellent illustration of how in a relatively short time and with many national interests clashing during the process, general agreement can be reached, conflicting national interests can be settled peacefully, and customary law can be created.

Although the United Nations Convention on the Law of the Sea (1982) is not yet in force, its section dealing with the EEZ reflects in essence the prevailing legal situation. In March 1983, President Reagan indicated that the convention norms on the zone did confirm international law and practice and balanced the interests of all states.

The convention states that the zone (200 nautical miles) is an area beyond and adjacent to the territorial sea in which the coastal state has sovereign rights. The state can use the zone to explore, exploit, conserve, and manage the natural resources, whether living or nonliving, of the waters superjacent to the seabed and of the seabed and its subsoil. The state can also economically exploit and explore the zone for such purposes as producing energy from water, currents, and winds. The coastal states also have jurisdiction over artificial structures and islands, marine scientific research, and the protection and preservation of the marine environment. This jurisdiction must be exercised with due regard to the rights and duties of other states (mainly those traditionally existing under the freedom of the seas), and these states must pay due respect to the rights and duties of the coastal states. Rights of landlocked and geographically disadvantaged states are protected. The convention prescribes in great detail what these various rights and duties are, primarily as they relate to fishing.

Jurisdiction over the Continental Shelf

In 1945, President Truman proclaimed that the United States regarded "the natural resources of the subsoil and seabed of the continental shelf beneath the high seas but contiguous to the coast of the United States as appertaining to the United States, subject to its jurisdiction and control." He was careful not to claim sovereignty and careful to emphasize that the waters over the continental shelf remained high seas and that freedom of navigation was in no way affected by the claim. Many other states ignored these qualifications as they rushed to follow the U.S. lead. Some claimed sovereignty over the shelf, the water above, the resources of both shelf and water, and anything else that might show up in that area.

Notwithstanding these many and very different claims, Lord Asquith in the *Abu Dhabi Award* (1951) denied that at that time the continental shelf doctrine had assumed the status of an established rule of international law. But by 1958 the situation had changed. Article 2 of the Convention on the Continental Shelf passed that year specified "The coastal State exercises over the continental shelf sovereign rights for the purpose of exploring the seabed and exploiting its natural resources." Eleven years later the International Court of Justice in the *North Sea Continental Shelf* cases (1969, p. 22) argued that the rights of a state over the continental shelf "exist *ipso facto* and *ab initio*, by virtue of its sovereignty over the land, and as an extension of it in an exercise of its sovereign rights for the purpose of exploring the seabed and exploiting its natural resources. In short, there is here an inherent right." The United Nations Convention on the Law of the Sea (1982) reaffirmed most of the conditions agreed upon in the 1958 convention, except that it elaborated in much greater detail the limits of the shelf as well as extending them.

What exactly the "sovereign rights" of a state are, as distinct from having sovereignty (which neither treaties nor courts speak about), may not always be clear. After affirming that states possess these rights, whether they use them or not, the conventions spell out some of them without being able to prevent disputes. (France and Brazil argued over lobsters as a resource, and the United States and Japan argued over Alaskan king crabs.) States may take necessary measures for exploration and exploitation without, however, interfering with navigation, fishing, or the conservation of living resources. States may establish necessary structures and surround these with a safety zone, although these are not to be considered islands and therefore do not affect the territorial limits of the state.

Jurisdiction on the High Seas

The legal fate of the high seas has undergone many changes in the course of history. At one time, virtually all oceans of the world were subject to the jurisdiction of Spain and Portugal. Now the freedom of oceans from jurisdiction by any state holds sway. The idea of the "freedom of the seas" means that no state can claim sovereignty in the area. Nevertheless, the definition of "the seas," specifically of what body of water is included, has changed.

As international traffic in and over oceans increased, as resources in and under oceans became valuable, and as technology made the exploitation of ocean resources feasible, states sought ways to narrow the parts of oceans free from any jurisdiction and then to subject the excluded parts to their own jurisdiction. The "creeping territorialization" of the oceans began in earnest after World War II. These inroads upon the freedom of the high seas are sanctioned in a number of general and special treaties—most comprehensively in the conventions of 1958 concluded at Geneva and the not yet in force United Nations Convention on the Law of the Sea (1982)—and in whatever customary law may exist.

What area of "high seas" is left after the scramble for an extension of territorial jurisdiction is discussed in Chapter 11. In regard to that area, the Convention on the High Seas (1958), says in Article 1, "The term 'high seas' means all parts of the sea that are not included in the territorial sea or in the internal waters of a State." The corresponding article (86) in the United Nations Convention on the Law of the Sea takes into consideration the narrowing of the high seas that had taken place between 1958 and 1982 through an extension of the territorial waters by also excluding from the area the Exclusive Economic Zone and archipelagic waters. Article 2 of the 1958 convention rules that freedom of the high seas comprises inter alia for coastal and noncoastal states freedom of navigation, freedom of fishing, freedom to lay submarine cables and pipelines, and freedom to fly over the high seas. Each state is to exercise these rights with mutual regard for every other state's right to do the same. Noncoastal states should be given free access to the sea by agreement with the state between the sea and the noncoastal state. In particular they should be granted free transit and equal treatment of their ships by that state. Article 87 in the U.N. convention adjusts this norm to subsequent developments. In addition, the Convention on Transit Trade of Landlocked Countries (1965) provides additional details of the obligations of the state interposed between the landlocked state and the ocean.

States have developed many new interests in the high seas, and some dissatisfactions growing out of the 1958 Geneva conventions are being dealt with in provisions of the United Nations Convention on the Law of the Sea (1982), either as new topics or as modernizations or alterations of old topics. The result has been that most issues, but not all, of concern to states form part of the very comprehensive convention. The convention attempts to establish a regime for the oceans so that as new developments take place, states can more easily reach agreements within the confines of the regime. But the comprehensiveness, presumably a beneficial characteristic of a regime, is also causing states not to commit themselves. It is a major reason so many states, the United States among them, have not yet signed or ratified the convention. The long and sometimes agonizing history of the debates between 1958 and 1982 offers a survey not only of the problems relating to the sea but also an illustration of many problems of international politics.

During the successive law of the sea conferences controversy seemed to turn around legal concepts such as sovereignty, jurisdiction, control, and international agencies. In fact, very often these concepts symbolized clashes of interest, many of them relating to the sea, some also relating to security issues, and occasionally a few having nothing at all to do with the issues at hand. In this last case, states used their votes on the convention as a bargaining counter to obtain concessions on topics quite unrelated to ocean issues.

The motives behind the positions taken by the various states were very mixed and sometimes obscure. There was the usual alignment of developed versus developing states. On some issues, however (such as landlocked states), lines were crossed because states had some common interests. The same was true about the USSR and the United States regarding certain similar military interests. Such coinciding interests led, for instance, to the introduction of the right of "transit passage" through straits as distinct from the well-established and more limited right to innocent passage. Under the second right submarines have to surface when going through straits located within the territorial sea; under the first right they may remain submerged.

Many states trailing in technology behind the most advanced states joined in trying to prevent the preemption of the values of the oceans because they feared that the more advanced states might use a new law of the sea to monopolize exploitation and research. Raw-material-producing states worried about competition from the same raw materials to be extracted from the deep seabed. Maritime transportation, oil production, coastal and distant-water fisheries, pollution prevention, defense, and scientific exploration became the basis of conflicts of interest or cooperation, both among states and within states. Yet in spite of the increasing territorialization of the sea, the principle of freedom of navigation was essentially maintained with the support of all states. It did not represent a subject for major debates or controversies.

The spirit pervading the negotiations at the law of the sea conferences was nationalism. There was little evidence that individual national proposals considered the high seas and its resources the "common heritage of mankind," U.N. declarations to the contrary notwithstanding. But it was also evident that any return to isolated sovereign independence could end only in chaos. States seemed compelled to pursue some form of cooperation, including an international authority, although it is now clear that acceptance of legal regulation of all the issues concerning the high seas is long in coming.

In the meantime, individual, mainly the most developed, states have taken provisional or even final steps to settle some of the most important issues. Some states have passed national legislation concerning seabed mining (United States, United Kingdom, France, West Germany, Japan, and the USSR, among them), pending general international agreement. They have entered into agreements to avoid competing claims. Some states have concluded regional agreements regarding fishery. And, as always, there remains the possibility that some of the innovative norms in the U.N. convention may become customary law.

Jurisdiction in the Polar Regions

Jurisdiction and sovereignty over polar regions are controversial. Antarctica raises more international problems than the Arctic does because it contains land and, presumably, natural resources. Under the "sector theory," various states are claiming either jurisdiction or sovereignty over portions of both arctic regions. According to this theory, lines are drawn from the state territory to the polar regions (on the basis of either continuous or contiguous territory) so that the area located between these lines becomes the sector claimed by the state. If, for instance, Argentina could draw these lines from its western border to the Falkland Islands instead of having to draw them from the western and eastern border of the mainland, its share in the Antarctic would be greater.

Other states claim jurisdiction or sovereignty resulting from discovery or annexation (but without effective occupation). These claims are occasionally recognized by other states, but most often they are not. The Antarctic Treaty of 1959 freezes existing claims, demilitarizes Antarctica, opens it to scientific activities of states, and stipulates that rights or duties under it do not affect past claims or serve new territorial claims. Though the treaty was ostensibly concluded in preparation for the International Geophysical Year, some states entertained additional considerations. Australia's real motivation, for instance, was to prevent the militarization of the Soviet sector.

The treaty is binding, of course, only upon its signatories. Whether they can enforce it—collectively, if at all—against third states is highly questionable. Tacit agreement to the treaty's arrangement by all other states when it was signed would be the likely and weak legal basis for such enforcement.

In June 1988, twenty states initialed the Convention on the Regulation of Antarctic Mineral Resource Activities. It replaces an informal moratorium during the preceding eight years and follows the Convention on the Conservation of Antarctic Marine Living Resources (1980). The growing understanding of the Antarctic ecosystem is reflected in the 1988 convention. There is repeated emphasis upon the protection of the Antarctic environment as a prime consideration in the exploration, development, and exploitation of the continent's mineral resources. Nevertheless, Greenpeace felt that the convention did a "disservice" to the Antarctic, a feeling shared by some other, similar organizations, but not all. Under the convention, any area of Antarctica may be opened up for exploration, development, and exploitation, providing all twenty parties approve. Testing that does not affect the environment is allowed without any further permission. Other approved activities will be supervised by a committee, of which the United States and Soviet Union will be permanent members. The question of sovereignty over parts of the Antarctic claimed by several countries was not addressed in the convention, presumably because several parties do not recognize it. States not parties to the convention are, of course, not bound by it. The hope was expressed, however, that they would not act contrary to its norms.

Jurisdiction over Ships and Airplanes
Outside Territorial Jurisdictions

In the *Lotus* case (1928, p. 25), the Permanent Court of International Justice proclaimed, "In virtue of the principle of the freedom of the seas, that is to say, the absence of any territorial sovereignty upon the high seas, no State may exercise any kind of jurisdiction over foreign vessels upon them." Since then, the Convention on the High Seas (1958) has codified and expanded the rules of customary law designed to maintain order on the high seas.

Every state, coastal or otherwise, has the right to sail ships under its flag on the high seas and has jurisdiction over these ships. The state must fix the conditions for the grant of its nationality to ships, for the registration of ships in its territory, and for the right to fly its flag, all of which give the ship its nationality. But there must be a "genuine link" between the state and the ship. In particular, the state must effectively exercise its jurisdiction and control in all matters concerning the ship. This condition aims at eliminating the special undue benefits to ships flying "flags of convenience." Such benefits include low taxes, low wages, low (if any) social security benefits, and, perhaps most important, evasion of the many treaties containing parts of the law of the sea to which the convenience flag state is not a party. In 1985, the U.N. Conference on Trade and Development drafted a convention detailing conditions to strengthen the measures against the undesirable consequences of flags of convenience.

According to the draft, a merchant ship should sail under one flag only. If it sails under two flags and uses them for its convenience, it will be treated as a ship flying no flag at all and lose the advantages of having a nationality that flying a flag provides.

Warships and merchant ships engaged in official state acts remain under the jurisdiction of their flag state even in territorial and internal waters of another state unless they violate the harbor's traffic laws. Over its merchantmen in foreign waters, the flag state retains jurisdiction only in regard to the internal order and discipline of the ship. But by general agreement, that jurisdiction ends and is replaced by that of the local state in cases of major crimes on board the ship or if activities on board "involve the peace and dignity of the country, or the tranquility of the port," as the U.S. Supreme Court formulated the norm in the *Wildenhus* case (1887, p. 18).

If the authorities of a state have good reason to believe that a foreign ship has violated the laws and regulations of the state in the internal waters, the territorial sea, or the contiguous zone, the state has the right of hot pursuit. Such pursuit may be undertaken only by specially authorized government service ships or airplanes, and it must begin while the ship is in any of these areas. The pursuit may continue beyond, into the high seas only, provided that it is uninterrupted. Details are regulated in the Convention on the High Seas (1958). It may be assumed—and has become frequent practice in fishing situations—that hot pursuit for the purpose of arrest and punishment may also begin when a foreign ship violates a state's rights in the EEZ or on the continental shelf. But in regard to violation of rights in any of the areas outside the territorial waters, the pursuit may take place only for the violation of those rights for whose maintenance the special zone was created. Article 111 of the United Nations Convention on the Law of the Sea (1982) brings the concept and norms of hot pursuit up to date. A merchantman who is engaged or suspected to be engaged in an activity considered criminal under international law may be visited and searched by a warship. (This topic is discussed in Chapter 13 in connection with international criminal law.) Many of the rules and regulations applying to ships are applied, mutatis mutandis, to airplanes.

11
ACQUISITION, LOSS, BOUNDARIES, OF SPATIAL SOVEREIGNTY AND JURISDICTION

Importance of Land

Because the physical-geographic extent of all forms of jurisdiction is measured mainly from or is related to a state's land base and because states originated from that land base, the definition of a state's land and other spatial boundaries is most important. Problems in defining existing boundaries and the manner and consequences of their changes are older than international law. Since the rise of the nation-state system, these problems have usually stemmed from the real or imagined need of all states to increase their power potential. Expanding the spatial boundaries to enhance sovereignty and jurisdiction, they often believe, is one way of achieving that result. There are many ways to establish and change these boundaries. Some are naturemade, some manmade. Some are legally well regulated, others not. Some apply to the entire land area of a state, others to parts of it. But whatever their origin and normative regulation, these means are frequent causes of political conflict and a challenge to the efficacy of international law.

Acquisition Through Natural Events

Several natural ways can increase or diminish a state's territory. Accretion is one, meaning an extension of land through such processes as volcanic activity, the drying up of a river, a receding ocean, or the formation of mud islands in the estuaries of rivers. Sir William Scott of the British High Court of Admiralty in the *Anna* (1805) case decided that the nature of the accretion was irrelevant; it would not affect the right of dominion. Another form of accretion is avulsion, the sudden, violent, and intensive washing of land onto seashore by the sea or by

a river from one bank to the other bank if the river marked a boundary
(a U.S.-Mexico problem). Alluvion, yet another form of accretion, is the
process by which a river or other body of water gradually washes more
and more land onto the shore, thereby increasing the land of a state.

Occupation

Territory not under any sovereignty can be brought under a state's
sovereignty on several conditions. In an original occupation, the occupant
must be a state. The territory must not be under any sovereignty at the
moment of occupation (*terra nullius*). The occupant must intend to bring
the territory under its sovereignty. The occupation must be effective—
that is, the occupant must exercise authority.

The last condition is crucial. But effectiveness is variable, and much
depends upon the nature of the territory—location, climate, population.
Arbitrator Max Huber in the *Island of Palmas* case (1928, p. 93) said
the manifestation of sovereignty must be "in a manner corresponding
to circumstances" and may assume different forms "according to conditions of time and place."

Continuous exhibition of sovereignty may differ according to whether
the territory is inhabited or uninhabited, thickly or thinly populated,
developed or undeveloped, easy or difficult of access. Making laws
applicable to the territory was sufficient "actual exercise or display" of
sovereignty, held the International Court of Justice in the *Eastern Greenland*
case (1933, p. 63). The king of Italy in the *Clipperton Island* arbitration
(1931) found that in the case of an uninhabited island, discovery and
raising the flag on that occasion were adequate to establish sovereignty.
Many international lawyers disagree, arguing that some form of occupation
must follow. Max Huber in the *Island of Palmas* case (1928) insisted that
discovery alone would merely establish inchoate (beginning, incomplete)
title, to be completed by occupation.

Because there is hardly any *terra nullius* left on the globe, acquisition
through occupation is relevant mainly to legitimize sovereignty or jurisdiction over territory acquired at an earlier time or possibly over the
seabed, polar regions, and celestial bodies—if that is not regulated by
treaty. The landing of *Sputnik* or U.S. spacecraft on the moon was
insufficient to establish sovereignty.

Military occupation during a war (*occupatio bellica*) does not create
sovereignty. It merely gives the occupying state jurisdiction within the
narrow limits of international laws of war.

Prescription

Sovereignty may be acquired, according to almost unanimous opinion,
through effective occupation of territory that was or may have been

under another state's sovereignty at the time of occupation. In the opinion of some international lawyers it is irrelevant whether the occupying state acted in good or bad faith. For such acquisition of sovereignty to occur, according to the *Chamizal* award (1911), the occupation must be undisturbed, uninterrupted, and unchallenged and undertaken with the intention of acquiring sovereignty. The former sovereign either may have renounced sovereignty expressly or by his or her behavior may have tolerated the continuing jurisdiction of the occupying state; over time that jurisdiction turns into sovereignty. This type of prescription was approved by the International Court of Justice in the *Temple of Preah Vihear (Cambodia v. Thailand)* case (1962).

The purpose of prescription is to create a stable social order, which is occasionally considered more important than right. The arbitral award in the *Grisbardana* case (1909, p. 130) referred to the "settled principle" in international law; this principle holds that a condition that has existed for a long time should be changed as little as possible. The circumstances of the case will define what "a long time" is. A less arguable criterion might be the assumed consequences of a situation existing for a long time—that is, the generally accepted prevailing order of things. Prescription could then be interrupted if any state failed to recognize this order by protesting the exercise of jurisdiction by the occupying state.

Cession

Cession is the transfer of a piece of territory (which may be all of the state) of one sovereign state to another. The reason for the transfer does not concern the law. It could be a gift, purchase, exchange, or result of defeat. The transfer is valid at the moment of treaty ratification if it is followed by the exercise of the new sovereignty. Decolonization would be a case of cession, where the transfer of territory takes place to a simultaneously formed new state.

Subjugation or Conquest

Before the League of Nations Covenant and the Charter of the United Nations, the acquisition of territory by conquest followed by annexation was legally possible. Now it is not. Nevertheless, in the absence of protest by the defeated state (which may have disappeared altogether) or any attempt to regain the lost territory, the territory may be acquired by the conquering state through prescription.

Treaty

Jurisdiction over space (without loss of sovereignty) can be acquired by one state through transfer by treaty from another state or from an international organization (as in the case of a mandate or trust territory). The various extraterritorial or consular jurisdictions by many European states in the nineteenth and early twentieth centuries in China and other parts of Asia were established in this manner.

Loss of Sovereignty and Jurisdiction

The loss of jurisdiction or sovereignty often means acquisition for the other party. Only secession has no counterpart. It usually occurs as a result of revolution and is completed when revolutionaries have succeeded in effectively creating a new state, either through force or through an agreement with the state from which they seceded.

The reason secession usually results from revolutionary action and involves international law is that states, even when their constitutions permit secession, rarely tolerate it in practice. The problem is acute in Africa and Eastern Europe today and poses the issue of a conflict between self-determination and secession.

The African states are most ardent defenders of "the right to self-determination of peoples." But they usually limit that right in practice to decolonization or the elimination of white minority governments. They have agreed in the Organization of African Unity and numerous African conferences that in regard to themselves, the principles of territorial integrity must prevail. Although boundaries between various African states were often arbitrarily established by the imperialist colonial powers, they are considered valid, and self-determination for the purpose of changing them (and often making them more rational) is declared inoperative. Self-determination is allowed to express itself until interference with national territorial integrity occurs; only federations and mergers are permitted.

The problem is also acute in the Soviet Union, the People's Republic of China, and the United Kingdom, to name just a few. In no case have demands for self-determination been permitted to lead to independence and a new state. The greatest concession made is to give the "minority" asking for self-determination more autonomy within the state. The limits of self-determination (other than against colonial powers) are guaranteed in the U.N. Charter (Article 2) in order to ensure the territorial integrity of states. The Declaration on the Granting of Independence to Colonial Countries and Peoples (1960) confirms that "any attempt aimed at the partial or total disruption of the national unity and the territorial integrity of a country" is incompatible with the principles of the charter.

Land Boundaries

Most land boundaries have been defined by treaties, often peace treaties, or by agreements giving colonies independence. In their absence and in the presence of uncertainties, said arbitrator Max Huber in the *Island of Palmas* case (1928, p. 93), "the actual continuous and peaceful display of state functions is in case of dispute the sound and natural criterion of territorial sovereignty." This dictum is an application of the principle of effectiveness.

Natural frontiers are never legal boundaries per se, although they are often chosen by agreement. Ridges of mountains or divides may serve as boundaries (as a convenience). For rivers, the middle is the frontier in the case of nonnavigable rivers. In the case of navigable rivers the deepest line of the main channel (*Talweg*) is the frontier. If the channel changes, the frontier changes with it. If the entire river changes its bed, the dry *Talweg* remains the boundary. The many complications that can arise were particularly evident in the U.S.-Mexican dispute concerning the Rio Grande between 1864 and 1970 and can also be found in numerous disputes between states of the United States regarding their borders. Frontiers across lakes or landlocked seas usually run across the middle. If several states border on a lake, agreement between them has to be reached. In the subsoil, the boundary runs where effective control of the state ends.

In *Delimitation of the Maritime Boundary in the Gulf of Maine Area (Canada/United States of America)* (1984), a chamber of the International Court of Justice pointed out that in the absence of a treaty, customary law applied and could do no more than provide a few legal guidelines for a decision. Customary law could not also be expected to specify equitable criteria to be applied or the technical methods to be used. Canada wanted to apply the equidistance line as the border; the United States wanted an equitable line. Because of the geographic configuration of the U.S. coastline in the gulf, under the Canadian proposal the United States would have received a smaller area than it felt it was entitled to. On the basis of an equitable solution of the conflict, the United States received about two-thirds of the gulf and three-fourths of the fishing grounds in the gulf.

Within the borders of the landmass, a state has sovereignty and, in principle, jurisdiction. The arbitrators in the *North Atlantic Coast Fisheries Arbitration* case (1910) asserted that one essential element of sovereignty is its exercise within territorial limits and that unless there is proof to the contrary, territory has the same limits as sovereignty.

Territorial Sea Boundary

There is no question that sovereignty and, in principle, jurisdiction also extend to the territorial sea. But sovereignty ends with the outer limit of the territorial waters, whereas jurisdiction does not necessarily end there. Two questions arise here: What is the breadth of the territorial sea? From where is that breadth (the baseline) measured? These problems bedeviled international law for hundreds of years. They have lost some of their importance in recent times through the creation of the Exclusive Economic Zone and the continental shelf, in which states have jurisdiction, although generally no sovereignty. But because states retain sovereignty in the territorial sea, its boundaries retain importance.

Under customary law, for several hundred years three miles was the extent of the territorial waters from the coast. Joined to the concept of territorial waters was the concept of the freedom of the high seas and the right of innocent passage of foreign ships through coastal waters. Most norms governing territorial waters have been codified mainly in the Convention on the Territorial Sea and the Contiguous Zone (1958), with some more specialized regulations embodied in the Convention on the Continental Shelf (1958), the Convention on Fishing and Conservation of the Living Resources of the High Seas (1958), the Treaty Banning Nuclear Weapon Tests (1963), the Convention on the Facilitation of Maritime Traffic (1965), and a few others. The United Nations Convention on the Law of the Sea (1982) sets the limit to the width of the territorial sea "not to exceed 12 nautical miles." All the other conventions, which are actually in force, leave the width undetermined because demands for fishing zones and territorial seas could not be reconciled. With the creation of new zones contiguous to territorial seas in which states have sovereign rights and jurisdiction over various matters, including fishing, the difficulty of agreeing on the breadth of territorial waters should fade into the background.

For the time being, therefore, states determine the breadth of their territorial seas. The International Court of Justice in the *Norwegian Fisheries (United Kingdom v. Norway)* case (1951, p. 132) made the ambiguous statement that the delimitation of a sea area is "necessarily a unilateral act, because only the coastal State is competent to undertake it." But the Court also argued that delimitation always has an "international aspect" because its validity in regard to other states "depends upon international law."

Once the scramble for an extension of the territorial seas and other zones in the high seas began after World War II, many states claimed limits to the territorial sea anywhere between 3 and 200 miles. For many years, several states, the United States and the United Kingdom among them (because their navies and high-sea fisheries would have more freedom of movement), held out for a 3-mile limit but did not succeed. Twelve miles is now the limit accepted by most states. (Note that those few states claiming a 200-mile limit are least able to enforce it, yet their security and coastal fisheries played a role in their claim to such a wide limit.)

The issue of determining the baseline for territorial sea measurement retains importance because other zones are or will be measured from the line established for the territorial sea. Several general principles apply to the drawing of the baseline. One is that it runs along the low-water line of the state's coast. Another is that the line must not deviate appreciably from the contours of the coast. This principle has caused difficulties in the case of heavily indented coasts (such as Norway's) or where submerged islands, reefs, and so on appear during low tide. For such situations, the International Court of Justice in the *Norwegian Fisheries* case (1951), while not rejecting the established principles, maintained that certain land formations in the sea that are closely linked to the mainland may turn the sea area into internal (sovereign) waters. This is particularly true, the Court amplified, if concrete and important economic links tie these land formations to the mainland. In such situations, drawing the baseline in straight sections between certain reasonable points as well as outside those land formations may be the proper procedure. The Convention on the Territorial Sea and the Contiguous Zone (1958) embodies the Court's decision in Article 4.

Islands situated some distance from the mainland have their own territorial waters. What this means for archipelagic states is uncertain. Indonesia and the Philippines have decided, against international protests, to draw their baselines in such a manner as to include all their islands, which turns the sea between the islands into internal waters. This has important consequences for the passage of ships, especially warships and submarines. In the case of the Hawaiian islands, the U.S. government has refused to declare them an archipelago, although the state of Hawaii wishes to be an archipelago.

Landlocked waters, such as lakes and rivers, represent no boundary problems. Internal waters—in which innocent passage need not be granted to foreign merchantmen—are those between the coast and the baseline from which territorial seas are measured. Harbors, shipyards, and similar installations are parts of internal waters.

In contrast, bays and gulfs do present problems. Following usual principle, states wish to nationalize as much water as possible. But under the law, only historical bays, such as the Chesapeake or the Delaware bays, are considered internal waters. For other bays, the width of the entrance to the bay or gulf from the sea is claimed to be the criterion that determines whether the bay is part of internal waters. (The situation becomes more complex when several states border on the bay or gulf.) The Convention on the Territorial Sea and the Contiguous Zone (1958) specifies in Article 7 that the specified entrance to a bay or gulf cannot exceed 24 miles. If it does, a straight 24-mile line is to be drawn within the bay or gulf, enclosing as much water as possible. The area of water so created is the bay or gulf over which the state has sovereignty. When the United States shot down two Libyan jets in 1981 in the Gulf of Sidra, it did so outside the area under Libyan sovereignty. Libya claimed the gulf as a "historical bay," an unsupportable claim because the "history" did not begin until the second half of the twentieth century.

The contiguous zone was permitted up to 12 miles from the baseline. But since the territorial seas have been extended to 12 miles, the contiguous zone has become obsolete. In the United Nations Law of the Sea Convention (1982), it will be extended to 24 miles.

Continental Shelf Boundary

The delimitation of the continental shelf boundary remains uncertain. One of two criteria could be applied. One criterion is geographic and determines adjacency to the coast to a depth of 200 meters and a natural prolongation of the shelf of the land—a relatively stable and feasible demarcation. Another criterion is exploitability, a variable demarcation moving the limit in accordance with the progressing technology to exploit.

Complications began after President Truman's 1945 proclamation created the continental shelf jurisdiction situation (discussed in Chapter 10). Peru and Chile, having no continental shelf, claimed not merely an extension to 200 miles from their coasts but also sovereignty over the seabed, the superjacent waters, and the airspace. Because other states protested this measure, customary law did not develop. But this extended claim to the continental shelf was typical for states trying to gain some control over the largest possible area. The Convention on the Continental Shelf (1958) (not ratified by Chile, Peru, and some other states) provides some precision by delimiting the continental shelf to 200 meters from the coast or, beyond that distance, to where the depth of the superjacent water admits of the exploitation of the natural resources of that area (Article 1). In other words, the convention allows the geographic criterion as well as the technical criterion, whichever is most favorable to the state. The United Nations Convention on the Law of the Sea (1982) has a different delimitation. It takes into account the shelf and the possible extension of its slope and other complications. In any case, the outer limit of the continental shelf, however defined, will not exceed 350 nautical miles from the baseline or 100 miles from the 2,500 meters isobath (Article 76).

Major problems have developed in the delimitation of continental shelves when those of two or more states overlap. The 1958 convention and the 1982 United Nations Convention on the Law of the Sea (Article 83) propose a delimitation. Failing this solution, the U.N. convention requires submission of the conflict to the settlement procedures it proposes if the parties cannot reach agreement on the basis of international law "in order to achieve an equitable result." The Court of International Justice has been called upon in a great number of cases to render a decision, in part because the 1958 convention bound only the signatories and did not become customary law. In some cases, the Court decided itself where the boundary was; in several others it ordered the parties to reach agreement on the basis of equitable principles leading to an equitable result.

The Exclusive Economic Zone Boundary

There is no convention delimiting this zone. It has developed as customary international law. Beginning about 1960, states began to claim exclusive fishing zones beyond their territorial seas. A compromise was attempted between claims to an exclusive fishing zone in the territorial seas and those fishing interests that had customarily fished in part of that zone. In 1974, the Court of International Justice held in the *Fisheries Jurisdiction (United Kingdom . . . v. Iceland) (Merits, Judgment)* case that states could claim an exclusive fishing zone within their territorial seas, that they could claim a preferential fishing right beyond the 12-mile limit if they were economically dependent on fishing, and that other states could not be entirely excluded from such areas if they had traditionally fished there and were dependent upon it economically.

The United Nations Law of the Sea Convention (1982) will overtake this arrangement by granting an exclusive economic exploitation zone extending to 200 miles from the baseline. But states have not waited until the Law of the Sea enters into force. Most of them are claiming an EEZ of slightly varying breadth, which must now be recognized as established customary law in principle, although details are uncertain. The International Court of Justice confirmed in the *Continental Shelf (Libyan Arab Jamahiriya Malta)* case (1985, pp. 1197, 1199) that the EEZ has become customary international law.

Many problems arising from this new institution await solution. For instance, the Indonesian zone overlaps with the Australian continental shelf in the Timor Sea. The two states concluded a treaty giving each one-third of the area in the Timor Sea (with Australia paying Indonesia 10 percent of the profits from its sector) and administering the middle sector jointly. If such a case were to come to the International Court of Justice, the rights of a state to the continental shelf might be declared better established than those to the zone, or the principle of equal distance or a division on an equitable basis might be the verdict. Similar problems arise in many parts of the oceans where EEZs overlap. Particular problems arise, for instance, in the Pacific where the zones of many islands overlap. Often, the U.S.-flag islands cannot settle border problems with neighboring independent state islands on a regional basis because the former are under Washington's control and are therefore subject to considerations not necessarily related to the region.

The Boundary of Space and Outer Space

Drawing the line between space and outer space is difficult. Rapidly progressing technology makes the definition of a state's interests uncertain and a state's reluctance to be committed great. In the meantime, innumerable proposals for the solution of the problem have come from several sides. Many tend to agree that the upper limit of air space ought to be the utmost reach of airborn aircraft, about 30 miles, and that the lowest limit of outer space ought to be the lowest limit of a spacecraft in orbit, about 90 miles. All such proposals suffer from the instability caused by technological uncertainties. Ignorance about the strategic and economic potential of outer space adds to the difficulty of reaching comprehensive international agreement. So far, only a few specific conventions have been agreed upon; these refer not to delimitation but to such matters as the return and rescue of astronauts, the return of space objects to the owner-state, the militarization of outer space, and broadcasting from satellites.

12
ACQUISITION, CONTENT, LOSS, OF PERSONAL JURISDICTION

Meaning of Personal Jurisdiction

Personal jurisdiction refers to a state's authority under international law over its own or foreign nationals. The importance of this jurisdiction rests in the rights and obligations it gives the state over individuals within its jurisdiction. From the individuals' viewpoint, their nationality creates their state's personal jurisdiction over them and may limit that of other states. Their nationality determines the protection they may expect from their own or another state when abroad; the claim a state may make in its own name against another state on behalf of one of its nationals; and the claims a national may or may not have against his or her state under international law—an important consideration lately in connection with the internationalization of human rights.

The International Court of Justice in the *Nottebohm (Liechtenstein v. Guatemala)* case (1955, p. 23) stated that nationality constitutes "the juridical expression of the fact that the individual upon whom it is conferred, either directly by the law or as the result of an act of the authorities, is in fact more closely connected with the population of the State conferring nationality than with that of any other state." The national remains under his or her state's jurisdiction wherever he or she is. The national's state can make laws binding the national abroad, but their enforcement is suspended where the jurisdiction of the state does not reach. The foreign state can be helpful, of course, by extraditing the individual to the home state or by permitting the home state to perform official acts in the other state (for example, congressional investigating committees). An alien does not "belong" to the state of his or her sojourn, although he or she is under its jurisdiction. Citizenship, in contrast to nationality, is in principle not relevant to international law. It is a quality regulated by municipal law and defines the political and civil rights of a state's national as well as those of aliens.

Acquisition of Personal Jurisdiction

A state acquires personal jurisdiction over an individual when it endows him or her with nationality or when an individual enters the space over which the state has spatial jurisdiction. Choice of the grounds on which an individual is granted nationality remains at present a matter of domestic jurisdiction, as the Permanent Court of International Justice confirmed in the case of *Nationality Decrees Issued in Tunis and Morocco* (1923). But the Convention on Conflict of Nationality Law (1930) confirms customary law when it states in Article 1 that the municipal law of nationality "shall be recognized by other states in so far as it is consistent with international conventions, international custom, and the principles of law generally recognized with regard to nationality."

This decision raises the question of what the general rules of international law regarding nationality are. Their occasionally controversial character is not too disadvantageous because nationality questions are regulated between states in innumerable bilateral treaties. The problem is more relevant in regard to corporations than to individuals.

In the *Nottebohm* case (1955, p. 23), the International Court of Justice decided that the basis of nationality must be "a social fact of attachment, a genuine connection of existence, interests and sentiments, together with the existence of reciprocal rights and duties." This requirement of a genuine link between the individual and his or her state to establish nationality was intended to nullify purely formal grants of nationality. The contemporary world is populated with individuals who in order to save their lives have had to flee from their own countries yet maintain their mobility across the globe with the help of a passport. They are often able to purchase both nationality and passport and thus become acceptable to countries of refuge. From the legal standpoint such formal nationality is rightly considered a subterfuge, if not fraud. There is no certain rule in international law to continue recognition of an individual's (for example, German) nationality for humanitarian reasons when a (for example, Nazi) state cancels that individual's nationality, and therewith passport, for inhumane reasons (such as racism). To the extent that human rights deal with the right or lack thereof of states to rob nationals of their nationality, the legal situation may change in favor of the refugee.

What represents a genuine link in the eyes of international law can be answered only pragmatically, although some links are generally recognized. Birth in the state's territory (*ius soli*) or the parents' nationality (*ius sanguinis*) is not necessarily conclusive, but either is a very strong link to justify nationality. Under international law, marriage may give the individual the nationality of the spouse. So may the acceptance of public office or permanent residence (but not the mere acquisition of real property).

Nationality cannot be foisted upon an unwilling individual. Compulsory naturalization is illegal under international law. The Universal Declaration of Human Rights (1948) specifies in Article 15 that everyone has a right to a nationality and cannot arbitrarily be deprived of it or the right to change it. Nevertheless, residence in a territory that is annexed or ceded can lead to the nationality of the new sovereign unless the individual abandons residence at the time of annexation or cession. A belligerent occupant cannot foist his or her nationality upon the residents of the occupied territory. These points were confirmed in *Schwarzkopf v. Uhl* by the Second Federal Circuit Court (1943).

An individual may possess dual nationality in spite of many efforts by states to avoid it. A number of judicial practices have developed to solve problems arising from this curiosity. An individual cannot invoke protection of one of the states against the other. He or she can usually not claim immunity in one if he or she were otherwise entitled to it as an organ of the second state. He or she is subject to certain duties when residing in one state, although nationals of the second state may be exempt from such duties in the state of residence. Third states usually recognize the nationality of the state with which the individual has the closest genuine and effective link. The Convention on the Conflict of Nationality Laws (1930) regulates most of these points in this sense following well-established precedents.

Loss of Personal Jurisdiction

A state may lose all or part of personal jurisdiction (enforcement of its laws) over individuals in a number of ways. One is when an alien leaves the state's spatial jurisdiction. Another is when a state deprives its national of his or her nationality (as happened frequently after World War I when states were trying to rid themselves of disliked populations or individuals). To what extent Article 15 of the Universal Declaration of Human Rights (1948)—which holds that no one shall be arbitrarily deprived of nationality—interferes with this possibility remains to be seen. The Convention on the Reduction of Statelessness (1961) enumerates four reasons for legitimate deprivation of nationality: taking of an oath of allegiance to another state, repudiation of allegiance to the state of existing nationality, rendering of public service to another state, and conduct seriously damaging to the interests of the state of nationality. Under international (but not necessarily under municipal) law, an individual may renounce his or her nationality.

An individual without a nationality is a stateless person. It is a miserable position to be in because such a person cannot travel from the country of residence unless he or she can obtain travel documents recognized by the country of destination and passage.

Personal Jurisdiction over Juridic Persons

Juridic persons, especially corporations, represent an unending number of problems. In general, juridic persons are treated by states as if they possessed nationality. Such treatment is important for purposes of jurisdiction, taxation, and diplomatic protection. But international law has no general rules or principles according to which the nationality of a corporation can be determined. Different states use different (and rarely precise) criteria by which to determine nationality. The United States and the United Kingdom follow the principle that the nationality is determined by where a corporation is incorporated. Other states judge by the *siège social*, the *siège réelle*, the administrative activity, the productive activity, the location of actual control (see *Interhandel [Switzerland v. United States of America]* [1959]), the location of the policymaking organ, or any combination of these. Many states are also willing to take up the case of the shareholders—if a significant number have the state's nationality—in cases of their claims against a corporation in a foreign country.

When a corporation is engaged in activities of considerable national interest, the state tends to consider it as having the state's nationality and to assume jurisdiction in order to gain more effective control over it. This political tendency is also noticeable in discussions to formulate a code of behavior for multinational corporations. The use of virtually every manner of determining the nationality of a corporation requires interferences with its anonymity. "The veil has to be lifted," as has been said, to find out who the directors, officers, workers, and shareholders are; to determine what activities are taking place and where; and to discover the "genuine link." Discovering the nationality of multinational corporations is more complicated, but similar criteria are being used.

13
MATERIAL JURISDICTION

Meaning

Material jurisdiction of states refers to the subject matter states are entitled to deal with under international law. This subject matter (for example, a person, an event, an action, a property) may not necessarily be located within a state's spatial jurisdiction (such as in the case of taxable income of a national earned abroad), personal jurisdiction (such as when an alien murders a state's national abroad), or temporal jurisdiction (for example, Israel trying Adolf Eichmann for killing German Jews before Israel became a state). Nevertheless, a state may promulgate laws addressed at subject matter beyond its territory. If the subject matter is located in a no-man's-land, no interstate complications arise unless another state also applies its material jurisdiction there. But if the subject matter is located within another state's jurisdiction, political trouble can develop. The saving grace is that material jurisdiction cannot be enforced unless the subject matter is within the legal power of the state. In other words, material jurisdiction requires territorial jurisdiction in order to be realized.

The Permanent Court of International Justice in the *Lotus* case (1927, p. 19) asserted that international law "far from laying down a general prohibition to the effect that states may not extend the application of their laws and the jurisdiction of their courts to persons, property and acts outside their territory . . . leaves them in this respect a wide measure of discretion." The judge in the case of *United States v. Laurence John Layton* (1981, p. 215) stated that the United States would have jurisdiction "for certain crimes where custody of the offender is sufficient."

Some international lawyers support a limitless competence of states to attach legal consequences to any condition anywhere (even though enforcement power is lacking). Such competence could create political resentment and social chaos as a result of competing and concurrent competences. An opposite doctrine holds that the competence of international law is unlimited and that states possess only the competence allotted to them by international law. But such a doctrine taken to its logical conclusion would leave states with no competence at all. They would disappear as self-governing units. Yet the function of international law is not to eliminate states but to regulate relations between them.

From this function follows a state's competence to regulate by its own methods any matter having some national implications. But the exclusivity of such jurisdiction ends and some competence of international law begins where a subject matter has international implications. The *Lotus* case (1927, p. 19) stated that "all that can be required of a state is that it should not overstep the limits which international law places upon its jurisdiction; within these limits, its title to exercise jurisdiction rests in its sovereignty."

The Limit of Material Jurisdiction

The difficulty is deciding when a subject matter has international implications. Growing mutual sensitivity among states leads to a growing internationalization of subject matter. The Permanent Court of International Justice in the *Nationality Decrees Issued in Tunis and Morocco* (1923, p. 19) declared that whether a matter is of purely domestic concern or has international implications is "relative" and depends on "the development of international relations."

This phenomenon worries states because it threatens sovereignty and the principle of nonintervention in domestic affairs. Virtually anything that happens within the major states sooner or later has consequences for other states. States are therefore most parsimonious in making concessions to the enlarging area of international concerns in the hope of retaining control over their fate—hence, for instance, their refusal in principle to let international organizations make binding decisions or to achieve effective regulations for the protection of the environment. Brazil objects to any outside interference with the lumbering activities in the Amazonas region as an internal affair, although the activity may have global meteorological consequences. Communist China claims that human rights are not universal and abstract and that how a country deals with human rights concretely is an internal affair.

The International Court's *Nationality Decrees Issued in Tunis and Morocco* (1923, p. 23) argued that matters solely within the domestic jurisdiction "seem" to be those "which, though they may very closely concern the interests of more than one state, are not, in principle, regulated by international law." This guideline for an age in which peace depends on internal as well as external affairs is supplemented by another: A state ceases to have exclusive material jurisdiction when a subject matter has actually and concretely (in contrast to potentially and possibly) a foreign element. But who can determine this, and when and how? When does a local rebellion turn into a threat to the peace and become of international concern? Has the rule *pacta sunt servanda* any domestic affairs aspect? Or what about mixed jurisdictions? For instance, piracy is illegal under international law, but how a pirate is to be punished depends upon national legislation. These many uncertainties make it very difficult to delimit the range of material jurisdiction.

The Passive Personality Principle

The counterpart to the principle that a state's exclusive material jurisdiction ceases when a foreign element is contained in the subject matter is the principle that a state's material jurisdiction should begin when a national element concerning the state is present. But the practice of states varies. In the *Lotus* case (1927), the Court decided that a state whose national was the victim of a crime committed abroad had material jurisdiction as part of the right of a state to protect its nationals—the passive personality principle. Several states follow that principle, especially in their criminal laws. But in the *Cutting* case (1886, p. 404) (a U.S. citizen, Cutting, had allegedly libeled a Mexican citizen in a newspaper published in Texas) and in the Convention on the High Seas (Article 11, 1958) (which overturned the *Lotus* case), this principle is rejected. The State Department denied—and the U.S. courts followed—that a state had any jurisdiction over foreigners committing acts criminal under the state's laws but committed outside its territory against their nationals. "To say . . . that the penal laws of a country can bind foreigners and regulate their conduct, either in their own or any other foreign country, is to assert a jurisdiction over such countries and to impair their independence."

These problems have importance in tax cases. A state cannot impose a tax on a foreigner living abroad who has no connection with the state. But if the foreigner is "effectively connected" economically with the state (as the U.S. Foreign Investors Tax Act of 1966 calls it)—for instance, by having a fixed place of business or owning land—the state may have material jurisdiction over that person's transactions. Often treaties determine the issue in order to avoid double taxation.

U.S. antitrust legislation is another important, very complex matter in such situations. The practice of U.S. courts, following *United States v. Aluminum Company of America et al.* (1945) heard in the U.S. Court of Appeals, Second Circuit, and similarly of the European Community Court on European Community trust legislation, is to claim jurisdiction over a foreign company's activities abroad that are incompatible with U.S. antitrust legislation if such activity was intended to and does affect U.S. commerce. This effect represents the link between the foreigner and the United States, thereby giving it material jurisdiction.

This practice has been found objectionable by foreign states as an infringement of their sovereignty. Their objection may be lessened following a Supreme Court's decision in January 1978 that foreign states may sue U.S. firms in U.S. courts if they, as customers, feel victimized by the anticompetitive practices of the U.S. firms with which they trade. The Court thereby established reciprocity, making U.S. antitrust legislation affecting foreigners more acceptable to them. In 1982, Congress attempted by legislation to define the extraterritorial reach of U.S. antitrust legislation but did so primarily to assist U.S. exports.

Another situation would be if a national performs an act abroad that is illegal in his or her home state but legal in the country where the act is performed. Many states, the United States among them, claim no criminal jurisdiction over the national unless the act has an effect in his or her home state.

The Protective Principle

The protective principle holds that a state has universal jurisdiction over persons regardless of their nationality or over acts regardless of where they are committed in order to protect its broadly defined national interests (such as security, government functions, social system, and currency). But such jurisdiction can be exercised only if the person is within the power of the state. There is agreement among states on the validity of the protective principle, although they do not agree on what it implies. The popularity of the protective principle stems from the fact that states can protect themselves against dangers emanating from the activities of individuals who reside in a state but are unconnected with its government. The protective principle was interpreted in a number of U.S. cases (for example, *United States v. Pizzarusso* [1968, p. 10], *Strassheim v. Daily* [1911, p. 285], and *Rocha v. United States* [1961, p. 545]) as meaning that a state has jurisdiction over conduct outside its territory that has or intends to have an adverse, detrimental effect upon the national interests of the state. None of the elements of the crime has to occur within the state.

This condition is in contrast to the objective territorial principle, which requires that at least one element of any crime (not just against the national interest) be located within the offended state. Under the protective principle the crime is completed and punishable even if the criminal never enters the United States. Thus, for instance, Ms. Pizzarusso obtained a visum to enter the United States by making false statements to the U.S. Consulate and thereby completed the crime. A "sham" marriage is a completed crime when marriage with a U.S. national has taken place abroad for the purpose of obtaining a nonquota immigration visum for the non-U.S. partner (when the quota system was still in force and regardless of whether the partners actually entered the United States). Foreigners forging U.S. money abroad have committed a crime whether that false money is ever used or not.

Material jurisdiction in all its forms is closely related to sovereignty but is internally contradictory. On the one hand, by extending the jurisdictional reach of a state, material jurisdiction is trying to assist in overcoming in matters of concern to that state the effect of the barriers established by the sovereign separation of states. On the other hand, because material jurisdiction cannot actually be exercised outside the territorial jurisdiction of the state, it does practically very little in overcoming the separation of states safeguarded by sovereignty.

Universal Material Jurisdiction

Universal material jurisdiction refers to acts declared to be crimes by international law. They are offenses against international law directly (*delicta iuris gentium*). They are acts so heinous that they have been declared crimes against humankind or the international community as a whole. They may be defined in conventions or in customary law.

So far, humankind has been unable to agree on a comprehensive definition or codification of international crimes in general or on what might be the legitimate responses to varying breaches of an international obligation. For this reason, each internationally wrongful act is treated separately, and the responses are usually left to the decision of each individual state unless some collective response has been agreed upon. Nor is there agreement on differences among "delicts" (a minor wrong), "crimes under international law" (usually referring to individual offenders), and "international crimes of states" (referring to offending states).

Development of the category of international crimes has occurred piecemeal. Piracy and slave trade are the oldest. Most others developed after World War II. Today there is wide agreement that, for instance, war crimes, genocide, officially sanctioned torture, racism, attacks on or hijacking of airplanes, and drug trade are international crimes. Although terrorism is not yet an international crime, the violation of human rights usually involved in terroristic acts may make it a crime. But in the absence of an international institution to determine that a wrong has been done and what the legitimate means and methods for reacting to it may be, every state may make this determination itself.

These crimes are punishable by any state because the jurisdiction of every state is global. This empowerment necessitates a distinction between individual offenders and state offenders. The tribunals prosecuting German and Japanese war criminals were confronted by this problem. They solved it by individualizing the offenders and trying those they considered most responsible—which left a great number of participants in the war crimes unpunished. By now, with so many crimes agreed upon, the difficulty is not with individual offenders but with states as offenders.

In regard to individuals, if a state can get hold of them, it can try them, regardless of their nationality or where the crime was committed. Several states have specifically incorporated acts considered international crimes into their municipal legislation, thereby providing penalties for their commission. In the United States, especially during the 1970s and 1980s, several such cases were dealt with by the courts. The judgments were frequently not unanimous, indicating the still tentative and complex nature of international crimes.

In the by now famous case of *Filartiga v. Peña-Irala*, Judge Kaufman of the Second Circuit (1980) decided that a Paraguayan official torturing a Paraguayan citizen to death in Paraguay could be condemned in the United States and could be fined for committing the international crime of torture. The court's jurisdiction was based on the Alien Tort Claims Act, dormant for almost two hundred years, whose §1350 gives district courts original jurisdiction of any civil action by an alien for tort committed in violation of the law of nations or a treaty of the United States. In the *United States v. Marino-Garcia* case (1982, p. 1381), the court argued, inter alia, that "all nations have jurisdiction to board and seize vessels engaged in universally prohibited activities such as the slave trade or piracy," although the vessel in the case was engaged in narcotic drugs trade. Incidentally, the *Filartiga* case established the most unusual principle that via international law individuals now may under very special circumstances have rights against actions of officials of their own governments and that officials may be responsible for their own actions (already established during the Nuremberg trials).

The *Tel-Oren [Hanoch] v. Libyan Arab Republic* case (1985) brought in the District of Columbia Circuit Court against the Palestine Liberation Organization for attacking a tourist bus in Israel was dismissed. But the three judges gave different reasons for holding for dismissal. Judge Edwards accepted the *Filartiga* precedent but maintained that terrorism was not yet recognized as an international crime and that in the case at bar the action was not performed by an official. Judge Bork, in a long statement, claimed that §1350, while giving district courts jurisdiction, did not provide a cause for action; the section would have to be implemented by congressional legislation supplying a remedy for the crime. Judge Robb supported dismissal of the case because of the inherent inability of federal courts to deal with cases such as this one. It seems to me that the political question doctrine controls. The case is non-justiciable" (p. 823). In the *Handel v. Artukovic* case (1985) heard in the Los Angeles, California, district court, the court accepted Judge Bork's argument and dismissed the case. Judge Fong in the Hawaiian District Court case *Trojanos v. Marcos* (1986) accepted Judge Robb's opinion. Plaintiffs accused former Philippine president Ferdinand Marcos of human rights violations. Several different arguments were produced, but the case was dismissed on the basis of the act of state doctrine. And because political actions were involved that the court was unable to examine, the case was declared nonjusticiable and a matter for the executive, not the judiciary, branch of government.

In contrast to some judgments based on the act of state doctrine or the Foreign Sovereignty Immunities Act, the court in the *Letelier v. Republic of Chile* case (1980, p. 674) maintained that if a state has no immunity under the act, it cannot excuse itself on the basis of the act of state doctrine because it "would totally emasculate the purpose and effectiveness of the Foreign Sovereign Immunities Act by permitting a state to reimpose the so recently supplanted framework of sovereign immunity as defined prior to the Act 'through the backdoor, under the guise of the act of state doctrine.' "

In regard to a state committing a crime against humankind, the situation is relatively novel and unexplored. Many problems await solution. Among them is that reactions to the offense are likely to affect innocent parties. The nearest to a solution is the suggestion that measures of coercion should be taken against the offending state that may spare innocent individuals as much as possible and that can be suspended when advisable. Another problem is determining whether a state is an offender and what the legitimate reaction of other states should be. This is a purely subjective act. Whether a state is powerful or weak will affect the actions of each. Instead of justice, politics and national interests will prevail.

In the case of apartheid, there was disagreement even within the United States as to what the reaction should be. U.N. resolutions, arms embargoes, and pressures of other kinds upon the South African government had no effect. When the United States and other states added severe economic sanctions, the government's stand on apartheid softened. A high point was reached when in February 1990 antiapartheid activist and leader Nelson Mandela was released from prison after almost three decades of incarceration. In many parts of the world, the economic coercion was credited with the South African government's step, although President F. W. de Klerk denied that South Africa was a "hostage" to the United Nations and that sanctions had no influence on his decisions, which were determined purely by the national interest. Mandela, however, expressed his conviction that the sanctions were having an effect and should continue until apartheid was abolished—even though innocent people were suffering from these sanctions.

Some trends favor the gradual acceptance of the principle of universal material jurisdiction. One is the slow metamorphosis of international law into community law. A second is the growing willingness of states to recognize international crimes. A third is that interaction causes such crimes to be offensive to more than one state. But the inconsistent, possibly schizophrenic, behavior of all too many states acts as a countertrend. Desirous of gaining prestige as civilized states subscribing to high values, they publicly support international action against violations of instruments such as the Universal Declaration of Human Rights (1948), yet in private (that is, domestically) act otherwise. The chances are therefore, at least as far as individual offenders are concerned, that countries in which such crimes are most likely to be prosecuted, among them the United States, will have to deal with them in ever greater numbers. There has already been critical talk in the United States that the "floodgates" should not be opened.

14
SPECIAL CASES
OF JURISDICTION

There are a number of special situations in international relations that either expand or restrict the normal scope of a state's jurisdictions. Some of these are of long standing; others have more recently arisen as a result of new developments in the relations between states. The older jurisdictions have recommended themselves by their practicability and preservation of states' cherished independence. They are hardly controversial. Others of relatively recent date, while generally accepted in principle, have yet to be universally accepted in detail. In addition, it is always possible to introduce or qualify jurisdiction (in relation to or independently of sovereignty) by means of treaties. This method has been followed for the regimes in the various new "territorializations" of what used to be the high seas (such as the EEZ and the continental shelf), for outer space, for certain rights and obligations relating to fishing, for resources and pollution of the high seas, and for the expansion of international crimes. All these principles apply, mutatis mutandis, to airplanes and ships.

Immunities

As was discussed earlier, the idea of sovereign immunity of a state from another state's jurisdiction is generally accepted by virtually all states as a principle flowing from state sovereignty. International organizations have immunity according to treaties among the member states. But states also instituted many exceptions to the general rule, so that many individual cases give rise to disputes and court cases. States, heads of states and their representatives (diplomats), government officials of all ranks, certain officials of international organizations, and property owned by governments or organizations have under defined circumstances and in defined respects immunity from the jurisdiction of another state, either under customary law, as a result of a treaty (such as the Vienna Convention on Diplomatic Relations [1961] and on Consular Relations [1963]), or under municipal legislation and practice. Existing immunity does not exempt these subjects from the laws of the state. Yet if these subjects break the laws, the state cannot sue them; it has no jurisdiction over them.

But there also are exceptions to immunity. Various countries (such as the United States and the United Kingdom) have enacted foreign sovereign immunities legislation. The result has been a fairly large volume of court cases; these have failed, however, to dissolve many doubts about when immunity is to be applied. (Compare, for instance, *Letelier v. Republic of Chile* [1980, 1984]; *Verlinden v. Central Bank of Nigeria* [1981, 1983]; *Broadbent v. Organization of American States* [1980]; and *Mendaro v. The World Bank* [1983].)

Armed Forces

Armed forces are considered organs of the state in peace and war. They are distinguished from a police force because they also deal with the external defense of the state, and they are distinguished from guerrillas because they are under the control of the legitimate government. The presence of armed forces on foreign territory with the permission of the foreign sovereign still does not subject them to his or her jurisdiction— except when individual soldiers act illegitimately when off duty. In virtually every case in which the armed forces of a state or of the United Nations are on foreign soil, agreements are reached between the respective sovereigns on details regarding the soldiers and their families. In most cases, the receiving state has no jurisdiction over these people.

Aliens

Although aliens are under the jurisdiction of the state of their sojourn, this jurisdiction is limited. The major restriction of the state's jurisdiction is that aliens must be treated according to certain international minimum standards regardless of how the state treats its own nationals. This view is not universally shared, especially not by the newer states. But it is fairly well established in international jurisprudence.

Ships

A merchant ship is under the jurisdiction of the state whose flag it flies and in which it is registered. Although until the twentieth century, the fiction was maintained that a ship was a floating piece of the state's territory, in the twentieth century the ship is treated as analogous to a national. Thus, although on the high seas no state has jurisdiction (treaty arrangements excepted), a state has jurisdiction over its ships on the high seas to enforce its national and international law. As the Permanent Court of International Justice maintained in the *Lotus* case (1927, p. 40),

"It is certainly true that—apart from certain special cases which are defined by international law—vessels on the high seas are subject to no authority except that of the State whose flag they fly."

One such current "special case" is the long-existing right of warships to visit and search a ship on the high seas suspected of engaging in some illicit trade or to ascertain its nationality. As part of the U.S. "war on drugs" the Coast Guard has "routinely" been stopping ships "at random" in international waters to search for drugs or violations of international fishing regulations. Whether such "routine" activity fulfills the prerequisite that the searched ship must be suspected of engaging in illicit behavior is a question of fact. The principle of search has been recognized as a universal rule of international law and has been confirmed in several decisions by United States and other courts (for instance, *United States v. Marino-Garcia* [1982] and *United States v. Williams* [1980]).

At the end of January 1990, to give some illustrations, the Coast Guard seized a Honduran freighter on the high seas west of Miami and found 1,100 pounds of cocaine. Ship and crew were taken to Key West. At the same time, the Coast Guard followed the freighter *Hermann* for about twenty hours asking it to stop and prepare for a search party from the Coast Guard cutter. The freighter was registered in Panama, was owned by a private Cuban company, had a Cuban crew, and, according to the master, carried chrome ore from Cuba to Tampico, Mexico. The Coast Guard claimed to have good reason for suspecting the freighter as a drug runner and obtained the unnecessary permission from the Panamanian government to board. But the *Hermann*, on orders from the Cuban government, refused to stop. Its crew stood ready with knives, machetes, and axes to receive the Coast Guard party. The Coast Guard cutter used water hoses and fired a shot across the freighter's bow without succeeding in stopping the freighter. Thereupon, the cutter fired at the freighter to disable it (according to the Coast Guard) or to sink it (according to the Cuban government). The freighter was hit in the engine compartment and the rudder. But it was still able to reach Mexican territorial waters. The State Department immediately asked the Mexican government to board and inspect the ship, which was done. No drugs were found.

In November 1989, the U.S. government announced a plan to station U.S. warships off the coast and outside the territorial waters of Colombia to control drug traffic. The plan was abandoned, however, for political reasons. Legally there could have been no objection. Indeed, the United Nations Convention on the Law of the Sea (1982) in Article 108 asks states to cooperate in the suppression of illicit traffic in drugs on the high seas and permits states to request the cooperation of other states in suppressing such traffic.

Another "special case" relating to vessels on the high seas is hot pursuit. Under its rules a government-owned ship may pursue a foreign vessel into the high seas if it has reason to believe that the ship violated the rules and regulations of the state while it was in the territorial waters of the state. This rule of customary law is defined in great detail in Article 23 of the Convention on the High Seas (1958).

In contrast to the *Lotus* decision, the same convention in Article 11 stipulates that in the case of a collision on the high seas, the responsible master or any other person in the service of the ship can be proceeded against only by the state whose flag the ship flies or by the state of which he or she is a national. In other words, no other state has jurisdiction.

Military Activities on the High Seas

Since the end of World War II, a number of states have established exclusion or warning or danger zones in the oceans when they have tested missiles or atom bombs. They have announced forthcoming tests, outlined the areas of the high seas that were involved, and expected shipping and fishing vessels to stay out of these areas. This practice is contrary to the high seas as no-man's-land and the guarantee of freedom of the seas. The United States points out that it was simply warning ships of the possible danger, whereas the Soviet Union states that it was merely requesting ships to avoid the areas. In each case, the warnings and requests were of a temporary nature and did not establish a claim to jurisdiction. Although atmospheric nuclear device tests have ceased, missile tests continue. They are presumably illegal on a variety of grounds if they interfere with shipping or fishing or otherwise do harm. Presumably, the testing state would be liable for any injury caused by its activities.

Pirate Broadcasting

Pirate broadcasting—that is, broadcasting (radio or television) from the high seas in such a way that it is directed for reception in a state—has been largely regulated by bilateral treaties and is incorporated in Article 109 in the United Nations Convention on the Law of the Sea (1982). Any person engaged in such unauthorized broadcasting may be prosecuted before the court of the ship's flag state, the state of registry of the installation, the state of which the person is a national, a state where the broadcast can be received, or any state where such broadcasting interferes with authorized radio communication. Any of these states may arrest the person and ship and seize the broadcasting installation.

Maritime Areas

Under customary law, implemented by numerous treaties, foreign ships have a right to innocent passage through the territorial waters and the various maritime zones of a state, thereby restraining the coastal state's jurisdiction. Certain conditions apply to make the passage innocent. They relate mainly to the security, peace, and order of the coastal state. Although the coastal state may for certain reasons close parts of the territorial sea to innocent passage, it may not do so in regard to straits connecting two sections of the high seas or connecting the high seas and the territorial sea of a foreign state.

Warships in time of peace also have the right of innocent passage, but they must comply with those rules and regulations of the coastal state that refer to its territorial waters. Some, mostly Communist states, insist upon prior authorization before a warship enters territorial waters. Otherwise, warships are immune as long as they are not engaged in commercial activity. The coastal state may request a warship's departure, but the state's authorities may not board the ship. Submarines must show their flag while passing through territorial waters of a foreign state. This requirement has become a cause of difficulty in signing and ratifying the United Nations Convention on the Law of the Sea (1982). For if the wider territorial sea and other "territorializations" of the high seas are accepted, submarines would have to surface in passing through certain straits, which they are loath to do. The U.N. convention seeks to arrange a compromise in Article 38 by speaking of freedom of navigation and overflight as "transit passage" through straits, which would permit submarines to pass submerged through straits used for international navigation.

The jurisdiction of a coastal state over foreign merchantmen is restricted to some extent. The restriction varies according to whether the ship goes through territorial waters or stays in the foreign port. Most of these restrictions are defined in bi- or multilateral agreements and in the United Nations Convention on the Law of the Sea (1982).

As long as states insist upon sovereignty, the need for delimiting jurisdiction remains undiminished. Fundamentally, jurisdiction remains bound to the territory of the state—an arrangement recommending itself for its neatness, if nothing else. Yet there are exceptions, and these will increase in number as the independent sovereign existence of states becomes anachronistic. There are simply too many uncontrollable matters, from viruses to multinational corporations to airwaves refusing to submit to the neat geographic division of traditional international law. States have tried to cope with these phenomena as they appeared by making special agreements. But as the volume of these phenomena grows and the exceptions turn into a rule, the patchwork of specific agreements is unlikely to keep order in the international society. Sooner or later a new community law will have to replace the traditional system based upon the strict separation of states in isolated existence.

REFERENCES AND READINGS FOR PART 4

Jurisdiction and Sovereignty

Akehurst, Michael. "Jurisdiction in international law." *BYIL* 46 (1972–1973):145–257.

Alexander, Lewis M., Scott Allen, and Lynne Carter Hanson, eds. *New Developments in Marine Science and Technology: Economic, Legal and Political Aspects of Change*. Honolulu: Law of the Sea Institute, 1989.

Bowett, Derek W. "Jurisdiction: Changing patterns of authority over activities and resources." *BYIL* 53 (1982):1–26.

Dunbar, N.C.H. "Controversial aspects of sovereign immunity in the case law of some states." *ADIRC* 132 (1972 I):197–362.

Elian, George. "Le principe de la souveraineté sur les resources nationales et ses incidents juridiques sur le commerce international." *ADIRC* 149 (1976 I):1–85.

Mann, F. A. "The doctrine of jurisdiction in international law." *ADIRC* 111 (1964 I):1–162.

———. "The doctrine of international jurisdiction revisited after twenty years." *ADIRC* 186 (1984 III):9–116.

Muela, Adolfo Miaja de la. "Les principes directeurs des règles de compétence territoriale des tribunaux internes en matières de litiges comportant un élément international." *ADIRC* 135 (1972 I):1–96.

Sucharitkul, Sompong. "Immunities of foreign states before national authorities." *ADIRC* 149 (1976 I):86–215.

Birth and Death of States

Kunz, Josef E. "Identity of states under international law." *AJIL* 49 (January 1955):68–76.

Marek, Krystyna. *Identity and Continuity of States in Public International Law*. Geneva: Droz, 1968.

Morvay, Werner. *Souveränitätsübergang und Rechtskontinuität im Britischen Commonwealth*. New York: Springer, 1974.

Succession

Bedjaoui, Mohammed. "Succession of states and governments: Succession in respect to matters other than treaties." *Yearbook of International Law Commission* (1969 II):69–100; (1970 II):131–169; (1971 II/1):157–191; (1972 II):61–69; (1973 II):3–73; (1974 II):91–115.

Cansacci, Giorgio. "Identité et continuité des sujets internationaux." *ADIRC* 130 (1970 II):1–94.

Chen, Ling-fong. *State Succession Relating to Unequal Treaties.* Hamden, CT: Archon Books, 1974.

International Law Association. *The Effect of Independence on Treaties.* London: Stevens, 1965.

Kearney, Richard D. "The twenty-fifth session of the International Law Commission." *AJIL* 68 (July 1974):454–474.

Mann, F. A. "The doctrine of jurisdiction in international law." *ADIRC* 111 (1964 I):1–162.

———. "The doctrine of international jurisdiction revisited after twenty years." *ADIRC* 186 (1984 III):9–116.

O'Connell, D. P. *State Succession in Municipal Law and International Law,* 2 vols. New York: Cambridge University Press, 1967.

———. "Recent problems of state succession in relation to new states." *ADIRC* 130 (1970 II):95–206.

Udokang, Okon. *Succession of New States to International Treaties.* Dobbs Ferry, NY: Oceana, 1972.

Waldeck, Humphrey (Francis Vallat from 1974). "Succession of states and governments: Succession in respect of treaties." *Yearbook of the International Law Commission* (1969 II):45–68; (1970 II):25–60; (1971 II/1):143–156; (1972 II):1–59; (1974 II):3–88.

Content of Spatial Jurisdiction: Air and Space

Benkö, Marietta, Willem de Graaff, and Gijsbertha L.M. Reijnen. *Space Law in the United Nations.* Dordrecht: Martinus Nijhoff, 1985.

Böckstiegel, Karl H. *Space Law: Changes and Expectations at the Turn of Commercial Space Activities.* Deventer, the Netherlands: Kluwer, 1986.

Christol, Carl Q. *The Modern International Law of Outer Space.* New York: Pergamon, 1982.

Dauses, Manfred E. "Neuere Fragen des Weltraumrechts." *AV* 17 (1976 I):46–80.

Dempsey, Paul S. *Law and Foreign Policy in International Aviation.* Dobbs Ferry, NY: Transnational, 1987.

Diederiks-Verschoor, I.H. Ph. *An Introduction to Space Law.* Deventer, the Netherlands: Kluwer, 1988.

Fawcett, J.E.S. *Outer Space: New Challenges to Law and Policy.* Oxford: Clarendon, 1984.

Goedhuis, D. "Telecommunications by satellite." International Law Association. *Report of the Fifty-Six Conference New Delhi, 1974,* pp. 467–510. London: International Law Association, 1976.

Goldman, Nathan C. *American Space Law.* Ames: Iowa State University Press, 1988.

Gorov, Stephan. "The geostationary orbit: Issues of law and policy." *AJIL* 73 (July 1979):444–461.

Jonsson, Christer. *International Aviation and the Politics of Régime Change.* New York: St. Martin's, 1987.

Kish, John. *The Law of International Spaces.* Leiden: A. W. Sijthoff, 1973.

Lachs, Manfred. *The Law of Outer Space.* Leiden: A. W. Sijthoff, 1972.

Lyall, Frances. *Law and Space Telecommunications.* Aldershot, England: Dartmouth, 1989.

Marcoff, Marco G. "Sources du droit international de l'espace." *ADIRC* 168 (1980 III):8–121.

Matte, Nicholas M., ed. *Space Activities and Emerging International Law.* Montreal: CRASI–McGill University, 1984.

––––––. "Outer space and international organizations." In Hague Academy of International Law. *A Handbook of International Organizations,* pp. 558–583. Dordrecht: Martinus Nijhoff, 1988.

McWhinney, Edward, and Martin A. Bradley, eds. *Freedom of the Air.* Dobbs Ferry, NY: Oceana, 1969.

Piradov, A. S., ed. *International Space Law.* Moscow: Progress Publishers, 1976.

Reynolds, Glenn H., and Robert P. Merges. *Outer Space Problems of Law and Policy.* Boulder, CO: Westview, 1989.

Snyder, Frederick E., and Surakiart Sathirathai, eds. *Third World Attitudes Toward International Law.* Dordrecht: Martinus Nijhoff, 1987, pp. 775–796.

"Symposium on international organizations and the law of outer space." *Journal of Space Law* 5 (Spring and Fall 1977):1–155.

Welck, Freiherr Stephan von, and Renate Platzöder, eds. *Weltraumrecht—Law of Outer Space.* Baden-Baden, West Germany: Nomos, 1987.

Young, Andrew J. *Law and Policy in the Space Station's Era.* Dordrecht: Martinus Nijhoff, 1989.

Zhukov, Gennady, and Yuri Kolosov. *International Space Law.* New York: Praeger, 1984.

Content of Spatial Jurisdiction: Maritime

Alexander, Lewis M., ed. *The Law of the Sea: Offshore Boundaries and Zones.* Columbus: Ohio State University Press, 1967.

Anand, R. P. *Origin and Development of the Law of the Sea.* The Hague: Martinus Nijhoff, 1983.

Andreyev, E. P. *International Law of the Sea.* Moscow: Progress Publishers, 1988.

Attard, David. *The Exclusive Economic Zone in International Law*. Oxford: Oxford University Press, 1987.

Bennett, T. W. et al., eds. *The Law of the Sea*. Cape Town: Juta, 1986.

Brown, E. D., and Robin Churchill, eds. *The UN Convention and the Law of the Sea: Impact and Implementation*. Honolulu: University of Hawaii Press, 1988.

Butler, William E. *The Law of Soviet Territorial Waters*. New York: Praeger, 1967.

————. "The Soviet Union and the continental shelf." *AJIL* 63 (January 1969):103–107.

————. *The Soviet Union and the Law of the Sea*. Baltimore, MD: Johns Hopkins University Press, 1971.

Clingan, Thomas A. Jr., ed. *The Law of the Sea: What Lies Ahead?* Honolulu: Law of the Sea Institute, 1988.

Colombos, John C. *The International Law of the Sea*, 6th ed. New York: Longmans Green, 1976.

Craven, John P., Jan Schneider, and Carol Simson, eds. *The International Implications of Extended Maritime Jurisdiction in the Pacific*. Honolulu: Law of the Sea Institute, 1989.

Dallmeyer, Dorinda, and Louis deVorsey Jr., eds. *Rights to the Ocean Resources: Deciding and Drawing Maritime Boundaries*. Dordrecht: Martinus Nijhoff, 1989.

Dickey, Margaret L. "Freedom of the seas and the law of the sea: Is what's new for better or worse?" *Ocean Development and International Law* 5 (1978 I):23–26.

Gustafson, Kristen, and Louis B. Sohn. *The Law of the Sea in a Nutshell*. St. Paul: West, 1984.

The International Law of the Sea. Moscow: Progress Publishers, 1988.

Johnston, Douglas M., and Norman G. Letalik, eds. *The Law of the Sea and Ocean Industry: New Opportunities and Restraints*. Honolulu: Law of the Sea Institute, 1984.

Kolodkin, Anatolii L., and Stepan V. Molodcov. *Seefriedensrecht: Das völkerrechtliche Régime der Territorialgewässer, der Anschlusszone und des hohen Meeres*. Frankfurt am Main, West Germany: A. Metzner, 1973.

Kwiatkowska, Barbara. *The 200 Mile Exclusive Economic Zone in the Law of the Sea*. Hingham, MA: Kluwer Academic Publishers, 1989.

McDougal, Myres S., and William T. Burke. *The Public Order of the Oceans: A Contemporary Law of the Sea*. Dordrecht: Martinus Nijhoff, 1987.

Miles, Edward L., and Scott Allen, eds. *The Law of the Sea and Ocean Development Issues in the Pacific Basin*. Honolulu: Law of the Sea Institute, 1983.

Park, Choon-Ho. *The Law of the Sea*. Honolulu: Law of the Sea Institute, 1983.

Platzöder, Renate. *Politische Konzeptionen zur Neuordnung des Meeresrechts*. Ebenhausen, West Germany: Stiftung Wissenschaft und Politik, 1976.

Platzöder, Renate, and Wolfgang Vitzthum. *Seerecht—Law of the Sea*. Baden-Baden, West Germany: Nomos, 1984.

Puñal, A. M. *Los derechos de los estados sin litoral y en situación geográfico desventajosa en la zona económica exclusiva*. Santiago, Chile: n.p., 1988.

Smith, Robert W. *Exclusive Economic Zone Claims and Primary Documents*. Dordrecht: Martinus Nijhoff, 1986.

Symonides, Janusz. "Geographically disadvantaged states under the 1982 Convention on the Law of the Sea." *ADIRC* 208 (1988 I):282–406.

Vallée, Charles. *Le plateau continental dans le droit positif actuel.* Paris: A. Pédone, 1971.

Van Dyke, Jon, ed. *Consensus and Confrontation: The United States and the Law of the Sea.* Honolulu: University of Hawaii Press, 1984.

Vicuña, Francisco O. "La zone économique exclusive: Régime et nature juridique dans le droit international." *ADIRC* 199 (1986 IV):9–170.

Vitzthum, Wolfgang. *Der Rechtsstatus des Meeresbodens.* Berlin: Duncker und Humblot, 1972.

Wani, I. J. "An evaluation of the Convention on the Law of the Sea from the perspective of landlocked states." *Virginia Journal of International Law* 22 (Summer 1981–1982):627–666.

Wulfrum, Rüdiger. "The emerging customary law of marine zones: State practice and the law on the Law of the Sea." *Netherlands Yearbook of International Law* 18 (1987):121–144.

―――. *Die Internationalisierung staatsfreier Räume: Die Entwicklung einer internationalen Verwaltung für Antarktika, Weltraum, Hohe See und Meeresboden.* Berlin: Springer, 1984.

Jurisdiction: Boundaries

Alexander, Lewis M. "Baseline determination and maritime boundaries." *Virginia Journal of International Law* 23 (Fall-Summer 1982):503–536.

Blake, Gerald, ed. *Maritime Boundaries and Ocean Resources.* Totowa, NY: Barnes and Noble, 1987.

Blecker, M. D. "Equitable delimitation of the continental shelf." *AJIL* 73 (January 1979):60–88.

Brown, E. D. "The continental shelf and the exclusive economic zone: The problem of delimitation at UNCLOS III." *Maritime Policy and Management* IV (1976–1977):377-408.

Caflisch, Lucius. "Les zones maritimes sous jurisdictions nationales, leurs limites et leurs délimitations." *RGDIP* 84 (1980):68–119.

Charney, Jonathan J. "Ocean boundaries between nations: A theory for progress." *AJIL* 78 (July 1984):582–606.

Goedhuis, D. "The problems of the frontiers of outer space and air space." *ADIRC* 175 (1982 I):366–407.

Hodgson, Robert D. "The delimitation of maritime boundaries between opposite and adjacent states through the economic zone and the continental shelf: Selected state practice." In Thomas Clingan Jr., ed. *Law of the Sea: State Practice in Zones of Special Jurisdiction,* pp. 280–316. Honolulu: Law of the Sea Institute, 1982.

Jagota, S. P. *Maritime Boundary.* Dordrecht: Martinus Nijhoff, 1985.

Johnston, Douglas M., and Philip M. Saunders, eds. *Ocean Boundary Making Regional Issues and Development.* London: Croom Helm, 1988.

Kapoor, D. C., and Adam J. Kerr. *A Guide to Maritime Boundary Delimitation.* Toronto: Carswell, 1986.

Luard Evan, ed. *The International Regulation of Frontier Disputes.* New York: Praeger, 1970.

Montiel-Arguello, Alejandro. "Frontières et lignes de délimitation." *RGDIP* 75 (1971):461–464.

Prescott, J.R.V. *The Maritime Political Boundaries of the World.* London: Methuen, 1985.

Weil, Prosper. *Perspectives du droit de la délimitation maritime.* Paris: A. Pédone, 1988.

————. *The Law of Maritime Delimitation—Reflections.* Cambridge: Grotius, 1989.

Polar Regions

Auburn, F. M. "International law and sea-ice jurisdiction in the Arctic ocean." *Int. & Comp. L. Q.* 22 (July 1973):552–557.

————. *Antarctic Law and Politics.* Bloomington: Indiana University Press, 1982.

————. "Aspects of the Antarctic treaty system." *AV* 26 (1988 II):203–215.

Boczek, Boleslaw A. "The Soviet Union and the Antarctic Regime." *AJIL* 78 (October 1984):834–858.

Dosman, E. J. *The Arctic in Question.* Toronto: Oxford University Press, 1976.

Joyner, Christoper C., and Sudhir K. Chapra. *The Antarctic Legal Regime.* Dordrecht: Martinus Nijhoff, 1988.

Myhre, Jeffrey D. *The Antarctic System: Politics, Law and Diplomacy.* Boulder, CO: Westview, 1986.

Peterson, M. J. *Managing the Frozen South.* Berkeley: University of California Press, 1988.

Polar Research Board. *Antarctic Treaty System: An Assessment.* Washington, DC: National Academy Press, 1986.

Schatz, Gerald S., ed. *Science, Technology, and Sovereignty in the Polar Regions.* Lexington, MA: D. C. Heath, 1974.

Triggs, Gilliand D. *The Antarctic Treaty Regime.* Cambridge: Cambridge University Press, 1987.

Wassermann, Ursula. "The Antarctic treaty and natural resources." *Journal of World Trade Law* 12 (March-April 1978):174–179.

Acquisition and Loss of Spatial Jurisdiction

Blum, Yehuda Z. *Historic Titles in International Law.* The Hague: Martinus Nijhoff, 1965.

Jennings, Robert Y. *The Acquisition of Territory in International Law.* Dobbs Ferry, NY: Oceana, 1963.

Acquisition and Loss of Personal Jurisdiction

Angelo, Homer G. "Multinational corporate enterprises." *ADIRC* 125 (1968 III):443–607.

Breuniz, Günter. *Staatsangehörigkeit und Entkolonisierung.* Berlin: Duncker und Humblot, 1974.

Grahl-Madsen, Ake. *The Status of Refugees in International Law,* 2 vols. Leiden: A. W. Sijthoff, 1972.

Mutharika, A. Peter. *International Regulation of Statelessness,* 2 vols. Dobbs Ferry, NY: Oceana, 1976.

Seidl-Hohenveldern, Ignaz von. "Multinational enterprises and the international law of the future." *Yearbook of World Affairs* (1975):301–312.

Universal Material Jurisdiction

Bassiouni M. Cherif, and Ved P. Nanda, eds. *A Treatise on International Criminal Law.* Springfield, IL: Charles C. Thomas, 1973.

Blum, Jeffrey M., and Ralph G. Steinhardt. "Federal jurisdiction over international rights and claims: The Alien Tort Claims Act after *Filartiga v. Peña-Irala.*" *Harvard International Law Journal* 22 (Winter 1981 I):53–113.

Harvard Research in International Law. "Jurisdiction with respect to crime." *AJIL* 29 (July 1935): suppl. 435–651.

Lillich, Richard B., ed. *Transnational Terrorism: Conventions and Commentary.* Charlottesville, VA: Michie, 1982.

Murphy, John F. *Punishing International Terrorists.* Totowa, NJ: Rowman and Allanheld, 1985.

Stone, Julius, and Robert K. Woetzel, eds. *Toward a Feasible International Criminal Court.* Geneva: World Peace Through Law Center, 1970.

Weiler, Joseph H.H. et al., eds. *International Crimes of States.* Berlin: Walter de Gruyter, 1988.

Yonah, Alexander et al., eds. *Control of Terrorism: International Documents.* New York: Crane Russak, 1979.

PART 5
PERSONS IN INTERNATIONAL LAW

The gradual evolution of sovereignty made states the highest authority vis-à-vis other states as well as their own citizens. States have remained intolerant of individuals having direct rights under international law and a legal status that is in competition with states. States have not accepted the argument of a few international lawyers (Georges Scelle, Nicolas Politis) that only individuals are real and exhibit behavior that can be regulated, so that all international law deals with individuals. But the point is that a society needs some individuals to regulate the behavior of other individuals, and the former comprise the collectivity called the state. States have been content for hundreds of years to deal with each other as social entities, just as nationalists enjoy being loyal to and identifying themselves with their state as such, not with each individual citizen. Nevertheless, international law has norms affecting directly the behavior of entities other than states, including individuals, although this remains the exception rather than the rule and often relates to duties rather than rights, especially when individuals are concerned.

The philosophical foundation for this practice of states is the dualist theory, which postulates a strict separation between the municipal legal system and the international legal system. But whatever the theoretical foundation may be, states have always taken political advantage of themselves as dominant social entities. Real or alleged mistreatment of nationals abroad has been used as an excuse for intervention by their state in the name of diplomatic protection; this intervention has ranged from protest to occupation (Japan and China in the nineteenth century). Such action in the name of humanitarianism has been common since the nineteenth century. More recently, political intervention ranging from withholding aid to sending occupation troops has taken place on grounds of supporting some faction's right to self-determination or a group's human rights. In brief, denial of legal subjectivity to individuals and monopolization of that subjectivity by the state have served as a convenient state tool to achieve political ends.

During the last hundred years, pressure for improvement of the individual's status under international law has presaged a change in the traditional position of states, in particular the sacrifice of some sovereignty over their nationals. States' apparent willingness to make concessions derived from a general change in the relationship between individuals and states. The involvement of the ordinary citizen in the politics of states generated insistence upon a greater political role. The mistreatment by governments of their own nationals stimulated demands for the international protection of human rights. Powerful corporations wished to be more than pawns of governments and made contracts with governments referring specifically to international law.

Some progress in the individual's status can hardly be denied. But many concessions states made have been more apparent than real. This situation becomes evident when one remembers that there are two methods by which the individual's status may be improved. One is the traditional method of giving the individual benefits by obliging the state internationally to grant these benefits in municipal legislation. The status of the individual remains a legal matter between states on which the individual depends and has no direct influence. The other method is to grant the individual rights derived directly from international law that can be asserted by the national against any state and that can be enforced through an international agency.

In general, the first method continues to be applied in regard to the improvement of the individual's status. Sovereignty remains intact. The individual is thus still denied full international legal personality and depends upon the goodwill of the state for the enjoyment of the improved status (the European Community and the International Bank for Reconstruction and Development are two exceptions). Mostly the individual obtains benefits as a by-product of international agreements and therefore of the state's fulfillment of these agreements. At worst, the more improvements states agree upon internationally to grant their nationals, the more pretexts they have to interfering in each other's affairs in the name of enforcing international obligations.

The great number of international declarations since the end of World War II relating to human rights and the creation of international agencies to which under very restricted conditions an individual may complain of a violation of human rights should not lead to premature euphoria. In principle and even more in practice, individuals are still not subjects of international law. The individual has more rights now than in the past, the enforcement of which a state can claim from another state on behalf of the individual. But it is rare indeed that an individual can turn directly to an international agency, and in any case these agencies have no effective means to enforce the individual's right. In fact, violations of human rights seem to be occurring with increasing frequency; or perhaps they have always occurred, but improved communications have created a greater awareness of their existence.

The individual may be said to possess limited legal subjectivity when international law imposes duties, obligations, or responsibilities directly upon him or her (for instance, as a pirate, war criminal, or slave trader), even though enforcement must still be up to states. The legal situation in such conditions is fairly clear, although it may be debatable, for instance, what crimes may be declared as such under international law. The legal situation is only a little less clear in regard to the individual's traditional, more beneficial status, such as nationality, immunity, diplomatic protection, extradition, immigration and emigration, asylum, or a contract partner with a government. The situation is quite unclear in regard to the more novel human rights, presumably because these rights can be claimed by the individual's own state against another state *and* in some states by the individual against his or her own state. States have always been more solicitous about preserving their own than another state's sovereignty. In other words, international norms are better developed when they protect an individual in some transnational position than when the individual is in a purely national position dealing only with his or her own government.

The legal situation is even more in flux regarding an individual's material interests (property, investments). The limited rights of protection in this respect that the newer and Communist states are willing to grant their own and foreign nationals have further confused a situation that was not clear among older states.

15
THE LAW OF ALIENS

Admission and Departure

In traditional international law, the alien is a national of another state. A stateless person is therefore not an alien. The difference results from the assumption—based upon the state's internal and external sovereignty—that the treatment of aliens is mainly a legal issue between states, with the alien being merely an object. The alien is considered to be an interest of his or her state. He or she, like all interests of the state, must be treated properly by other states. Any mistreatment entitles the injured state to diplomatic protection of its interests. When a state takes up a case of its national with another state, the issue is one of rights and obligations between states and is subject to international law. This was confirmed by the Permanent Court of International Justice in the *Mavrommatis Palestine Concession (Jurisdiction)* case (1924, p. 12). As soon as Greece took up a suit of Mavrommatis against the United Kingdom for its refusal to acknowledge certain rights (Mavrommatis, a Greek citizen, had previously initiated the suit as a private person), the issue became one between Greece and the United Kingdom, so that international law became relevant. The Court asserted that by taking up the case of a national, "a state is in reality asserting its own right— its right to ensure, in the person of its subjects, respect for the rules of international law." Nevertheless, the person retains some relevance because the injury suffered by the individual triggers the international case and generally forms the basis of the claim. The umpire in the Mixed Claims Commission (United States–Germany) in *Administrative Decision V* (1924, p. 153) warned that considering the injury to the national as an injury to the state and thereby converting a private into a national claim "must not be permitted to obscure the realities or blind us to the fact that the ultimate object of asserting the claim is to provide reparation for the private claimant."

The difference in status and treatment between aliens and stateless persons, or for that matter between aliens and nationals, may disappear when states live up to their protestations that the protection of human dignity should be an international obligation. Then the relevant basis for decent treatment will be the fact of being a person, not of being a national, an alien, or a stateless person. The consequences of treating human beings as human beings are so far-reaching (for example, free migration across the globe, equal and full rights under any law) that this chimera is not likely to be realized in the foreseeable future, except perhaps within limits in the European Community when it becomes a full community.

In traditional international law, no rule obligates states to admit aliens either as transients or permanent residents. The U.S. Supreme Court in the *Nishimura Eiku v. United States* case (1892, p. 659) declared that a state "has the power, as inherent in sovereignty and essential to self-protection, to forbid the entrance of foreigners within its dominions, or to admit them only in such cases and upon such conditions as it may see fit to prescribe." The development of human rights law has not affected this situation. Only treaties can change it, as, for instance, does the Convention on the Privileges and Immunities of the United Nations (1946), which exempts member representatives and officers of the organization from immigration restrictions, alien registration, or national service obligations, or the Headquarters Agreement Between the United Nations and the United States (1947), which stipulates that U.S. laws and regulations regarding the entry of aliens shall not be applied in such a manner as to interfere with the transit of persons having official business in the United Nations. (This stipulation became a matter of controversy in regard to the projected appearance of Yasir Arafat before the General Assembly in 1988.)

The Supreme Court's declaration was directed to a natural person, but it has taken on particular importance in recent times in regard to corporations doing business abroad. The transfer of rules relating to natural persons is applicable to juridic persons only within limits. These limits are likely to become even more stringent when human dignity rather than nationality becomes the basis for a person's legal position as an alien. To avoid difficulties and to protect corporations abroad, states as well as corporations tend to conclude agreements either between states or between a state and a corporation. These agreements regulate whether a corporation may be established (enter) abroad or may be dissolved (expelled or deported) and under what conditions. In the absence of agreements, insofar as is reasonable, the traditional rules developed for natural persons are applied to juridic persons (for example, suing in courts, being taxed or expropriated).

The voluntary or forced departure of an alien from a state is a more controversial legal situation. It has recently become acute especially in connection with foreign labor. The International Covenant on Civil and Political Rights (1966)—ratified by few states—stipulates in Article 12 that everyone "shall be free to leave any country, including his own." The more troublesome situation is expulsion of an alien. Several court cases decided in the United States gradually established some criteria that are now accepted in a number of countries as a prerequisite for the expulsion of an alien, although the right of a state to expel an alien is generally admitted in principle (see, for example, *United States ex rel John Turner v. Williams* [1903] and *Boffolo* [1903]). These criteria are the existence of extreme circumstances, obtaining an entrance permit under false pretenses, violating the conditions of entry, violating laws while residing in the country, becoming a public charge, and violating the *ordre public*. The expulsion should be in a manner least injurious to the alien. This last condition is connected with the duty of every state to treat aliens according to certain minimum international standards. If human rights begin to permeate the relations between states, expulsion may also be affected in favor of the alien.

Nevertheless, the municipal legislation of many countries reserves the right to expel aliens without giving reasons. The Covenant on Civil and Political Rights (1966) states in Article 13 that an alien may be expelled from a country "in pursuance of a decision reached in accordance with law and shall, except where compelling reasons of national security otherwise require, be allowed to submit the reasons against expulsion" and to have his or her case reviewed by a competent authority. This clause is obviously subject to a great variety of interpretations. Would it, for instance, allow the by now quite customary expulsion of journalists from totalitarian countries for expressing their ideas, opinions, and information when doing so is permissible under the Universal Declaration of Human Rights (1948)?

The Standard of Treatment and Its Enforcement

Once a state admits an alien, it enters into an obligation toward the alien's state to treat the alien's person and interests in certain ways. This obligation relates to the receiving state's activities, not to those of a private person in the receiving country. Thus, the state may be responsible either for those of its acts that have an effect upon the alien (such as expropriation of the alien's property) or for normal action or nonaction in response to a private individual's acts (such as protection against a criminal). If the alien cannot get satisfactory enforcement of the obligation by the state itself, the alien's state may enforce it with all legal means, usually diplomatic means.

This diplomatic protection has an unsavory history. In the past, it led to political and military intervention and was frequently used as a pretext for imperialism. Quite often, the "protective" action was disproportionate to the alleged injury to the alien. The alien was merely the trigger for extensive imperialistic enterprises. This practice of the older states explains, at least in part, why the newer (mainly ex-colonial) states and to some extent the Communist states are opposed to important aspects of traditional customary law. The result is that today the treatment of aliens has been thrown back into the political arena and has not yet firmed into new international law. The issue is the manner—substance and method—in which the alien must be treated in international law.

A basic principle has been that the alien must be treated according to the ordinary standards of civilized states. Depending upon how a state treats its own nationals, this principle obligates a state to treat aliens better or entitles it to treat them worse. Not equality of treatment of nationals and aliens, but "whether aliens are treated in accordance with ordinary standards of civilization" is "the ultimate test of the propriety of acts of authorities in the light of international law," said the U.S.-Mexican General Claims Commission in the *Harry Roberts (United States) v. United Mexican States* case (1927, p. 361). Mexico was found guilty of violating its obligation because Harry Roberts, a U.S. citizen, was imprisoned for a long time before his trial and the prison was in extraordinarily bad condition (although Mexicans suffered the same treatment).

The Latin American states, which were later joined by many newer states, attacked the principle of ordinary standards on substantive and procedural grounds. Under the early leadership of the Argentinian jurist Carlos Calvo, these states insisted that aliens were entitled to the same protection as nationals—no more, no less—and that the implementation of this protection was a sovereign, national matter. They denied the legitimacy of intervention in the name of the alien's diplomatic protection.

Latin American states then introduced the Calvo clause into contracts between aliens and their governments. The clause holds that the alien thereby renounces any appeal to his or her government for the protection of his or her rights. The clause was upheld as well as denied by tribunals. The most telling argument against it was that protecting nationals was a right of the state under international law that the national could not renounce. Since the 1930s the clause has played no role in international disputes.

The problem the clause was intended to solve remains acute, however. To many states special treatment for aliens remains a symbol of imperialism. To Communist states the ordinary standards principle also signifies a disguised imposition of bourgeois legal principles upon the world to perpetuate the superior status of the "imperialist" states, their citizens, and their corporations.

The newer states are trying to preserve the effects of the Calvo clause by reformulating traditional legal principles. They are arguing that national standards and equal treatment with the state's nationals are the norm of international law. Some even find equal treatment too much because aliens are relieved from the burdens of citizenship. The main concern of these states is not so much the physical treatment of aliens as their property (investments, concessions, contracts), which is suspect as evidence of neocolonialism. The newer states' general argument can be summed up as, "Poor countries need protection through international law more than rich investors do."

The newer and Communist states usually join forces in international organizations to pass resolutions that in fact represent attacks upon the substantive and procedural aspects of the traditional principle of the treatment of aliens. For instance, the Trade and Development Board of the United Nations Conference on Trade and Development passed Resolution 88 (XII) in October 1972, which states that a dispute arising from the nationalization of foreign-owned property lies within the "sole jurisdiction" of the nationalizing state. A very similar proposal was included in General Assembly Resolution 3171 (XXVIII) of December 1973, in Resolution 3281 (XXIX) of the Charter of Economic Rights and Duties of States adopted by the General Assembly in December 1974, and in implied ways in documents sponsored by developing countries that proposed the New International Economic Order (NIEO).

The attitude of these states creates a dilemma for them. They need foreign experts and investments but want to keep both under state control. States solve this dilemma by standing on their proposals in principle and granting special rights and protection of aliens in treaties and contracts. Furthermore, movement of people and resources is no longer the one-way street from developed to developing countries that it used to be. There are millions of foreign workers from poorer countries in richer countries. For some Third World countries exports of goods and investments have become important sources of their well-being. Some governments in the new states are becoming quite interested in accepting the principle of ordinary international standards from which their citizens abroad could benefit as much as aliens in their countries could. Finally, references to human rights, which deal with human beings not nationals, have been hailed in the Third World as a "common standard of achievement." These developments could be steps toward the restoration of ordinary standards as a universally valid legal principle for treating aliens.

The public stance of these states of insisting upon their national standard principle has not turned this principle into a binding legal norm. On the contrary, the International Court of Justice in *Barcelona Traction, Light and Power Co. Ltd. (Judgment)* (1970, p. 33) reaffirmed "the universally recognized rule of customary international law concerning every state's right of diplomatic protection over its nationals abroad, that is, the right to require that another State observe a certain standard of decent treatment to aliens in its territory."

This pronouncement does not solve the basic problem, however. What is the ordinary standard states have to apply? What methods of diplomatic protection are legal? Broad agreement on an answer to the first question has always been difficult to achieve, even when the culture of international society was relatively homogeneous. Every state attempts to demand higher standards from others than it is willing to apply to itself. In addition, there are different national legislations regarding aliens, there are differences between words and deeds everywhere, there are different perspectives on the rights and duties of individuals, and there are enormous cultural differences. If the ordinary standard is some amalgam of the practice of civilized states, the practice of Communist and newer states must be included in the mixture as much as that of the older states. What is the amalgam, for instance, between cutting off the hand of a thief and sending him or her to prison?

There are numerous decisions illustrating what some people may mean by an ordinary standard that others condemn. In the *Chattin (United States) v. United Mexican States* case (1927, p. 682), Mexico's judicial proceedings were found to be "highly insufficient." But a minority opinion in the case accused the majority "of a lack of knowledge of the judicial system and practice of Mexico" and of applying to the Mexican proceedings "tests belonging to foreign systems of law." In the *Neer and Neer (United States) v. United Mexican States* case (1926, p. 214), the commission tried to define some standard by saying that "the treatment of an alien, in order to constitute an international delinquency, should amount to an outrage, to bad faith, to wilful neglect of duty, or to an insufficiency of governmental action so far short of international standards that every reasonable and impartial man would readily recognize its insufficiency." But this valiant attempt at a definition does not avoid subjectivity of judgment. And where is the borderline between an insufficiency and an overabundance of (for instance, totalitarian) governmental action?

A diminution of the conflict might occur if states could agree on human rather than national values. The incipient human rights law points the way. Arbitrator Max Huber in the *Spanish Zone of Morocco Claims (Spain v. United Kingdom)* (1924, p. 151) pleaded that at some point the interest of the state in protecting its citizens and their goods must overcome respect for territorial sovereignty. Otherwise international law would be powerless to protect the human personality. Sixty-five years after Huber's reference to human values, the humane foundation of the treatment of an alien's person remains mostly rhetoric and the treatment itself a delicate political issue.

The protection of an alien's material interests is even more controversial than protection of the person is because the trend is away from protection of material interests. National differences in this area are particularly pronounced and are often a matter of pride so that no rhetoric is needed to cover them up. These differences show themselves in disputes about private versus public property, capitalist versus socialist economy, foreign development aid versus neocolonial domination, and the sanctity of acquired rights versus the imperialist origin of such rights. The conclusion drawn by the newer and (former) Communist states is that the protection of an alien's material interests is a matter for municipal law exclusively. Their stance appears firm and ideological, hence non-negotiable in the abstract, but it is softened by the fact that they are willing to negotiate exceptions when expedient.

What methods of diplomatic protection are legal is much debated. There is agreement that a state is not obliged to protect its nationals abroad under international law and that its right to protect them arises only after the alien has exhausted all local means of obtaining redress for injury. (This was called a "well-established" rule of customary international law by the International Court of Justice in *Interhandel (Switzerland v. United States of America)* [1959, p. 25]). Diplomacy is one means; retorsion and reprisal if they do not involve illegal use of force or other illegalities may be others. The use of international organizations is yet another. Because the use of force has become illegal, forceful intervention could at most be justified in the name of self-defense if there is an immediate threat to the life (but probably not to the material interest) of the alien. The United States used this argument as one excuse for the 1983 invasion of Grenada and the 1989 invasion of Panama. If the concept of force as broadened by the newer states to include pressure of all kinds is accepted, there is little room left for the diplomatic protection of aliens (or any diplomacy at all!).

The uncertainties prevailing in regard to the protection of aliens have served as an incentive for many states to conclude bilateral treaties regulating the treatment of their nationals' person and interests in their respective states. Increasing political and economic interaction makes the treatment of nationals in other countries a matter of mutual interest. Reciprocity becomes established and exercises its usual beneficial effect. Conceivably, new customary law could emerge from these treaties. But comprehensive multilateral treaties have not yet been concluded in spite of some interesting proposals from the International Law Commission. In fact, many bilateral treaties and a number of international resolutions refer to existing norms. Innovations are at best very slow in coming. In the meantime and in spite of all the controversies, the present international law on aliens retains considerable importance.

Aliens as Objects of Municipal Law

Aliens are subjects of their state of sojourn. International law demands that the alien be granted certain rights by the state but also that the alien accept certain duties. International law prescribes the means and methods for the fulfillment of these rights and duties. Neither rights nor duties have to match those of the state's nationals. Customarily, aliens have no right to vote, may be restricted in the exercise of certain professions or the performance of security-sensitive jobs, and may not acquire land near military installations. They may not have to perform military duties. These regulations of the alien's behavior flow from the state's sovereign right to regulate the entry and the conditions of sojourn for aliens. This right includes unequal treatment of different groups of aliens, to which now probably has to be added the qualification that the inequality must not be counter to those parts of human rights that have become law.

The principle of the ordinary standard of treatment applies here, too. But when the regulations or treatment of the alien by an official state agency falls below that standard remains uncertain as long as the standard cannot be defined. Unfavorable treatment of an alien and a state's failure to fulfill minimal obligations can amount to what is known as "denial of justice."

The General Claims Commission in the *Laura B. Janes (United States) v. United Mexican States* case (1926, p. 214) stated that in the broadest sense of the term *denial of justice*, such a failure could occur in any branch of government: legislative, administrative, judicial. In this sense, the government could be held responsible only for what it committed or omitted itself. The commission elaborated further that denial of justice in the narrower sense would make the government responsible for what a private individual did to the alien by preventing the alien from obtaining redress for an injury through wrongful governmental procedures. In the *Janes* case, for instance, the Mexican authorities were found guilty of not making any reasonable effort to apprehend the murderer of Byron E. Janes. In the *William E. Chapman (United States) v. Mexico Claims* (1930), the same commission found Mexico guilty because the police at Puerta Mexico had not provided Consul Chapman (who was shot and wounded) with proper protection after he informed the police that he had received several threats to his life.

This distinction between a broader and a narrower sense of the denial of justice concept is not significant. The important point is always whether a state has acted or has failed to act according to international law, for there are many ways in which a state can act illegally. It can pass or not pass a law contrary to a commitment under international law. It can have a corrupt administration or judiciary. It can deny aliens proper access to courts. It can fail to protect the person or property of the alien.

The main use of the denial of justice rule is in the alien's obligation to exhaust all local remedies to obtain satisfaction before the alien's state can go into action. Exhaustion of local remedies certainly includes normal administrative and judicial procedures, which the alien must use even if there is a suspicion that these procedures may be unfair. If that can be proved, a denial of justice may have taken place.

Foreign juridic persons, especially corporations, represent a special problem in regard to legal subjectivity. As "artificial beings" (Chief Justice John Marshall) created under special national laws, other states may refuse to acknowledge their existence altogether or under special conditions or in a limited manner. States could therefore deny legal subjectivity to foreign corporations under national law. In practice, virtually all states have legislation solving this problem in their fashion, with some more generous than others in granting legal subjectivity.

The Protection of an Alien's Private Rights

Under traditional international law, a state is obligated to respect the vested private rights of an alien. The Permanent Court of International Justice in the *German Interests in Polish Upper Silesia* case (1926) declared that respect for the vested interests of aliens formed a part of generally accepted international law. This principle has been solidly established in numerous national and international court decisions, arbitral awards, and diplomatic practice. It comprises all private rights: those inherent in the human person and those acquired by a person (mainly property, investments, contracts, and concessions). Although respect for private rights is established in general international law, many states stipulate in treaties protection of their nationals' rights specifically—and for good reason. The validity of the principle has lately been questioned and in the practice of most states has been applied in limited fashion at best.

A state's respect for the private rights of aliens has never been an absolute obligation. Like most other obligations, it is subject to the legitimate higher interests of the state. Unless a state invokes these interests in an arbitrary fashion, thus abusing its right, it is entitled to interfere with private rights of aliens. In regard to acquired rights, including those established by contract between the alien and a government, international law has always permitted a recognized government—unless prohibited by treaty—to expropriate an alien's property within its jurisdiction in a nondiscriminatory manner for a genuinely public purpose and by legal procedures according to the state's municipal legislation and international law. If a government makes use of this right, it is obligated to pay compensation (not damages) to the alien promptly, adequately, and effectively, according to contested traditional legal rules.

If any of these conditions is not fulfilled, the act of the government is not legitimate expropriation but illegal confiscation. Similarly, a government has the usual right to tax an alien's property and impose certain other conditions upon it. But if such measures are tantamount to a disguised confiscation (such as prevention of the alien's access to the property or direct or indirect forcing of its sale), the measures are illegal. Although there is far-reaching agreement about the right of a state in principle to "affect" acquired private rights of an alien, there are vast differences of opinion and practice on the consequences after a state has made use of that right.

The traditional legal situation regarding acquired private rights was created when economic liberalism and orthodox capitalism were dominant. Since then, Communist states have appeared and have rejected the idea of private vested rights altogether. New states emerging from colonial status have tried to overcome their traumatic experience with special foreign rights by subjecting these to their sovereign control and trying to adapt private rights of aliens to social reforms. Even in capitalist states the concept of accountability of private rights and the prevalence of the common welfare over individual interests have affected municipal legal systems to the disadvantage of absolute private rights. The result of these changes has been that the traditional rule of prompt, adequate, and effective compensation for a government's interference with an alien's private property no longer corresponds to the ordinary standard principle and is no longer justified.

The practice of states provides examples of expropriation with no compensations to compensation in accordance with traditional norms of international law. In many instances, especially in cases of nationalization of entire categories of property, disputes have been settled by political, rather than legal, means because political considerations and the relative bargaining positions of the parties proved more relevant than their legal positions. Indeed, the U.S. Supreme Court in *Banco Nacional de Cuba v. Sabbatino* (1964, p. 431) belittled the legal as compared to the political route for obtaining compensation. Diplomacy, it argued, "will often be able, either by bilateral or multilateral talks, by submission to the United Nations, or by the employment of economic and political sanctions, to achieve some degree of general redress. Judicial determinations of invalidity of title can, on the other hand, have only an occasional impact." The Court also said, "when one considers the variety of means possessed by this country to make secure foreign investment, the persuasive or coercive effect of judicial invalidation of acts of expropriation dwindles in comparison."

Congress also took a hand in the situation. It passed the Hickenlooper amendment to the Foreign Assistance Act of 1962 following Brazilian expropriation of the assets of a local subsidiary of International Telephone & Telegraph. The amendment directs the president to suspend all assistance to any government that expropriates U.S.-owned property, breaks an existing contract with a U.S. national, or by other means in effect deprives a U.S. citizen of his or her property without discharging "its obligation under international law."

The nature of this obligation is changing. For all practical purposes, the requirement of prompt, adequate, and effective compensation has disappeared. The trend toward a lower standard is therefore an adjustment of the law to reality. But the approach of many newer states appears to go to an opposite extreme that is unacceptable to the older states and discouraging to foreign investors. An indication of this approach can be found in the previously cited General Assembly Resolution 3171 (XXVIII), the Declaration on the Establishment of a New International Economic Order of the General Assembly of May 1, 1974, and the Charter of Economic Rights and Duties of States adopted by majority vote in the General Assembly in 1974. These resolutions, although differing somewhat in detail, make nationalization and expropriation the "inalienable" right of the state. There is no mention of nondiscrimination. Compensation is in essence a domestic matter and regulated exclusively by municipal legislation. There is no longer mention of any influence of international legal principles or what the amount of compensation should be. (In Resolution 1803 [XVII] on sovereignty over natural resources [1962] there was still talk of "appropriate" compensation.)

The U.S. government tried to fight this development. In a statement in January 1972, the president enumerated the conditions under which expropriation was legal under international law. Should a state violate these conditions in expropriating "a significant U.S. interest," the United States would not extend new economic benefits to such a state; it would withhold its support from loans to be granted by "multilateral development banks"; but it would still give special consideration to humanitarian assistance.

The Special Case of Concessions

Concessions granted to a foreign person are sometimes considered a special category of acquired private rights for two reasons. First, concession contracts, usually to extract natural resources or to develop and run utilities of the granting state, tend to have greater general significance than the usual sales or purchase contract does. They normally run for a long period of time, have many secondary effects upon the state's economy, and touch upon many political and social policies. Second, as one of the parties is the government and the subject matter is closely related to public policy, the legal nature or applicable law may be in doubt (for example, whether the contract is private or public, whether the state acts as contractor or sovereign).

The possibilities are that international public law, the local or some other law of contracts, or general principles of law may apply. A vexing problem is that the government as a partner to the contract, even when committed under the rule of *pacta sunt servanda*, is also a lawmaker and can by legislation change the rules of the game under which the contract is to be carried out. In this last instance, the state uses its prerogative as a sovereign, which it cannot limit by agreement with a private person (only by agreement with another state). In most disputes involving concessions, the application of any established legal system is unsatisfactory because it does not fit the mixed nature of the contract, it has inadequate provisions for handling the dispute, it is unacceptable to one or both parties, or it comprises all of these conditions.

In many contracts of this kind concluded in recent years, the parties have specified what law is to govern. When they have failed to do so, the tendency has been to develop a new type of law ("transnational") that seeks to rely upon universally recognized general principles of law combined with parts of the municipal law of the parties involved that may be relevant and useful for the solution of the dispute.

From the standpoint of international law, the important question remains when a breach of contract—under whatever applicable law—

has taken place so that the alien may eventually invoke diplomatic protection by his or her home state. Given that a state is simultaneously a contract partner and a guardian of the public interest, the tendency in international law has recently been to insist upon stricter requirements for declaring a state guilty of a violation of international law in these kinds of contracts than in other kinds or, for that matter, in other kinds of interference with acquired rights of aliens.

The Special Case of Nationalization

The legal situation regarding concession contracts with aliens has most often become acute in cases of nationalization of a state's natural resources, financial institutions, or utilities. Several U.N. resolutions (for example, General Assembly Resolution 1803 [XVII] [1962]) adopted by overwhelming majorities and with very few opposing votes have distinguished between nationalization and expropriation, but have not spelled out what the difference is. In both cases ownership of property is compulsorily transferred from the individual to the state; the reason for the transfer must relate to public interest. In the general case of expropriation, however, only a specific item of property may be involved (such as a piece of land to build a railway across), and the purpose to which it is turned may not be the same as under private ownership. In the case of nationalization, an entire category of property is expropriated and the purpose remains the same, with the beneficiary changing from the former private owner to the general public (as in the case of public utilities). Perhaps the most important clue to the difference is in the political and social context in which the processes take place.

Nationalization is likely to be part of a political and social reform of the entire social system of the state. Indeed, in cases of nationalization international lawyers and states tend to favor states and disfavor aliens, a response that rests on the changing attitude toward the sacred quality of private property versus the social responsibility of private ownership. Thus, aliens will find it more difficult to prove a state's violation of international law in cases of nationalization than of straight expropriation.

The actual legal situation regarding nationalization as distinct from expropriation is very controversial. Some nationalizing states have rejected any demand for compensation or for fulfillment of other conditions to make nationalization legal. They insist that nationalization is part of the absolute sovereignty of the state itself. Others have conceded a duty to compensate and thereby express majority opinion. But from this point on, differences in the legal consequences of expropriation and nationalization are difficult to define. The major difference is probably to be found in the attitude of the alien's state toward the nationalizing state. There is a tendency to take a less rigid diplomatic stand in the case of nationalization than in the case of expropriation. In other words, the difference is more noticeable in the political than in the legal sphere.

The Protection of an Alien's Personal Rights

Great diversity among states in the treatment of individuals, whether nationals or aliens, has caused considerable differences in the practice of states concerning the inherent, personal rights of aliens. Aliens are quite well off in democratic states. They enjoy most of the constitutional rights enjoyed by nationals (with some exceptions mentioned earlier). In very many other states, however, aliens as well as nationals are deprived of rights considered elemental in democratic states. In many instances, this situation derives from a difference in ideology (type of economy, type of punishment, role of classes and sexes, due process). But in other cases deprivation of rights is also a denial to the human person of honor, dignity, and right to existence—freedoms that in principle very few ideologies, if any, deny.

These differences in attitude also extend to the departure or deportation of the alien (which was discussed earlier). The fundamental principle underlying his or her treatment—whether, for instance, the alien has the right to appeal against a deportation order, what happens to him or her before deportation takes place—is the respect a state shows to the person as a human being. But quite apart from the specific legal recourse that the alien may have in theory, in practice states circumvent theoretically granted rights (such as by accusing the alien of subversion or spying). There is no evidence, however, that such state actions have had much impact upon the international minimum or ordinary standard of treatment of aliens.

Extradition and Asylum

Extradition is the delivery of an accused or convicted person by one state (into which the person has fled) to the state in whose territory a crime was allegedly committed. There is neither an international legal norm nor a universal multilateral treaty regulating extradition. Its regulation is left to treaty arrangements between interested states or even to comity. With greater mobility of people in modern times have come a large number of such treaties showing a great variety of characteristics. To achieve some uniformity, Latin American states and the European Community have signed multilateral treaties. But whether certain clauses found in many of these treaties have turned into customary law is a moot question. Usually, when a state extradites a person, it expects that the person will be tried by the receiving country only for those crimes for which the extradition took place.

When a case arises between states having no treaty, they have to negotiate the fate of the individual. Very frequently, extradition takes place only if the crime for which the criminal is wanted is also a crime in the surrendering country. In some cases a state's refusal to extradite a criminal has led to political retaliation by the country demanding the extradition. Or in other cases a country that will not extradite its own citizens does nevertheless try them for the crime committed in the other country. A frequent practice has been to apply the principle of reciprocity—namely, if one country is willing to extradite its nationals, the other country will do the same.

When a fugitive is suspected or convicted of a political crime, the international legal situation does not change, but the practice changes. In the absence of a treaty, a state is free to extradite or not. A decision is often complicated in such cases by a liberal state's reluctance to deliver a political criminal to a different type of state. The obvious problem is to define "political" in this context, and the problem is aggravated in the case of "mixed" crimes, such as murder or a terroristic act. (The government repression and murder of prodemocracy activists in China in June 1989 raised several such questions in regard to the refugees who fled abroad from the governmental terror.)

In the absence of an objective or incontrovertible definition, the political culture of time and place determines whether a crime is political or not. In general, during the last two hundred years the category "political" has been broadened, and political more than legal considerations have influenced the decision to extradite. The rise of so many totalitarian or dictatorial countries in which the treatment of political prisoners was considered inhumane or the crimes were not even considered political in the more liberal countries affected this change. For the same reason, escapees from their own governmental authorities persecuted for reasons of race, religion, nationality, or political beliefs are often granted political asylum in other countries. The cases of *Castioni* (1890, p. 491), *Kavic, Bjelanovic and Arsenijevic* (1952, p. 374), and *United States v. Mackin* (1981) are indicative of the changes that have taken place in the definition or consequences of political crimes.

The Universal Declaration of Human Rights (1948) states in Article 14, "Everyone has the right to seek and to enjoy in other countries asylum from persecution. This right may not be invoked in the case of prosecutions genuinely arising from non-political crimes or from acts contrary to the purposes and principles of the United Nations."

In this respect, Manuel Noriega's case was clear as far as his involvement in drug dealing was concerned. But the U.S. government also wanted to replace his government with a more democratic regime, which would make him a political refugee. Moreover, his drug dealings took place while he was in fact the head of state, which presumably gave him immunity. His allegedly voluntary surrender reduced some of the complexity of his case.

In the light of the masses of refugees populating the globe since World War II (usually political fugitives), the U.N. high commissioner for refugees has been able to supply some aid to them. He has also been partially successful in obtaining from some states of refuge the assurance of treatment at least equal to that of aliens and the issuance of identity papers. Stateless persons who are not refugees are faring worse as long as the Convention Relating to the Status of Stateless Persons (1954) does not come into force. Article 15 of the Universal Declaration of Human Rights (1948), that "everyone has the right to a nationality," has basically failed to motivate the signers of the declaration into action.

16
INTERNATIONAL LAW
OF NATIONALS
AND HUMAN RIGHTS

One state has no obligation toward another state for a certain treatment of its nationals unless a treaty stipulates otherwise. The state has far-reaching freedom to treat its nationals as it sees fit; this freedom is unhampered by universal norms of international law. This competence results from sovereignty. But just as external sovereignty is undergoing limiting changes, so improvements of the individual's legal position under international law are very slowly making inroads on internal sovereignty. For the time being, however, it remains true that a national in his or her own state does not possess the minimum protection and its minimal effectiveness that an alien may enjoy through international law with the help of diplomatic protection. This is particularly true of the national as an individual. Nationals as members of specified groups (such as national minorities) fare slightly better.

The paradox is that at least since the end of World War II, the protection of the human rights of every natural person as a general international obligation has been a most prominent topic in international meetings. Yet it has become binding on only those states that have ratified the relevant conventions (none of which has been ratified by the United States). Moreover, the individual still has to rely mainly on the state to get his or her rights when most likely that very state is violating those rights. In fact, the maltreatment of nationals by their own states, including even by those states that have signed the Universal Declaration of Human Rights (1948) and other documents promising rights to individuals, has increased. Although human rights apply to human beings regardless of nationality, the touchstone by which to evaluate the effective grant of human rights is the ability of an injured individual to turn for the fulfillment of his or her rights to an international agency against the national's own government. That possibility exists in only a few very exceptional cases. For instance, the Optional Protocol, which supplements the Covenant on Civil and Political Rights (1966), grants an individual the right under very stringent conditions to complain about a violation of his or her human rights to an international committee of experts and thereby trigger an investigation.

Since 1945 this situation has improved somewhat in, for instance, the European Community and in Latin America (at least in theory). There has been an improvement regarding complaints by individuals but not necessarily regarding remedies. In formal legal terms the individual's human rights are better taken care of today than they used to be; in practice, this is hardly the case.

Beginnings of International Protection

A brief survey of the history of agencies, conventions, and declarations relating to the human rights of nationals shows an abundance of such instruments quite disproportionate to their concrete results. Rudolph Rummel has demonstrated that since World War I more people have been killed by their own governments than by wars. The overwhelming majority of guilty parties are nondemocratic governments.

The earliest attempts to guarantee certain rights to individuals (as a group) referred to freedom of religion for minorities, although these rights were hardly enforceable through international law. Early instruments regarding international obligations for the protection of individuals referred to the treatment of sick and wounded soldiers and prisoners (from 1864 on). This protection was comprehensively regulated in the two Hague conferences of 1899 and 1907, which aimed at the humanization of war. In addition, scattered laws appeared safeguarding the health of workers in certain occupations. These arrangements were part of a growing awareness of and agitation for the welfare of individuals in an age when, in the aftermath of undiluted capitalism, the person's labor was more an object of consideration than the person was.

World War I demonstrated the inadequacy of the Hague agreements, which led after World War II to the Geneva conventions of 1949 and later to the Diplomatic Conference Protocols in the 1970s and 1980 on the humanitarization of violent conflicts. World War I encouraged the labor movement to demand a share in its spoils of war, from which sprang the International Labor Organization (1919) and its preoccupation with the social improvement of workers' status. The Treaty of Versailles created a precedent by granting the peoples of the mandates system freedom of conscience and religion and rights of petition directly to international agencies for violation of their rights. (The rights of petition were also extended to the minorities of eastern Europe.)

World War II gave an enormous impetus to the emergence of numerous agencies primarily or secondarily concerned with human rights, mainly as a result of the U.N. Charter, and to the creation of an even greater number of declarations and recommendations. Reference to human rights has since become an almost de rigueur practice in international conferences and at least an auxiliary justification for all kinds of demands by states. It has become a political weapon.

The Status of Human Rights

As the following (partial) list of agreements, both international and regional, makes clear, there is hardly any area of human existence not touched upon by some agreement.

- Articles 1, 13, 56, and 76 of the U.N. Charter (the promotion of human rights)
- Convention on the Prevention and Punishment of the Crime of Genocide (1948)
- Universal Declaration of Human Rights (1948)
- Convention Relating to the Status of Refugees (1951)
- Convention on the Political Rights of Women (1953)
- Declaration on the Granting of Independence to Colonial Countries and Peoples (1960)
- International Convention on the Elimination of All Forms of Racial Discrimination (1965)
- Covenant on Civil and Political Rights and Covenant on Economic, Social, and Cultural Rights (1966) (implementing Universal Declaration of Human Rights)
- International Convention on the Suppression and Punishment of the Crime of Apartheid (1973)
- Helsinki Accords (1975) (renewed and expanded in 1989)
- Convention on the Elimination of All Forms of Discrimination Against Women (1979)
- Convention Against Torture and Other Cruel, Inhuman, or Degrading Treatment or Punishment (1984)

When all these conventions and declarations are added up, it would be difficult to imagine the human rights of any individual or group of individuals remaining unprotected, especially when some highly specialized conventions aimed at special groups of people, such as diplomats (1973) or fugitives (1968), are added. The real problem is therefore not so much agreement on protection as implementation and enforcement. The main burden for enforcement must be carried by international organizations because in the majority of cases an individual's rights are violated by his or her own state, and so he or she can hardly count upon that state for satisfaction.

There are innumerable organs (commission, committees, subcommittees) of main U.N. agencies, their specialized agencies, and specially created agencies that occupy themselves with supervising adherence of states to human rights, interpreting these rights, suggesting additions, and reporting on the fate of these rights in individual states. In several cases states can complain to these agencies about the failure of other states to fulfill their commitments. In a very few really exceptional cases individuals or groups of individuals can complain about the violation of their human rights to a commission or subcommission, which in turn can handle such complaints only in the most discrete, and therefore inefficient, manner.

There are several difficulties with enforcement. First, U.N. agencies have to justify a violation as a threat to peace because the major function of the United Nations is maintenance of peace. Second, because such matters are always highly political as well as cultural, interpretation of just what right is protected is variable. Third, U.N. agencies cannot interfere in essentially domestic jurisdiction. Fourth, giving individuals the right to address themselves directly to an international agency would make them subjects of international law—a quality all states are most reluctant to grant. Fifth, these agencies have no real sanction to enforce their verdicts. Sixth, several sovereign states legislate specific rights based on universal, generally stated, but abstract human rights; international documents cannot override national laws.

Nevertheless, it is hardly deniable that the manner in which international society deals with human rights has had some effect upon the internal and external behavior of states. The many conventions, declarations, and recommendations have served as a guide for many states and have had political and possibly some moral impact. It is also true that some of the crimes enumerated in these documents are now generally accepted as such—for instance, torture, genocide, and the older piracy and slave trade. But it is very much debated whether most of the other crimes and rights mentioned in these understandings have indeed become binding upon states, if not as treaty law then as customary law. Court decisions can be found on either side of the argument; so can government statements.

When the practice of states as a very important criterion for the development of customary law is examined, there can be little doubt that the neglect of human rights in many, if not most, states is customary behavior. In other words, neither the objective criterion of customary law—habitual behavior—nor the subjective criterion—*opinio iuris*—has been fulfilled. What states hypocritically say in innumerable international meetings and in what documents they sign (as opposed to ratify) cannot create international law as such when so often their practice belies their words. In contrast to this opinion, the International Court in the *Nicaragua (Merits, Judgment)* case (1986, pp. 1066, 1070) felt that participation in U.N. declarations and resolutions confirms the existence of an *opinio iuris*.

But even if agreement could be reached on what violation is a crime and what the definition of the crime is, purely national enforcement machinery is unlikely to be adequate for the enforcement of human rights. The European Court of Human Rights, inadequate as it may be but nevertheless having influence, is an indication that supranational machinery can be developed. Obviously, the prerequisite of concern for human rights as it existed in Western Europe is not likely to exist in other parts of the world for a long time to come. This inadequacy applies in particular to the complaints of Third World states that multinational corporations in collusion with "internal colonialists" are violating many human rights of the local population and that these abuses cannot be eliminated because the home governments of the corporations do not feel responsible and the local governments are either incapable of enforcement or belong to the same class as the internal colonialist. Underlying this complaint is the often cited internationalization of capitalism without the simultaneous internationalization of the controls over it. In other words, part of the basic difficulty in enforcing human rights is the incompatibility of sovereignty with the internationalized violation of human rights.

The situation of the United States in regard to international human rights is paradoxical. It has not ratified a single one of the many agreements relating to human rights. The genocide convention, for instance, has been before the Senate for about four decades. President Bush sent the convention on torture to the Senate in 1989. Among the reasons for the hesitancy of the Senate to agree to ratification of these instruments are three worthy of mention here. First, under some conventions U.S. citizens might be tried before foreign courts on grounds of racism, sex discrimination, intervention in foreign countries, and so on. Second, the death penalty existing in some states might come into conflict with a convention ratified by the United States. Third, more generally, the norms of some convention might amount to an interference with U.S. values (as, for example, the International Covenant on Economic, Social, and Cultural Rights [1966] could be interpreted to do). Yet the enforcement of human rights in the United States is considerably better than in very many states having ratified these conventions. Nevertheless, the argument is being made that ratifying these conventions would have considerable political and legal value at a time when the guarantee of human rights is demanded by peoples across the globe.

Self-Determination of Peoples

The precise meaning of self-determination is controversial. Its formulation as the fifth principle in the 1970 Declaration on Principles of International Law Concerning Friendly Relations and Co-operation Among States in Accordance with the Charter of the United Nations has not been helpful. The idea of self-determination refers to collectivities, rather than individuals, not yet subjects of international law but potential recipients of direct rights under the law. Such collectivities wish to secede from or have autonomy within their state, create their own state, or join another state. The idea is frightening to existing states. They usually do everything possible to restrain self-determination, both in method and substance, as a matter of self-preservation. This, too, is a right, for the U.N. Charter forbids all action against the territorial integrity of a state. Numerous later international declarations specifically assert that any attack upon the territorial integrity of states or the disruption of their unity is illegal.

Yet support of self-determination can also be a political tool in the hands of states supporting groups agitating for self-determination in other states to embarrass or even dismember those states. These possible consequences led Secretary of State Robert Lansing to say that the idea was full of "dynamite" and that states should treat it with great circumspection. Each state, depending upon its interests, defines the right to self-determination differently so as to reap benefits when the right can serve as a tool against other states and to avoid disadvantages when confronted with claims to self-determination within its own borders.

The U.N. Charter embodies self-determination of peoples as a principle in Article 1. By the time the General Assembly passed Resolution 1514 (XV) in 1960, Declaration on the Granting of Independence to Colonial Countries and Peoples, the principle had probably become a right of all peoples. The United States and Great Britain, and some other older states, wavered between calling it a right or a principle. The Soviet Union claims credit for introducing the idea into international society as a legally binding norm resulting from the October Revolution and untiring Soviet efforts in international councils. The Chinese Communists also recognize self-determination as a right, as do the states of Asia and Africa. Indeed, to these states the right has become a foremost norm of international law, matching sovereignty in importance, but is used by them as a political weapon against the First World, in support of the Third World, and for political ends also in their own world.

Legally, self-determination could mean interference in a state's internal affairs. It could also mean independence or secession for revolutionary or irredentist groups. The vagueness of the concept makes it serviceable for a multitude of political purposes, including antiracism and decolonization. For some states, self-determination is an internal matter. For other states, it is a matter of international concern.

There is much agreement, however, that self-determination means relieving a people from rule it opposes. But there is disagreement on how this end is to be achieved, when it has been achieved, and what collectivity represents a "people" entitled to self-determination. In addition, the older states have tended to attach qualifications to the grant of self-determination that can be subsumed under the heading of "readiness" or "preparedness" for self-government or independence. These states also favor plebiscites in some democratic form on whether a people wants independence, self-government, autonomy within a state, or something else.

The newer and totalitarian states have been less concerned with democratic plebiscites. In practice, they have taken it for granted that peoples of color under white (racist) governments or colonial rule want independent self-government. Thus, self-determination has become practically synonymous with absolute independence of a territory outside the existing state and with decolonization. These states limit self-government within a larger political unit to autonomy within a state or protected minority status. Any doubt has been cleared up by ex-colonial states referring to those entities entitled to self-determination aiming at independent states as being "geographically" separated from the state (so that the Soviet Union and China could lend their support because the Asian peoples in their empires are not "geographically" separated). For all practical purposes, self-determination directed toward forming a new, separate state has become limited to white-dominated colonies. When, for instance, the Tibetans asked for sovereign independence, China did not grant it. India acceded to the human rights covenants in 1979 on the understanding that the right to self-determination would apply only to peoples under foreign domination; the right would not apply to sovereign and independent states or to a part of one people or nation. Likewise, when some rebellious minorities in the USSR and the Baltic states demanded sovereign independence in 1989, President Gorbachev spoke of sovereignty and autonomy in somewhat nebulous terms, certainly not as decolonization. Although the Soviet Union recognized the illegality of the Stalin-Hitler Pact, which incorporated the Baltic states into the Soviet Union, he made clear that secession from the Soviet Union would not be tolerated (President Bush spoke of these demands as an "internal affair"). Except for actual decolonization, self-determination may not include the right to secession in the view and practice of states, at least not within their own borders.

The political reason for such a narrow interpretation of the right to self-determination is obvious. Many newer states in Asia and Africa would fall apart if self-determination were allowed to go as far as the formation of a new, independent state from part of an existing state—although the wording in the U.N. Charter and elsewhere could easily be understood in this sense. The newer states therefore argue—now that they are independent—that the right to self-determination ends where the right to the territorial integrity of the state begins. The African summit conference at Addis Ababa in 1963 suggested respect for existing boundaries (originally mostly created by the colonial powers). In 1967 the summit conference formally condemned "secession in any member state" when the Biafra issue was acute. The Charter of the Organization of African Unity does not directly refer to any right of self-determination. By tailoring the concept to fit Western colonialism or white racist regimes, many newer states of Asia and Africa have been able to attack such regimes without having to fear that the United Nations might deal with their own violent or oppressive methods against national minorities inside or peoples outside their borders. Incidentally, such tailoring also relieves these states from struggling with the problem of who is entitled to self-determination and how it is to be achieved.

These states have no monopoly on the expedient use of self-determination. Although Stalin maintained that self-determination must be a means of revolutionary struggles, he also said that it must be subordinated to socialism, and his country unhesitatingly interfered in Hungary in 1956, Czechoslovakia in 1968, and Afghanistan in the 1980s to prevent changes in regimes. U.S. presidents have declared they would find regimes engaging in genocide or enslavement of other peoples intolerable and the creation of Communist regimes in the U.S. continent impermissible. Yet the Soviet Union and the United States have an impressive record in interference with self-determination in other states, notwithstanding their championship of self-determination as a principle.

The disappearance of colonies is not likely to solve the problem of self-determination. Many disadvantaged minorities are scattered across the globe, and many others, although not disadvantaged, nevertheless agitate for at least more autonomy within their states. The narrowing of the concept by the previously colonized countries has not been useful to them. Nevertheless, these newer countries continue to use the concept in this way and are now applying it against attempts to gain control of their economies.

As a protection against this newer form of economic control, they were instrumental in the passage of General Assembly Resolution 1803 (XVII) in 1962 on permanent sovereignty over natural resources. Out of this resolution again emerges a right of states, not individuals. It could even be argued that this resolution and subsequent others based upon it diminish rather than increase the right of the individual. For they explicitly allow states to expropriate or nationalize resources in the national interest "which are recognized as overriding purely individual or private interests, both domestic and foreign."

The arrival of new states has not improved the fate of the individual under international law. Indeed, although they and the Communist states ostensibly champion the right to self-determination and rights of the individual, they also insist that the source and protector of these rights is the state, although it is the state that denies its citizens human rights. All too often, self-determination, instead of being a means for freeing people from unwanted political control, is being degraded into an instrument for narrow political purposes of the state. As a high-minded principle potentially entitling individuals directly under international law to be their own political masters, self-determination has been thoroughly corrupted.

REFERENCES AND READINGS FOR PART 5

Individuals: General

Dahm, G. *Die Stellung des Menschen im Völkerrecht unserer Zeit.* Tübingen, West Germany: J.C.B. Mohr, 1961.

Korowicz, Marek St. "The problem of the international personality of individuals." *AJIL* 50 (July 1956):533–562.

Mosler, Hermann. "The international society as a legal community." *ADIRC* 140 (1974 IV):1–320.

Norgaard, Carl A. *The Position of the Individual in International Law.* Copenhagen: Munksgaard, 1962.

Obieta, D. José A.C. *El derecho internacional de la persona humana.* Bilbao, Spain: Mensajero, 1974.

Alien Natural and Juridic Persons: Diplomatic Protection

Akehurst, Michael. "The use of force to protect nationals abroad." *International Relations* (London) 5 (May 1977):3–23.

Beyer, Sigurd. *Der diplomatische Schutz der Aktionäre im Völkerrecht.* Baden-Baden, West Germany: Nomos, 1977.

Caflisch, Lucius. *La protection des sociétés commerciales et des interêts indirects en droit international public.* The Hague: Martinus Nijhoff, 1969.

Dawson, Frank, and Ivan L. Head. *International Law, International Tribunals, and the Right of Aliens.* Syracuse, NY: Syracuse University Press, 1971.

Fourlanos, Gerassimo. *Sovereignty and the Ingress of Aliens.* Stockholm: Almqvist and Wiksell, 1986.

International Legal Center. *Law and Public Enterprise in Asia.* New York: Praeger, 1976.

Kronfol, Zouhair A. *Protection of Foreign Investments: A Study of International Law.* Leiden: A. W. Bijthoff, 1972.

Lillich, Richard B. *The Protection of Foreign Investments.* Syracuse, NY: Syracuse University Press, 1965.

————. "The diplomatic protection of nationals abroad: An elementary principle of international law under attack." *AJIL* 69 (April 1975):359–365.

Lowenfeld, Andreas F. "Diplomatic intervention in investment disputes." *Proceedings*, pp. 96–102. Washington, DC: American Society of International Law, 1976.

McDougal, Myres S., Harold D. Lasswell, and Lung-chu Chen. "Nationality and human rights: The protection of the individual in external areas." *Yale Law Journal* 83 (April 1974:)901–998.

————. "The protection of aliens from discrimination and world public order: Responsibility of states conjoined with human rights." *AJIL* 70 (July 1976):432–469.

Denial of Justice

See other sections on aliens.

Aliens: Private Rights and Expropriation

Akinsaya, Adeoye A. *The Expropriation of Multinational Property in the Third World.* Boulder, CO: Westview, 1980.

Katzarov, Konstantin. *The Theory of Nationalization.* The Hague: Martinus Nijhoff, 1964.

Lapres, Daniel A. "Principles of compensation for nationalised property." *Int. & Comp. L. Q.* 26 (January 1977 I):97–109.

Miller, Richard S., and Roland J. Stanger, eds. "Responsibility of states for injuries to the economic interest of aliens." *AJIL* 55 (July 1961):545–584.

White, Gillian. *Nationalisation of Foreign Property.* New York: Praeger, 1961.

Aliens: Government Contracts and Nationalization

Bowett, Derek W. "State contracts with aliens: Contemporary Developments on compensation for termination or breach." *BYIL* 59 (1988):49–74.

Carasco, Emily. "A nationalization compensation framework in the new international economic order." In *Third World Attitudes Toward International Law*, edited by Frederick E. Snyder and Surakiart Sathirathai, pp. 659–690. Dordrecht: Martinus Nijhoff, 1987.

Domke, Martin. "Foreign nationalization: Some aspects of contemporary international law." *AJIL* 55 (July 1961):585–616.

Francioni, Francesco. "Compensation for nationalisation of foreign property: The borderland between law and equity." *Int. & Comp. L. Q.* 24 (April 1975):255–283.

Lillich, Richard B. *The Valuation of Nationalized Property.* Charlottesville: University Press of Virginia, 1972.

Monreal, Eduardo N. *Nacionalisación y recuperación de recursos naturales ante la ley internacional.* Mexico City: Fondo de Cultura Económica, 1974.
Przetacznik, Franciszk. "Responsibility of the state for nationalization of foreign property." *Revue de Droit International de Sciences Diplomatiques et Politiques* 51 (July-September 1973):161–183.

Aliens: Personal Rights

Blaser, Pierre M. "La nationalité et la protection juridique internationale de l'individu." Ph.D. diss., University of Neuchatêl, Lausanne, 1962.
Goodwin-Gill, Guys S. *International Law and the Movement of Persons Between States.* Oxford: Clarendon, 1978.
Lillich, Richard B. "Duties of states regarding the civil rights of aliens." *ADIRC* 161 (1978 III):329–442.
————. *The Human Rights of Aliens in Contemporary International Law.* Manchester: Manchester University Press, 1984.
Plender, Richard. *International Migration Law.* Leiden: A. W. Sijthoff, 1972.

Aliens: Extradition and Asylum

Evans, Alona. "The new extradition treaties of the United States." *AJIL* 59 (April 1965):351–362.
García-Mora, Manuel R. "The nature of political offenses: A knotty problem of extradition law." *Virginia Law Review* 48 (November 1962):1226–1257.
Gold, Martin E. "Non-extradition for political offenses: The communist perspective." *Harvard International Law Journal* 11 (Winter 1970):191–211.
Shearer, Ivan A. *Extradition in International Law.* Dobbs Ferry, NY: Oceana, 1971.
Sinha, S. Prakash. *Asylum and International Law.* The Hague: Martinus Nijhoff, 1971.

Nationals and Human Rights

Beddard, Ralph. *Human Rights and Europe: A Study of the Machinery of Human Rights Protection of the Council of Europe.* London: Sweet and Maxwell, 1973.
Buergenthal, Thomas, ed. *Human Rights, International Law and the Helsinki Accord.* Montclair, NJ: Allanheld, Osmun, 1978.
Campbell, Tom et al., eds. *Human Rights: From Rhetoric to Reality.* Oxford: Basil Blackwell, 1986.
Carey, John. *U.N. Protection of Civil and Political Rights.* Syracuse, NY: Syracuse University Press, 1970.
Cassese, Antonio, ed. *UN/Law, Fundamental Rights: Two Topics in International Law.* Alphen, the Netherlands: Sijthoff and Nordhoff, 1979.
Cingranelli, David Louis, ed. *Human Rights Theory and Measurement.* New York: St. Martin's, 1988.

D'Amato, Anthony A. "The concept of human rights in international law." *Columbia Law Review* 82 (October 1982 VI):1110–1159.

Forsythe, David P. *Human Rights and U.S. Foreign Policy Congress Reconsidered.* Gainesville: University of Florida Press, 1988.

Gastil, Raymond D. *Freedom in the World.* New York: Freedom House, 1987–1988.

Haksar, Urmila. *Minority Protection and International Bill of Human Rights.* Bombay: Allied Publishers, 1974.

Henkin, Louis, ed. *The International Bill of Rights. The Covenant on Civil and Political Rights.* New York: Columbia University Press, 1981.

"The international human rights treaties: Some problems of policy and interpretation." *University of Pennsylvania Law Review* 126 (April 1978):886–929.

Jacobs, Francis G. *The European Convention on Human Rights.* Oxford: Clarendon, 1975.

Laqueur, Walter, and Barry Rubin. *The Human Rights Reader,* rev. ed. New York: New American Library, 1990.

Luard, Evan, ed. *The International Protection of Human Rights.* New York: Praeger, 1986.

McDougal, Myres, Harold D. Lasswell, and Lung-chu Chen. *Human Rights and World Public Order.* New Haven, CT: Yale University Press, 1980.

McKean, W. A. "The meaning of discrimination in international and municipal law." *BYIL* 44 (1970):177–192.

Meron, Theodor, ed. *Human Rights in International Law,* 2 vols. Oxford: Clarendon, 1984.

———. *Human Rights Law-Making in the United Nations: A Critique of Instruments and Process.* Oxford: Clarendon, 1986.

Milne, A.J.M. *Human Rights and Human Diversity.* Ithaca: State University of New York Press, 1986.

Mower, Glenn A. Jr. *Human Rights and American Foreign Policy: The Carter and Reagan Experiences.* Westport, CT: Greenwood, 1987.

Porter, Jack N., ed. *Genocide and Human Rights: A Global Anthology.* Washington, DC: University Press of America, 1982.

Ramcharan, B. G. *The Concept and Present Status of Human Rights: Forty Years After the Universal Declaration.* Dordrecht: Martinus Nijhoff, 1989.

Renteln, Alison Dundes. *International Human Rights Universalism Versus Relativism.* Newbury Park, CA: Sage, 1990.

Schwebel, S. "The Implementation of the International Convention on the Elimination of all Forms of Racial Discrimination." International Law Association. *Report of the Fifty-Fifth Conference New York, 1972,* p. 585–608. London: International Law Association, 1974.

Schwelb, Egon. "Law of treaties and human rights." *AV* 16 (1973 I):1–27.

Sieghart, Paul. *The International Law of Human Rights.* Oxford: Clarendon, 1983.

———. *The Lawful Rights of Mankind: An Introduction to the Legal Code of Human Rights.* Oxford: Oxford University Press, 1985.

Snyder, Frederick, E., and Surakiart Sathirathai, eds. *Third World Attitudes Toward International Law,* Part 4, pp. 259–360. Dordrecht: Martinus Nijhoff, 1987.

Sohn, Louis B., and Thomas Buergenthal. *International Protection of Human Rights.* Indianapolis: Bobbs-Merrill, 1973.

Takemoto, Masayuki. "The scrutiny system under international humanitarian law." *Japanese Annual of International Law* (Tokyo) 19 (1975):1–23.

Vierdag, E. W. *The Concept of Discrimination in International Law.* The Hague: Martinus Nijhoff, 1973.

Vincent, R. J., ed. *Foreign Policy and Human Rights: Issues and Responses.* Cambridge: Cambridge University Press, 1986.

Self-Determination and Neocolonialism

Buchheit, L. C. *Secession: The Legitimacy of Self-Determination.* New Haven, CT: Yale University Press, 1978.

Chowdry, Subrata R. "The status and norms of self-determination in contemporary international law." *Netherlands International Law Review* 24 (special issue 1977):72–84.

Dinstein, Yoram. "Collective human rights of peoples and minorities." *Int. & Comp. L. Q.* 25 (January 1976):102–120.

El-Ayouty, Yassin. *The United Nations and Decolonization: The Role of Afro-Asia.* The Hague: Martinus Nijhoff, 1971.

Emerson, Rupert. "Self-determination." *AJIL* 65 (July 1971):459–575.

Guilhandis, Jean-François. *Le droit des peuples à disposer d'eux-mêmes.* Grenoble: Presses Universitaires de Grenoble, 1976.

Menon, K. P. "The right to self-determination: A historical appraisal." *Revue de Droit International de Sciences Diplomatiques et Politiques* 53 (October-December 1975):272–281.

Ofuatey-Kodje, W. *The Principle of Self-Determination in International Law.* New York: Nellen, 1977.

Pomerance, Michla. "Methods of self-determination and the argument of 'primitiveness.'" *Canadian Yearbook of International Law* 12 (1974):38-66.

———. *Self-Determination in Law and Practice: The New Doctrine in the United Nations.* The Hague: Martinus Nijhoff, 1982.

Sinha, S. Prakash. "Has self-determination become a principle of international law today?" *Indian Journal of International Law* 14 (July-December 1974):332–361.

Sureda, A. Rigo. *The Evolution of the Right of Self-Determination: A Study of United Nations Practice.* Leiden: A. W. Sijthoff, 1973.

Umozurike, U. O. *Self-Determination in International Law.* Hamden, CT: Archon Books, 1972.

Veiter, Theodor. *System eines internationalen Volksgruppenrechts.* Vienna: W. Baumüller, 1972.

Yonah, Alexander, and Robert A. Friedlander. *Self-Determination: National, Regional and Global Dimensions.* Boulder, CO: Westview, 1980.

PART 6
INTERNATIONAL ACTIONS WITH LEGAL CONSEQUENCES

Social order requires that the socially relevant actions of society's members be governed by certain principles or have certain consequences in general. These principles and consequences apply independently of the members' will. They apply in addition to and regardless of any specific consequences or purposes intended by the members. They do not have to be spelled out with every international transaction because they are fundamental. They form, so to speak, the framework within which states and other subjects act.

These principles and consequences can be classified into four categories, all universally agreed upon in international society in general but not in detail. One is good faith, permeating all international actions. The second is consent, expressing the intended and voluntary (sovereign) character of legal consequences. The third is responsibility, committing the actor legally to the consequences of his or her actions, regardless of will or intent. The fourth is humanitarianism. Although not so generally recognized, the principle was assumed, for instance, in the *Corfu Channel* case (1949). The International Court of Justice called humanitarianism elementary and absolute.

The specific meaning of good faith depends upon the given situation and contemporary mores. In general, it requires that a party must carry out obligations honestly, without mental reservations or deceitfulness, and must fulfill the letter and spirit of a commitment. Numerous international declarations and juridic decisions refer to good faith in this sense. The preamble of the Vienna Convention on the Law of Treaties (1969) notes, for instance, "that the principles of free consent and good faith and the *pacta sunt servanda* rule are universally recognized." Equally universal is disagreement over the meaning of good faith in concrete cases. In the *Right of Passage over Indian Territory (Portugal v. India) (Merits)* case (1960), Portugal claimed a right of passage over certain Indian territory between some Portuguese enclaves in the Indian Peninsula. Portugal argued that Indian regulations and control of passage through its territory should be exercised in good faith. The International Court of Justice found on this point that India had acted in good faith given the tensions in the region following the 1954 overthrow of Portugal's rule over the enclaves.

Because good faith is a principle in virtually all legal systems and informs the manner in which rights are to be exercised and obligations fulfilled, it is not basically a source of rights and obligations itself. Good faith is more a quality of a state's legal behavior. Largely for this reason, there can be much disagreement about whether good faith has been applied in a given situation, and as in so many cases of interpretations, it lends itself to extensive political manipulation.

Consent means that the subject agrees to the circumstances creating the legal consequences. States have virtually unlimited capacity to create legal consequences by consent. International organizations possess such capacity within the limits of their legal personality. Consent is of particular importance in international law because states can be bound only in conformity with their will and because they can create through consent their own international law. They can now do so, within limits, even in regard to affecting *ius cogens* (peremptory norms) under Article 53 of the Vienna Convention on the Law of Treaties (1969).

The form of consent is determined largely by the nature of the transaction. Because of its importance and states' reluctance to bind themselves, consent cannot be presumed when there is doubt about its existence. If consent is claimed as having been given formlessly, tacitly, or implicitly, the behavior must exhibit it unequivocally. In the *Island of Palmas* case (1928), the award stated that silence could not be interpreted as consent if a reaction from the silent party was not to be expected. In the *Norwegian Fisheries (United Kingdom v. Norway)* case (1951, p. 138), the International Court of Justice pronounced Norway's method of delimiting its territorial waters legally binding upon other states because its "general toleration" by foreign states for many decades was an unchallenged fact. The Permanent Court of International Justice decided in the *Eastern Greenland* case (1933, p. 71) that a statement by Norway's foreign minister, Nils Claus Ihlen, in the course of a conversation with his Danish colleague that his country "would not make any difficulty" in the settlement of the Greenland question created a binding obligation for Norway. Finally, in the *Temple of Preah Vihear (Cambodia v. Thailand)* case (1962), the International Court of Justice held that Thailand's silence for forty years after having seen a map showing the temple on the Cambodian side of the frontier prevented it from claiming ownership of the temple. These decisions were strictly bound to each case. No generally valid rules for all cases emerged.

Responsibility means that a subject is accountable for some wrongful action. Responsibility is thus a narrower term—at least as used in international law—than accountability, which means to be generally answerable for an act and its consequences—good or bad, right or wrong. The act goes on the "account" of the actor. Responsibility in legal parlance is connected to an act or omission breaking a legal norm. The U.S.-Mexican Special Claims Commission in the *Dickson Car Wheel Co. (U.S. v. United Mexican States)* case (1931, p. 678) said, "Under International Law apart from any convention, in order that a State may incur responsibility, it is necessary that an unlawful international act be imputed to it, that is, that there exist a violation of a duty imposed by an international juridical standard." In other words, international responsibility requires a wrongful act causing damage or injury for which the actor must provide some form of reparation or satisfaction to the injured party. This principle implements all international norms. Without it there is no international law. For if there is no responsibility, there can hardly be an obligation to obey it.

Recently, states have shown a tendency, often for political reasons, to acquire goodwill and to make themselves accountable (not merely responsible) for repairing damage or injury caused by legal acts (for example, damage by a nuclear ship in a foreign port). Because such accountability is still not customary law, it can arise only as a result of a treaty or a unilateral declaration.

Responsibility by its nature is independent of the parties' will. But because its prerequisite is the existence of an obligation, responsibility is dependent upon a preexisting violation of a legal norm.

17
UNILATERAL TRANSACTIONS

Nature of Transaction

Legally relevant international transactions are those by subjects of international law having desired and direct legal consequences for other states. Such transactions are limited formally in their consequences by the principle that one subject cannot obligate another subject without the latter's consent. Nevertheless, several types of unilateral transaction by a state have legal consequences affecting other states. There is usually no problem when a unilateral transaction creates rights and benefits for another state. But a problem can arise when another state is disadvantageously affected by the transaction. When a state by unilateral action occupies unoccupied no-man's-land, other states are excluded from it, and they have to treat the acting state as the sovereign, providing that all necessary conditions have been fulfilled. On several occasions a state unilaterally derecognized an existing government (for example, in 1979 the United States derecognized the Republic of China and recognized the People's Republic of China, and in 1940 Great Britain withdrew recognition of Italian sovereignty over Ethiopia).

Whether a state can undo a unilateral transaction depends upon the nature of the transaction. It could happen that through the behavior of affected states, the transaction leads to a treaty and withdrawal is no longer possible. It could also be that withdrawal would greatly damage other states that have relied upon the unilateral transaction, in which case a question of responsibility of the acting state might arise (for example, when a state promised financial aid). In general, the rule that certain unilateral transactions may have legal consequences for other as well as the transacting state rests upon a fundamental requirement of social order. The members of society must be able to rely upon behavior in good faith of all other members. *Pacta sunt servanda* applies not only to completed bilateral agreements but also to every subject standing by its words and actions. Ultimately, the issue goes beyond law and is simply the consequence of the social fact that what happens anywhere is likely to affect conditions elsewhere—a fact law cannot ignore. The nature of the consequence depends upon the nature of the transaction as well as the intent behind it.

Recognition

Recognition as a unilateral transaction has been dealt with earlier in this book in connection with new states and new governments, but it can be applied to many other situations. Recognition simply means that a fact is acknowledged as legally relevant and can apply to many different situations.

Notification

Notification is a communication from one legal subject to another about facts or events of legal relevance. Examples include information to another state about the outbreak of war, the establishment of territorial limits, a change in the form or leadership of the government, or the mining of sea-lanes normally open to foreign shipping. In this age of rocketry, many states are publishing warnings to foreign shipping to stay out of certain areas of the high seas because tests are being conducted. This has become such common practice that it may develop into a legitimate interference with the freedom of the high seas in the name of "reasonable use."

Declarations

Declarations are a very broad category. Some may simply be actions without further legal consequences for other states, such as an expression of an intention or outlines of future policies—which, however, could amount to a warning. Many unilateral declarations of international bodies fall into this category. Declarations become transactions with legal consequences when their wording, their context, or the intention of their maker indicates unequivocally that they are meant to have legally relevant content. Declarations of war or neutrality are examples.

Apropos of the public statements by France in 1974 that it would no longer undertake atmospheric nuclear tests in the Pacific, the International Court of Justice in the *Nuclear Test (Australia v. France)* case (1974, p. 267) stated that it was "well recognized that declarations made by way of unilateral acts, concerning legal or factual situations, may have the effect of creating legal obligations." If an interpretation of an act demonstrates that the state intended to be bound, it is "legally required to follow a course of conduct consistent with the declaration." No reaction from other states is required to give the declaration that legal effect. (France ceasing nuclear atmospheric tests and the United States ceasing mining Nicaraguan harbors, although both refused to appear before the International Court of Justice, may be indications that public pressure may force states into legal behavior.)

Promises

A promise is a declaration in which the maker commits itself to another subject to a specific action. The difference between a promise and a declaration is that the former always involves an obligation. When states announce that they are planning to devote 1 percent of their gross national income to foreign aid, this is a declaration with no particular obligation toward any particular state or group of states. When a state declares that it will donate $1 million to another specified state in foreign aid, it is making a legally binding promise.

Protest

A protest is a declaration denying the legality or legitimacy of a fact or event. The most frequent purpose of a protest is to prevent the interpretation of silence as tacit agreement or acquiescence. On several occasions, international courts and tribunals have made such interpretations, as, for instance, in the *Norwegian Fisheries (United Kingdom v. Norway)* case (1951, p. 139) and in the *Minquiers and Ecréhous* case (1953). In both cases, the International Court of Justice decided that long practice by one state without protests by any other state established a right for the practicing state. If a protest was reasonably to be expected but is not forthcoming, the silent state or organization can no longer deny the legality of the fact or event (estoppel).

Renunciation

In a renunciation, a subject voluntarily and deliberately abandons a right. This can be done expressly or tacitly. But before an assumption of renunciation can be made, conclusive evidence that renunciation has occurred is required. For instance, failure to exercise a right during a long period of time cannot be presumed to indicate renunciation because in international law rights do not expire through mere lapse of time. (This statement should not be confused with the loss of a right through prescription. In that case, a state may lose a right that another state has exercised for a long time uncontested by the first state.) Nevertheless, long neglect by a state of its supposed rights may justify a belief in their nonexistence and be evidence to that effect, as the arbitrator of the Mixed Claims Commission in the *Gentini (Italy v. Venezuela)* case (1903, p. 730) pointed out. Gentini had waited thirty-one years before making a claim against the Venezuelan government. The arbitrator rejected the claim because the long wait justified a belief in its nonexistence. The "necessities of mankind" required that an end to a dispute should be brought about by the efflux of time.

Interdependent Unilateral Transactions

Unilateral transactions by states may be mutually dependent without becoming bilateral or multilateral transactions. A state may make an offer to another state. This is one unilateral transaction having the legal consequence that acceptance by the other state, another unilateral transaction, may create a treaty that then becomes a bilateral transaction having its own legal consequences. Each state can withdraw its transaction before the other has obtained knowledge of it. But once the two unilateral transactions have created a treaty, no such unilateral withdrawal is possible.

18
MULTILATERAL ACTIONS (TREATIES)

Value of Treaties

Treaties are the bilateral or multilateral transactions of international law. They dominate the legal system because they are now the main sources of rules binding the behavior of states. They also regulate the bulk of international transactions. Moreover, a treaty (or else a non-solution) is the main legal alternative for settling international disputes now that the use of force has become illegal.

The contemporary state of international relations adds further to the value of treaties. They correspond better than other sources of law to the dynamics of the international society. As was pointed out in the discussion of the sources of law, treaties are the best response to the growing volume and relevance of international interaction, to the increasing speed of change in the international society, and to the expanding need for detail, specificity, and precision in international economic activities.

This value of treaties does not make customary law obsolete. Often treaties are little more than the codification of customary law. Customary law often contains the universal legal norms of international law, usually not repeated but assumed and underlying treaties. And, perhaps most important, the existence of a treaty does not rule out the continuing development of customary law, which affects treaties, modifies treaty law, and brings it up to date. Otherwise, in the present rapidly changing world, the advantages of treaties may turn into disadvantages if they remain unchangeable. They could rapidly become dead letters. The International Court of Justice (*Nicaragua (Merits, Judgment)* [1986, pp. 107–109]) in a lengthy elaboration concluded "customary law continues to exist alongside treaty law" even where the two categories of law have an identical content. But the principle of sovereign equality requires that treaties remain equal in effect for the parties and presumably dominant in case of differences with customary law.

Most of the newer and Communist states prefer treaties to all other types of international law because of their consensual character. Having been nonexistent or in a minority when much international law was created, these states are now trying to recoup lost opportunities of participating in the making of law by insisting that only a state's consent to a legal norm binds that state and that all states should have the right to participate in multilateral treaties from which general rules of international law are likely to emerge. This last argument is an admission, of course, that treaties containing legal norms may have an impact beyond the signatories—either leading to or confirming general international law. Communist states ascribe special significance to treaties because in their view relations between states in a multicultural world can be based only or mainly upon explicit agreement.

The long history of treaty making enabled states to conclude the Vienna Convention on the Law of Treaties in 1969 and the Vienna Convention on the Law of Treaties Between the States and International Organizations or Between International Organizations in 1986. This codification provides some clarity, but its comprehensiveness is not synonymous with completeness or with the need for interpretation in given cases.

Nature of Treaties

A treaty is an agreement under international law between two (bilateral) or among more than two (multilateral) states for the achievement of the purpose specified in the agreement. It is a meeting of wills, a consensus. Whenever such an agreement is achieved, it represents a treaty, whatever name the parties give to it, and the legal consequences international law attaches to treaties apply.

Because many names have been given to such agreements and because the conclusion of such an agreement can be quite formless (for example, oral or conduct indicating mutual consent), the existence of a treaty must be concluded from the available evidence regarding the will of the parties. In most instances, there is little doubt when states have concluded a treaty. The doubt begins when the meaning of a treaty is to be defined. For the major legal consequence of a treaty intended by the parties is to bind each other to the fulfillment of obligations and the enjoyment of rights—with states preferring the latter to the former. Each side will attempt to interpret the meaning in its favor.

As the purposes of a treaty are virtually unlimited (the limit is an illegal purpose), attempts have been made to categorize treaties into bilateral or multilateral, ordinary or lawmaking, conditional or unconditional, self-executing or requiring implementation, legal or political. These categories are merely descriptive. Occasionally, political use is made of them (for example, between legal and political agreements), or they may be relevant for municipal law and politics. From the international legal standpoint, there is no difference in the norms governing all treaties. All treaties are binding under the rule *pacta sunt servanda*. A party, whether a state or an international organization, cannot invoke its internal law as justifying failure to perform.

Capacity and Authority to Conclude Treaties

Only subjects of international law can conclude treaties: states, international organizations, exceptionally the Roman Catholic church (as distinct from the Vatican state), and individual states of a federation. Indeed, these subjects are presumed to have capacity to conclude treaties. If for reasons of internal legislation they do not have it, a treaty concluded by them is nevertheless valid unless a violation of internal law was manifest or concerned an internal legal rule of "fundamental importance" (Article 46, Vienna Convention on the Law of Treaties [1969]; hereafter in this chapter cited as 1969 convention).

The organ of the subject entitled to conclude a treaty is a person with full powers or a person customarily in the practice of the given subject considered by other subjects to represent the subject for the purpose of concluding treaties. Persons with full powers include a head of a state or its foreign minister. Persons acting as representatives but without full powers include an ambassador or a head of a mission, who can "adopt" texts of treaties (the second step, after negotiation, in the making of treaties) but not conclude them. Nevertheless, any act relating to the conclusion of a treaty performed by an unauthorized person can afterward be confirmed and thereby validated by the subject (1969 convention, Article 7 and 8). If an organ of a subject exceeds its powers in concluding a treaty, the subject can claim invalidity of the treaty only if the other party to the treaty was informed previous to the conclusion of the limitation on the organ's power (Article 47). If the subject's organ concludes the treaty as a result of direct or indirect coercion or corruption, the treaty is invalid (Articles 50 and 51). As long as wars were legal, peace treaties were legal. Because wars are illegal now, peace treaties are equally so.

Under Article 52, a treaty is void if its conclusion was achieved by the threat or use of force in violation of the principles of the U.N. Charter. Iceland, for instance, declared an exchange of notes with the United Kingdom in 1961 void because it was under "difficult circumstances"—the British Navy was threatening Iceland at the time. The International Court of Justice in the *Fisheries Jurisdiction (United Kingdom . . . v. Iceland) (Merits, Judgment)* case (1974) agreed with Iceland on this point.

The controversial nature of the concept of force has made the validity of some treaties questionable. If the interpretation of the newer and Communist states is accepted—that "force" is not limited to violence but may include political, economic, and social pressures of various kinds—it would become almost impossible to determine the validity of a treaty. Most treaties result from the pressures and counterpressures between the parties.

Closely related to this problem is the refusal of China and other states to recognize "unequal" treaties as valid. The question here is the meaning of "unequal." It could refer to the manner in which a treaty was concluded or to the substance of the treaty or both. To paraphrase Anatole France: A treaty granting equal rights and obligations upon the parties is not necessarily any more equal than a law forbidding the prince and the beggar from sleeping under the bridges of the Seine. Soviet writers argue that treaties that are forced upon a state, that enslave a state, that disregard the principle of equality, or that do not correspond to the "real will" of a party to the treaty are invalid as unequal. But these same writers provide no definition of these concepts. Chinese writers emphasize that mutual benefit and equality are connected. A treaty of mutual benefit in form but not in substance (because, for instance, the parties are unequal in economic status) is not an equal treaty and hence is invalid. Moreover, the obligations of the parties must be "identical and reciprocal" to make an equal treaty. In the practice of these states, the terms are variously defined, thereby making the application of the principles quite flexible and subservient to political requirements. The Chinese, for instance, approve the veto right of the major states in the Security Council. The Soviets insisted upon rights against China on the basis of tsarist and clearly unequal treaties. The Third World's New International Economic Order proposes inequalities favorable to its members (to compensate for past injustices against them).

Consent

An essential part of a treaty is the mutual consent of the parties. If the consent is faulty, the nature of the fault determines whether the treaty is valid or not. If a party was in error about a fact or a situation that it assumed existed and that formed an essential basis for its consent, the party can invalidate the treaty (1969 convention, Article 48). But if the party itself contributed to the error or was forewarned of the possibility of error, it is bound to the treaty. If all parties are in error, the treaty is invalid. Fraud makes consent faulty and the treaty invalid (Article 49) because a party was under a misconception as to what it consented to or why.

International customary law prescribes no particular form for the consent and leaves it to the parties. The 1969 convention, Article 11, suggests signature, ratification, acceptance, approval or accession, and exchange of documents; the article then defines what behavior constitutes these various forms. The several steps the formation of a treaty passes through, from negotiation to final conclusion, could make doubtful when a concordance of wills or opinions (consent) has been achieved, the more so as some of these forms (for example, signature) may be either the final step or a preliminary step. In view of the large number of treaties needed under modern conditions, the tendency has been to simplify procedures at least for the less important treaties. But many newer states oppose this development. They are very cautious about binding themselves to treaties, and, they claim, they lack some of the experience and expertise necessary to recognize quickly all the implications of a treaty. Insisting upon all the formalities, especially ratification, gives them a better (or at any rate longer) opportunity to examine their commitments.

Until consent has been given, the treaty is not binding upon the parties. But the 1969 convention in Article 18 stipulates that after signature and before the final step, or that between the final step and the entry into force of the treaty, the parties shall not defeat the object and purpose of the treaty.

When a treaty (usually a multilateral treaty) is open to accession by states not parties to it, the method of consent by these states is either specified in the treaty (usually "acceptance") or is within the choice of the acceding state. According to customary law and Article 5 of the 1969 convention, a treaty is accessible when the parties concluding the treaty agree that it shall be. But many newer states argue that in regard to "law-making" treaties, accessibility is not a matter of consent by the original parties but a matter of the right of all states wishing to accede. Otherwise, they insist, international society could again be dominated by a few major powers. Some of these states go further and argue that they have a right to participate in the making of such a treaty. In support of their contention, they cite the advisory opinion of the Court of International Justice in the *Reservations on the Convention on the Prevention and Punishment of the Crime of Genocide* (1951, p. 24) case, in which the Court stated that the convention seeks to accomplish the highest moral purpose. In such a convention, there can be no question of individual advantage or disadvantages of states or of the maintenance of a perfect contractual balance between rights and duties. "The object and purpose of the Genocide Convention imply that it was the intention of the General Assembly and the States which adopted it that as many States as possible should participate."

Reservations, Amendments, Modifications

In this same opinion, the Court of International Justice elaborated at length on the effect of the reservations a party may have in concluding or acceding to a multilateral treaty. A reservation is the exclusion or modification of the legal effect of certain provisions of a treaty (1969 convention, Article 2). A reservation is equivalent to a new offer or a counteroffer by the reserving party or, in other words, a change in the nature of its consent, which therefore requires a corresponding change in the consent of the other parties to produce a concordance of wills.

The problem, which does not arise in bilateral treaties, is that some parties may consent to the reservation while others may object and therefore consider the reserving party as having rejected the treaty and be no party at all, which in turn may make the entire treaty uninteresting to these objecting parties. Such a situation could be legally very confusing indeed. Yet states make reservations quite frequently, and a solution to the problem is imperative. For this reason, practice often is to stipulate in the treaty itself the permissibility and effect of reservations.

When a treaty has been silent on reservations, views have differed widely in the past on the solution of the problem. There was agreement only that the norms governing a reservation were merely a special application of the general principle of consent as the basis of a treaty. This principle allowed the parties to make the reservation and then accept or reject it. But the question remained open what the legal effect was for all the other parties. Was the treaty invalid for all, invalid only between the reserving and the objecting parties, invalid for the reserving party, invalid for the parties not accepting the reservation, or partially invalid?

The International Court introduced as a major criterion whether the reservation was "compatible with the object and purpose" of the treaty. The Court suggested consideration of various alternatives in that light without being able to define compatibility. The Secretariat of the League of Nations and of the United Nations had followed the principle that a reservation was admissible before the treaty entered into force and after its entry with the consent of all parties to the treaty.

The 1969 convention (Articles 19–23) stipulates in some detail the admissibility, forms, and legal consequences of reservations. The convention follows in principle the opinions of the International Court— that is, the reservation by a party does not necessarily invalidate the entire treaty. How it remains valid among the various parties is made dependent upon a combination of their consent with the reservation's compatibility with the object of the treaty.

In the absence of a neutral agency to define compatibility authoritatively, this solution of the problem suffers, as so many others do, from the subjectivity of the criterion. Each state is its own judge. Many newer states urge liberality in allowing reservations. They hope that when they are unable to prevent conclusion of a treaty or to achieve a desired modification, a reservation allows a better adjustment to their own interests.

The parties may wish to amend or modify an existing treaty. Such a method may prevent a treaty from becoming a dead letter altogether. The proposed method in this case is the same as the method that governs the conclusion of a treaty—unless the parties agree otherwise. Because in the case of multilateral treaties problems similar to those arising in relation to reservations may exist, the 1969 convention (Articles 39–41) details possibilities and procedures. The convention thus deals with one problem of peaceful change in international society. By regulating revision of treaties (read adjustment to new situations), the convention at least provides for regular methods if revision is desired. Article 14 of the U.N. Charter deals with the same problem when it empowers the General Assembly to "recommend measures for the peaceful adjustment of any situation, regardless of origin, which it deems likely to impair the general welfare or friendly relations among nations." But neither of these methods can force a party to a treaty to agree to its revisions. The fact remains that the conflict between the essential need for the fulfillment of treaties and the equally essential need of adjustments to new social conditions can be settled only by political, not legal, means. These problems raised by social change highlight politics as the primary instrument of social order.

Object and Purpose

The object of every treaty is to create obligations for one or all of the parties. Because treaties are subject to general rules of international law, the limit upon states to choose any object or purpose they wish to pursue with the treaty is their legality. Legal prohibition of an object or purpose makes the treaty invalid from the beginning. There are several categories of such prohibitions.

A treaty is invalid when it conflicts with an existing peremptory norm or becomes invalid when it conflicts with a new peremptory norm (1969 convention, Articles 53 and 64). It is invalid when its purpose is immoral or physically impossible. But what immorality is cannot be defined any better in international law than, for instance, obscenity can be defined in municipal law. A treaty is invalid insofar (or possibly altogether) as its obligations are inconsistent with previously established and continuing obligations. The obligations of members of the United Nations under Article 103 of the charter prevail over all other obligations. Finally, a treaty is invalid when its purpose is to impose obligations upon a third party.

Entry into Force

A treaty enters into force (becomes binding) after all requirements of international law have been fulfilled and the proper moment by the parties chosen has arrived. The 1969 convention (Article 24) stipulates that a treaty enters into force either according to agreement among the parties or "as soon as consent to be bound by the treaty has been established for all the negotiating states." The convention thus relies upon customary law. If the treaty is valid according to the behavior of the parties, the treaty's object and purpose, and the authority of the parties' organs to conclude it, the last step—to "establish consent"—is whatever the parties intend it to be. Usually, this last step is either the exchange among the parties or the deposit with the agreed agency in due course of the signatures or ratifications, but this step can also be a less formal measure. The opinion of the Permanent Court of International Justice in the *Territorial Jurisdiction of the International Commission of the River Oder* (1929, p. 20) that under "ordinary rule" of international law treaties are binding only "by virtue of ratification" is supported neither by state practice nor by the convention. Conditional or partial ratification is tantamount to an offer for a new, different treaty. The other party may accept the offer and a new treaty is born. If the offer is rejected, the planned treaty is dead.

Interpretation

Once a treaty has entered into force, the question of its meaning may arise. Parties may interpret the treaty differently, even when both or all act in good faith, as they are expected to do. Differences can lead either to an agreed authentic interpretation by the parties themselves or to an interpretation by a third party: an arbitration tribunal or an international court. International law does not—because it cannot— provide guidance for "correct" interpretation of a treaty. All that can be and has been done is to suggest what factors should be considered, what methods should be followed, and what principles should be applied. The 1969 convention, Articles 31–33, stipulates some of these, following fairly closely the voluminous jurisprudence on this issue.

The three basic factors to be considered in arriving at a proper interpretation are the ordinary meaning of words used in the treaty, the intentions of the parties negotiating (not later acceding to) the treaty, and the object and purpose of the treaty. There is no predetermination of the emphasis to be placed on any one factor. Because all three go into the making of the treaty, that none should prevail over the others is likely to yield the nearest desired meaning of the treaty. (If an interpretation of the words leads to an apparent defeat of the treaty's purpose, the interpretation is not adequate.) The achievement of this result affects the methods and principles of the interpretation. A given method or principle should not be applied if its use would exclude one of the remaining factors.

Within the framework of this overall desirable result and in the absence of any international legal norms, any or all methods for achieving the result are permissible. The Permanent Court of International Justice in the *Factory at Chorzów (Jurisdiction)* case (1927, p. 24) exhausted almost all possibilities by referring to a treaty's "historical development," "terminology," "grammatical and logical meaning," and "function" as methods. But both International Courts have consistently held—for example, in *Postal Service of Danzig* (1925), *Lotus* (1927), *Conditions of Admission of a State to the United Nations* (1948), and *Competence of the General Assembly for the Admission of a State to the United Nations* (1950)— that if the text of a convention is sufficiently clear in itself, there is no occasion to resort to preparatory work. But the Court also pointed out in the *Postal Service of Danzig* case that although the ordinary wording of a treaty should be the primary method of interpreting it, this method is inadequate if it leads to "unreasonable or absurd" results. In that case—as the Court maintained in *Factory at Chorzów*, *Rights of Minorities in Upper Silesia (Minority Schools)* (1928), and *Competence of the International Labor Organization with Respect to Agricultural Labor* (1922)— the meaning and the purpose of the treaty may be obtained from the arguments of the parties or their behavior subsequent to the conclusion of the treaty.

Because words may have several meanings, the Court in the *Factory at Chorzów* case also held that the meaning of the terminology used in one case cannot simply be transferred to another case. That meaning will have to be discovered each time anew by considering the entire article or section of the treaty, its historical development, its preparatory work, or the broader context and the prevailing conditions during the conclusion of the treaty. This opinion has been expressed in many cases, among them *Interpretation of the Statute of Memel Territory (Judgment)* (1932), *Access to or Anchorage in the Port of Danzig of Polish War Vessels* (1931), *Lighthouses Case Between France and Greece* (1934), *Interpretation of Article 3 Part 2 of the Treaty of Lausanne (Frontier Between Iraq and Turkey) (Mosul Case)* (1925), *Acquisition of Polish Nationality* (1923), and *Competence of the International Labor Organization with Respect to Agricultural Labor* (1923). At times, the Court even interpreted the meaning of a treaty "by inference" from the "entire framework" of the treaty (*Competence of the International Labor Organization to Regulate, Incidentally, the Personal Work of the Employer* [1926, p. 18]) or "within the framework of the entire legal system prevailing at the time of the interpretation" (*Legal Consequences for States of the Continued Presence of South Africa in Namibia* [1971, p. 31]).

The principles to be applied are based on common sense, on the assumption that states do not want to commit themselves more than necessary, or on a combination of both. Here belongs the principle of effectiveness—that an interpretation must give effectiveness to a treaty rather than destroy it—as the International Court pointed out in the *Acquisition of Polish Nationality* case (1923).

But the application of this principle, warned the International Court of Justice in the *Interpretation of Peace Treaties with Bulgaria, Hungary and Romania (Second Phase)* (1952), should not lead to a reading into the treaty provisions contrary to its letter and spirit. The possibility exists, however, that the parties may wish to continue the object and purpose of the treaty even though the conditions needed to achieve them may change greatly over time as a result, for instance, of technological developments unforeseen at the conclusion of the treaty. In such a case, the U.S. District Court (New York) in *Eck v. United Arab Airlines* (1964, p. 812) decided that the proper procedure is "to examine the treaty as a whole, along with its history, and, in particular, to look into the problems which it was intended to solve." This procedure may then lead to realization of the intent of the treaty by means not necessarily covered by a literal reading of the text.

Another principle is that in case of doubt the interpretation that involves the minimum of obligations for the parties should be chosen. So said the Permanent Court of International Justice in the *Interpretation of Article 3 Part 2 of the Treaty of Lausanne* case (1925) and in the *Lotus* case (1927). The trouble with this principle is that reducing the obligations of one party diminishes the rights of the other or possibly increases its obligations. Somewhere lost in the middle between these two principles is the principle, stated by the International Court of Justice in the *Right of Passage over Indian Territory (Portugal v. India) (Merits)* case (1960), that a treaty should be interpreted to yield an effect in conformity with rather than contrary to existing international law.

Almost no principle has been followed for differences in interpretation when a treaty was concluded in several authentic languages. In some cases, the narrower meaning has been used, in others the more liberal meaning has been applied, and in yet others an interpretation has been used compatible with all texts. The 1969 convention suggests in Article 33 that the meaning shall be used that best reconciles the text with the object and purpose of the treaty—which, unfortunately, may well lead to circular reasoning or a begging of the question.

The charter and constitutions of international organizations represent a special case for interpretation. Often political organs of the organizations interpret the meaning of these instruments. Where the interpretation has been delegated to the International Court of Justice, as in the cases of *Reparation for Injuries Suffered in the Service of the United Nations* (1949) or *Certain Expenses of the United Nations* (1962), the Court has tended to interpret in the light of the general structure of the basic instrument and especially of the functions assigned to the organization. The Court has then granted to the organizations means for fulfilling those functions that were not mentioned in the basic instrument. In other words, the Court has enlarged the power of the organization to permit a more effective fulfillment, or even any fulfillment at all, of its functions.

Although the entire problem of interpretation is especially significant in relation to treaties, it exists in many other contexts of the law. There is almost always a subjective element present, which is why a dispute over meaning initially develops. What this subjectivity implies for the parties is that the meaning of law and treaty is not fully known until the judge determines it. In this sense, the judge makes the law or the treaty, although he or she would strenuously deny this. Yet if law or treaty were incontrovertibly clear, the judge would be superfluous. Within states, especially democratic states, there are enough safeguards (appeal, legislature, public opinion) of the citizens' interests to make the situation acceptable without much questioning. In international society these safeguards hardly exist. Power is the ultimate arbiter and the more powerful state is likely to win—to the dismay of the weaker state and almost everyone else.

Termination and Suspension

A treaty may be terminated or its operation suspended for all parties, or for one of the parties to a multilateral treaty, for a number of reasons. The parties can agree to terminate the treaty either by setting a date in the treaty, by stipulating a (resolutory) condition under which the treaty shall be terminated, or by expressly or implicitly agreeing to do so (Articles 54, 56, 59, and 60). When a treaty is silent on a date for termination or on withdrawal or denunciation, opinion is divided on whether silence excludes termination if that exclusion is implied by the intention of the parties or the nature of the treaty. In the case of multilateral treaties, the reduction in the number of parties through legitimate withdrawals below the number required for the entry into force of the treaty is not by itself a reason for termination (1969 convention, Article 55). All or part of a treaty may be suspended (instead of terminated) under conditions very similar to those applying to termination (convention, Articles 57 and 58).

A treaty may also terminate as a result of its voidance (as distinct from its invalidity *ab initio*) for several reasons. The performance by one of the parties may become impossible after conclusion of the treaty (if, for example, an object indispensable for the execution of the treaty disappears permanently). In that case a party may claim termination of the treaty or withdraw from it, providing that this party has not caused the impossibility (1969 convention, Article 61). Where the situation is not permanent, a party may call for suspension of the treaty for the duration of the situation. If one of the parties disappears, the treaty becomes void, or the principle of succession may apply.

The impossibility does not necessarily have to be an absolute physical impossibility. It may be a moral impossibility, when, for instance, a party would suffer unduly from performance. In the *Russian Indemnity (Russia-Turkey)* case (1912), the Arbitration Tribunal granted that performance could not be expected if it would imperil the state's existence. Because states rarely disappear these days, "existence" must be broadly defined and may include bankruptcy (for example, the repayment of loans by Third World countries). When an act of God prevents a party from performing permanently or temporarily, the treaty is void or suspended.

Another case of voidance is the invocation of the *clausula rebus sic stantibus* by one of the parties. This controversial clause is defined in the 1969 convention, Article 62 as follows: "A fundamental change of circumstances which has occurred with regard to those existing at the time of the conclusion of the treaty, and which was not foreseen by the parties." Unless a party itself has produced the change by any breach of any obligation to a party of the treaty or the treaty establishes a boundary, the party may invoke the clause if the circumstances in question constitute an essential basis of consent of the parties to the treaty or if the effect of change radically transforms the obligations still to be performed under the treaty.

The exact meaning and applicability of the clause are much debated. But whatever position is taken, many of its details are purely subjective, and no two parties have in practice ever agreed upon a justification for invoking the clause. International courts have avoided deciding any of the clause's fundamental aspects, although the International Court of Justice in the *Fisheries Jurisdiction* case (1973) ventured a pronouncement on some details. Obviously, the clause is a danger to the stability of an international society based upon adherence to agreements. In the few cases in which the clause has been invoked, the invoking party indicated that a change in the power relations between the parties to the treaty had made it restrictive. Attempts have been made to limit the applicability of the clause—for instance, by excluding it from treaties referring to property rights—or to submit the application of the clause in a given case to an objective international agency. At any rate, the clause remains tempting for states wanting to escape from treaty obligations experienced as onerous.

The usefulness of establishing legal conditions under which the clause may be applied is greatly diminished by the fact that in the end political calculations will determine whether a state will use the clause or not. In the meantime, the possibility that the clause may be invoked by a party to a treaty is likely to make the other party more willing to renegotiate an existing treaty to save what it can. Perhaps the major reason for the reticence of states to use the clause is, first, that treaties would become useless if the clause were invoked unhesitatingly, and, second, that reciprocity exerts a restraining influence. In favor of the clause is the possibility that the refusal by one party to change a treaty may cause an explosive situation; as John Stuart Mill pointed out, although it may be wrong to throw off an obligation, it may be even more wrong to insist upon its continuation. This moral consideration has in fact been used by states invoking the clause and provides legal respectability to a party wanting to escape from treaty obligations.

A treaty may also be voided when one or more parties commit a breach of the treaty, although whether this breach has to be substantial or can be minor is much debated. The 1969 convention, Article 60, opts for a material breach, meaning violation of a provision essential to the accomplishment of the treaty's object and purpose. In no case, however, are the consequences of the breach automatic. The injured party has some options that it may exercise in proper form (such as notification in writing, observation of time limitations, or use of judicial or arbitration procedure). The innocent party to a bilateral treaty may continue the treaty, demanding fulfillment, or else it may suspend or terminate the treaty and retaliate by legal (peaceful) means. Demand for damages resulting from the breach is a separate, independent action. On May 7, 1955, for instance, the Presidium of the Supreme Soviet of the USSR annulled the nonaggression, alliance, and friendship treaties with the United Kingdom (May 26, 1942) and France (December 10, 1944) on the grounds that the inclusion of a "remilitarized" Germany in the North Atlantic Treaty Organization had in effect unilaterally broken these treaties.

In the more complex case of a multilateral treaty, any injured party in exercising its options must always consider the effect upon other innocent parties to the treaty. The 1969 convention in Article 60, following customary law, allows all parties in the case of a material breach to suspend or terminate, by agreement, the treaty between themselves and the defaulting party only or among all parties. A specially affected party may suspend the treaty between itself and the defaulting party. Any party may suspend all or part of the treaty in respect to itself if the breach radically changes the position of every party in regard to the further performance of its treaty obligations.

Consequences of Invalidity, Termination, Suspension

When a treaty is found to be invalid, its provisions lack legal force. But the question arises what happens to the results of their performance by the parties while the treaty was believed to be valid. The 1969 convention, Article 69, stipulates the restoration of the status quo ante if any party so requires, which in many cases is easier said than done. Acts performed before the invalidity was invoked are not rendered invalid by reason only of the treaty's invalidity. If the treaty was invalid because of some misdeed of one of the parties (fraud, coercion), that party has no rights. If one party's consent to a multilateral treaty was invalid, the same rule applies between that party and the other parties to the treaty.

After termination of the treaty, the parties have no further obligations. But rights, obligations, or any other legal situations created during the execution of the treaty remain unaffected. If only one party to a multilateral treaty withdraws from the treaty or denounces it, the same rules apply to that party in relation to all others (Article 70).

During the suspension of a treaty, the parties are relieved from their performance. But they must not do anything to obstruct the resumption of the treaty's operation (Article 72).

The great problem regarding the law of treaties, as in many other legal subjects, is how to determine the facts objectively. This is particularly true when one party withdraws from the treaty, denounces it, or declares it invalid. Probably the most effective deterrent to arbitrary action is the danger to the whole fabric of international treaty relations that such an action poses. The 1969 convention proposes in Articles 65 through 68 procedures that minimally preserve the peacefulness of any dispute by referring to Article 33 of the U.N. Charter and that maximally call for judicial or arbitration procedures if no solution under the U.N. procedure has been accomplished. Nevertheless, these solutions by a neutral third party are suggestions, not obligations. In any case, the law of treaties has been working well and the reason is not difficult to find. Treaties are means to ends. Conflicts of interest arise mostly concerning the subject matter regulated by treaties, not the form and technicalities of treaties themselves. These will generally be the object of a dispute when the parties use the form to affect the substance—when they try to find fault with the treaty's form because they do not like its substance. In such situations, the settlement of the conflict is more likely to come from political arrangements regarding the treaty's substance than from rectification of the treaty's form.

In the opposite situation, which is occurring with increasing frequency, treaties are used for essentially symbolic purposes—mainly on politically neutral subjects—to signal new or growing "friendship" between states formerly on less than friendly terms. In such situations, the substance of the treaty is often most vague, general, and politically "neutral." The fact of concluding the treaty is more important than its content. Such political use of the treaty form is likely to undermine the usefulness of treaties as one of the most important instruments of social change in international society and as a good means for the reconciliation of differing interests.

19
RESPONSIBILITY OF SUBJECTS

The Principle

Every subject of international law is at least responsible for an internationally wrongful act and owes amends for the wrongful act to the injured subject. The argument has been made occasionally that responsibility is incompatible with sovereignty. But the practice of states and of international courts has firmly established the principle in international law. The Permanent Court of International Justice confirmed the principle in the *Wimbledon* (1923), *Factory at Chorzów (Jurisdiction)* (1927), and *Phosphates of Morocco* (1938) cases. The International Court of Justice confirmed it in the *Corfu Channel* case (1949); in its advisory opinions in *Reparation for Injuries Suffered in the Service of the United Nations* (1949) and *Interpretation of Peace Treaties with Bulgaria, Hungary and Romania (Second Phase)* (1950); and in *Barcelona Traction, Light, and Power Co. Ltd. (Judgment)* (1970) and *Nicaragua (Merits, Judgment)* (1986).

A subject of international law can become responsible by either committing or omitting an act. Responsibility can be direct just as the injury can be suffered directly. But both may also be vicarious (for example, when a national for whom the state is responsible acts, or when a national is injured abroad).

During the first few hundred years of international law, responsibility became an acute problem usually with regard to the treatment of aliens and their diplomatic protection. Indeed, for many newer, ex-colonial states, treatment of diplomats and aliens remains the area of greatest concern. Aliens, especially corporations, as investors or traders from developed states are feared as tools of neocolonialism or triggers of intervention. These newer states want to have the sovereign right to deal with these aliens and their property as state interests dictate without having to account to outsiders. But the expansion of international contacts and the corresponding expansion of international law have also expanded the possibilities of state responsibility. The rise of liberation movements and their international implications or the protection of the human environment, for instance, has generated entirely new aspects of the principle of state responsibility. The growth, albeit hesitant, of an international criminal law has shaken the foundation of state responsibility, which hitherto has been treated as the equivalent to civil responsibility in municipal law. So far, the growth of a criminal law among states has produced many questions, few answers, and some innovations.

Whatever innovations are occurring, violation of international law with the consequence of responsibility remains unchanged but is no longer exclusive. States may be responsible without such violation—for instance, in the case of ultrahazardous action. Yet under customary law, causing damage or injury alone is not sufficient. In 1931, the U.S.-Mexican Claims Commission in the *International Fisheries Co.* case could still say, "States, according to a thoroughly established rule of international law, are responsible only for those injuries which are inflicted through an act which violates some rule of international law" (p. 275). The injury may be nonmaterial, such as an insult or the mistreatment of a state's flag. Or the injury may be the violation of an obligation itself without further damaging effect upon another state. In the *Corfu Channel* case (1949), the International Court of Justice found that Great Britain had violated Albania's sovereignty by clearing mines in its territorial waters without its permission. Confirming this injury was, the Court stated, appropriate satisfaction for the injury.

As in the cases of good faith and consent, there is no absolute standard for judgment. The innumerable questions usually arising in concrete disputes can be answered only individually in the light of all the circumstances. In addition to these questions of interpretation in individual cases and their fit into the conditions for responsibility, there are more weighty questions of principle regarding the nature and details of responsibility itself.

Controversial Aspects of the Principle

One question is whether for a subject to be responsible for a wrongful act, guilt or fault (*culpa*) must be present or whether responsibility exists absolutely and objectively regardless of any guilt as long as a legal norm was violated. Majority opinion holds that responsibility exists once a norm has been broken regardless of guilt or fault. The U.S.–Great Britain Claims Arbitration Tribunal in *Jessie, the Thomas F. Bayard, and the Pescawha* (1921, p. 115) held that responsibility was absolute. U.S. naval officers had interfered with the operation of British sealing vessels in the belief that Anglo-British regulations justified their action. Neither malice nor negligence was involved. The United States was held responsible "for errors in judgment of its officials purporting to act within the scope of their duties and vested with power to enforce their demands." The U.S.-Canada Arbitral Tribunal in the *Trail Smelter Arbitration (United States–Canada)* case (1941) supported a similar view.

A tribunal of the Permanent Court of International Justice in the *Russian Indemnity (Russia-Turkey)* case (1912) held that responsibility required guilt. In the *Corfu Channel* case (1949, p. 23) the Court also insisted on guilt. The Court had come to the conclusion that Albania had knowledge of the existence of mine fields in its territorial waters but had neglected to warn all shipping so that consequently some British warships were severely damaged. "These grave omissions involve the international responsibility of Albania." The same position was taken in the *Home Missionary Society* case (1920) before the U.S.–Great Britain Claims Arbitration Tribunal. The arbitrator held that there was no responsibility for damages by a government that was neither guilty of lack of good faith nor negligent in doing its duty. In some judgments both views seem to be represented simultaneously (compare *Spanish Zone of Morocco Claims [Spain v. United Kingdom]* [1927] and *Harry Roberts [United States] v. United Mexican States* [1925–1926] before the U.S.-Mexican General Claims Commission).

A second question raised in connection with state responsibility regards damage and injury suffered by a state as the result of a legal action by another state. The problematic situation has become particularly acute now that aspects of modern technology threaten not only the environment but the very life of human beings everywhere. Customary law leaves no doubt that a state cannot be responsible for injurious consequences of a legal act. But that law leaves states unprotected against catastrophic consequences of ultrahazardous technological activities, such as accidents at nuclear power plants. Under customary law states may at best be able to construe some foundation for claims on such vague principles as good neighborliness, abuse of rights, or violation of sovereignty and perhaps some parts of human rights to the extent that these are becoming customary law (the right of everyone to live in a decent environment).

This highly unsatisfactory situation is now undergoing change. There is much talk of an absolute responsibility when such activities cause injury. Liability is said to exist regardless of guilt or even neglect of a state. Causality is the only criterion. If the activity—legitimate or not—has caused the damage, the acting state is liable. Fault can possibly enter into consideration in assessing the amends the acting state has to make. So far, such responsibility has not yet become customary law. For example, no claim could be made on the basis of any specific norm against the Soviet Union for damage arising from the accident at the nuclear power plant in Chernobyl. But a large number of conventions are now in existence creating just such responsibility and liability. Examples include several conventions concluded in the 1960s and early 1970s relating to specific risks such as the pollution of oceans by oil and liability for damage caused by space objects or dumping of wastes into the ocean, the Treaty on Principles Governing Activities of States in the Exploration and Use of Outer Space (1967, Article 7), and several conventions on maritime or transboundary air pollution. There are also unilateral commitments such as U.S. Public Law 95-513 (December 6, 1974), which declares that claims for damages from nuclear reactors carried on U.S. warships will be entertained and settled. The United Nations Conference on the Human Environment (1972) states in Article 22 that "states shall co-operate to develop further the international law regarding liability and compensation for the victims of pollution and other environmental damage caused by activities within the jurisdiction or control of such states to areas beyond their jurisdiction."

Liability of states for activities of private armies on their soil against a neighboring state is even more uncertain now. The traditional rules for such cases were clear. The state was liable for hostile actions from its soil. Reciprocal guarantees of sovereignty and of the territorial inviolability of states required such liability. If a state failed to control such hostile activities, the injured state conceivably had the right of unilateral coercive action of abatement on the other state's soil. Israel held Lebanon responsible for an invasion by some PLO members from Lebanon who killed some Israeli nationals. But some newer and Communist states argue that the actions of liberation movements are legal as self-defense against aggressors. There could therefore be no question of liability by the state from whose soil the liberation movement operated.

A third question raised by liability is the distinction, if any, between criminal and civil liability. Until recently, such a distinction was rejected by majority opinion. Or more correctly, the possibility of criminal responsibility by states was denied. The main argument against such responsibility was that the commission of a crime required the attributes of natural persons: thought, will, feeling, conscience, motivation. But under the impact of war crimes and genocide during and after World War II as well as later crimes against international law, agitation for international criminal laws applying to states and their organs was strong and mildly successful.

The question of whether states can be criminally responsible remains controversial. The possibility of a violation by a state of international norms concerning the international community as a whole (*erga omnes*) is recognized. Such a violation is a breach of obligations toward the international society, a crime against humankind, in whose enforcement every state is interested and for which every state can hold the violating state responsible. But war crimes apart, there has not yet been a case of the prosecution of a state—as distinct from officials of a state—for committing a crime against international law. It would be nearly impossible to think of one state prosecuting another state or its organs for a crime. Such prosecution would have to be performed by an international criminal court whose creation cannot yet be forseen.

Occasionally international tribunals have awarded damages of a punitive character, which implies the existence of criminal liability. The war crimes trials assumed criminal liability of state organs. The genocide convention and some other U.N. resolutions regarding acts that have become crimes directly against international law call for punishment of such acts whether committed by private individuals or organs of states. In 1976 the International Law Commission agreed on a clause on codification of responsibility of states that held that "an internationally wrongful act which results from a breach by a State of an international obligation, so essential for the protection of fundamental interests of the international community that its breach is recognized as a crime by that community as a whole, constitutes an international crime." Examples given were aggression, denial of self-determination, slavery, genocide, apartheid, and massive pollution of sea and air.

Raising the question regarding principles of state accountability, responsibility, and liability demonstrates the extremely controversial nature of the issue. The agencies occupied with the codification of international law have long since reached the conclusion that the time is not ripe for a codification of state responsibility and liability. Yet the need for it is great. Dangers of injury and damage are worldwide, regardless of which state is initially responsible for the danger or where it originates. Oil spills, nuclear radiation, and terrorism ignore national boundaries. The tendency of some states to exempt themselves from responsibility—a contemporary form of isolationism—and blame other states for hazardous behavior in which they are not likely to engage for some time to come ignores the worldwide effects of such behavior and, consequently, the worldwide concern in a regulation of state responsibility.

The Forms of Injury

Injuries and their perpetrators have been classified in many ways. The usefulness of this enterprise is in defining more precisely the nature of responsibility or liability and its relation to the type of injury, the persons causing it, and the amends due.

One class of injuries is that caused by one subject (such as a state) to another (such as a state). A state may break a treaty or violate another's sovereignty or inviolability. Such cases are usually settled by diplomatic means. A second, and frequent, class of injuries is that caused by a state to an alien. This situation is covered by the law of aliens (and has been covered in Chapter 15). A third class of injuries is caused by individuals to states, increasingly so with the rise of terrorism, subversion, and insurgency from foreign territory. The wrongful act— in the eyes of international law—consists in a state neglecting its obligation toward the injured state in forbidding the individuals to use its territory as a base for their activities. A fourth class of cases, often settled within the national legal system, is injury done by a national to a foreign national and the state neglecting its duty to give the alien the justice due him or her.

No one general legal principle can be formulated for the settlement of all these cases. The types of injuries and the ways of causing them are too varied. Responsibility may be established in many different forms. The damages, reparations, compensations, and satisfactions demanded by the injured subject can vary accordingly. Each case must be examined individually, and its settlement must take the route most appropriate to the particulars of the case. Settlement can run the gamut from a simple acknowledgment of guilt by the guilty subject, to an apology, payments of money (Iran to the United States for its kidnapping of U.S. diplomats), restoration of the damage, punishment of the perpetrators of the injury, military action (in the past), or the use of force in the name of self-defense (in the present).

The Subjects and Objects of Responsibility

Only subjects of international law (or their organs) can be made responsible under international law or can benefit from it. This corresponds to the basic principle that persons have no legal personality under international law. Any breach of an international obligation by a subject toward an individual person can be an obligation only toward that person's state or an international organization. But the U.S.-Mexican Claims Commission in the *North American Dredging Co. of Texas (United States) v. United Mexican States* case (1926, p. 802) denied "that the rules of international Public Law apply only to nations and that individuals cannot under any circumstances have a personal standing under it." Nevertheless, the opinion remains prevalent that under *lex lata* an injured individual cannot rely on any responsibility by the violating foreign state. Also prevalent is the belief that to give the individual standing before a state or an international organization would be of little help. But this belief should be reexamined. The position of individuals in the European Community (in relation to the Court of Human Rights) and under conventions on human rights is gradually changing. Large corporations in small countries could conceivably have an opportunity to enforce state responsibility toward them.

In principle, only the injured subject can make claims against the responsible subject. A general customary rule that every subject may enforce international law because every subject is interested in maintaining international law does not yet exist. This problem has been discussed earlier in connection with material jurisdiction of states. Yet such a rule may be in the making. There certainly are a number of breaches of the principle. Their beginning can be seen in the Treaty of Utrecht (1713), which formally established a European balance of power, obligated states to maintain it, and respectively entitled every participating European state as a matter of right to restore it if another state disturbed it. This right was still considered to exist at the end of the nineteenth century. A similar rule can also be seen, this time in regard to the maintenance of peace, in the principle of collective security as embodied in the Charter of the United Nations. According to the charter, states not injured may or even must take action against an aggressor state (one incorrect assumption being that war anywhere means war everywhere). Such a rule can likewise be seen in the right of states to enforce responsibility for crimes against humankind to the extent that such rights are becoming international law.

Soviet lawyers, foremost G. I. Tunkin, are advancing the opinion that in cases of crimes against humankind, all states and international organizations are entitled to make claims against responsible states and to act against them even when such states have not been injured directly. Soviet lawyers argue that interaction among states and the mutual sensitivities to their behavior make the observation of such rules the concern of every state. A state committing such crimes is responsible to every state. States should have not only the right but the duty to demand observation of these rules and, within the limits of the law, see to their enforcement. In support of their argument they quote the International Court of Justice in the *Barcelona Traction, Light, and Power Co. Ltd.* case (1970, p. 32):

> A distinction must be drawn between the obligations of a State towards the international community as a whole, and those arising vis-à-vis another State in the field of diplomatic protection. By their very nature, the former are the concern of all States. In view of the importance of the rights involved, all States can be held to have a legal interest in their protection; they are obligations *erga omnes*.

Because states and international organizations can act only through individuals, two major questions arise. Which individuals' actions and omissions are imputable to the subject of international law? Is the action or omission of such individuals a breach of international obligation if the subject itself had behaved in such a manner?

Responsibility for the Subject's Organs

Inevitably, the subjects are responsible for the acts and omissions through their organs. Who the organs are is determined mostly by international law independently of the subject's internal organization, as was discussed earlier. One basic principle is that in matters of responsibility the state is not identified (as it often is) with the entire population; the state is identified only with officials, usually on all levels from the president to the local police. In the case of the attack upon the U.S. Embassy in Teheran, there was initially no state responsibility by Iran because the attackers were private individuals. But, according to the International Court, when the Iranian government supported the attack and held U.S. personnel hostage, the attackers became organs of the state and Iran became responsible (*Diplomatic and Consular Staff in Teheran [U.S.A. v. Iran]* [1980, pp. 34–35]).

According to the theory that an organization is an indivisible entity, which legal entity is responsible depends upon in whose name and for whom the person was acting, not where the person belonged organizationally. (So decided an Oberlandesgericht in Austria, *N. K. v. Austria* [1979, p. 472].)

In relation to government officials, the theory has been advanced that there are degrees of responsibility and that responsibility diminishes with the rank of the official. Nevertheless, the responsibility internationally is by the state, not by any one official because each acts on behalf of the state.

In relation to parliaments and constitution-making bodies, there is agreement that subjects are responsible for passing laws that may themselves be contrary to international obligations, for not passing laws required according to an international obligation, or for passing laws inadequate in enabling the subject to fulfill its international obligations (for example, the U.S. Congress may not allot funds to pay damages). Nevertheless, the state remains responsible because a subject cannot plead inadequacy of municipal law in failing to fulfill international obligations.

The judiciary of a state can create responsibility by breaking a rule of international law. Cases occur most often when aliens ask for court action to right some wrong. The abundant literature and case law on this situation are contradictory, and few basic, generally accepted norms have emerged, probably because nationalism may bias judges against aliens and states are sensitive to any outside interference in their judicial system.

As was pointed out in the discussion of the legal position of aliens, the state becomes responsible if it denies justice to the alien. This concept can be interpreted broadly to include many ways in which the state defaults on its duty toward the alien. This concept can cover refusal of access to a court, failure to execute a court's judgment, or delay in giving a judgment—although the International Court of Justice in the *Interhandel (Switzerland v. United States of America)* (1959) did not feel that nine years of litigation in U.S. courts to obtain justice amounted to an undue delay.

Cases of denial of justice were found when a court deliberately showed bad faith and willful neglect of duty—*Chattin (United States) v. United Mexican States* (1927), U.S.-Mexican Claims Commission; when a court was packed by judges who usually decided against an alien—*Robert E. Brown Claim* (1925), U.S. and British Claims Arbitration; and *Idler, Jacob v. Venezuela* (1890), United States v. Venezuela Arbitration; when a court manifestly discriminated against an alien—*Salem, Egypt v. United States* (1932), special arbitration; or when there were no courts at all.

In the last case, as in all others as a last resort, a state becomes responsible for its judiciary when the international standard regarding the existence and behavior of a judiciary is not observed. The application of this standard sustains international responsibility of a state even if its own internal system is highly inadequate. The difficulty, as always, is to define such a standard and to find an impartial agency to do so. A state whose judicial system is clearly below the international standard is not likely to submit to a definition by an outside agency as to what the standard is. Moreover, such states have little difficulty disguising a denial of justice by using formally and superficially acceptable procedures.

The Behavior Creating Responsibility

Responsibility exists only for acts of state or, more precisely, for acts performed by the organs of subjects as acts of the subject. If a state or an international organization runs a business, such as a postal service, a railroad, or an economic aid program, the actions related to such enterprises are not considered acts of state. The U.S.-Mexican General Claims Commission in the *Home Insurance Co.* claim (1926) held that activities of this kind should be treated like the activities of private companies. But two recent developments make a reconsideration of this opinion advisable. One is that states are becoming increasingly involved in enterprises that in the past were not normally considered state activities. The other is that when states engage in such enterprises, their capabilities are considerably greater than those of private persons; thus, the degree of state responsibility should be increased accordingly.

A related but different problem is posed by behavior of state or international organization organs that exceeds their competence, function, or official powers. Majority opinion holds that the subjects remain responsible at least as long as organs seemingly act with authorization and use the power their official position provides them, unless the organs' excess is very obvious (compare *Florida Bonds* [1898], Great Britain v. U.S. Arbitration; and *Youman's Claim* [1926], U.S.-Mexican General Claims Commission). The arbitrator in the *Jean-Baptiste Caire* case (1929, p. 148), France and Mexico Mixed Claims Commission, stated that for acts committed by officers beyond the limits of their competence, "it is necessary either that they should have acted, at least apparently, as authorised officers, or that, in acting, they should have exercised powers or measures connected with their official character."

Behavior by organs of the subject unconnected with their status or function does not create per se state responsibility. It is the behavior of a private person.

Responsibility for Private Persons

There is general agreement that subjects of international law are not responsible for injuries caused to other subjects by private persons. A responsibility can arise only if the subject has failed in fulfilling a duty to prevent the injury or to seize and punish the perpetrator of the injury and to force him or her to make restitution for the injury, as prescribed by international law. In other words, the subject's responsibility is related to how it handles the injurious act and its perpetrator.

International law expects the subject to act with "due diligence"—a term that is virtually impossible to define consensually. It is clear only that due diligence requires adequate preventive measures to avoid injury or adequate remedial measures once the injury has occurred. *Alabama Claims, United States–Great Britain Arbitration* (1872), illustrates the first point; *Laura B. Janes (United States) v. United Mexican States* General Claims Commission (1926), illustrates the second point.

The legal situation is not different when the injury has been perpetrated by a group of persons: a mob, insurgents, revolutionaries. As long as the state has shown due diligence in preventing or remedying an injury and treats aliens and nationals alike in such a situation, it has discharged its international obligation and no responsibility arises. Nor is the situation different if the injury has been caused by a state's organized forces to suppress a rebellion. The arbitrator in the *Rosa Gelbtrunk* case before an arbitral tribunal (1902, p. 465) stated that the state of which the injured person is a national

> has no right to claim for him as against the nation in which he is resident any other or different treatment in case of loss by war—either foreign or civil—revolution, insurrection, or other internal disturbance caused by organized military force or by soldiers, than that which the latter country metes out to its own subjects or citizens.

Once a state recognizes revolutionaries or insurgents on its own territory as belligerents, or another state so recognizes them, neither state has any more responsibility, and neither can make claims related to the action of the insurgents.

Conditions Excluding Responsibility

Apart from conditions that make an otherwise wrongful act right (such as an act of God, self-defense), conditions exist that although not necessarily annulling the wrongfulness of the subject's action nevertheless excuse the action legally so that no responsibility or liability exists. Among these conditions are the following.

Responsibility is excluded if fulfillment of the obligation involves self-destruction, as was pointed out in the *Russian Indemnity (Russia-Turkey)* case (1912) before the Permanent Court of International Arbitration. Responsibility is also excluded if an obligation is broken through a self-protecting action (for example, sinking an oil tanker outside of territorial waters to prevent an oil spill near the coast). Similarly and rarely, a case of necessity may excuse an injurious action of one subject against another. If in a given case under any of these circumstances the subject's responsibility is not completely eliminated, extenuating circumstances may cause a reduction in the amends to be made.

Neither responsibility nor liability, however, is affected by municipal legislation. Either exists even if under municipal law a government acted legally or had no power to act in conformity with its international obligation. Conversely, behavior prescribed by municipal law may nevertheless be wrongful according to international law and may cause liability.

Amends

The kind of reparation owed by the responsible subject to the injured subject depends upon the kind of injury. Two major kinds may be distinguished: material and nonmaterial.

For the material damage situation, the Permanent Court of International Justice in the *Factory at Chorzów (Jurisdiction)* case (1927, p. 47) formulated what is a far-reaching consensus:

> Reparation must, as far as possible, wipe out all the consequences of the illegal act and reestablish the situation which would, in all probability, have existed if that act had not been committed. Restitution in kind, or, if this is not possible, payment of a sum corresponding to the value which a restitution in kind would bear; the award, if need be, of damages for loss sustained which would not be covered by restitution in kind or payment in place of it—such are the principles which should serve to determine the amount of compensation due for an act contrary to international law.

The Permanent Court of Arbitration in the *Norwegian Claims* case (1922), p. 73) put it more briefly: "Just compensation implies complete restitution of the *status quo ante.*"

In the *Factory at Chorzów (Jurisdiction)* case (1927, p. 29), the International Court made clear that there exists a norm of international law requiring the responsible state to repair the damage. But there is much uncertainty regarding the nature of the repair.

Restitution in kind is the restoration of the situation that would in all likelihood have existed had the damage not been done. If the demand for restitution is unreasonable (abuse of rights!), the injured party must be satisfied with some form of reparation.

If restitution in toto or in part is impossible, the responsible subject must pay indemnity or must partially restitute and partially indemnify. Indemnity is owed for direct as well as indirect damages, as long as there is a causal nexus between the act and the damage. Damages include lost profits and, according to majority opinion, interest on money owed. There are no fixed rules regarding the amount of indemnity, the percentage of interest, or similar details, in spite of a great number of court decisions and arbitral awards.

Satisfaction for nonmaterial damage is designed to pacify the hurt feelings and sense of justice of the injured subject. To some extent, only the injured party can express the degree of injury and must therefore be entitled—within the limits of reasonableness and international standards—to determine the form of satisfaction (for example, an official apology, honoring of the flag and other symbolic acts, or punishment of the perpetrator of the injury). Payment of damage directly to the subject is very rare, but it is quite frequent in cases of damage to a national of an injured state or an official of an international organization on whose behalf the injured subject is acting.

The parties involved in cases of responsibility may agree to let either the International Court of Justice (Article 36 of the statute) or an arbitrator determine the nature and extent of reparation to be made by the responsible subject. Iran made use of this possibility when it applied to the International Court of Justice in May 1989 (*ILM* 27 [1989 IV]:843–844, 896–940) for a determination of the violation of several conventions, of the allocation of compensation, and of the amount of compensation in regard to military action by the United States. The *USS Vincennes* was patrolling in the Gulf of Persia to protect neutral shipping from attacks by Iran. On July 3, 1988, the *Vincennes* mistakenly shot down an Iranian commercial airliner. The airplane and many lives were lost. This generated the request for a judgment—in spite of U.S. willingness to accept responsibility and pay compensation. The case of *Amoco International Finance Corporation v. Islamic Republic of Iran* before the Iran-U.S. Claims Tribunal (1987) is a good illustration of the great difficulty in determining damages and compensation, especially when the injured party is a juridic person.

Procedure

When one subject of international law is responsible to another for damage done directly to it—for instance, as a result of injury to a state organ or state property—proper diplomatic channels can be used to serve the claim. The situation becomes more complex when a subject has suffered indirect damage, usually through the injury of a person under the protection of the damaged subject. Because an injury under international law can be caused only by one subject of international law to another subject, injury to a person can create responsibility of a subject only if through the injury to the individual person another subject has been injured.

The problems created by indirect damage to the subject of international law are, first, what the relationship of the injured person must be to the subject to entitle it to claim damages from the responsible subject and, second, what measures the injured person must take before international procedures may be initiated. The answer to the first problem is that usually the person must be a national of the state before that

state can claim damages (or an agent of an international organization
if the organization wishes to bring a claim for injury). Such status is
assumed when the national acquired nationality by birth. If nationality
was acquired by naturalization, the relationship between the person and
the protecting state must be more than nominal. It must be substantial,
real, and effective. There must be a genuine link connecting the person
to the state, as the International Court of Justice elaborated at great
length in the case of *Nottebohm (Liechtenstein v. Guatemala)* (1955).

But at what point the person must have been a national is in some
respects controversial, as the great number of cases decided differently
indicates. There is little doubt that the person must have possessed the
nationality of the state when the injury occurred. But there can be
complications if the person loses or changes nationality after the deed,
if the person dies and the heirs (possibly of different nationality) inherit
the claim, or if the person has dual nationality. See, for examples, the
claim of *Caccamese*, American-Italian Conciliation Commission (1952);
the case of *Canevaro (Italy v. Peru)*, Permanent Court of Arbitration
(1912); *Panevezys-Saldutiskis Railway, Estonia v. Lithuania,* Permanent
Court of International Justice (1939); and *Burthe v. Denis,* U.S. Supreme
Court (1889).

An interesting aspect for the future development of international law
is the possibility of a claim transferring from one state to another when
an injured person changes nationality. Because the new state has not
been injured, the new state presumably has no claim; but if it was
found to have a claim, this would mean that the injured person rather
than the state had an international legal claim. In the European Community the injured person can directly complain to the Commission on
Human Rights, providing the responsible state has recognized the commission's jurisdiction.

There are some rather rare exceptions to the principle of nationality.
A state may claim when a person not yet a national but having declared
the intention of becoming a national has been injured. Or the nationality
of a merchant vessel may entitle the flag state to make claims, although
the owners of the vessel may not have the state's nationality. Or
shareholders of a company who are not nationals may nevertheless be
protected by the state whose nationality the company possesses. (Compare
Koszta, United States–Austria, diplomatic negotiations [1853]; *Wimbledon,*
Permanent Court of International Justice [1923]; and *Agency of Canadian
Car and Foundry Co.,* U.S.-German Mixed Claims Commission [1939]).

The second problem—what measures an injured person may have
to take before the matter can be brought to the international level—
relates to the exhaustion of local remedies. According to this principle,
before raising the matter to the international level, the injured person
must exhaust all possible remedies within the responsible state to obtain
satisfaction. The International Court of Justice in *Interhandel* (1959, p.
27) formulated the principle as follows:

The rule that local remedies must be exhausted before international proceedings may be instituted is a well-established rule of customary international law; the rule has been generally observed in cases in which a
State has adopted the cause of its national whose rights are claimed to
have been disregarded by another State in violation of international law.
Before resort may be had to an international court in such a situation, it
has been considered necessary that the State where the violation occurred
should have an opportunity to redress it by its own means, within the
framework of its own domestic legal system.

One rationale of the principle is that the responsible state should
have the chance to right a wrong by its own means. This rationale also
obviates the requirement of exhausting local remedies when there is
clearly no remedy available. The absence of such a remedy may itself
be a breach of an international norm or a quasi-norm under the "soft"
law of human rights. There should be no confusion, however, that the
act causing responsibility precedes the exhaustion of local remedies. The
act, not the denial of justice, justifies the international claim. The
exhaustion of local remedies is a rule of procedure unrelated to the
substance of the claim (that is, the injury caused by the act). This
principle is also controversial, however. See *Panevezys-Saldutiskis Railway*
(1939); *Finnish Vessels in Great Britain During the War* (1934); *Certain
Norwegian Loans*, International Court of Justice (1957); and *Interhandel*
(1959). Exceptionally, the Convention on International Liability for Damage Caused by Space Objects (1971), Article 11, permits the presentation
of claims for damages without prior exhaustion of local remedies.

The issue of whether local remedies have been exhausted and of
whether the injured party is therefore entitled to bring the case to the
international level suffers from an absence of a neutral, objective agency
to make such a determination. Nevertheless, the great number of cases
decided by international courts or settled through international arbitration
indicate that states are willing to submit such matters to rulings by
third parties, presumably because vital interests of states are rarely
involved.

Expanding and Contracting Claims

The expansion of the right to make claims by every state in crimes
against humankind suggested by the Soviets is counterbalanced by the
narrower, although ambiguous, position taken by the Chinese. Their
practice is inconsistent and seems to depend on the political relationship
the PRC has with a given state. For example, during the initial phases
of Sino-U.S. relations, the property of U.S. nationals was not confiscated
outright but was subject to "controls" and to "freezing." For all practical
purposes, this amounted to a complete loss of property. Some British
property was "requisitioned"; other property was to be purchased. During
the period of "unbreakable friendship" between the USSR and the PRC,

Soviet nationals were treated most generously. The Chinese, by avoiding customary terminology such as expropriation, socialization, nationalization, and confiscation, obscure the legal consequences of their actions and are thus able to obtain foreign property without formally breaking the rules of international law. But their writers have made one thing very clear: They do not subscribe to the law requiring compensation for property no longer available to its owners—whatever semantic excuse is being used. Only lately, as China has begun entering the mainstream of international political and economic relations, are the Communists submitting more to the normal rules of international law in regard to foreign property.

The states of the Third World deal with state responsibility mainly from the standpoint of the treatment of aliens. They are not sympathetic to traditional principles. First, they believe these were largely developed to protect imperialists and imperialism in their countries when these were colonies. Second, they feel that the principles relating to responsibility toward aliens and their property frequently disadvantageously affect the programs of these states for political, economic, and social reforms. As a result, the newer states would prefer to see a change in the concept of responsibility that emphasizes the duty of older states to help the development of the newer states.

The dilemma of the newer states is that they need foreign investments and advisers but do not want to surrender their sovereignty to get them. These states are working toward a compromise. They acknowledge, for instance, that a foreign corporation should not be punished for the inequalities in the international economic system. But in making a concession to compensation for nationalizing such enterprises, these states are willing to pay only an absolute minimum, although some flexibility is built into their proposals. They are willing to pay only direct losses, not anticipated profits, on the grounds that nationalization of the corporations' property is only taking what rightly belonged to the state all along.

Responsibility of International Organizations

Because international organizations can have international personality (are subjects of international law to the extent granted them by their member states directly or implicitly), responsibility and related claims have been dealt with here as being those of subjects rather than of states. For obvious historical reasons, the principles have been developed mainly for states. But they should be applied in analogous fashion and mutatis mutandis to international organizations as well. In fact, the International Court of Justice has so applied them. It could not help doing so. For once it is agreed that international organizations possess international rights, they must of necessity also have international responsibilities.

REFERENCES AND READINGS FOR PART 6

General Principles

Ago, Roberto. "Reports on state responsibility." *Yearbook of the International Law Commission* (1969 II):125–156; (1970 II):177–197; (1971 II/1):193–199.
Brownlee, Ian. *State Responsibility*. Oxford: Clarendon, 1983.
"Kolloquium über Staatsverantwortlichkeit." Z 45 (1985 II):193–389.
Schwarzenberger, Georg. "The fundamental principles of international law." *ADIRC* 87 (1955 I):195–384.
———. "Use and abuses of the 'abuse of rights' in international law." *Transactions* (Grotius Society) 42 (1956):147–179.
Vallée, Charles. "Quelques observations sur l'estoppel en droit des gens." *RGDIP* 77 (1973):949–999.

Unilateral Actions

McGibbon, I. C. "Some observations on the part of protest in international law." *BYIL* 30 (1953):293–319.
Rubin, Alfred P. "The international legal effects of unilateral declarations." *AJIL* 71 (January 1977):1–30.
Suy, E. *Les actes juridiques unilatéraux en droit international public*. Paris: Librairie Générale de Droit et de Jurisprudence, 1962.
Tomasi de Vignano, Alessandro. *La rinuncia in diritto internazionale*. Padua: CEDAM, 1960.
Venturini, Gian C. "La portée des effets juridiques des attitudes et des actes unilatéraux des états." *ADIRC* 112 (1964 II):367–467.

Nature of Treaties

Binder, Guyora. *Treaty Conflict and Political Contradiction: The Dialectic of Duplicity*. New York: Praeger, 1988.
Fawcett, J.E.S. "The legal character of international agreements." *BYIL* 30 (1953):381–400.

Myers, Denis P. "The names and scope of treaties." *AJIL* 51 (July 1957):574–605.

Reuter, Paul. *Introduction to the Law of Treaties*. New York: Columbia University Press, 1989.

Triska, Jan F., and Robert M. Slusser. *The Theory, Law and Policy of Soviet Treaties*. Stanford, CA: Stanford University Press, 1962.

Villiger, Mark E. *Customary International Law and Treaties*. Dordrecht: Martinus Nijhoff, 1985.

Waldock, Humphrey. "First report on the law of treaties." *Yearbook of the International Law Commission* (1962 II):27–83; and subsequent 1962 issues.

Capacity and Authority to Conclude Treaties

Blix, Hans. *Treaty-making Power*. New York: Praeger, 1960.

Brosche, Hartmut. *Zwang beim Abschluss völkerrechtlicher Verträge*. Berlin: Duncker und Humblot, 1974.

Detter, Ingrid. "The problem of unequal treaties." *Int. & Comp. L. Q.* 15 (October 1966):1069–1089.

Elias, T. O. *The Modern Law of Treaties*. Dobbs Ferry, NY: Oceana, 1974.

Lissitzyn, Oliver J. "Territorial entities in the law of treaties." *ADIRC* 125 (1968 III):1–91.

Malawer, Stuart S. *Essays on International Law*. Buffalo, NY: W. S. Hein, 1986.

Okeke, Chris N. *Controversial Subjects of Contemporary International Law*. Rotterdam: Rotterdam University Press, 1974.

Pernice, Ingolf. "Völkerrechtliche Verträge internationaler Organisationen." Z 48 (1988 II):229–250.

Przetacznik, Franciszek. "The validity of treaties concluded under coercion." *Indian Journal of International Law* 15 (April-June 1975):173–194.

Steinberger, Helmut. "Constitutional subdivisions of states or unions and their capacity to conclude treaties." Z 27 (1967 III):411–428.

Stone, Julius, "De victoribus victis: The International Law Commission and imposed treaties of peace." *Virginia Journal of International Law* 8 (December 1967):356–373.

Varma, Prem. "Unequal treaties in modern international law." *Eastern Journal of International Law* 7 (April 1975):56–79.

Consent to Treaties

Bolintineau, Alexandru. "Expression of consent to be bound by a treaty in the light of the 1969 Vienna convention." *AJIL* 68 (October 1974):62–86.

Lukashuk, I. I. "Parties to a treaty—the right of participation." *ADIRC* 135 (1972 I):231–328.

Tammes, A.J.P. "The status of consent in international law." *Netherlands Yearbook of International Law* 2 (1971):1–28.

Reservations to Treaties

Fitzmaurice, G. G. "Reservations to multilateral conventions." *Int. & Com. L. Q.* 2 (January 1953):1–26.

Horn, Frank. *Reservations and Interpretative Declarations to Multilateral Treaties.* New York: Elsevier Science, 1988.

Hoyt, Edwin C. *The Unanimity Rule in the Revision of Treaties: A Reexamination.* The Hague: Martinus Nijhoff, 1959.

Ruda, José M. "Reservations to Treaties." *ADIRC* 146 (1975 III):94–218.

Ius Cogens and Treaty Objects

Barberis, Julio A. "Liberté de traiter des états et le jus cogens." *Z* 30 (1970 I):19–45.

Jenks, C. Wilfred. "Conflict of law-making treaties." *BYIL* 30 (1953):401–453.

Nahlik, S. E. "The grounds of invalidity and termination of treaties." *AJIL* 65 (October 1971):736–756.

Rozakis, Christos L. *The Concept of Jus Cogens in the Law of Treaties.* New York: North Holland, 1976.

Scheuner, Ulrich. "Conflict of treaty with peremptory norm of international law." *Z* 27 (1967 III):520–532.

Simma, Bruno. *Das Reziprozitätselement im Zustandekommen völkerrechtlicher Verträge.* Berlin: Duncker und Humblot, 1972.

Sztucki, Jerzi. *Jus Cogens and the Vienna Convention on the Law of Treaties.* New York: Springer, 1974.

Whiteman, M. M. "Jus cogens in international law, with a projected list." *Georgia Journal of International and Comparative Law* 7 (Fall 1977):609–626.

Entry into Force of Treaties

Lewan, Kenneth. "Which states must be bound before a multilateral treaty enters into force if nothing is specified?" *Z* 29 (1969 III):536–542.

Interpretation of Treaties

Fitzmaurice, Gerald. "The law and procedure of the International Court of Justice 1951–4: Treaty interpretation and other treaty points." *BYIL* 33 (1957):203–293.

Germer, Peter. "Interpretation of plurilingual treaties: A study of article 33 of the Vienna Convention on the Law of Treaties." *Harvard International Law Journal* 11 (Spring 1970):400–427.

Gottlieb, Gideon. "The interpretation of treaties by tribunals." *Proceedings,* pp. 122–131. Washington, DC: American Society of International Law, 1969.

Gross, Leo. "Treaty interpretations: The proper role of an international tribunal." *Proceedings*, pp. 108–121. Washington, DC: American Society of International Law, 1969.

Haraszti, György. *Some Fundamental Problems of the Law of Treaties.* Budapest: Akadémiai Kiadó, 1973, pp. 13–228.

McDougal, Myres, Harold D. Lasswell, and J. C. Miller. *The Interpretation of Agreements and World Public Order.* New Haven, CT: Yale University Press, 1967.

Sohn, Louis B. "Settlement of disputes relating to the interpretation and application of treaties." *ADIRC* 150 (1976 II):195–294.

Sur, Serge. *L'interprétation en droit international public.* Paris: Librairie Générale de Droit et de Jurisprudence, 1974.

Yambrusic, Edward Slavko. *Treaty Interpretation Theory and Reality.* Lanham, MD: University Press of America, 1987.

Yasseen, Mustafa K. "L'interprétation des traités d'après la convention de Vienne sur le droit des traités." *ADIRC* 151 (1976 III):1–114.

Suspension and Termination of Treaties

Briggs, Herbert W. "Unilateral denunciation of treaties: The Vienna Convention and the International Court of Justice." *AJIL* 68 (January 1974):51–68.

Capotorti, Francesco. "Extinction et suspension des traités." *ADIRC* 134 (1971 III):417–587.

Elias, Tashin O. "Problems concerning the validity of treaties." *ADIRC* 134 (1971 III):332–416.

Haraszti, Geörgy. *Some Fundamental Problems of the Law of Treaties.* Budapest: Akadémiai Kiadó, 1973, pp. 229–425.

———. "Treaties and the fundamental change of circumstances." *ADIRC* 146 (1975 III):7–93.

Lissitzyn, Oliver J. "Treaties and changed circumstances (*rebus sic stantibus*)." *AJIL* 61 (October 1967):895–922.

"Report of the International Law Commission on the work of its 18th session (*clausula rebus sic stantibus*)." *Yearbook of the International Law Commission* (1966 II):172–274.

Schwelb, Egon. "Fundamental change of circumstances." *Z* 29 (1969 I):39–70.

Vamvoukos, Athanassios. *Termination of Treaties in International Law.* Oxford: Clarendon, 1985.

State Responsibility: General

Green, N. A. Maryan. *International Law of Peace.* London: Macdonald & Evans, 1973, pp. 243–245.

Wengler, Wilhelm. *Völkerrecht*, vol. 1. Berlin: Springer, 1964, pp. 489–498.

Responsibility for Hazardous Action

Hailbronner, Kay. "Liability for damage caused by spacecraft." Z 30 (1970 I):125–141.

Hoog, Günter. *Die Konvention über die Haftung der Inhaber von Atomschiffen vom 23, Mai 1962.* Frankfurt am Main, West Germany: A. Metzner, 1970.

Jenks, C. Wilfred. "Liability for ultra-hazardous activities in international law." *ADIRC* 117 (1966 I):99–200.

Criminal Liability of States

Bassiouni, M. Cherif, and Ved P. Nanda, eds. *A Treatise on International Criminal Law,* 2 vols. Springfield, IL: Charles C. Thomas, 1973.

Iluyomade, B. O. "The scope and content of a complaint of abuse of rights in international law." *Harvard International Law Journal* 16 (Winter 1975):47–92.

Schlochauer, Hans-Jürgen. "Die Entwicklung des völkerrechtlichen Deliktsrechts." *AV* 16 (1975 III):239–277.

Schwarzenberger, Georg. *The Frontiers of International Law.* London: Stevens, 1962, pp. 181–209.

Subjects and Objects of State Liability

García-Amador, F. V. "State responsibility in the light of the new trends in international law." *AJIL* 49 (July 1955):339–346.

State Responsibility for Treatment of Aliens

Adede, A. O. "A fresh look at the meaning of denial of justice under international law." *Canadian Yearbook of International Law* 14 (1976):73–95.

———. "A survey of treaty provisions on the rule of exhaustion of local remedies." *Harvard International Law Journal* 18 (Winter 1977):1–17.

Amerasinghe, Chittharanjan F. "The rule of exhaustion of local remedies in the framework of international systems for the protection of human rights." Z 28 (1968 II):257–300.

Broches, A. "The convention on the settlement of investment disputes between states and nationals of other states." *ADIRC* 136 (1972 II):331–410.

Carella, Gabriella. *La responsibilità dello stato per crimini internazionali.* Naples: Jovene, 1985.

Chappey, Jean. *La règle de l'épuisement des voies de recours internes.* Paris: A. Pédone, 1972.

Dawson, Frank, and Ivan L. Head. *International Law, Tribunals and the Rights of Aliens.* Syracuse, NY: Syracuse University Press, 1971.

García-Amador, F. V., Louis B. Sohn, and Richard R. Baxter. *Recent Codification of the Law of State Responsibility for Injuries to Aliens*. Dobbs Ferry, NY: Oceana, 1974.

Haesler, Th. *The Exhaustion of Local Remedies: Rule in the Case Law of International Courts and Tribunals*. Leiden: A. W. Sijthoff, 1968.

Responsibility of International Organizations

Günther, Konrad. *Die völkerrechtliche Verantwortlichkeit internationaler Organisationen gegenüber Drittstaaten*. New York: Springer, 1969.

Special Responsibilities of States

Bloomfield, Louis M., and Gerald F. Fitzgerald. *Crimes Against Internationally Protected Persons: Prevention and Punishment*. New York: Praeger, 1975.

Przetacznik, Franciszek. "International responsibility of the state for failure to afford special protection for foreign officials." *Revue de Droit International de Sciences Diplomatiques et Politiques* 52 (October-December 1974):310–326; 53 (January-March 1975):29–49.

Queneudec, Jean-Pierre. *La responsabilité internationale de l'état pour les fautes personelles de ses agents*. Paris: Librairie Générale de Droit et de Jurisprudence, 1966.

Ress, Georg. "Mangelhafte diplomatische Protektion and Staatshaftung." Z 32 (1972 II–IV):420–482.

PART 7
INTERNATIONAL COOPERATION

When used in the context of international law, the term *cooperation* normally implies something desirable, something beneficial for the parties involved (if not for the entire international society), something that will lead to mutually favorable results at the least and to eventual community at the most. But cooperation can also be a strategy for the realization of each party's purposes. Indeed, as a Soviet lawyer expressed it, confrontational cooperation is a strategy that has none of those desirable results.

Article 1 of the U.N. Charter lists as one of the organization's purposes the achievement of "international cooperation in solving international problems." Clearly, the charter intends the first meaning of cooperation, as do innumerable other international organizations and declarations. They usually specify the goals to be reached through cooperation—for example, Article 22 of the Universal Declaration of Human Rights (1948) empowers everyone to realize the rights indispensable for achieving dignity and full personality through national effort and "international cooperation."

The United Nations and all other international organizations presumably aim at stimulating and facilitating cooperation toward a common goal. But practice has demonstrated that cooperation can also take place for a host of purposes between benefit and nonbenefit, notwithstanding these organizations' clear announcement that they mean to support the maintenance of peace and the welfare of states. The cooperation of states has not always led to this laudable goal because there are many different ways to reach it. States may have common, like, or antagonistic interests in whose pursuit they may have to cooperate. But they do not necessarily share a common goal. It was not until 1988 that a Soviet historian, Yevg. Bazhanov (*Izvestia*, July 22, p. 5), suggested cooperation among the three superpowers (the USSR, the United States, and the PRC) as a means toward world stability, and even then, Bazhanov's suggestion was more reminiscent of the Holy Alliance than it was a plan to achieve a world state. Therefore, it is not appropriate to assume automatically that cooperation, even within international organizations, is necessarily of benefit for international society or for all those states engaged in cooperation.

The tendency of international law to regulate and institutionalize cooperation among states is only about eight or nine decades old. Before that time, the main role of law was to safeguard and reconcile the sovereign existence of states with their inevitable coexistence. Law's emphasis was therefore on the essentially negative aspects of state behavior—namely, what states may not do to each other. Even when cooperation was to some extent institutionalized, as in guarantees to maintain a balance of power, the main purpose was to guarantee isolation of states, not to promote their common well-being. Sovereignty epitomized this function of the law.

This function was in accord with the relative self-sufficiency of states. Few national interests required cooperation for fulfillment. This function was also in accord with the early-nineteenth-century philosophy of liberalism. According to liberalism, the role of the state was to be a "night watchman." The state was a security mechanism for the citizens or, as Marxists would have it, for capitalists in suppressing the working masses. The state was to maintain law and order or the protection of "natural rights." Anything beyond this activity was considered an undue usurpation of power. Economics, social welfare, religion, and culture belonged to the sphere of private activity, unless they could directly serve the political ends of the state.

But the formal separation of politics from other human activities has always been unfeasible, except for purposes of discussion and, occasionally, of social organization. Maintaining law and order, for instance, had to mean a certain distribution of property or ways of acquiring it—an economic question. The formal separation of the political subsystem of a society could not mean autonomy of every subsystem or its separation from the political subsystem. Law and order, then understood as the essence of politics, are comprehensive and must be maintained in every social activity. Thus, politics penetrates all social activity, making the social system an integrated system. Subsystems always have effects upon each other; and the political subsystem, by ordering all social behavior, of necessity affects every other subsystem. President Gorbachev may have had this inseparability in mind when he told the United Nations (December 7, 1988) that the "new world" called for "a revolutionary revision of views on the sum total of problems of international cooperation as a highly universal element of universal security."

These early liberal or capitalist philosophies did not leave society without some restraints. An underlying value system (usually religiously based) permeated and controlled all social institutions and affected all social behavior. This value system was taken for granted and in some ways substituted for law and often more effectively so. A natural harmony (*ordre naturel*) formed a unifying and controlling base for the entire society. This value system as much as the law set the limits for social action.

The fundamental social control exercised by this ethical system broke down for a number of reasons, among them developing technology, a growing scientific mentality (for example, social analysis), and a multiplication of ethical systems. Subsystems became independent and functioned under controls inherent in themselves (for instance, religion became a private affair, and economics and law became "pure" sciences, unspoiled by moral considerations). The free marketplace ruled the competitive economic system; power dominated the political system; positivism determined the legal system (law is what states consent it to be). The broadening membership of international society secularized its character. Legal norms changed from "Christian principles" or a "natural order" to "civilization." This last integrating principle vanished with the universalization of international society and the elevation of all states to the level of "civilized." Chief Justice Marshall in the *Antelope* case (1825) came to the morally abhorrent decision (for him) that under prevailing—that is, positive—law, slave trading was legal. The absolutism of sovereignty and the subservience of international law to its arrogance can be explained by this loss of an integrating principle.

Legal commitment to cooperation by states for peaceful purposes fits poorly into a system based upon the pursuit of selfish interests by states. Also, agreement to keep states apart from each other is easier to achieve than agreement to commit them to cooperation for peace and general welfare. This is especially true when standards of welfare vary widely and when individual contributions to it would have to be very unequal.

Yet at the beginning of the twentieth century, many lawyers, politicians, and analysts understood that even the selfish pursuit of individual national interests required international cooperation. Their fulfillment became difficult in a political and legal system geared to increasingly antiquated conditions. The rising number of multilateral international agreements on politically "harmless" matters, such as communications, health, and even trade, persuaded some forward-looking writers to draw optimistic conclusions for the future. Max Huber (in 1910), then Paul S. Reinsch, and then later still J. W. Garner predicted the conversion of international society into a closely knit community in which cooperation and interdependence would produce a law emphasizing the duties of states, collective responsibility, international controls, and supranational, instead of merely international, institutions. Ever since, there have been calls for more cooperative laws and euphoric anticipation of a universal obligation to cooperation as the foundation of beneficial international norms. Of course, cooperation is an indispensable condition of community, but cooperation does not necessarily lead to that goal. There are international lawyers doing much wishful thinking in interpreting verbal commitments to cooperation as an obligation to cooperation or who see in actual cooperation steps toward an international community. On festive occasions, such language can still be heard from the highest officials.

But in the daily processes of international relations, the traditional institutions of the nation-state system survive almost unchanged, reinforced by the first seductive taste of many new countries experiencing the reality of these institutions as a novelty. The nationalist mentality keeping them alive has hardly been affected by contrary ceremonial rhetoric, except perhaps in Western Europe, where states are old enough at least to doubt the usefulness of absolute independence. Sovereignty continues to dominate. No ultimate conclusions have been drawn from the admitted realization of its inadequacy for modern needs. No political or legal institutions have been created to assure effectively the political cooperation without which states can no longer satisfy their individual interests, let alone peace.

Mutual needs have led to an enormous volume of treaties and declarations relating to commerce, communications, environmental protection, the limitation of hazardous action, health measures, cultural exchanges, and the advancement of human rights. Technically, these documents represent international cooperation, although for limited, specific purposes. These documents are motivated by selfish interests, not heart. Inevitable mutual needs and the high cost of war make "cooperation" necessary and cheaper. As soon as a state perceives cooperation's cost or disadvantage, it ends. The cutting of the Amazon forests becomes an internal, sovereign matter, even though it may change the world's climate. The killing of whales continues, now allegedly for research, not commerce. Chinese and Americans playing ping-pong was a political signal. The visits of the New York Philharmonic Orchestra and the Bolshoi Ballet to each other's country were suspended when the cold war became colder. The proclaiming of human rights in unending international declarations, and even binding covenants, is belied by the death of mounting numbers of citizens within (mostly undemocratic) countries, surpassing deaths from all wars since 1914. Racism is in practical application the discrimination by whites of people of color, never by one nonwhite group of another. Self-determination of peoples is praised if it does not lead to the dismemberment of states. The list is endless. But quite apart from this expediency, there is a major barrier to cooperative law. Cooperation, in general and in the abstract, cannot be legislated. A blanket rule can forbid the use of force, violence, and coercion, but it cannot command cooperation.

States do not initiate relations to provide an opportunity for cooperation; they do so to satisfy demands of interests. Cooperation as a method for satisfying interests must be preceded by interests. The nature of these interests determines whether, when, and how states cooperate, for better or worse. These conditions cannot be specified in advance. No legal rule can anticipate them. The most a law of cooperation can do is to prescribe that any relationship generated by a common or antagonistic interest between states must be peacefully cooperative. Such a rule would hardly amount to more than prescribing what international law has always prescribed: that states must respect each other's sovereignty and integrity. The refusal, or at least extreme reluctance, of the developed states to grant developing states unequal and favorable treatment under the NIEO demonstrates the veracity of this proposition. Even economic aid, which is presented to the public as an altruistic gesture, is most often justified to those holding the purse strings (Congress, parliaments) as in the national interest.

The much-vaunted and ambivalent United Nations Declaration of Principles of International Law Concerning Friendly Relations and Cooperation Among States in Accordance with the Charter of the United Nations (1970) (hereafter called the Declaration on Friendly Relations) stresses the importance of institutionalizing international cooperation. But, in fact, the declaration merely reaffirms sovereignty and its legal consequences and elaborates on the charter. The declaration retains the tradition features—it remains an instrument for the application of traditional political and legal principles of the nation-state system.

Joint political action by states can be promoted by international organizations mainly within the framework constructed by the charter. The most to be said, in general, for progress toward a law of beneficial cooperation is that in accord with firmly established traditional principles based on sovereignty, the United Nations and all international organizations (again with the possible exception of some European organizations) facilitate and may even stimulate international political cooperation when there is willingness to cooperate.

There has been much talk lately of regimes as expressions and stimulants of cooperation. Stephen D. Krasner defined regimes "as sets of implicit or explicit principles, norms, rules, and decision-making procedures in a given area of international relations" (1968, p. 3). They are presumed to provide guidance for states in future behavior. Regimes may be expanded or contracted. New developments in any given area (oceans, air pollution, outer space) are expected to fit into the general framework established by the regimes. But they remain subject to the principles of sovereignty, and any state can choose to subject itself to the regime or not.

It also remains true—as state practice amply demonstrates—that international organizations in political and other arenas are used for confrontations and entirely hostile purposes and often represent the functional equivalent of impossible hot wars. For example, speeches and debates can function as a constructive attempt to solve a dispute; they can also be used to disseminate propaganda.

On the usually less emotionally charged economic issues, the basic approach of international society is not much more encouraging. The need for cooperation is clearly recognized, and the pressure for it by selfish interests is greater. But the process of securing general economic cooperation as a broad legal obligation is strangely skewed in practice. The emphasis in the 1960s, 1970s, and early 1980s was not on reciprocity or mutual benefit—normally the most reliable basis for well-functioning international law—but on the duties of the developed states, claimed by the developing states, to help in the achievement of development goals. Ambassador Pardo's concept of the "common heritage of mankind" is a good example from an abundance of examples. It is applied to the exploitation of the deep seabed and to the exploration and use of outer space and means that although only a few technically advanced states may be able to extract resources or other advantages from these areas, the benefits should accrue to all states. In fact, this principle is a demand for (one-sided) altruism hitherto unknown in international relations and essentially rejected by those who would have to pay the price.

If the basic economic documents produced by the developing states (the Declaration of the New International Economic Order [1974], the Program of Action on the Establishment of a New International Economic Order [1974], and the Charter of Economic Rights and Duties of States [1974]) are taken jointly with the U.N. Charter and the Declaration on Friendly Relations (1970) as the blueprints for the political and economic future of international society—beyond the early post–World War II agencies—one sees that an international law of cooperation has not advanced noticeably beyond the vague obligation "to cooperate" or beyond specific treaties. This failure is not surprising. States are notoriously reluctant to commit themselves to broad, general principles whose consequences are practically unforeseeable.

The situation is better in regard to narrower and more specific purposes stipulated in bilateral and multilateral treaties. A few such purposes (for example, the General Agreement on Tariffs and Trade [GATT], which the United States was accused in 1989 of violating; the International Monetary Fund [IMF], which France has been accused of violating; economic antidumping; aspects of the most-favored-nation clause; cultural exchanges; transboundary air pollution; marine pollution by dumping wastes and other matters; limitation of the use and production of chlorofluorocarbons; and currency arrangements) are of sufficient concern to a sufficient number of states and sufficiently specific to be introduced in cooperative treaties. These purposes benefit all parties and do not interfere with sovereignty; and when they do, they are disobeyed. The absence of an obligation to cooperate permeating and conditioning all international norms is emphasized by state practice to talk simultaneously of sovereignty whenever there is talk of cooperation in conferences. This practice is not an attempt to dissolve the possible legal discrepancy between the two concepts but to stress that all cooperation is subject to sovereignty. Evidently, states place their individuality above their solidarity.

In this hierarchy of values, states exist, of necessity, side by side, with no common, higher decisionmaking authority that could enforce beneficial cooperation. Each state is a power center. And as almost everything can increase the power potential of a state, the international society is heavily politicized—to the detriment of cooperation. Even cultural exchanges can be as political in intent and effect as a military alliance. UNESCO, intended as a cultural and politically "neutral" institution par excellence, is almost as often a political battlefield as the General Assembly or the Security Council is. When some of the struggles over the freedom of the press or over the Israeli-Arab conflict are recalled (to name only two examples), it becomes clear how far removed UNESCO is from the cooperative scientific humanism advocated as its basis by its first general secretary, Julian Huxley. In an area in which cooperation should be relatively easy to achieve, political battles take place as in most other international agencies. The greatest hope for progress in cooperation lies in the European Community—but that is still mostly a hope.

20
POLITICAL COOPERATION

Cooperation as a Legal Obligation

The most comprehensive and general, although still limited, commitment for cooperation in the political sphere is embodied in the U.N. Charter. The limitation exists in the focus of the United Nations upon the maintenance of peace—a comprehensive purpose to be sure, but not all-encompassing. Moreover, the term *cooperation* first appears in Article 1, #3 of the charter in connection with problems of an economic, a cultural, or a humanitarian character. There is no reference to politics, only to collective measures to be taken by the states to achieve the maintenance of peace. A degree of cooperation involving politics is inevitable in the collectivity of the measures to be taken, of course. But avoiding an explicit reference to cooperation in political matters may be symptomatic of the reluctance of states to be bound in this respect and to sacrifice part of their sovereignty.

The Declaration on Friendly Relations (1970) reflects this spirit. Its bulk, insofar as political matters are concerned, is merely another elaboration on the duties of states to abstain from behavior interfering with other states' sovereignty and its consequences. In a brief section on "the duty of states to co-operate with one another in accordance with the Charter," the duty for cooperation for the maintenance of peace and security is mentioned. But no hint is given what this duty specifically involves and when states would be in default of this duty. This section relates at most to the type of state behavior, not the goal. The creators of the declaration in the International Law Commission were not only puzzled by what the meaning might be of what they were formulating as a duty of states; they were totally frustrated in specifying any detail. Even though it was claimed that in spite of all the uncertainty the duty to cooperate in the political sphere had become a legal obligation, agreement also prevailed that cooperation was too subjective a concept for legal definition. Too much would depend upon the capacity of an individual state, its needs, and its exercise of sovereignty.

The continuing emphasis in the Declaration on Friendly Relations (1970), following the charter, upon abstention rather than joint action as the major substance of political cooperation shows that in all these decades states have not changed their preference for a right to individual existence over an obligation to cooperate in political matters. Aleksandr Prokhanov, in an article in *Literaturnya Rossia* (May 6, 1988), expressed frankly a thought not limited to the Soviet mind when he wrote that "it is to our glory and honor that we preserved, as the germ of future possibilities, the great ethical ideals: . . . the idea of sovereignty."

Subsequent articles in the charter relating to the activities of the General Assembly in political matters are permissive, perhaps suggestive, but not binding. The General Assembly is authorized to "consider the general principles of cooperation in the maintenance of international peace and security." It may initiate studies and make recommendations for the purpose of "promoting international cooperation in the political field." All these proposals are far from binding legislation, a power the General Assembly was not intended to have.

The Security Council's activities in maintaining peace could involve some obligation to cooperate. Parties to a dispute may be obliged to cooperate toward its peaceful settlement. All member states may be obligated to cooperate in taking collective measures against a disturber of the peace. These are possible, but not necessary, obligations. And they are limited in scope and purpose. They do not amount to a general obligation to cooperate, and in the few cases when the Security Council decided upon collective opposition to aggression (such as in the case of North Korea), a large number of states refused participation.

The cooperation envisaged by the U.N. Charter in political matters is limited to the maintenance of peace as the common purpose of states. This could be a very broad or a very narrow purpose. At any rate, it is of dubious effectiveness as an incentive for cooperation because there are many ways to peace. Indeed, the maintenance of peace may not even be the common purpose of states. Some states may favor war between some other states (the United States and the USSR together supply about two-thirds of the Third World's weapons) and may foster wars between satellite or client states. Even for themselves, states want only a peace determined by such self-defined qualities as justice, dignity, or honor. (Depending upon the definition of war, there have been dozens of wars since the end of World War II.)

The use states have made of the United Nations and some of its specialized agencies indicates that a very narrow definition of peace (the absence of physical violence) allows the organization to be used as a tool to carry out hostilities and turn it into a battlefield, albeit a bloodless one, as much as an instrument for obligatory beneficial cooperation.

Differing Views on the Law of Political Cooperation

Given the varied and sometimes contradictory political activities in the United Nations, the existence of differing views on its character and influence on international law or as a tool of cooperation is not surprising. The ever-increasing activity in the United Nations and especially in its specialized agencies and their commissions has encouraged the idealists who expect that the inevitably augmenting volume of international interaction needing coordination, regularity, predictability—in other words, needing social order—will eventually turn international organizations, with the United Nations at its head, into something resembling a world government. The organization would not merely be assigned the coordination of other actors (mainly states) but would become an actor in its own right, with all the appurtenances of a government, including legislative power.

Somewhat related is the view that considers the United Nations a potential world executive. Trygvie Lie, first secretary general of the United Nations, spoke of his assistant secretaries as his cabinet. The purpose of maintaining peace, in this view, includes concern with, and to some extent management of, all possible conditions guaranteeing and causing war and rightly so because no one knows the causes of war. This view is favorable to an active promotion of beneficial cooperation and to its institution as a legal obligation. The charters creating international organizations are considered constitutions, thereby making these organizations relatively independent from their creators (the states) and organs in their own right. There are a few international organizations to which this description already applies if one wants to stretch the point (for example, the international financial organizations).

The treatment meted out to and the use made of international organizations by their member states make the views that they will develop into a world government extremely Pollyannaish. The fact remains that states tend to force new norms and institutions into the existing traditional—and admittedly anachronistic—framework of the international system.

Another view, nearer the present and the very likely future reality, considers the United Nations and other international organizations as little more than a permanent conference for the settlement or disputes and the avoidance of violent hostilities. As an instrument to facilitate peaceful international relations, the United Nations should not assume even a shade of supranationalism or an international personality of its own. This view is not affected by the existence of specialized agencies or commissions that have had success in sponsoring beneficial political cooperation and even some covenants binding its parties—to which, however, their agreement remained necessary! This may be taken as additional evidence that in principle an international organization—even where it has had success—remains a servant, not a master, of states.

The Communist states initially rejected the more optimistic views of international organization. But in the mid-1950s, they had begun to change their views. At first, the Communist states granted international subjectivity to the United Nations, and then gradually, as they together with the states of the Third World began to have majorities in many organizations, they granted subjectivity to other organizations.

Under President Gorbachev, the point has been reached where Soviet (and Chinese) lawyers have admitted the absolute need for "cooperation" in an "interdependent world." This greater emphasis upon "cooperation" rather than—as hitherto—upon "peaceful coexistence and competition" could signify a less reserved acceptance of classical international law. It could mean a change in the Soviet Union's view of classical international law as class law and the USSR's acceptance of it as the "higher form" of international law, which so far has been considered possible only between socialist states.

Nevertheless, these lawyers rigidly adhere to the institution of sovereignty and accuse Western lawyers of introducing concepts of constitutional law by talking of charters as constitutions. These concepts, according to the Soviets and Chinese, introduce an unjustifiable flexibility in the interpretation of the organizations' charters and an expansion of their activities that was not originally intended. The Soviets and Chinese consider such action merely another "bourgeois" attempt to bend the United Nations to "imperialistic" purposes and to justify "violations" of the charter (for example, the Uniting for Peace Resolution of 1950). The Soviets are correct at least insofar as they evaluate international organizations as another political instrument of states, responding to modern needs, whose employment the Communist states find as useful as the "bourgeois" states.

Whatever the views held by international laws and governments, international organizations are political instruments. They share with politics the dynamics of responding to the needs and interests of states. There is both awareness of the increasing political activities of international organizations beyond specific provisions of their charters and agreement on their inevitability. On September 26, 1989, Soviet foreign minister Eduard Shevardnadze told the U.N. General Assembly that the world must develop a "new model of security" based on "political and legal guarantees." In October, other Soviet delegates told the General Assembly that their country was working to develop through the United Nations "a comprehensive strategy for establishing the primacy of the rule of law in relations between states." But this strategy was nothing newer than the arrangements incorporated in the U.N. Charter under the heading "Pacific Settlement of Disputes." Nevertheless, this was a new tone for the Soviet Union. It could also be heard from Soviet lawyers and from President Gorbachev. He spoke on December 7, 1988, in the General Assembly on the priority of a universal legal order over state policies for the sake of humankind's survival, of a "common security" to be achieved not by deterrence but by cooperation. He also suggested that "universal human interests will be the basis of progress" and therefore that world politics must be determined "by the priority of universal human values."

He will find much agreement on this view. But disputes will still arise over legal meanings. Those construing charters narrowly argue that these broader activities are legitimate because in each individual case states agree to them. Those construing charters more liberally argue that organizations have a right to these activities regardless of specific consent of states. These analysts are resting their case on the doctrines of the "implied powers" and the "inherent jurisdiction" of international organizations.

The International Court of Justice in the *Reparation for Injuries Suffered in the Service of the United Nations* case (1949, p. 168) decided, as had the Permanent Court of International Justice before it, that "under international law, the Organization must be deemed to have those powers which, though not expressly provided in the Charter, are conferred upon it by necessary implication as being essential to the performance of its duties." In the *Certain Expenses of the United Nations* case (1962, p. 168), the Court reflected the "inherent jurisdiction" doctrine by saying, "When the Organization takes action which warrants the assertion that it was appropriate for the fulfillment of one of the stated purposes of the United Nations, the presumption is that such action is not *ultra vires* the Organization."

There is no denying that political cooperation through and in international organization has made progress—although the organization as the arena for the conduct of the cold war should not be forgotten. This progress was inevitable in any case, as international society grew in membership and interaction. Examples of some advances are the settlement of international disputes through cooperative action in global or regional organizations, the development of peacekeeping and truce-supervising activities, the formation of international "peace" forces, and contributions to the regulation and control of atomic weaponry and international spaces. The bases for such cooperation—whether voluntary or obligatory—may have differed in the minds of participating governments. There is, however, no evidence that political cooperation has yet become a universal legal rule, as some newer states are claiming. It may be more correct to say that international organizations are there when they are wanted, especially for informal conversations, but they do not have to be used. Jeane Kirkpatrick, when she was the U.S. representative to United Nations, was even said to consider the organization "a dangerous place" rather than a step toward world government because the increasing membership of the United Nations was leading to bloc formations, logrolling, polarization, and Third World states' exploitation of their majority.

As a matter of fact, the U.N. peacekeeping record is mixed; as the cold war receded some of the major world politics issues were handled by the major powers on a bilateral or multilateral basis outside the international organizations—as was often the case when these powers wanted to achieve results. They did so not to fulfill some legal obligation to cooperate but because they considered it the best way to take care of their national interests—by avoiding the glass house atmosphere of the United Nations or the "nuisance" of the small states.

Whatever amount of cooperation in international organizations is taking place, Kurt Waldheim's judgment has been that international organizations will never be able to guarantee the maintenance of peace as long as the decision of states "as sovereign entities" is not subject to a higher authority. In other words, whether or not cooperation is a legal duty is not decisive to the ends of the United Nations.

21
ECONOMIC COOPERATION
AS A LEGAL OBLIGATION

The Roots

The need for institutionalized economic cooperation dawned on states between the two world wars. The economic catastrophes during that period brought the realization that peace could not be maintained only by political measures; because the origins of the threats to peace were often economic, economic activity would have to be organized to prevent peace's deterioration. But this initial analysis was of very limited scope and undertaken by few people. The organizational results, emerging just before the outbreak of World War II, were meager. Few laws related to economic behavior.

Until that time, states were conducting their economic relations by norms heavily influenced by the liberal doctrine of laissez-faire. This approach derived from ideological convictions as well as from its easy reconciliation with political sovereignty. In operation, this approach meant granting states and their nationals freedom to pursue public and private interests selfishly, regardless of the effects upon other states. The corresponding, albeit almost nonexistent, legal framework remained, and to some extent still remains, unchanged; the laws of an orthodox capitalist system were extended to the global level, unless a state rejected the relevant legal norms. Governments strongly committed to capitalism tended to oppose international controls, regulatory agencies, or any other measures that might have interfered with a free market system.

But now the system of unrestrained capitalism is losing popularity, and even though Gorbachev and the 1989 Paris summit of the major capitalist states appealed for an integrated economic world system, the inherited legal system is difficult to reconcile with the demands of a modern global economic system. International arguments over acquired rights or compensation for expropriated private property illustrate the situation. Because there is no feasible global legal system, these ultimately ideological differences are overcome by specific bilateral treaties between the Communist and capitalist countries or between states of each group, thereby adding to the agglomeration of individual treaties already in existence. When Switzerland announced that it would not join a future European Community, it also announced that, typically, it would relate to the EC's members by a set of individual treaties.

Advances in many fields and a European division of labor after World War II produced treaties for specific beneficial economic purposes. These obviated to some extent wars for economic ends but also pointed to the structuring of a comprehensive economic order based on numerous individual treaties. Each treaty leads its own existence, fulfills its own purpose, and is based on the sovereign consent of its partners. This situation is unaffected by the fact that (1) some of these treaties relate to minor matters and others to major matters of multilateral interest, such as the IMF and the World Bank; (2) some are global in scope and some are regional in scope; and (3) some are of significance to some states only at a certain stage of their development.

These treaties reinforce established principles for the preservation of reciprocal national interests and usually for the sanctity of private property. States were bound for centuries according to customary law to protect each other's nationals, their property, investments, trade, and acquired rights. A network of bilateral agreements implemented the traditional general legal commitments. But in the spirit of liberalism, many of these are enabling instruments.

The legal treatment of states in the international economic process is almost as "negative" as that in the political process. The business of states is to maintain the play of a free, competitive, global economic system—unless the struggle for power corrupts the system. At any rate, there is no thought of active, positive international cooperation for the promotion of a common welfare. At most, states will engage themselves not to act in a manner harmful to the other party. But even this is a general norm of international law applicable to all matters. Pope John Paul II severely criticized such an international economic system in his encyclical letter *On Social Concern* (1987, p. 72). He reminded states that "interdependence must be transformed into *solidarity*, based upon the principle that the goods of creation are meant for all. That which human industry produces through the processing of raw materials, with the contribution of work, must serve equally for the good of all." Perhaps not too far removed from this pronouncement was President Gorbachev's statement to the United Nations (December 8, 1988) that the world economy is now a "single organism outside of which no state can develop normally, no matter what social system it belongs to."

What international society failed to foresee or notice even after World War II were widespread changes in economic processes and the state's role in them. These changes, nationally and internationally, caused a move away from laissez-faire economics and straight into an international legal vacuum. Among the more significant aspects of these changes were four. First, economic interaction became voluminous and was further augmented when colonialism ended. The end of colonialism not only increased the membership of the international society; it turned relations between the metropolitan power and the colony from a domestic into an international affair. Second, the participation of states in economic processes uninterested in or opposed to any guarantee of the free market introduced problems considered novel, and therefore ignored, by existing international law. Third, economics became a foremost element in the power potential of states and in the process rendered outdated those legal regulations still based on an international laissez-faire system and demolished any attempt to separate politics from economics. Fourth, and probably most important, the entrance of the Third World into the global economic area brought with it a division in the economic existence of states quantitatively so different as to be also qualitatively different.

The U.N. Charter at least stipulates international cooperation for the solution of economic problems as one of the organization's purposes. In contrast to the League of Nations Covenant, the charter devotes two chapters to economic cooperation and its institutionalization through the Economic and Social Council. Joint and separate action for the improvement of people's living standards and the solution of economic problems is made a duty of states in Article 56. These are not only unspecified duties; they also are not self-executing. They require additional international conventions for their implementation. A large number of such conventions have been concluded for the formation of specialized agencies, commissions, committees, and special conferences devoted to particular economic problems. No aspect of international economic life has remained untouched. But with a few exceptions, these conventions do not bind their members.

If discussions, research, recommendations, and resolutions can be called cooperation, great progress has been made, essentially in the spirit of capitalism. Yet out of these talks a number of important multilateral treaties have also emerged. Their substantive scope is always limited and specialized, but the number of signatories is often so large that in fact some new international law has been created—for example, the GATT, the IMF, the International Bank for Reconstruction and Development. But these treaties were concluded voluntarily and set no precedent for obligatory economic cooperation in general. They all preserve the principle of sovereign equality. They do not fulfill the charter's vision of legally required, comprehensive international cooperation to solve the world's economic problems. Regional organizations have turned out to be more successful in this regard.

In drawing up the Charter of the United Nations, the founding states tried to recoup what they had missed before the war. Though not anticipating the full impact of novelties in economics, they demonstrated a change of mind in at least suggesting that the new type of economics required new or additional regulation.

The implementation of the charter with new rules and organizations as time went on showed a previously lacking flexibility. Nevertheless, not only did binding norms—as compared to suggested regulations—lag behind newly arising needs. When at various times the world economy went through depressions, even binding norms were disobeyed, regardless of what they did to other states (for example, unilateral devaluation of currencies, protectionist trade measures, and economic sanctions justified as self-defense). Cooperation went out the window, and every state tried to save its own economic existence, as it still does, all talk of "interdependence" notwithstanding. In fact, a number of multilateral treaties foresee and allow individual members exceptional action if they feel the need to do so—for instance, to adjust "a fundamental disequilibrium" (Article 4, Section 5 of the Agreement on the International Monetary Fund, 1945) or to cooperate for the preservation of the environment "in such a way that due account is taken of the sovereignty and interests of all states," (Declaration of the United Nations Conference on the Human Environment, Article 24, 1972).

Development as a Right

When the issue of the developing states became acute, it tended to overshadow most other economic problems, at least as an enduring problem. The states of the Third World were not satisfied with an international economic law whose rules referred to the behavior of states but not to the goals of such behavior. At the Algiers Conference in 1972, the Third World states agreed that the real-world issue was elimination of economic neocolonialism and the creation of a just and equitable economic system. With the help of the NIEO, these states suggested in 1974 that international law not only regulate the behavior of states but also establish the specific overall objective—namely, elimination of the inequality between the developing and the developed states and allotment to the former of their due share in the world's economic progress. Recently, however, this preoccupation is at least matched by the problem of reducing the enormous Third World foreign debts. At the same time, changes in First World preoccupations have reduced the interest of the major powers in the fate of the smaller, especially weaker states.

Although the united effort of the Third World states brought their plight and problems into the forefront of international discussion, events within the Third World have weakened that effort to the point where their joint action has lost credibility and power. Development is now only one of many international economic problems to be solved. Among the many reasons for the deemphasis on development within the Third World are mutual antagonisms and wars as well as differing problems. In Africa the problem is food; in Asia it is industrialization; in Latin America it is use of raw materials and inflation. Everywhere there is ethnic strife, and many parts of the Third World are in disarray. The members of the Third World are growing apart—for instance, Taiwan or South Korea would find it difficult to assume the same positions vis-à-vis the First World as some poor African state would. In addition, some members permitted themselves to be coopted by their former colonial masters (for example, the Lomé agreements); on ocean policy and hence on ocean law the relevant Third World members differ greatly in some of their goals (India is building a navy that will eventually surpass Britain's Royal Navy); considerable disagreement prevails between and within Third World countries on the right path to development; and in all too many Third World countries, development means little more than augmenting the foreign bank accounts of the ruling classes.

In the face of such a situation, it becomes difficult to speak of legalizing the relatively undifferentiated New International Economic Order for a group of such disparate states and nearly impossible to think of a normative order aiming specifically at cooperation to solve the development problems of the Third World.

The norm "taking into account, in particular, the interests of developing countries," which is found in virtually all multilateral agreements, has lost much of its meaning when the conditions of these countries differ so greatly and some of their interests have become antagonistic. Nevertheless, the debate continues, if in a lower key, as to whether these states have a right to development, although the debate largely ignores the differences prevailing among the developing countries and what gives legal norms concrete content.

The parties to this debate confront each other from opposing sides. Those favoring the existence of a right to development (Philip Alston, Wil D. Verwey, and Maurice Flory, among them) refer to a number of international statements since World War II from which a right to development is said to have gradually emerged. Foremost is the pledge in the U.N. Charter, Articles 55 and 56, of all members to take joint and separate action with the United Nations to promote welfare, higher standards of living, education, social welfare, human rights, and so on. Advocates cite in support of their argument the implementation of this pledge, which includes the granting to developing states of special privileges in treaties and international organizations (for example, the GATT, the IMF, nonreciprocity in a number of international dealings, and many unilateral privileges in bilateral agreements) and the references to a duty for cooperation in development in innumerable resolutions in the General Assembly and other bodies of international organizations.

These advocates refer to meetings of UNESCO and the Commission on Human Rights in the 1970s in which a right to development was suddenly considered a fait accompli. They use the Universal Declaration of Human Rights (1948), the two covenants on political and social rights, and dozens of international declarations in toto as justifying a right to development. To this foundation advocates have added ethical considerations, especially justice in general, as proving the existence of a right to development, for which a number of precedents in international resolutions could be cited. The absence of a specific legal document establishing a right to development, say the advocates, is merely indicative of a failure to adapt international law to new conditions and should be rectified. If the individual covenants calling for feeding, clothing, educating, and granting special trading and financial rights to underdeveloped peoples are taken together, they represent a new type of legal order amounting to a right to development. This right, it is contended, reflects the injection of ethical considerations into the international legal system as a constantly progressing trend.

The right to development, advocates contend, becomes merely a logical consequence of the granting of independence and decolonization to peoples. The obligation of the First World is to undo the consequences of the suppression of colonial peoples for hundreds of years. In a world with two such unequal parts, sovereign equality is in fact denied unless the economic imbalance between the two is eliminated. Finally, they argue, principles of solidarity of states for the preservation of peace, which underly the idea of the United Nations, cannot be realized without implementing the suggestions to be found in the NIEC, including the right of Third World states to development.

Taken together with binding covenants such as the U.N. Charter— as the advocates interpret these—all these resolutions merely reinforce the existence of a right to development. Advocates are particularly insistent in using legal language because it permits access to a wide range of legal norms that would be helpful in enforcing development as a right. They will not admit that these international instruments referring to development have mainly hortatory significance or are of a recommendatory nature. They insist that a right to development is not to be established at some future date or in the process of emerging. For them, it exists now. Some do admit, however, that much of the right's foundation rests on "soft" law, which, however, is to them no reason to accept a positivist straightjacket.

On the other side of the debate are those (for example, Jack Donelly) who insist that there is no international instrument affirming or founding development as a legal right. The constant reiteration of the existence of such a right does not create it. Most of the documents used to demonstrate a right to development treat development as a goal, not a right, that may eventually emerge from the practice of all human rights. Self-determination neither explicitly nor implicitly recognizes a right to development, only a right to self-determination.

The Universal Declaration of Human Rights (1948) as base for customary law, opponents argue, even though accepted publicly by many states, suffers from any demonstration of *opinio iuris* as an indispensable element of its existence. One way of determining its existence is the domestic behavior of a state. The behavior within a very great number of Third World states fails to show respect for human rights. Therefore, one essential part of human rights as customary law, and therefore of a right to development derived from them, is missing—quite apart from the fact that human rights refer to individuals, not peoples. The many sources allegedly demonstrating a right to development, mainly General Assembly resolutions, UNESCO declarations, and regional charters and recommendations, not only fail to mention any right to development but lack the universal acceptance to create one. Moreover, a law of development is not equivalent to a right to development. Moral arguments as a foundation of a right to development are rejected on various grounds as a source of a positive right to development. Finally, this group argues, there is no agreement, even if there is mention of, who possesses the right to development, who has the duty to assist in development, what is to be supplied as assistance to development, and how the use of aid to development for purposes of development could be supervised, especially in view of the developing states' insistence upon their sovereignty.

The Economic Division
of the World and the Law

The division of the world into East-West and North-South is a hurdle preventing the growth of a comprehensive economic legal system. East and West have more or less solved their problem through bilateral negotiations and agreements. This is not the case between the developed and the developing states. The developing states do not cherish the free market, although it is useful for the preservation of sovereignty. They have changed their initial tactics from making demands to assuming active roles in international forums. They are trying to use international law to obtain a greater share of the world's wealth, but they differ from the developed states, and from each other, in how they approach the regulation of economic relations. As some of the Third World states are nearing developed status, this difference becomes less pronounced. But it still exists to some extent, and, quite often, for the sake of unity, the more developed states are inclined to accept the position of the least developed.

Most of the developed states remain attached to the institutions, legal and otherwise, of laissez-faire, concessions to state intervention domestically and internationally notwithstanding. Their conception of an international economic cooperative law is maintenance of a free international market or prevention of future controlling interference by states. Developed states consider this approach to be most responsive to the U.N. Charter, Article 55, which calls for "respect for the principle of equal rights and self-determination of peoples" as the basis of economic cooperation.

Most developing states would not necessarily deny these principles. But as an Indian official once expressed it, because "equitable treatment is equitable only among equals," developing states have their special interpretation of equality. Before laws supportive of a free market can be just, gross inequalities must be eliminated. Developing states insist therefore upon the creation of equality in some material sense, which is to be achieved by granting them unequal, favorable (preferential) treatment, as proposed in the NIEO. In some cases, preferential treatment has been granted. At the same time, however, developing states implicitly object to the customary rule of international law permitting discriminatory behavior among states in the economic sphere (as when developed states grant each other most-favored-nation treatment).

The solution of this apparent paradox of creating equality through inequality lies in the claim of the developing states that formal equality without some material equality is meaningless. They can therefore not go too far in demanding nondiscrimination and equality in economic behavior, lest they undermine their insistence upon favorable, unequal treatment themselves. The Declaration on Friendly Relations (1970), for instance, contains no explicit prohibition of discriminatory treatment in international trade relations. Presumably, until these states have reached some level of equality satisfactory to them, their emphasis is upon their special, unequal, favorable treatment.

The developing states argue therefore that a future economic order must be based upon some (unspecified) substantive equality, not on a formal equality that in fact leads to increasing inequalities. Far from negating equality or cooperation, interpretation by developing states of these concepts gives them reality and acceptable meaning. The basic principles and rules developing states are demanding in scores of international resolutions are therefore diametrically opposed to those cherished by economic liberalism. Developing states insist as legal obligations upon the protection of their developing economies, upon a cooperation that strengthens weak economies, upon aid as rectification of economic imbalances, upon preferential treatment to close gaps between rich and poor states, upon the right to form cartels for their own raw materials, and upon many other kinds of one-sided advantages. In many of their joint declarations, the developing states reject the principle of reciprocity or free competition as inapplicable between developed and developing states. These are the kinds of demands with which some of the more advanced developing states either do not go along or are making clear that they do so hesitantly and for the sake of unity in the Third World.

With the help of the majorities they command in U.N. organs and conferences, the developing states have passed numerous broad resolutions embodying these principles. In addition, they have done the same in resolutions of more limited scope dealing with economic matters such as trade, tariffs, raw materials, shipping, and transfer of technologies. As a justification, developing countries not only cite the principles they have already employed; they also use the "common heritage of mankind" concept wherever the developed states are clearly too far ahead for the developing states ever to catch up, such as in deep seabed mining and exploration and exploitation of outer space. The success of the developing states in introducing some of their demands into more limited, specialized treaties has not been matched by attempts to convert such treaty rules into universal norms of state behavior. It is therefore premature to talk of the existence of a comprehensive international law of cooperation, at least as the developing states interpret this concept. The Indian author R. K. Sinha felt constrained in 1985 in speaking of the attempt to create the NIEO to state that because of the failure of the North to cooperate with the South, "no fruitful results have come out so far" and "the prospect appears ever gloomier." Although such pessimism appears justified in regard to an overall universal global economic system, it can hardly be applied to the narrower, more specific privileges that the developed states have granted the developing states. These privileges are based on the preparedness of sovereign states to make these concessions, and there is no way to insist on further concessions. But this behavior is based less on arbitrariness or individual political considerations than on the unwillingness of all states to commit themselves to broad, unspecified obligations.

The common denominator of developing and developed states is, after all, their approach to the problem of cooperative law on the basis of their national interests. This approach has not prevented some advances in cooperative law. But the growth has been selective and piecemeal. The rise of interests requiring international cooperation has produced some new phenomena in international law, not all of them favorable to the future of a global cooperative international law. The frequently asserted assumption that the greater the volume of international interaction, the better are the chances for a universal international law of cooperation has not been borne out in the past, and there is no reason to believe that it will be in the future. What can be expected with certainty is only that the volume of international law, but not necessarily any specific kind of law, will grow parallel to the increasing volume of new international interactions. Recent trends in the international legal system in this respect illustrate the point.

One discernible trend regarding cooperation is a great volume of mostly bilateral or limited multilateral treaties regulating specific aspects of new economic relations on a reciprocal national-interest basis. A second trend is pressure for a more truly international cooperative law, mainly in the economic sphere, to which the developed states are slow to surrender. A third trend is the emergence of developing states as a new category of international law subjects, with groups of states at different stages of development forming subcategories. Attached to these categories are carefully graded rights and privileges (but rarely obligations). The phenomenon is not new (there have been landlocked states), merely more obvious and more frequent. Finally, there is the fact—not favorable to the universalization of international law or to the developing countries—that the bulk of new treaty law of economic cooperation covers relations between developed states for the simple reason that they have the most new interests and relations. That law is based mostly on traditional principles of reciprocity and is strongly influenced by economic liberalism.

Two opposing views may be taken about this development. One is that this type of law will survive and will eventually expand throughout the world as developing states reach a certain level in their development. The other is that the legal, hence the political-economic, arrangements between the presently developed states will widen the gap between rich and poor states.

This last possibility appears at present the more likely (with some rapidly developing states joining the group of the rich). The quasi-universal, nonbinding declarations that are often sponsored by the Third World have little chance of turning into binding, global international law of cooperation because much of the time they lack the support of the most developed states. The most important documents of this kind (such as the 1974 Declaration of a New International Economic Order and related instruments and the 1974 Charter of Economic Rights and Duties of States) tend to divide the world into two mutually exclusive groups subscribing to incompatible legal systems. One can see in them the symptoms of a divided world as readily as one can see the heralds of a future one world.

A U.S. delegate once pointed out during an international conference on economic matters that the successful passage of grandiloquent resolutions on new economic orders in the world by majorities of developing and Communist states could produce only illusions about political and legal realities. He reflected more than the U.S. stance on these matters. If, as Sinha claims, the outlook for the developing states remains gloomy, the fault lies to some extent in the unwillingness of developed *and* of developing states to make concessions. The stubbornness of First World states and the militancy of many Third World states have helped to delay the growth of an international economic and political law of cooperation from which all states could benefit.

The delayed arrival of some new international economic order can be traced ultimately to the continuing dominance of sovereignty. It leads to the fragmentation into national economies and political units of what in fact are a world economy and a global polity. All states, developed as well as developing, are equally attached to their sovereignty, which is increasingly becoming a facsimile rather than a representation of reality. But the developed states take their independence for granted. They are more relaxed about sovereignty (and in Western Europe possibly even willing to sacrifice it to the European Community) and show very little anxiety about being dominated by some foreign power. Developing states feel insecure largely because of differences in economic status.

Their partly real, partly imagined dependence upon developed states for their own progress reminds them of the colonial era. They are therefore of two minds in international economic matters. Their predicament leads them to urge a greater volume of economic relations and cooperation in their favor but also to stipulate conditions of stringent national control that frustrate cooperation.

While proposing an economic legal order asking for concessive actions by the developed states (some of these actions would be difficult to reconcile with "sovereign equality"), developing states are concerned (not always without reason) that a favorable response to their demands might generate neocolonialism. They are hoping to prevent this eventuality by fencing in their economic relations with norms heavily relying on sovereignty (such as compensation for expropriation according to national laws only, forbidding of very broadly defined "coercive" use of economic matters, no reciprocity). Developing states are more prepared to slight the sovereignty of developed states by demanding structural changes in the economic activities of developed states and by, so to speak, imposing international taxes upon them for the purpose of helping the developing states in the name of an international duty toward cooperation and solidarity (see, especially the Charter of Economic Rights, Articles 14 and 17, and demands for forgiving the repayment of loans.)

These conditions make economic relations quite unattractive for developed countries, which reject the legitimization of these unequal conditions by fairness and justice as inadmissibly mixing morals and economics. The basic discrepancy in interests between the developing and the developed states results in an inability of the parties to agree to legal norms and is responsible for the long delay in the creation of some legally binding new international economic order. In the meantime, some of the more rapidly developing states have appeared willing to deal with the developed states on the basis of essentially traditional legal rules, thereby encouraging the impression of their continuing validity.

22
ENVIRONMENTAL
PROTECTION

Protection of the environment is a subject that demands international cooperation. Damage to the environment is usually not limited to any one state. Many of the causes of this damage have transboundary effects. Yet although a few treaties for the protection of birds date back to the beginning of the twentieth century, no progress was made to protect the environment, mainly because there was little awareness of the problem until the middle of the century. Then the issue became almost explosive, but little has been achieved to defuse it. There is an abundance of plans but a dearth of action in relation to the size of the problem and the number of resolutions. Although environmental protection officials with Cabinet rank have been appointed in several countries, the percentage of money spent on protecting the environment compared to the gross national product in most countries has declined since 1975.

There is much discussion but no comprehensive legal regime devoted to the protection of the environment. There are only narrow treaties, broad declarations, some inconsistent national practices, and some possibly customary laws relating to specific issues. In their totality, these documents and actions cannot even euphemistically be called the "legal order for cooperation on environmental protection." Moreover, many measures protect individuals rather than the environment.

There is no legal rule upon which a binding cooperative order for the protection of the environment could be built, unless it be some very vague norm, such as good neighborliness or state use of rights in such a way as not to damage others. Even if a legal rule were adopted as a foundation, it would be subject to a great variety of interpretations and would be negative in the sense that it would tell states what they should not do to each other rather than what must be done positively to protect the environment.

New binding rules specifically focused on the environment are difficult even to suggest, mainly because the environment encompasses all aspects of life. Whether there can be a comprehensive, systematic solution to a problem of such dimension is a legitimate question. An international legal order would have to fuse virtually every aspect of human existence into a consistent system, for which there is neither a precedent nor a prospect. The complaint about the absence of a coherent conceptual framework for a legal order of the environment can at best lead to a multitude of specific agreements that are consistent with each other and that represent some groping toward a comprehensive regime.

There are many reasons for this situation, apart from the magnitude of the problem.

1. The topic is so broad and complex and the environment is such an interdependent unit that an overall codification to cover all possibilities is virtually impossible.
2. Some issues are of interest to only a limited number of states.
3. Many causes of environmental damage are unknown, and new ones arise from time to time.
4. States fear the supranational institutions that are likely to be needed for effective remedies, especially because a very high percentage of all pollution originates from land-based (national) sources. States worry that the need to "inform and consult" might be used as interference in internal affairs.
5. Developing states worry that developed states will use pollution controls as a trick to interfere with development or reduce their competitiveness by requests for expensive controls.
6. Developing states are convinced in any case that pollution is a problem of developed states. They are, however, now beginning to realize either that they have their own environmental problems or that their development causes damage regardless of the stage of development. (See General Assembly Resolution 2849 [XXVI] 1972.)
7. The principle that "the polluter pays" is considered another trick of the developed countries by the developing states to reduce their competitiveness.
8. Capitalist states fear state control, in particular if environmental controls are connected to the common heritage of mankind concept.
9. Communist states opposed any kind of international supervision until they began to realize that damage to the environment was transgressing ideologies as much as national borders. Gorbachev, in a speech at Murmansk (*Pravda*, October 2, 1988), made an ardent plea for national and international protection of the environment. During his visit to Western Europe in 1989 he placed environmental protection above ideology and class struggle.
10. The "creeping territorialization" of the sea aggravates all the problems that derive from insistence upon sovereignty.
11. Potential military uses that might damage the environment (such as weather control or crop destruction) interfere with an international solution to the environment problem.

12. The materialist character of capitalism and communism makes any restriction on consumption or any other measures interfering with their quest for "more, more, more" extremely difficult.
13. The benefits and burdens of protective measures are likely to be unevenly distributed, so that "equitability" will be very difficult to achieve and any incentive to act diminished.
14. The solution must be global—a near-impossibility in the face of the multitude of sovereign, different types of states.
15. Many of the subjects to be protected and many of the measures to be taken relate to the problem of collective goods (clean air, oceans, outer space, resources, epidemics). An international system based upon sovereignty of states is poorly equipped to deal with such matters.

In sum, insistence on sovereignty is only a part, albeit a large part, of the difficulty of creating a comprehensive legal order enjoining cooperation. Even if such an order could be generated (and Western Europe has made considerable progress toward it), regulations would most likely have to be based on the lowest standard acceptable to the largest number of states. Hence, the entire enterprise would probably be of very limited value. Basically it is a human problem in the sense that although many causes of damage are natural, humans can do something about them. And while humans are in fact doing something about these problems, they also add to existing problems through new inventions and technology. Humans are creating problems faster than they can solve them.

The general answer to the problem is not an end to development, for the developing or the developed states, but a legally regulated, adequate management of development that renders it harmless to the environment. In particular, a legally binding balance between growth and protection of the environment is needed—a goal toward which Western Europe has moved a considerable distance. This would include not only measures directed to the protection of the environment but also equitable access to the resources already available (for example, better distribution of food, equitable access to raw materials, transfer of technology).

The existing legal situation for state cooperation is highly inadequate, as the nature of the topic makes almost inevitable. There is an abundance of global, regional, and local declarations and conferences dealing with environmental protection in general. Few binding norms have emerged. The U.N.-sponsored, comprehensive Stockholm Declaration on the Human Environment (and Plan for Action) (1972) raised high hopes but led to meagre results. Although the Stockholm declaration had no legally binding force, it did draw the world's attention to the totality of environmental problems and addressed itself to the entire world, including the seas, oceans, individual people, and states. The declaration clarified thereby that environmental protection is the problem of humankind.

The declaration also created the United Nations Environmental Program (UNEP), which is responsible for promotion, coordination, stimulation, assistance (international or municipal), standardization, and every other conceivable activity helpful to further the protection of the environment. But as an official of UNEP summarized the results after a decade, they were not encouraging, partly because of the attitude of states, partly because of the speed with which environmental problems changed, and partly because of scientific ignorance about what causes ecological damage.

The usefulness of these instruments and declarations lies in their stimulating much more restricted and more effective (binding) conventions about specific aspects of environmental problems, again of a universal, regional, or local kind. There are dozens of these agreements. They relate to transboundary air pollution; maritime pollution from ships, air, or land; the disposal of noxious and other wastes; acid rain; and so on. Some suggest new and imaginative features such as mutual licensing, common standards, mutual supervision, and international inspection. All could promote cooperation, albeit on limited subjects. But they are far from satisfying existing needs.

These conventions are inadequate in scope. The participation of states is uneven; not all states ratify all conventions. Legislative implementation by the parties is often required but not forthcoming. Even when these conventions are binding, their formulation makes an escape by states from their commitments easy. Terminology such as "as far as possible," "as appropriate to a state's needs," "subject to national laws," and "taking into account the needs of developing states" are indeterminate and facilitate the circumvention of obligations. There are no international institutions for the effective enforcement of agreements. And there are no agreements at all (other than those, such as the Amazon Basin Compact, that draw attention to a danger) on such serious threats to the environment as destruction of rain forests or desertification. In other words, the multitude of agreements is deceptive because in fact they fail to generate adequate action, even though they demonstrate full awareness of existing threats to the environment.

How far the preoccupation with the environment has gone can be measured by the introduction of relevant references in documents even when their main purpose is not the preservation of the environment. See, for example, the United Nations Law of the Sea (1982), the Coyoc Declaration (1974), the Dai Dong Declaration (1972), and the Universal Declaration of the Rights of Peoples (1976).

The inadequacy of this legal situation has led many writers to search for existing rules to which states can be held in protecting the environment. The major legal precedent was the lone *Trail Smelter Arbitration (United States–Canada* case (1941), in which Canada was held liable to the United States for damages caused by air pollution originating in Canada. The *Lac Lanoux (France v. Spain)* case (1957) and the *Lauca River (Chile v.*

Bolivia) case (1961–1962) were at least tangentially of interest to environmental protection because all parties recognized the rights to water resources of downstream states against upstream states.

The *Trail Smelter* case—in which suit was brought for damage done in the state of Washington by fumes from a smelter in British Columbia— was decided mainly on the ground that a state must not knowingly allow its territory to be used for acts contrary to the rights of other states. In addition to this well-established legal principle, states and writers have found innumerable other general legal principles, some of dubious validity, on which activities damaging to the environment could be stopped, such as absolute territorial integrity, community of states, good neighborliness, abuse of rights, equality of rights, and peaceful coexistence. Many of these principles are, at best, "soft" law. This is particularly true when, more recently, damage to the environment was considered unlawful under the various documents on human rights, which guarantee every individual a right to live in a healthy environment, and in connection with development in the Third World.

There is even less agreement on the definition of what damage to the environment is. The most that can be said about this problem is that the definition may legitimately depend upon what aspect of the environment is at issue. And there is no agreement at all on what the responsibilities for damage to the environment are. Is damage or risk to be assessed? How is it to be assessed, and who is to assess? What preventive action can be demanded, and what sanction can be imposed after the act? States tend to shy away from such questions, presumably knowing beforehand that agreement is most unlikely to be reached. Nevertheless, at the summit meeting of seven major states and the European Community in Paris in July 1989, agreement was reached that uncertainties about some aspects of environmental protection should not prevent decisive, immediate action. There was also awareness, however, that a grand vision on the subject of environment protection was missing and that dread alone could not solve the problem.

The accident at the nuclear power plant in Chernobyl in April 1986 demonstrated how very poorly international society has dealt with humankind's ecosystem. Although the Soviet Union acknowledged negligence at the plant, the atmospheric pollution across the globe, and the damage done to persons and property, no claim was made against the Soviet Union. It turned out that among the mass of conventions, accords, declarations, and resolutions relating to the environment in general or to nuclear matters specifically, not one could be used to hold the Soviet Union legally responsible. Either there was no binding agreement fitting the situation, or if there was, the Soviet Union had not ratified it. Public concern was sufficiently great to lead to two conventions dealing with an obligation to inform about a nuclear accident and to assist the state where it had happened. Earlier conventions dealing with civil liability for nuclear damage dating back to the early 1960s were updated in the

1980s. But they cover only a fraction of nuclear plants. What was true in the Chernobyl case—namely, that all the agreements and institutions relating to the protection of the environment failed to affect the situation— is nearly as true for the entire globe.

The issue of environmental legal controls is so difficult to settle not merely because of the nature of the issue but because it has not yet been settled politically. It is an excellent illustration of the principle that effective law must be preceded by effective political agreement. Otherwise states will take refuge in those existing legal principles giving them the widest freedom of behavior. In this case that principle is territorial jurisdiction based on sovereign independence. This issue of legal controls is also an illustration of the state practice of solving new problems by adjusting existing norms rather than by making radical innovations in the existing legal system.

REFERENCES AND READINGS FOR PART 7

Political Cooperation

Butler, William E. "International Law, foreign policy and the Gorbachev style." *Journal of International Affairs* 42 (1989 II):362–375.

Dohna, Bernt Graf zu. *Die Grundbeziehungen über die freundlichen Beziehungen and die Zusammenarbeit zwischen Saaten.* Berlin: Duncker and Humblot, 1973.

François, Louis. *Les institutions internationales: La coopération et son organization.* Paris: Hachette, 1975.

Huber, Max. "Beiträge zur Kenntnis der soziologischen Grundlagen des Völkerrechts und der Staatengesellschaft." *Jahrbuch des öffentlichen Rechts der Gegenwart* 4 (1910):56–134.

Sahovic, Milan. "Codification des principes du droit international des relations amicales et de la coopération entre les états." *ADIRC* 137 (1972 III):242–310.

————, ed. *Principles of International Law Concerning Friendly Relations and Cooperation.* Dobbs Ferry, NY: Oceana, 1972.

Sanders, David. *Lawmaking and Co-operation in International Politics: The Idealist Case Reconsidered.* New York: St. Martin's, 1986.

Schwarzenberger, Georg. The Frontiers of International Law. London: Stevens, 1962.

Waldheim, Kurt. "The United Nations: The tarnished image." *Foreign Affairs* 63 (Fall 1984):93–107.

Economic Cooperation

Adelman, Carol C., ed. *International Regulations: New Rules in a Changing World Order.* San Francisco: Institute for Contemporary Studies, 1988.

"The Charter of Economic Rights and Duties of States." *Proceedings,* pp. 225–246. Washington, DC: American Society of International Law, 1976.

Grzybowski, Kazimierz. *The Socialist Commonwealth of Nations: Organizations and Institutions.* New Haven, CT: Yale University Press, 1964.

Kapteyn, P.JG., and P. V. van Themat. *Introduction to the Law of the European Community.* London: Sweet and Maxwell, 1973.

Petersmann, Ernst U. *Wirtschaftsintegrationsrecht und Insvestitionsgesetzgebung der Entwicklungsländer.* Baden-Baden, West Germany: Nomos, 1974.

Rao, P. Chandrasekhara. "Charter of Economic Rights and Duties of States." *Indian Journal of International Law* 15 (July-September 1975):351–370.

Singh, Jyoti S. *A New International Economic Order.* New York: Praeger, 1977.

Sinha, R. K. *New International Economic Order.* New Delhi: Deep and Deep, 1985.

Sørensen, Max. "Institutionalized international co-operation in economic, social, and cultural fields." In *Manual of Public International Law,* edited by Max Sørensen, pp. 605–671. New York: St. Martin's, 1968.

Tomuschat, Christian. "Die Charta der wirtschaftlichen Rechte und Pflichten der Staaten." Z 36 (1976 I–III):444–491.

Wallace, Don Jr., and Helga Escobar, eds. *The Future of International Economic Organization.* New York: Praeger, 1977.

White, Robin C.A. "A new economic order." *Int. & Comp. L. Q.* 24 (July 1975): 542–552.

Economic Development

Alston, Philip. "The right to development at the international level." In Frederick E. Snyder and Surakiart Sathirathai, eds. *Third World Attitudes Toward International Law.* Dordrecht: Martinus Nijhoff, 1987, pp. 811–824.

British Institute of International and Comparative Law. "The encouragement and protection of investments in developing countries." *Int. & Comp. L. Q.* (supplementary publication no. 3, 1962).

Colliard, C. A., ed. *Les résolutions dans la formation du droit international du développement.* Geneva: Institut Universitaire des Hautes Etudes Internationales, 1971.

Donnelly, Jack. "In search of the unicorn: The jurisprudence and politics of the right to development." *California Western International Law Journal* 15 (Autumn 1985):473–509.

Dorsey, John F. "Preferential treatment: A new standard for international economic relations." *Harvard Law Journal* 18 (Winter 1977):109–135.

Flory, Maurice. "Souveraineté des états et coopération pour le développement." *ADIRC* 141 (1974 I):255–329.

———. "Adapting international law to the development of the Third World." In *Third World Attitudes Toward International Law,* edited by Frederick E. Snyder and Surakiart Sathirathai, pp. 801–810. Dordrecht: Martinus Nijhoff, 1987.

Geiger, Rainer. "The unilateral change of economic development agreements." *Int & Comp. L. Q.* 23 (January 1974):73–104.

Lillich, Richard B., ed. *Economic Coercion and the New Economic Order.* Charlottesville, VA.: Michie, 1976.

Luchaire, François. *Cours de droit international du développement* Paris: Les Cours de Droit, 1971.

McWhinney, Edward. "The international law-making process and the new international economic order." *Canadian Yearbook of International Law* 14 (1976):57–72.

Petersmann, Ernst U. "Die dritte Welt und das Wirtschaftsvölkerrecht." Z 36 (1976 I–II):492–550.

Société Française de Droit International. *Pays en voie de développement et transformation du droit international.* Paris: A. Pédone, 1974.

Tunc, André, ed. *Les Aspects juridiques du développement économique.* Paris: Dalloz, 1966.

Verwey, William D. *Economic Development, Peace and International Law.* Assen, the Netherlands: Van Gorcum, 1972.

————. "The New International Economic Order and the realization of the right to development and welfare." In *Third World Attitudes Toward International Law,* edited by Frederick E. Snyder and Surakiart Sathirathai, pp. 825–851. Dordrecht: Martinus Nijhoff, 1987.

Woart, Paul de et al., eds. *International Law and Development.* Dordrecht: Martinus Nijhoff, 1988.

Economic Discrimination

Ferguson, Clarence C., Jr. "Redressing global injustices: The role of law." *Rutgers Law Review* 33 (Winter 1981 II):410–422.

Hyder, Khusid. *Equality of Treatment and Trade Discrimination in International Law.* The Hague: Martinus Nijhoff, 1968.

Kaplan, G. G. "Equality and discrimination in international economic law (II): The UNCTAD scheme for generalised preferences." *Yearbook of World Affairs* (1972):267–285.

Kewenig, Wilhelm. *Der Grundsatz der Nichtdiskriminierung im Völkerrecht der internationalen Handelsbeziehungen.* Frankfurt am Main, West Germany, Athenäum, 1972.

Verbit, Gilbert P. "Preferences and the public law of international trade: The end of most-favored-nation treatment in international trade agreements?" In Académie de Droit International. *Colloque 1968,* 19–84. Dordrecht: Martinus Nijhoff, 1969.

————. *Trade Agreements for Developing Countries.* New York: Columbia University Press, 1969.

Protection of the Environment

Académie de Droit International de la Haye. *Transfrontier Pollution and International Law.* Dordrecht: Martinus Nijhoff, 1985.

Brown-Weiss, Edith. *In Fairness to Future Generations: International Law, Common Patrimony and Intergenerational Equity.* Dobbs Ferry, NY: Transnational, 1989.

Caldwell, Lynton K. *In Defense of Earth.* Bloomington: Indiana University Press, 1972.

————. *International Environmental Policy: Emergence and Dimensions.* Duke Press Policy Studies. Durham, NC: Duke University Press, 1984.

Cameron, Peter et al., eds. *Nuclear Energy after Chernobyl.* London: Graham and Trotman, 1988.

Carroll, John E., ed. *International Environmental Diplomacy.* Cambridge: Cambridge University Press, 1988.

Conservation Foundation. *State of the Environment: An Assessment at Mid-Decade.* Washington, DC: Conservation Foundation, 1984.

Diwan, Paras, ed. *Environment Protection.* New Delhi: Deep and Deep, 1987.

Dupuy, René-Jean, ed. *Workshop 1984: The Future of the Law of Environment.* Dordrecht: Martinus Nijhoff, 1985.

Flinterman, C. et al. *Transboundary Air Pollution.* Dordrecht: Martinus Nijhoff, 1986.

Keohane, Robert O. *After Hegemony, Cooperation and Discord in the World Political Economy.* Princeton, NJ: Princeton University Press, 1984.

Kiss, Alexandre. *Droit international de l'environnement.* Paris: A. Pédone, 1989.

Krasner, Stephen D., ed. *International Régimes.* Ithaca, NY: Cornell University Press, 1968.

Lang, Winfred. "Luft and Ozon: Schutzobjekte des Völkerrechts?" *Z* 45 (1985 II):261–285.

Lücke, Jörg. "Das Recht des Einzelnen auf Umweltschutz als ein internationales Menschenrecht." *AV* 16 (1975 IV):387–396.

Munro, Robert. "Twenty years after Stockholm: Past achievements and future issues." *Mazingira* 6 (1982 I):46–57.

Organization for Economic Cooperation and Development. *Nuclear Third Party Liability.* Paris: OECD, 1976.

Sands, Philippe J. "The environment, community and international law." *Harvard International Law Journal* 30 (Spring 1989):393–420.

Schneider, Jan. *World Public Order of the Environment.* Toronto: University of Toronto Press, 1979.

Springer, Allen L. *The International Law of Pollution.* Westport, CT: Quorum Book, 1983.

Utton, Albert E., and Ludwik A. Teclaff. *Transboundary Resource Law.* Boulder, CO: Westview, 1987.

Young, Oren R. *International Cooperation: Building Regimes for Natural Resources and the Environment.* Ithaca, NY: Cornell University Press, 1989.

PART 8
THE PACIFIC SETTLEMENT OF INTERNATIONAL DISPUTES

The effective functioning of international law requires states to accept its substantive norms, which allocate rights and duties, and its procedural norms, which define the manner in which all norms are to be applied and executed. Conflicts of interest would then be settled in an orderly fashion. Such an ideal situation does not exist. The acceptance of substantive norms alone would not suffice to preserve social order unless states also accepted procedural norms. But the distribution of power in international society encourages resistance to these norms. The diffusion of power among states makes it tempting—and almost irresistible to the most powerful—to settle disputes through the arbitrament of power. And the more important the interests involved in the dispute, the greater becomes the temptation.

There are many reasons states prefer reliance upon their own resources over submission to third parties for the legal settlement of disputes. This is true of major as well as minor states, as long as one of the parties calculates that it can win the dispute by use of its own resources. One reason is that the outcome of a legal process is always uncertain. The leeway left to a third party in interpreting the law will introduce, states fear, political considerations. Marxist and some new states consider much international law class law in any case, to which they are reluctant to submit as a general principle. Another reason is that in the contemporary, interconnected world, many states doubt that any third party, whether a state, a judge, or an arbitrator, can be truly disinterested in an international dispute. A third reason is that even if the settlement is fair, the objectivity of its enforcement is dubious. A fourth reason is that third parties are usually inclined to look for precedents in settling disputes, and many states, especially the newer states, feel that this would perpetuate the status quo, which they do not find favorable to themselves. Much of the time, they desire a change in the law, which is a political, not a judicial, role. A fifth and very strong reason is that states have greater confidence in the use of their own resources because the use of force in settling disputes is becoming increasingly unfashionable and even unfeasible. States therefore do not have to fear defeat or annihilation in a conflict as the worst outcome, only delay in a settlement, for which states generally have considerable tolerance and that may in any case be preferable to settlement.

In addition to the legal settlement of disputes, other peaceful and often faster means are relatively more popular. There is a variety of reasons for this phenomenon. One may be that internal politics motivates a government to end a dispute. A second reason is that a stalemate has been reached so that continuation of the dispute is likely to remain without results. A third reason, especially if violence is involved, is exhaustion of one or all parties. A fourth reason is that a settlement is worthwhile compared to the likely alternative. A fifth reason is that increasing interaction or pressure from outside states, particularly neighbor states, will lead to more disputes requiring settlement. And a sixth reason is that the cost of wars has risen to such an extent as to make a peaceful settlement preferable.

The strong inclination of states to rely upon their own resources has very often led states to the misuse of pacific methods for political ends. Organs of the United Nations and other institutions for peacefully settling international disputes have been degraded into instruments for denunciatory rather than peace-preserving purposes. Thus, the means for fostering cooperation and friendly relations among states have been turned into items in a state's political arsenal. Even worse for the peaceful settlement of disputes is the circumvention of international organizations altogether on various grounds, a practice engaged in by small and large states as long as one of the parties believes it can settle a dispute by its own means in its own favor.

23
APPLICABILITY OF
METHODS FOR
PACIFIC SETTLEMENT

Political Versus Legal Methods

The U.N. Charter, in Article 33, suggests that parties to a dispute likely to endanger peace shall "first of all" seek a solution by negotiation, enquiry, mediation, conciliation, arbitration, judicial settlement, resort to regional arrangements, or any other peaceful means of their own choice. Because states often prefer to settle disputes with their own means, neither the charter nor general international law obligates them to have disputes settled by disinterested third parties; law leaves a peaceful settlement to the parties themselves. With the use of force no longer being a legal means, negotiation is the primary legal way to settle. But negotiation, especially in international relations, is always a political process. Thus, the actual settlement of disputes is transferred by law from the legal to the political arena.

This transfer corresponds to the general politicization of international society. The strong feeling of states about this issue is indicated by their insistence on distinguishing between legal and political disputes. Legal disputes, they allege, turn around purely legal questions and are justiciable. Political disputes turn around political interests and are solvable only by political means. By branding a dispute political, even when it involves the interpretation of a legal norm or a treaty and could be settled by legal methods, states can avoid an obligation to settle it by judicial means and can settle instead with their own political means.

In spite of many attempts to find objective criteria to distinguish legal from political disputes, none has been found. The political interests of states are the decisive factor in determining the nature of the dispute. This became clear, once again, in the case of *Nicaragua (Merits) (Judgment)* (1986, p. 26), when the United States denied the jurisdiction of the International Court of Justice because, among other reasons, the unlawful use of armed force is a political question assigned to the Security Council and because an ongoing armed conflict cannot be dealt with by the

Court without overstepping its proper judicial bounds. For different reasons, the U.S. Supreme Court in *Banco Nacional de Cuba v. Sabbatino* (1964, pp. 428, 432), after having stated that it is evident that "some aspects of international law touch much more sharply on national nerves than do others; the less important the implications of an issue are for our foreign relations, the weaker the justification for exclusivity in the political branches" of government, also suggested that the political rather than legal settlement of a dispute might cover a wider ground and be more effective (enforceable) than a legal decision.

The disadvantage of purely political settlements of disputes usually is that little or no attention is paid to justice. One of the parties may therefore find that settlement unsatisfactory and try to circumvent it at the first opportunity. When law is the basis for a settlement, there is likely to be a modicum of consent to the underlying norm, and the settlement is likely to be more acceptable to all the parties.

Legal settlements are not without disadvantage, however. Formulating a dispute to make it susceptible to legal treatment and settlement may narrow the subject matter unduly, sharpen differences, and prevent the parties from reaching the underlying cause. A dispute is very often the overt evidence of a much broader covert conflict of interests.

This is particularly true of the struggle for power between two states as a broad, general conflict suitable neither to legal formulation nor political settlement. Yet this struggle is an integral and inevitable part of the contemporary international system. The specific disputes the struggle for power generates and symbolizes might be settled legally or politically, but this would be settling a symptom, not a cause. Nevertheless, their legal settlement could contribute, in however piecemeal and tangential a fashion, to preventing the struggle for power from deteriorating into violence and war. The cause of social order may sometimes be well served by avoiding confrontation on basic issues and by dealing merely with their manifestations. In addition, if, as in the case of the struggle for power, there is a psychological element of tension between the states involved, there is virtually no other way but to deal with manifestations.

When the interests involved in a dispute were not considered too important, states did not always take advantage of the rule "that no State can, without its consent, be compelled to submit its disputes with other States either to mediation or to arbitration, or to any other kind of pacific settlement" (*Eastern Carelia* [1923, p. 27]). Especially since the end of the nineteenth century, states have quite frequently submitted disputes to settlement involving the participation of third parties. In the process, they have developed the peaceful methods that they have agreed to follow in their disputes in certain, on the whole rather limited, circumstances.

The use of these methods remains subject to agreement by the parties, and the methods themselves have been generally outlined in various conventions, foremost the Hague Conventions for the Pacific

Settlement of International Disputes (1899 and 1907), the Covenant of the League of Nations (1919), the General Act on Pacific Settlement of International Disputes (1928), the Charter of the United Nations (1945), and the Declaration on Friendly Relations (1970). Thus, neither the methods nor the rules for their application are part of general international law. Nevertheless, both have been developed so well by far-reaching agreement among states that their treatment here in the context of general international law is justified.

What Are International Disputes?

International disputes are nowhere defined in conventions or treaties. Yet legal consequences for states can arise from their existence. The finding that there is a dispute and, if so, that it is international is important. The Permanent Court of International Justice in the *Mavrommatis Palestine Concession (Jurisdiction)* case (1924, p. 11) defined a dispute "as a disagreement on a point of law or fact, a conflict of legal views or of interests between two persons," with the consequences, it should be added, that one party denies the other the satisfaction of some interest.

Recently, the international character of a dispute has become more difficult to define. The division of states (Korea, Germany, China) raised the question as to whether a dispute between the two parts is internal or international. The international implications of insurgency and even more the pressure of the newer and Communist states to consider the fighting of liberation movements not civil war but self-defense against aggressors have made the dividing line between internal and international disputes even more uncertain.

Because the whole purpose of defining an international dispute aims at maintaining peace, the concept should not be construed too narrowly. States, liberation movements, and insurgents may have varying reasons for affirming or denying the international character of their disputes. In recent practice, international society has been almost invariably drawn into these situations, and they should therefore be subject to international arrangements, including laws, designed to prevent them from threatening the social order. The Declaration on Friendly Relations (1970) takes such a broad view. The first principle—that states shall refrain from the threat or use of force against other states—is especially extended to apply to "international lines of demarcation, such as armistice lines," and to all parties involved. As long as the parties are organizationally and territorially effectively separate from each other, and regardless of their status of recognition, a dispute between them is international. A liberation war would also be an international dispute between the liberation forces and the colonial power if liberation wars were accepted as legitimate self-defense against aggressors. Civil wars have not traditionally been considered international disputes unless they have assumed an international character—for example, through outside intervention or through threats to the peace of other states. In that case, the difficult decision would have to be made by any outside state regarding which is the legitimate government and which faction is the insurgents. For if the outsiders intervene on the side of the legitimate government, the conflict would remain "internal," whereas assistance to the insurgents would technically internationalize the dispute.

When an international dispute is found to exist, it is now considered to be universal international law that states are obliged to settle it by peaceful means in such a manner "that international peace and security, and justice, are not threatened" (Declaration on Friendly Relations, 1970). Article 33 of the U.N. Charter provides a fairly exhaustive catalogue of methods available to states.

The Choice of Methods

The suggestion that states should use "other peaceful means of their choice" is most useful. For the nature and stage of the dispute determine to some extent the effectiveness of the means for its settlement. Success may depend upon how well means are adapted to the dispute. In recognition of this relationship between dispute and means for settlement, states have begun to develop means, or at least forums, specifically designed for specific subjects and going beyond traditional methods.

Some regions have their own institutions for the settlement of regional disputes (for example, the European Community, the Inter-American Court of Human Rights and the Administrative Tribunal, the Andean Court of Justice [the Organization of American States now allows use of inter-American courts parallel to the U.N. agencies], the less formal arrangements of the Organization of African Unity). Many specialized agencies have their own dispute settlement procedure (for example, the International Labor Organization, the International Civil Aviation Organization, the GATT). The World Bank and the IMF have at their disposal the International Centre for Settlement of Investment Disputes. Many other international agencies have established their own procedures, often because their specialized, sometimes technical character requires experts for the settlement of disputes that the established global organizations (such as the International Court of Justice) cannot furnish. The Helsinki Accords (1975) refer to peaceful settlement of disputes among the participating states themselves. The United Nations Convention on the Law of the Sea (1982) foresees the creation of an international tribunal for the law of the sea. Thus, there are a multitude of international organizations and agencies within which disputes can be settled peacefully. But the fundamental form of the methods available to the disputing parties has essentially remained unchanged from the time they were first developed. It is more in the nature of subject matter and the character of parties involved in disputes that changes have taken place.

This development is particularly evident in civil wars and other conflicts in which only one party is a subject of international law. For in principle, the methods for peaceful settlements are designed as applicable only between states. But in view of the potential danger of modern civil wars to international peace and the development of human rights, the principle has been broken on many occasions.

Occasionally, the government involved in civil war will object to any outsider's attempt to settle the conflict as unlawful intervention. But in many more cases, the question of the status of the nongovernmental party does not prove to be an insurmountable obstacle. Third states or prestigious individuals have successfully helped in settling such conflicts. All secretaries general of the United Nations have considered the peaceful settlement of conflicts between states or of civil wars to be part of their inherent powers, whether asked to do so by some political international organ or not. Some of these efforts have taken place on an unofficial or even secret basis. But there are limits beyond which states, international officials, or private persons cannot go or beyond which some methods of settlement cannot be applied. Private parties to a conflict, for instance, cannot appear before the International Court of Justice. In the final analysis, the choice of methods is a political question whose use cannot be foisted on either a government or a private party.

24

SETTLEMENT METHODS NOT INVOLVING DECISIONS BY THIRD PARTIES

There are a number of methods available to disputing parties. But there is no international legal or other standardized structure for all of them or their details. Nevertheless, the methods are well established and their nature well known. As they are all voluntary and have no legally binding features, their flexibility is heightened without hurting the settlement process they represent. As J. L. Brierly has pointed out, all these methods for settling disputes without decisions by third parties have as their main purpose to facilitate a decision by the parties, not make a decision for the parties.

Negotiation

Direct negotiation between the parties to a dispute is the most frequent method for the pacific settlement of international disputes. The International Court of Justice in the *North Sea Continental Shelf* cases (1969) declared it an obligation for the parties to negotiate, and the Permanent Court of International Justice in its *Railway Traffic Between Lithuania and Poland* (1931, p. 116) advisory opinion had previously stated that the parties must "not only enter into negotiations but also pursue them as far as possible with a view to concluding agreements." The same Court in its advisory opinion on *German Settlers in Poland* (1923) had found, however, that a treaty to submit disputes to the Court did not imply an obligation to try to settle the dispute by negotiation first. The Declaration on Friendly Relations (1970) confirms this principle by giving the parties the choice to settle their disputes by any pacific means.

The advantage of negotiation, which sometimes can also be a disadvantage, over other means is that the parties conduct direct conversations. They may settle their dispute in any way they agree, regardless of constraints binding arbitrators or judges. They remain in control of the settlement procedure. They can avoid the glare of public attention and the political pressures of groups at home. If the parties to a dispute have a comparable power potential, settling by negotiations has the advantage that there is no "victor," an important consideration among prestige-conscious states. Compromises and adjustments are less likely to be branded as "sellouts," and the agreement reached has the likely approval of both sides.

Negotiation is also well adapted to a dispute over changes in the law rather than over interpretation of existing law. Many disputes between First and Third World states do not turn around what is right but around what is equitable. If, however, the power potential of the disputants is uneven, the settlement may reflect this inequality. The weaker party may therefore want to bring the dispute into some forum of an international organization, although the usual allegations, accusations, and resolutions that emerge cannot be considered negotiation (contrary to the opinion of the International Court of Justice *South West Africa Cases (Preliminary Objections, Judgment)* [1962]).

A quite different consideration favoring negotiation over (national) judicial processes was expressed by the U.S. Supreme Court in *Banco Nacional de Cuba v. Sabbatino* (1964, pp. 431–432). Although the case involved the expropriation of one U.S. national's property by the Cuban government, the Court made some statements of general validity in comparing legal versus political (diplomatic) procedures. In "contrasting the practice of the political branch [of government] with the limitations of the judicial process," the Court reached several conclusions. The executive may obtain some degree of general redress from the foreign government for all affected nationals, not just one, through talks, submission to the United Nations, or the employment of political or economic sanctions. Judicial determinations are much more limited, and redress can usually be obtained effectively only if the foreign state has "by fortuitous circumstance" property that can be seized in the state of the forum. A decision by the (national) court that the foreign state's acts were invalid may offend that state and make agreement difficult. The narrow, piecemeal decisions by courts could interfere with negotiations of a much broader scope designed to benefit more persons than the plaintiff. If the court should find the foreign state's acts legal, the finding could undermine negotiations between the two states aimed at redress regardless of the legal situation for the damaged nationals. The situation could be worse still, the Court argued, if the court's finding of the legality of the state act flew in the face of the executive's claim to the contrary. Such an embarrassing situation could happen because "the Executive Branch speaks not only as an interpreter of generally accepted and traditional values, as would the courts, but also as an advocate of standards it believes desirable for the community of nations and protective of national concerns." (One may wonder whether the court of a small, powerless state would have reached the same conclusions.)

Good Offices

"Good offices" is the intercession of a third party (a state, an international organization, a private individual) in a dispute between parties that do not negotiate, are at war, or, at any rate, are not on speaking terms. The aim of good offices is to bring the parties into direct negotiations for the settlement of their dispute. (Theodore Roosevelt acted in this capacity in the Russo-Japanese War of 1904–1905, the United States did in the Israeli-Egyptian War in 1973, and France probably did in the U.S.-Vietnam War in the 1970s.)

Any party to a dispute may ask for good offices, and no party has to accept good offices. Nobody has the duty to offer good offices, even when asked to do so. The offer is always advisory, is never binding, and cannot be considered an unfriendly act. Presumably for these uncertainty-producing reasons, the dispute (or war) continues unaffected in any way by the offer. Yet an outside state may consider the good office service as "meddling" in other people's affairs, as China did regarding U.S. attempts in South Africa and Rhodesia and Soviet attempts in Lebanon in 1976.

Special treaty provisions may, of course, alter the voluntary nature of good offices for all parties. In the League of Nations Covenant and the U.N. Charter, the members are obligated to do something about those disputes likely to endanger the peace and security of the world. At a minimum, such action would include that good offices be offered and accepted. As in all cases of a third party participating in some settlement, the third party's important function may be to rectify misperceptions the disputants have about each other.

Mediation

The rules relating to mediation are essentially the same as those applying to good offices, except that there is greater activity on the part of the mediating agent. The action of mediation consists in reconciling opposing views of the disputants and appeasing their feelings of mutual resentment. The mediation effort ceases when one of the parties or the mediator determines that the proposed means for conciliation are unacceptable.

The mediator—who goes further than the agent offering good offices—deals with the substance of the dispute and may even participate in its settlement by making proposals. This role may make a mediator less acceptable to the parties, even though his or her proposals are merely advisory. The final settlement remains a matter of agreement between the disputants. The nature of the proposals thus becomes more important than the mediator and may explain why mediation has been successful in a relatively large number of international disputes.

Under the U.N. Charter, mediation, although used on a number of occasions, is not fully exploited because a dispute must have reached the point where its continuance "is likely to endanger the maintenance of international peace and security" (Article 33) before organs of the United Nations can go into action. By that time, the positions of the disputants are likely to be rigid, and public mediation efforts become difficult. The practice has therefore developed that the secretary general or his representative engages quietly and discreetly in mediation efforts when they are invited by the disputants—states or liberation movements—to do so. This would amount to a "means of their own choice" to which they are entitled and would also transfer the task of peacekeeping to organs other than the Security Council to a minor degree.

The alternative for the United Nations is offered in Article 34: a declaration that a "situation" exists that "might lead to international friction or give rise to a dispute" and with which the organization is allowed to deal. But the possibilities of dealing with a "situation" are fewer and less effective and do not necessarily include, if they do not actually exclude, good offices or other means of pacific settlement. Nevertheless, if the situation turns around the status quo that some state wishes to change, Article 34 may initiate peaceful change, for which few other organizational means exist in international society.

Enquiry

As disputes may be based mainly on differences over facts, the Hague and other conventions established international commissions of enquiry created and constituted by agreement between the disputants as impartial bodies. The Security Council, Article 36, or the General Assembly, Articles 10, 11, and 14, may establish such a commission or may recommend to the disputants to do so. The commission's task is to find and report the facts of the situation without evaluating them or drawing conclusions from them. The disputants can do with the report as they please.

A number of international organizations have instituted commissions of enquiry with the proviso that while the commission is active, the disputants have to refrain from further antagonistic action. The idea here is to provide a "cooling off" period, which could, however, also be used by one or the other disputant to recover enough strength to continue the dispute after the commission's task is ended. Such commissions have not been used in abundance. The last one was sent to Teheran in 1980 to investigate Iran's grievance against the United States and the shah. But circumstances in Iran prevented the commission from fulfilling its task.

An example of how such a commission of enquiry can also be misused to evade rather than live up to responsibility was provided by the Lytton Commission of Inquiry. It was appointed in 1932 by the

League of Nations to investigate the Japanese invasion of Manchuria. In fact, it served as a device for the League members to avoid taking protective action for China. Its ambiguous report was used by Japan as a pretext to leave the League of Nations.

Conciliation

Conciliation is a combination of mediation and fact-finding. Upon request of the disputants, the commission of conciliation ascertains the facts of the dispute and proposes a settlement on the basis of its findings. But the proposal is only recommendatory and advisory. Since 1918 several hundred conciliation commissions have been established. But there have been almost no cases of conciliation, except in the League of Nations and the United Nations as part of their peacekeeping machinery. The Security Council in particular has created a number of commissions whose function included, more or less, those of a commission of conciliation (for example, the Netherlands-Indonesia dispute, the India-Pakistan dispute over Kashmir, the Palestine issue, and the Greek frontier incidents).

In practice, U.N. commissions tended to act more and more as commissions of enquiry, leaving recommendations and activities for settlement of disputes to the major organs. To some extent this development resulted from the insistence of the Soviet Union that only the Security Council had authority to make decisions in matters relating to the maintenance of peace. The risk always exists that activities within the United Nations, being public, turn into political battles, with the result that sometimes disputes worsen rather than diminish. Trying to settle disputes out of the public eye, even with the help of commissions of conciliation, may eliminate many factors introduced by the disputants essentially for public consumption but may also lead to results having little to do with justice.

25
SETTLEMENT METHODS INVOLVING DECISIONS BY THIRD PARTIES

Arbitration

Arbitration is among the oldest methods involving decisions by third parties. It became popular in modern times after the United States introduced it in the Jay Treaties (1794). But there was no widely agreed formalization of the arbitration procedure until the Hague Conventions of 1898 and 1907 and the Model Rules on Arbitral Procedure (adopted by the General Assembly in 1958). Even then, however, these rules did not have to be used.

The Hague Conventions define arbitration as "the settlement of disputes between states by judges of their choice and on the basis of respect for law." The definition is not quite correct, however. The "judges" are arbitrators, not judges. Nevertheless, the definition points to the basic differences between arbitration and judicial procedure. In arbitration—but not in court procedure—the parties may choose the arbitrator(s). The basis of the decision has to be respect for the law, but need not be the rules of law. The decision is an award, not a judgment, although both are binding upon the parties, and both are final unless new facts can be produced that would decisively affect the decisions.

The parties to an arbitration may choose the principles and procedures to be followed in arriving at the award, unless they prefer to follow those proposed by the Hague Conventions. They may define the subject matter to be dealt with by the arbitrator. They may agree on the power and jurisdiction to be granted the arbitrator, the composition of the arbitration tribunal, the limits of the subject matter the tribunal may not overstep, the basis for the award, possibly the interpretation of the principles to be applied to the case, and the alternative awards the arbitrator may make. In a judicial procedure, most of these matters are prescribed by law.

The chosen details are laid down in a *compromis* before the arbitration begins. Without the *compromis*, there can be no arbitration, even if the parties have a treaty obligation to submit disputes to arbitration. Violation of any details of the *compromis* makes the award null and void—although who decides whether a violation has occurred is an unanswered question.

As the arbitration must proceed with respect for the law, generally accepted fundamental principles must be obeyed. Both sides must be heard; the arbitrator must be impartial; the proceedings must be fair.

Arbitration's attraction for states is that it gives them fair control over the entire procedure once they are in agreement on it. Their relative proximity to the procedure obviates the need for a political, and presumably less satisfactory, decision. Moreover, states ever-conscious of their prestige hestitate to submit to a court judgment declaring one party right, the other wrong. They prefer the very great chance that an arbitrator will decide according to what is just rather than legal so that each side may save face by gaining some and losing some.

At the first Hague Conference, an agreement was reached to create the Permanent Court of International Arbitration, again an incorrect terminology. Arbitration is not court procedure. In fact, the "court" consists of a panel of available arbitrators from among whom the parties can choose, some administrative offices, and rules applicable to arbitration if the parties do not agree on rules of their own. The "court" was used on several occasions. Its more important contribution to the peaceful settlement of international disputes was the incorporation of its procedures into hundreds of bilateral and multilateral treaties. Subsequent attempts to formulate a universally valid code of arbitral procedure failed, however. Presumably, the leeway given to states to establish their own condition for arbitration was one of its attractions (there are arbitration clauses in many treaties, and other treaties specifically create an obligation of the parties to use arbitration in all their disputes).

Adjudication

Adjudication as an international process is relatively new and rarely employed. Adjudication is a procedure before a permanent tribunal with a fixed number of judges using law as a basis of their decisions. Central America had the first international court, created in 1907, which died an early death for reasons of inefficiency in 1918. The Court of Justice of the European Communities is the only successful attempt to create a general regional international court.

The International Court of Justice in the Hague was established in 1946, following its predecessor, the Permanent Court of International Justice, established in 1921. The Court is an integral part of the United Nations. Its statute provides the details for its structure and functions. The notorious underemployment of the Court has little to do with the quality of the statute, whatever reasons states pretend for ignoring the Court. Underutilization results from the nature of international politics, more specifically the unwillingness of states to have third parties decide their interests. Notwithstanding some notable contributions of the court to the development of international law, its significance in settling dangerous international disputes is small.

As an integral part of the United Nations, all members of the organization are parties to the statute, which, however, does not commit them to its use. The basic principles and purposes of the United Nations therefore apply to the Court. Its fifteen judges are elected for overlapping periods of nine years in an elaborate procedure designed to prevent a deadlock in the choice of the judges. The appointment procedure also guarantees the judges' high qualifications, impartiality, and representation of the world's civilizations and legal systems. The judges act as private individuals, and several studies show that in their judgment juridical considerations outweigh national considerations most of the time. The exceptions are ad hoc judges—judges whom a party before the Court can nominate in its own case when there is no judge of its own nationality. This arrangement implies doubt in the impartiality of the judges and is a concession to nationalism and politics. Only states can be parties before the Court. Individuals are excluded altogether, although international organizations may at least work closely with the Court in cases concerning them. They (but not states) may also, with authorization of the General Assembly (and like the General Assembly and the Security Council), ask the Court for nonbinding but nevertheless influential advisory opinions. Now that international organizations have expressly been given a modicum of legal personality, one can assume that they can also be regular parties before the Court in matters affecting their functions.

States not members of the United Nations may become parties to the statute only, and with the authorization of the Security Council, the Court may be opened to states neither members of the United Nations nor parties to the statute. States that are co-signatories of a treaty representing the object of a dispute between other signatories may join the case, and they are bound by the Court's judgment. This great number of opportunities available to states for the use of the Court is in stark contrast to the very small number of cases actually submitted to it.

The institution of advisory opinions has generated a number of legal problems that turn mainly around the legal nature of these opinions. Because the procedure is very similar to that followed in contentious cases, advisory opinions, although not binding, in fact tend to have that effect. For this reason, the Court has been very careful in examining each request for an advisory opinion as to its exact nature (legal or political) and in justifying its acceptance or rejection of the request (see, for example, *Eastern Carelia* (1923); *Interpretation of Peace Treaties with Bulgaria, Hungary and Romania* (1950); and *Certain Expenses of the United Nations* [1962]).

The Court is faced with the problem of having to distinguish legal from political disputes (already discussed earlier). The statute specifies that legal disputes are those concerning the interpretation of treaties, questions of international law, facts that if established would represent the breach of an international obligation, and the nature and extent of a reparation to be made for the breach of an international obligation. In spite of attempts by courts (U.S. Supreme Court, German Reichsgericht) to define political disputes, none has succeeded in doing so and very likely never will because such definition depends upon the subjective element of a state wanting or not wanting to submit its case to the court.

The statute specifies the law the Court is to apply. Its decisions are binding and final. The parties have usually fulfilled the judgments, mainly because they would submit cases in the first place only if the outcome is not of very great interest to them or because their weakness precludes the use of other means. The Security Council could, under Article 94 of the charter, make recommendations or take measures to give effect to the judgments. It has done so once, and then incompletely.

The relative insignificance of the Court is built into its statute. Use of the Court is voluntary. Under Article 36 of the statute—the "optional clause"—states may commit themselves to the use of the Court in certain, limited types of disputes if the other disputant has also committed itself. But in addition to the limited range of disputes envisaged, parties may add their own, additional conditions under which they commit themselves. Thus, the United States, for instance, has introduced the Connally amendment. It stipulates that the "compulsory jurisdiction" of the Court under Article 36 would not apply to disputes relating to matters essentially within the domestic jurisdiction of the United States "as determined by the United States of America." This stipulation nullifies the U.S. signing of Article 36 altogether. Since then, the International Court has further narrowed use of the Court by deciding that a state committed to this "compulsory jurisdiction" without any condition may nevertheless refuse to use the Court if the other party to the dispute is committed under a Connally-type condition—even if that party is willing in a given case to submit a dispute to the Court. To make doubly sure that the United States is completely free to use the Court or not, it withdrew in 1985 from the "optional clause" in Article 36 in connection with the *Nicaragua (Merits, Judgment)* (1986) case. After the United States introduced the Connally amendment, other states followed suit, thereby attempting to reduce the International Court's jurisdiction (compare, for example, *Certain Norwegian Loans* [1957], *Nuclear Test Cases [Australia v. France; New Zealand v. France]* [1973], and *Nicaragua [Jurisdiction]* [1984]).

The statute does not mention enforcement of its judgments. The U.N. Charter (Article 94, possibly combined with Articles 39, 41, and 42) obliges the parties before the Court to comply with its decisions and provides some means for enforcing this obligation.

Many suggestions for adjusting its statute have been made to make the Court more acceptable. They result from the general illusion that politically motivated mis- or nonuse of institutions can be overcome by the manipulation of the constitutions of these institutions. The likelihood is that the services of the Court are neglected for two main, essentially political reasons. The first is that many disputes involve a change in the status quo based on law. As has been pointed out before, the function of the judiciary is not to change the law (although in fact it does so through interpretation). In the international system especially, there is an inclination among international lawyers to substitute a court for the nonexistent legislature to cope with the problem of social change. But states do not use this route. They rely on politics as the more effective way, they believe, to bring about or handle social change.

The second reason for neglect follows from the first. The heavy politicization of international society resulting from the horizontal organization of power induces states, indeed almost obliges them, to keep their affairs under their own control as much as possible. Their insistence upon sovereignty is an important part of the evidence. Tinkering with the statute of the International Court of Justice could not affect this fundamental condition of a state's existence.

The newer states of the Third World are often said to have their own, additional reasons for bypassing the adjudicative procedure. The most often cited reason is cultural differences. Non-Western societies are said to prefer conciliation to litigation. Available statistics do not bear out this contention, however. Per capita litigation in Asian countries is as great or greater than in many Western states. In Africa, tribal justice is based largely on decisions by "judges." Among the judges of the International Court of Justice disagreements are virtually never based upon their cultural differences. A considerable number of Third World states have signed the optional clause, and several have brought their disputes to the Court. They have signed a great number of treaties with each other stipulating use of the Court in case of disputes.

The reluctance of Third World states to use the Court is based on political, not cultural, grounds. In many cases, these states desire a change of law, which the Court cannot provide. Going to the Court forecloses other means of obtaining justice. These states fear that the inequality of power will affect the Court's judgment. The argument can also be heard that the Hague is far away from, say, Mali or Vanuatu. Yet the remedy of establishing regional courts has not worked. The difficulties these states have experienced in relying upon their own culture-bound "regional" law have not occurred when they decided to go to the Hague. The more convincing reasons Third World and Communist states tend to shun the adjudicative procedure are essentially the same as are valid for all states: preference for reliance upon their own means to settle disputes, settlement through nonjudicial methods, and the general weaknesses of the international system as they affect the peaceful settlement of international disputes.

There is some hope, however, that the Court's importance may grow. President Gorbachev suggested at the U.N. General Assembly (December

7, 1988) that in the application of agreements on human rights, all states should recognize the mandatory jurisdiction of the Court. On February 10, 1989, the Supreme Soviet adopted a decree to that effect. Gorbachev followed up this step throughout 1989 with speeches and appeals emphasizing the importance of international law and the Court to the survival of humankind. In August of that year, President Bush and Gorbachev agreed to submit seven cases regarding drug traffic and terrorism to the Court (following an agreement in 1988, reported in the *New York Times*, October 8, 1989, to submit disputes over such cases to binding Court arbitration). There was speculation that these measures were responsible for the U.S. agreement to appear before the International Court of Justice to answer charges by Iran that the shooting down of a civilian airliner by the *USS Vincennes* in the Persian Gulf on July 3, 1988, violated various conventions and deserved compensation from the United States. This appearance was not taken for granted after the refusal of the United States to appear at any point in the *Nicaragua* case and the cancellation of the U.S. subscription to the optional clause.

REFERENCES AND READINGS FOR PART 8

Legal Character of Disputes

Davies Memorial Institute of International Studies. *International Disputes: Legal Aspects*. London: Europa, 1972.

Patchen, Martin. *Resolving Disputes Between Nations: Coercion or Conciliation?* Durham, NC: Duke University Press, 1988.

Rogers, William P. "The rule of law and the settlement of international disputes," *Proceedings*, pp. 285–291. Washington, DC: American Society of International Law, 1970.

Verzijl, J.H.W. *International Law in Historical Perspective, Part VIII: Inter-State Disputes and their Settlement*. Leiden: A. W. Sijthoff, 1976.

Young, Oran R. *The Intermediaries: Third Parties in International Crises*. Princeton, NJ: Princeton University Press, 1967.

Settlement Methods Not Involving Third-Party Decisions

American Society of International Law. "United Nations mediation of regional crises." *Proceedings*, pp. 135–190. Washington, DC: American Society of International Law, 1980.

Assefa, Hizkias. *Mediation of Civil Wars Approaches and Strategies—The Sudan Conflict*. Boulder, CO: Westview, 1987.

Azar, Edward, and John Burton. *International Conflict Resolution, Theory and Practice*. Boulder, CO: Lynne Rienner, 1986.

Beusalah, Tabrizi. *L'enquête internationale dans le règlement des conflits*. Paris: Librairie Générale de Droit et de Jurisprudence, 1976.

Bilder, Richard B. "An overview of international dispute settlement." *Emory Journal of International Dispute Resolution* 1 (Fall 1986 I):1–32.

Cot, Jean Pierre. *International Conciliation*. London: Europa, 1972.

Finnegan, Richard B., Robert S. Yum, and Clifton Wilson. *Law and Politics in the International System Case Studies in Conflict Resolution*. Washington, DC: University Press of America, 1979.

Lall, Arthur. *Modern International Negotiation*. New York: Columbia University Press, 1966.

Merrills, J. G. *International Dispute Settlement*. London: Sweet and Maxwell, 1984.

Shore, William I. *Fact Finding in the Maintenance of Peace*. Dobbs Ferry, NY: Oceana, 1970.

Snyder, Frederick E. and Surakiart Sathirathai, eds. *Third World Attitudes Toward International Law*. Dordrecht: Martinus Nijhoff, 1987, pp. 161–218.

"Symposium international dispute resolution: Enforcement and awards from arbitration, mediation and conciliation." *Loyola of Los Angeles International and Comparative Law Journal* 10 (1988 III):567–627.

Thakur, Romesh. *International Conflict Resolution*, Boulder, CO: Westview, 1988.

Trevelyan, Humphrey. *Diplomatic Channels*. London: Macmillan, 1973.

Settlement Methods Involving Third-Party Decisions

Anand, Ram P. *Studies in International Adjudication*. Dobbs Ferry, NY: Oceana, 1970.

————. *International Courts and Contemporary Conflicts*. New York: Asia Publishing House, 1974.

Bernhardt, Rudolf. "Homogeneität, Kontinuität und Dissonanzen in der Rechtsprechung des internationalen Gerichtshofs." Z 33 (1973 I):1–37.

Damrosch, Lori F., ed. *The International Court of Justice at a Crossroads*. Dobbs Ferry, NY: Transnational, 1987.

Gross, Leo, ed. *The Future of the International Court of Justice*, 2 vols. Dobbs Ferry, NY: Oceana, 1976.

Keith, Kenneth J. *The Extent of Advisory Jurisdiction of the International Court of Justice*. Leiden: A. W. Sijthoff, 1971.

Lias, Toslim. *The International Court of Justice and Some Contemporary Problems*. The Hague: Martinus Nijhoff, 1983.

Mangoldt, Hans von. *Die Schiedsgerichtsbarkeit als Mittel internationaler Streitschlichtung*. New York: Springer, 1974.

Pomerance, Michla. *The Advisory Function of the International Court of Justice in the League and the U.N. Eras*. Baltimore, MD: Johns Hopkins University Press, 1973.

Prott, Lyndel V. *Der internationale Richter im Spannungsfeld der Rechtskulturen*. Berlin: Duncker und Humblot, 1975.

Reisman, William M. *Nullity and Revision: The Review and Enforcement of International Judgments and Awards*. New Haven, CT: Yale University Press, 1971.

Rosenne, Shabtai. *The World Court: What It Is and How It Works*. Dobbs Ferry, NY: Oceana, 1974.

Schwebel, Stephen M., ed. *The Effectiveness of International Decisions*. Leiden: A. W. Sijthoff, 1971.

Stuyt, Alexander M., ed. *Survey of International Arbitrations, 1794–1970*. Dobbs Ferry, NY: Oceana, 1972.

Thirlway, H.W.A. *Non-Appearance Before the International Court of Justice*. Cambridge: Cambridge University Press, 1984.

PART 9
THE USE OF FORCE

The unregulated, arbitrary use of force is a major threat to social order. A political and legal system must make the controlled use of force a foremost task. Generally, national societies have done better than international society has in this regard. They have a central government with sufficient power, including force, to overcome force used by citizens. More important, they educate their members not to use force in the first place by making the survival of the society the members' highest social value. Citizens will abstain from fulfilling or even developing their interests by means threatening their society.

In international society, that value is lacking. National interests supersede all others—hence the diffusion of power, with force one of its important components. Indeed, until World War II force was such an important element that states refused, even verbally, to abandon its use (contrary treaties notwithstanding). International politics without the use of force was unthinkable and still is today. But the arrival of "ultimate" weapons has imposed restraint upon the use of force by nuclear powers, reinforced that restraint by some conventions, and substituted vicarious wars through use of satellite states. The efficacy of international law has not profited much. The solution to the problem lies primarily outside the area of law because international society must rely heavily upon the abdication by states of the use of force either through free will or fear of deterrence. Law can make only a minor contribution toward that step. To expect the Charter of the United Nations to prevent the illegal use of force is overburdening a legal instrument with a task that is located primarily in political, social, and other arenas.

Even when states have occasionally abdicated the use of force, no reliance could be placed upon their always limited commitment. States therefore invented all kinds of schemes to deter each other from using force. Alliances, balances of power, arms competition, and collective security were all designed to make the use of force by any one state predictably unsuccessful. A chain of treaties beginning with the Pact of Paris (1928) was intended to give legal support to these arrangements by declaring war illegal. This finally led up to the Charter of the United Nations, which makes the unilateral use of force by individual states illegal, except in cases of self-defense or possibly some means of forcible self-help. But all legal instruments are subject to interpretation. And those states having used force since 1945 have been able to justify their actions, at least to their own satisfaction, by an expedient interpretation of the charter or no reference to the charter at all (for example, the Soviet Union in Afghanistan and the United States in Grenada and Panama).

A major difficulty in making law against the use of force effective is the great variety of motivations of states for using force. The lawmaker cannot adjust norms to every possible reason for a state's use of force. Nor can functional substitutes be provided to satisfy states in all cases. Under these conditions, international law can only forbid the use of force in general and provide some formal methods for the peaceful settlement of disputes as a substitute. The usefulness of such an arrangement is severely limited. There is an additional need of providing opportunities for the adjustment and compromise of clashing interests on a continual basis before they escalate into the confrontation stage of a dispute. This is the problem of maintaining social order in the face of social change. No society has been able to solve it perfectly.

In national societies the approach to a solution is objective and subjective. Objectively, there are such institutions as popular legislatures, an effective judiciary, public debates, plebiscites, brainwashing, and expression of real or alleged public opinion to manage changing conditions in the society. Subjectively, the citizens, or enough of them, have been socialized into nationalists and endowed with a sense of community intolerant of any threat to their nation. Their attachment to the nation is based on interests as well as sentiments. In combination, the objective and subjective factors usually succeed in setting a terminal point to a dispute before it becomes a threat to the existence of national society.

International society is coping most inadequately with social change. The fragile bond between states is interests alone. The love of humankind preached by some religions is not a political reality upon which a legal system can be built. The vast network of international organization has been designed to provide states with forums for the adjustment of their interests by either suggesting changes in conditions or by evaluating the effect of past changes upon their interests. In this manner, a state's purpose may be achieved without resort to force. But if the arrangement fails, no sentiment moderates the temptation to use force, and the structure of international society makes surrender all too easy.

Modern weapons render the use of force self-defeating or at any rate so costly that it is difficult to imagine a national interest worth paying the price of war, at least one involving major states. One alternative is adjustment of interests and recourse to international law and international organization. Mainly for this reason the attempt to develop and maintain law and to provide legal substitutes for the use of force remains sensible.

But as long as some states use force because they judge it profitable, and to the extent that they cannot be prevented from doing so, they will advance legal and moral justifications for their behavior. Most often their explanation will be that they are acting in self-defense, adjusting a wrong, engaging in "anticipatory self-defense" or "preemptive retaliation," executing a sanction against illegal action by another state, or fighting a "just" war. There are great opportunities for borderline cases. From the standpoint of international law and the illegal use of force, such explanations or rationalizations lack credibility, especially in the absence of any objective agency to which states are willing to submit the case. On the contrary, in the *Nicaragua (Merits, Judgment)* case (1986), the United States claimed that an ongoing war is always a political dispute beyond the reach of judicial decision.

The efficacy of any law forbidding the use of force must therefore continue to depend upon the unpredictable outcome of every state's profit and loss calculation, which weighs expected benefits from the use of force against expected costs. The decision about whether, when, and how to use force thus remains subjective with each state. This condition applies more or less to three broad areas to which international law has devoted itself: the conditions under which the use of force may be legal, the rules for its application, and the position of uninvolved third states. An additional problem, created mainly by the newer states, is the definition of force in the context of making its use illegal.

There was virtually unanimity among older states that force essentially meant armed force. But for transparent reasons, many newer states, with the support of Communist states, are challenging this meaning, at least in a legal context. They are arguing that the effect rather than the means of an action should be legally regulated. If that is done, their argument continues, economic, social, and other forms of pressure can under modern conditions achieve the same results as force. They are making force synonymous with coercion and are interpreting coercion very broadly. Where the law forbids the use of force, it should also forbid the use of economic and other pressures (at least, some of these states concede, if such use means violation of sovereignty, violation of a specific norm of international law, or destruction of the state). In that case, violent self-defense, for instance, would be allowed.

Opposing states point out that such a broad interpretation of force would make virtually all politics illegal because politics always involves some form and measure of pressure. Moreover, the legal regulation of force so conceived would be extremely difficult technically because drawing a line between illegal pressuring and legitimate influencing would be impossible. Indeed, the inability of a state, for instance, to fulfill another state's economic demand, the withdrawal of an ambassador, the breaking of diplomatic ties, or the limiting of travel by diplomats might be interpreted as the application of force and declared an illegal act.

International documents continue to make a distinction between force as armed force and coercion. The Charter of the Organization of

American States (1948) speaks in Article 16 of "coercive measures" as distinct from force (Article 18). The U.N. Charter in Article 2 speaks of use or threat of force and does not mention coercion. The Declaration on Friendly Relations (1970) speaks of coercion separately from armed intervention. A Soviet proposal in the United Nations in 1976 spoke of the nonuse of force, and that was generally understood in the debate as armed force. Only a few states (for example, Nepal, Trinidad and Tobago) advocated an expansion of the concept to include economic and other nonviolent forms of compulsion. In 1987, the General Assembly passed the Declaration on Enhancement of the Effectiveness of the Principle of Refraining from the Threat or Use of Force in International Relations. In this declaration, states are asked to abstain from threats against the economy and to avoid economic, political, or any other measures to "coerce" another state.

Nonviolent, mainly economic coercion as a means of diplomacy has been used by the United States, many other states, and the Security Council for a long time. Nonviolent coercion expresses dissatisfaction with the behavior of the target state and is legal unless it is forbidden by treaty, represents a threat to peace or to the integrity of the target state, or is out of proportion to the criticized behavior. The United States, for instance, has used nonviolent coercion during the last few decades against Cuba, Chile, Nicaragua, the Soviet Union, Libya, Rhodesia (Zimbabwe), China, and South Africa. In the case of Libya, nonviolent coercion was described in the president's proclamation as a response to a threat against the security and foreign policy of the United States. In the case of South Africa, the Anti-Apartheid Act of October 2, 1986, was passed by Congress (over President Reagan's veto) as a punishment of the international crime of apartheid and racism and as an incentive to stop the offense. Lifting of the economic sanctions was made conditional upon the ending of apartheid, including the release of Nelson Mandela and other political prisoners.

A continuing distinction between physical and other forms of force seems desirable. Force as physical violence is qualitatively different from other forms of coercion, notwithstanding the possibility of borderline cases. Because physical force is overt and fairly readily identifiable, it can be defined legally with greater precision. Expanding the concept of force to encompass all forms of pressure or coercion could conceivably encompass all human relations. Such a concept would escape precise legal regulation. If states wish to eliminate economic and other forms of coercion, they can agree, as they have occasionally done, on the requisite rules.

26
CONDITIONS FOR THE
LEGAL USE OF FORCE

The use of force continues to be permitted by general international law. It is restricted by global multilateral treaties (such as the U.N. Charter) and by regional multilateral treaties. As virtually all states of the world are parties to one or another treaty banning the use of force, it has become illegal for all states, unless permitted under special circumstances. For all practical purposes, the United Nations was meant to have a legal monopoly on the use of force when there was a threat to peace. Nevertheless, states continue to use force, in war and short of war, under conditions hardly reconcilable with the charter or regional conventions forbidding the use of force. States never admit that they are doing so. They justify their actions by their own interpretation of treaties or by semantic circumvention of legal norms—such as calling the U.S. blockade of Cuba a quarantine (1962), the French-British war on Egypt a police action (1956), the Japanese aggression against China an incident (1932), the Soviet invasion of Eastern European countries a move to save Communist regimes (1956 and 1968), and the U.S. invasion of Panama a measure to restore democracy (among other things) (1989). There are, however, a number of situations in which the use of force and some more or less peaceful measures of a forceful retaliation are permitted under international law, most of which could be eliminated under a more communitarian international system.

Unilateral (Legally Peaceful) Methods

Suspension of diplomatic relations, withdrawal from a treaty, cancellation of membership in an international organization, reciprocity (doing to one state what it did to another state), and economic boycott are legally peaceful measures indicating disapproval of the actions of another state or an organization. Those are not necessarily illegal but are experienced as unfriendly or discourteous. These measures occur in abundance, almost routinely. Hersch Lauterpacht called them "peaceful, although not amicable." Very often, as time heals all wounds, the disagreement between the parties disappears, and normal relations are restored, sometimes with the intermediary of third parties.

Retorsion

These situations are closely related to what technically is called retorsion. To quote Lauterpacht: "The essence of retorsion consists in retaliation for a noxious act by a noxious act." Neither side's action need be unlawful. The aim of retorsion is simply to stop the first state from engaging in its noxious behavior. Occasionally, retorsion (legal action) may also be undertaken against an initial act that was unlawful. Examples of retorsion are (1) restrictions upon the movement within a country of the citizens of another country, (2) the boycott by the United States and other countries of the Moscow Summer Olympic Games as a protest against the Soviet Union's invasion of Afghanistan and the Soviet retorsion by boycotting the Los Angeles Summer Olympic Games, and (3) trade restrictions by one country followed by trade restrictions by the other country. Retorsion may be considered a form of compulsion. Hence, if the new states succeed in expanding the interpretation of the concept of force, the lawful actions of retorsion could become unlawful and considerably complicate matters. Relatively harmless international actions could be turned into major crises.

Reprisal

When a state acts illegally toward another, either in peace or war, the retaliation of the wronged state is a reprisal. In contrast to war, reprisal is a limited interference by one state with the rights of another state or its citizens. In the *Naulilaa Incident Arbitration* case (1928, p. 1026), the arbitrator said:

> Reprisals are acts of self-help by the injured State, acts responding to acts contrary to international law committed by the offending State which have continued after a fruitless demand for amends. Reprisals have the effect of temporarily suspending—between the two States—the observance of this or that rule of international law. They are restricted by considerations of humanity and the rules of good faith generally applicable between States. They are illegal unless they are motivated by previous acts contrary to international law. They seek to impose upon the offending State reparation for the offense or the return to legality with a view to the avoidance of new offenses.

Reprisals can take place during peacetime or during war. The enforcement of the laws of peace or of war is their purpose. When they have been successful, they must end or themselves become unlawful. Reprisals can be counteracted legally. Their means can be anything suitable to reach their end, from seizing the offending state's property to bombarding its cities, although under the U.N. Charter force as a means is unlawful. Few states obey this restriction.

A broadening of the concept of force would open up the complex relationship between international law and economic warfare. The increasing interaction between states multiplies opportunities for economic "aggression" and therefore for reprisals in about the same proportion that it multiplies opportunities for cooperation. Many states have already shown considerable ingenuity in using economic measures either to stop or prevent what they believed to be illegal actions by other states, sometimes even when these actions were directed at third states (for example, U.S. economic measures against the Soviet Union for Soviet activities against Poland and Afghanistan).

In recognition of these newer possibilities, states have created a large number of international organizations to deal with these problems. In several (such as the GATT and the IMF), they have committed themselves to act unilaterally for any purpose only within severely narrowed limits. But in the absence of general rules of international law dealing in any detail with aspects of economic warfare, these organizations have been unable to control effectively the use of economic measures for individual purposes in disregard of international social order. Economic sanctions (embargoes, boycotts, export or import controls, "freezing" of assets, pacific blockade [a controversial measure]) have played a large role in instituting reprisals (if they are not actually an illegal intervention in the domestic affairs of the other state).

In reprisals, the inequality of states becomes particularly relevant. Obviously, a powerful state can insist more easily than a weak state that a wrong has been done and can proceed to right it by reprisal. The weaker state has only some, not easily enforceable, protection. The offending state must be given an opportunity to right the wrong before reprisals can begin; any legal use of force must be in proportion to the wrong done; and the reprisal cannot do what is forbidden under laws of war because it is a lesser sanction than war (for the same reason, the Geneva conventions of 1949 and so on apply). Nevertheless, under favorable circumstances, weaker states may at times be able to engage in reprisals if they possess resources needed by more powerful states or can otherwise damage their economy (for example, the Arab oil embargo of 1973 or the dumping of cheap goods).

Self-Defense and Aggression

That self-defense permits the use of force is a generally recognized principle. But what constitutes self-defense in a specific case, what means the defending state may use, and when and against what acts the defending state may move are usually controversial among the parties. They are the only, obviously subjective, judges. Occasionally, an evaluation of a concrete case comes ex post facto and then not always by an objective third party. The League of Nation's Lytton Commission investigating the Japanese-Chinese situation in 1933, the Nuremberg and Tokyo war crimes trials, and the judgment by the International Court of Justice of the Nicaragua situation came after the relevant events had occurred. Probably most often, the case is never investigated. It should be remembered that almost every war in history has been justified by all parties as an allegedly defensive war. Yet as the Nuremberg tribunal states, "Whether action taken under the claim of self-defense was in fact aggressive or defensive must ultimately be subject to investigation and adjudication if international law is ever to be enforced."

The controversy raging over abstract definitions of the elements involved in self-defense indicates that they are unlikely to be helpful in given cases. Self-defense may be defined as the forcible rejection of an illegal existing or impending interference, usually by force, with a state's rights. Self-defense shares with reprisal the probable condition that the state must have committed an unlawful act. The condition is probable because an argument has been made that self-defense may be permissible even in response to a legal act as long as that act threatens, say, the security or independence of the defending state (for example, the sudden cutting off of aid may mean the ruin of a developing state). Whereas a reprisal can be an offensive action inherently unrelated to the action of the other state and an independent interference with the offending state's rights (as in the case of retaliation), self-defense aims directly at rejecting the interference. Moreover, the right of reprisal presupposes that the offending state be given the opportunity to right the wrong. Self-defense can be undertaken immediately and directly, probably even in anticipation of the illegal action contemplated by the offending state.

It is now widely agreed, as is true in cases of reprisal, that the right of self-defense is subject to certain conditions. Daniel Webster stated them in the case of the *Caroline* (1837, p. 412). There must be a necessity of self-defense, "instant, overwhelming, and leaving no choice of means and no moment for deliberation." The action must not be "unreasonable or excessive, since the act justified by the necessity of self-defense must be limited by that necessity and kept clearly within it." Nevertheless, there is doubt regarding virtually all details of self-defense: the action against which self-defense is allowed, what rights a state is allowed to defend, the proportionality of the defense measure in relation to the illegal interference, and the timing of the defense, especially in cases of "indirect" interference (such as subversion) when the effect is cumulative during a period of time.

The U.S. invasion of Grenada in 1983 and bombardment of Libya in 1986 were justified by the administration as self-defense. Later, the invasion of Panama on December 20, 1989, with an army of about twenty-five thousand troops was justified by the administration on various grounds at different times. One was to seize Manuel Noriega and "bring him to justice." He had been indicted on drug traffic charges in the United States in February 1988. There can be little doubt that this was an invalid ground. Another was that the United States wanted to restore democracy in Panama, which had been destroyed by Noriega's voiding of the May 1989 election that had been won by his rival, Guillermo Endara. This, too, was an arguably invalid ground.

Most of the time, the administration cited "preemptive" self-defense against a "pattern" of aggression as a justification, based on Article 51 of the U.N. Charter, which allows the use of force in self-defense; on the Charter of the Organization of American States; and on Article 4 of the Panama Canal Treaty (1979), which confirms the canal's neutrality and manner of its operation. The administration did not mention a 1977 "understanding" between the United States and Panama to defend the canal's regime of neutrality against any threat to it but not to intervene in Panama's internal affairs or violate its territorial integrity and independence.

The "armed attack" against which self-defense is permitted consisted, according to the administration, in the killing of a U.S. marine in Panama, the harassment of U.S. citizens, a threat to U.S. installations in Panama, and Noriega's declaration of war when he said in a speech that Panama was in a "state of war" with the United States. The administration also announced that the new "democratically elected" government of President Endara, sworn in at a U.S. military base forty minutes before the invasion began, had been informed of the intended invasion and "welcomed" it. Finally, the Department of Justice was reported to have constructed a theory according to which the United States would be allowed under international law to arrest a person indicted for a crime on the soil of another state without that state's permission.

In the Security Council, only Great Britain and Canada fully supported the United States. Finland called the invasion a disproportionate response and hence unjustified. In the Organization of American States all members condemned the invasion as a violation of Panama's sovereignty and a denial of self-determination (although in the preceding November, the organization had called Noriega's government "devoid of constitutional legitimacy"). In Congress, arguments could be heard that the president lacked constitutional and international rights for his action. From international lawyers came criticism to the effect that self-defense was directed against threats to the state itself, not against some "rhetorical" threats from some foreign leader or incidents harming U.S. citizens abroad.

Even more indefinite than the term *intervention* and its legal meaning is the concept of interference or aggression on which the legality of self-defense depends. The definition of aggression has been obscured rather than clarified by U.N. Resolution 3314 (XXIX) (1975), which attempts such a definition. A main reason for this indefiniteness is the confusion stemming from the increasingly complex political use states intend to make of the definition (for example, that colonialism is permanent aggression against which forceful self-defense is permitted).

The U.N. definition is replete with concepts subject to most varied interpretations. Article 1 says, "Aggression is the use of armed force by a State against the sovereignty, territorial integrity or political independence of another State, or in any manner inconsistent with the Charter of the United Nations as set out in this Definition." The subsequent articles elaborating on this definition create confusion by paying no attention to the motivation for using armed force, by relying on the principle of "first use" of armed force as prima facie evidence of aggression, by ignoring the role of economic coercion as a provocation to the use of armed force by the victimized state, and by omitting reference to "peoples" or armed bands fighting for freedom. Uncertainty culminates in the Security Council's authority either to determine that an act of aggresssion has not been committed "in the light of other relevant circumstances" or to determine that acts other than those enumerated in the resolution constitute aggression. This jurisdiction of the Security Council means that it need not pay any attention to the definition of aggression and can reach its own conclusions as it sees fit.

This relationship as laid down in the resolution and in the Security Council's authority highlights the illusion that political realities can be forced and controlled by logical formulations or semantic tricks. Governments will base their decisions about "aggressive" acts not on preconceived definitions but on their expectations of consequences. The authority granted the Security Council does in fact nullify the significance of the definition and takes into account exactly the reality of the situation: Politics dominates the law.

This attitude is further evidenced by the specific exemption from the definition of aggression of the struggle of a people to end "colonial or racist regimes or other forms of alien domination" and "to seek and receive support." By the simple device of declaring such regimes and forms "aggression," the resolution qualifies wars of liberation as self-defense. Perhaps anticipating such wars within its own realm, the Soviet Union has pointed out that the definition of aggression in no way affects a state's right to take "police action" against dissident movements.

The legal situation regarding the use of force by liberation movements is in flux. The point has now been reached with the help of newer and Communist states where the peoples agitating for self-government (recognized as their right, at least, if directed against colonial or racist or oppressive governments) may not be forcefully attacked. Whether they themselves may use force—according to the nonbinding resolution they may—is dubious, not to themselves but to the states confronted by their force and to most Western states. Equally dubious is whether self-defense against the force used by liberation movements is lawful, regardless of whether that force originates from within or without a state. Wars of liberation movements are no longer considered civil wars, except by Communists as long as they support these wars.

The trend in contemporary international law is to improve the legal status of liberation movements, including their right to use armed force in pursuit of self-determination. Against such a legitimate use of force in pursuit of a legitimate goal (such as self-determination), self-defense of a dominating state is presumably illegitimate. Communist and Third World states were the main protagonists of this trend. But the 1989 police action against minorities within the Soviet Union seeking more autonomy is likely to stop that trend.

The regulation of the use of force and of self-defense in the U.N. Charter has also failed to solve such problems in international law. The regulation's interpretation is highly controversial. The right of individual and collective self-defense granted in Article 51, combined with the duties outlined in Article 2, paragraphs 3 and 4, to use peaceful means for the settlement of disputes and to refrain from the threat or use of force against a state's territorial integrity or political independence, is variously interpreted.

The narrow view is that the limited right to use force in self-defense is the single exception to the charter's general prohibition of the use of force. The broadest view is that states retain their "inherent" right to self-defense as granted by general international law against various forms of attack. In concrete cases, governments will interpret the right to self-defense (and they have done so many times) to cover whatever forceful action they deem necessary.

The International Court of Justice in the *Nicaragua (Merits, Judgment)* case (1986) argued that customary law coexists with treaty law (as demonstrated, for instance, by Article 51, which speaks of the "inherent" right of self-defense and therefore can refer only to customary law). From this verdict it follows that the right to self-defense is not limited to that granted by the charter; it includes rights granted by customary law. The Court then concluded that the self-defense must be necessary and proportionate (also customary law); that an armed attack, against which self-defense is legitimate, can be undertaken by a state sending armed bands, groups, irregulars, or mercenaries into another country if this is done on a sufficiently large scale; that provision of weapons or logistical and other support to rebels can also represent an armed attack and thereby justify self-defense; that collective self-defense requires a request of the attacked states for such assistance; and that the act provoking the response of collective self-defense was an armed attack.

The Court did not decide whether self-defense against an imminent threat of an armed attack (anticipatory self-defense or preemptive self-defense) is lawful. Article 51 of the charter speaks of the inherent right to self-defense "if an armed attack occurs." Taken literally, this would exclude anticipatory self-defense. That may have been adequate when the charter was written. It certainly is not adequate any longer. Because the spirit of self-defense is to protect a state against a forceful interference, the only sensible interpretation to give effect to the intention of Article 51 is to allow self-defense against an impending threat of interference. The risks of such an interpretation are obvious because it is based upon the purely subjective evaluation by the self-defending state of the antagonist's intention. But this is an unsolved problem bedevilling international law in many other cases.

Self-Preservation

Self-preservation is one of those principles in international law whose inherently dubious character is worsened by its misuse as a decoy for illegal intervention and aggression. The concept is broader than self-defense, although closely related to it. Self-preservation may not be a response to some other state's action, or if it is, that state's action may be legal and innocent. Self-preservation differs from reprisal because it does not aim at righting a wrong committed by some other state. Self-preservation is violation of another state, in particular disregard of respect for its personality, through use of force or any other means in order to protect the conditions of survival by the violating state.

If general international law did indeed recognize a right to self-preservation, there would have to be a corresponding duty of states to suffer violation of their personality. International chaos would result. Writers have therefore denied the existence of such a law—leaving the underlying problem to political solutions—or have argued that self-preservation can be taken only in cases of necessity, when no other means to preserve the vital interests of a state are available. Here again, autojudgment about whether all the conditions are fulfilled renders self-preservation a danger to the international social order and its use unpopular, but nevertheless not infrequent.

Until early in the nineteenth century, when the balance of power system was more openly acknowledged as an important and desirable political principle, an argument was often made for the legality of any state action restoring a disturbed balance of power in the name of self-preservation. More recent historical examples of actions claimed to have been undertaken in the name of self-preservation are the cases of the Caroline in 1837, U.S. intervention in Mexico's civil war (1916–1919) for the protection of U.S. citizens, the German invasion of neutral Belgium in 1914, the destruction of the French (Vichy) fleet at Oran in 1940, and the breach of traditional neutrality rules by the United States in transferring warships to Great Britain in 1940 and executing the Lend Lease Act of 1941.

Since the end of World War II, the balance of power has had no legal standing, although it has remained a foremost principle of foreign policy. The balance of power principle usually includes the maintenance of dominance in what the major powers consider to be their spheres of influence. Maintenance by almost any means and under whatever name by the Soviet Union (the Brezhnev Doctrine, since 1989 abandoned verbally by President Gorbachev) and the consequences of the Monroe Doctrine by the United States testify to the vitality of the balance of power principle (out of date as it may be in the age of mutual deterrence) and the use of force to maintain it.

In virtually all cases, action for self-preservation amounts to intervention or the threat of it. Self-preservation takes many different forms, depending upon the means used, the purpose pursued, and the nature of the prevailing situation. As, in principle, intervention by one state in the affairs of another is illegal, the right to self-preservation would be an exception to the general principle. Because the reasons for intervention and the kind of changes sought in the other country are legion, these possibilities illustrate to what extent the claim of self-preservation can be used to cover political and selfish goals by a state and make them appear legitimate. One only has to think of the numerous and different activities of the United States in Latin America or the Soviet Union in its contiguous areas, which are frequently excused as counteracting intolerable threats to these states, to realize the popularity and widespread acceptance of the right to self-preservation.

Closely related to the principle of self-preservation is the principle of self-protection. This principle, out of fashion for some time, has experienced a revival in connection with oil pollution on the high seas near a state's coastline. Under general international law, a state has the right "to secure itself from injury" beyond the limits of its territory, said Chief Justice Marshall in Church v. Hubbard (1804, p. 234) when referring to any kind of injury. General Assembly Resolution 2749 (XXV) (1970) reconfirms this right in regard to a state's coastline. Self-defense does not apply to accidental pollution because it is not an armed attack. Therefore, abatement activity to prevent injury on the high seas can involve use of force only within the limits permitted by the U.N. Charter and must be proportional to the injury. The International Convention Relating to Intervention on the High Seas in Case of Oil Pollution Casualties (1969) spells out the rights of coastal states in some detail for those states that are parties. Abatement by force is not restricted to terra nullius. It may be applied to a neighboring country, for instance, if uncontrolled danger threatens to spill over into the abating country. The International Court of Justice also permitted the threat of force to enforce a right that another state intended to deny in the Corfu Channel case (1949, p. 30).

War

By almost any definition, war is the most typical and extreme use of force. For many centuries a debate has been raging about whether under general international law war is legal under any circumstances or only under certain conditions. The first view has at least two merits. It obviates the practically unfeasible distinction between legal and illegal wars in any concrete case, and it legitimizes what states will do. The second view—that war is legal or "just" only against states having committed illegal acts (war as a sanction)—is morally more appealing but practically inapplicable. In brief, the voluminous theoretical and philosophical argumentation has not provided a final answer to the question of the legality of war. There is no agreement among states upon the justness of a given war, on its aggressive or defensive nature, or on any of the other conditions suggested as criteria for distinguishing legal from illegal wars. There is not even agreement on what a war is: whether it is an action or a status, whether it must involve force, whether it can be fought unilaterally or only bilaterally, whether behind the use of force must be the intent to make war, whether it must be "hot" or may be "cold."

This lack of agreement results from the nature of the prevailing international system in which states are sovereign and power (including force) is diffused among them, available to their unilaterally determined disposition. Until, for instance a central organ is established with sufficient power to enforce its decisions, the effective definition and control of war as such and in general are beyond the reach of law.

Partly to approach such a situation, partly to prevent semantics from circumventing the illegality of war, and to clarify the illegality of war, the focus of discussion and regulation shifted after World War II from the status called war to the broader and, it was hoped, less easily circumvented concept of use of force or threat to peace. The law of armed conflict rather than the law of war became the subject on which international society concentrated its efforts at regulation. A number of factors favored this shift. There was hope that regardless of the legality or illegality of war, states would use force in accordance with some legal rules. There was hope also that the more humane aspects of the use of force (as, in any case, the aspects most susceptible to legal regulation) could be improved and agreed upon. The change in focus also took into account the increasing number of situations in which the use of force in internationalized conflicts (as in foreign intervention, liberation wars, internationalized civil wars, indirect aggression, and vicariously applied violence) did not amount technically to any definition of war. These situations especially justified preoccupation with legal rules even in the age of atomic weapons because the conflicts envisaged were fought in a "limited" and "traditional" manner (so-called conventional wars), short of all-out war.

In contrast to untold earlier attempts to "abolish" war, notably the League of Nations and the Pact of Paris (1928), the Charter of the United Nations mentions war only in the preamble. The binding articles speak of "threat or use of force" and "threat to the peace, breach of the peace, or act of aggression." This language intended to avoid, or at least reduce, semantic squabbles, and the legitimacy or illegitimacy of the use of force became a consideration subordinated to the primacy of maintaining peace, meaning essentially absence of violence.

The risks involved in the international diffusion of power were to be diminished by centralizing force and giving the Security Council a monopoly in the use of force, except in cases of self-defense and possibly some other measures of forcible self-help still permitted under the charter. According to the charter plan, what triggers the use of the Security Council's monopoly are those broad conditions endangering or breaching the peace—however the Security Council may define them and establish their presence and whoever may be responsible for creating those conditions. For the members of the United Nations and, by now, for every state, war has become an illegal act.

The historical record shows the charter arrangement for the legal control of force to be a failure. The basic reasons for this failure are, as has been mentioned earlier, that under the prevailing international system law is impotent in the matter and politics is largely beyond the controlling reach of the United Nations. Additionally, the seemingly clear-cut arrangement of the charter is qualified by the charter in so many ways that a state would find an escape from it easy. The mechanism for the actual operation of the arrangement is such (for example, the veto of the permanent members) that it could be successful only in rare and unusual circumstances. Moreover, every legal rule (and facts) is usually subject to evasive interpretation in application to a concrete case. States can frustrate the charter's arrangement and have done so on many occasions with relative ease. The conclusion regarding the use of force as war must be that under the charter and many other treaties it is illegal under general international law for all states but that a state would have little difficulty in finding some legal norm justifying its use of force.

The attempt to outlaw war has been significantly and unfavorably affected by the pressure to legalize liberation wars against colonial and (white) racist regimes, mainly in Africa. The tendency is to change the characterization of these wars from self-defense against aggression to something approaching "just wars." The division of view on this point between the newer and Communist states and the mainly Western states became very clear when the Diplomatic Conferences on the Reaffirmation and Development of International Humanitarian Law Applicable in Armed Conflicts (1974–1977) discussed the extent to which the international legal protection of combatants, prisoners of war, and so forth should be extended to participants in civil, liberation, and similar (traditionally noninternational) wars.

The older, mainly Western states had a number of primarily legal arguments designed to keep some neatness in the legal system but also to preserve some political situations intact. One argument was that to be international a conflict must involve participants of more than one state and must be of an intensity that can normally be produced only by states. A second argument was that for the application of humanitarian laws the moral character of the armed conflict (just or unjust) should be irrelevant. A third argument was that international law deals with states, not "bands" or "peoples." This is a particularly important consideration in armed conflicts because reciprocity as a main incentive for obeying international norms can hardly be safeguarded in a confrontation between a state and a revolutionary group (such as guerrillas). A fourth argument, as a U.S. delegate put it, is that terrorism should not be legalized by simply classifying it as an international conflict. These states were not opposed to making humane treatment of participants in internal armed conflicts an international obligation. They merely felt that internal and international conflicts should be treated separately because their consequences, going far beyond the problem of humanitarianism, were quite different.

The arguments of the newer states, usually with the support of the Communist states, were more openly political. One was that violent actions against colonial and racist regimes had by their nature become international, however they might be fought. A second argument was that the question of justice in the conflict should be a determining factor so that participants in (traditionally) internal wars would benefit from the humanitarian laws of war. A third argument was that liberation and resistance movements were recognized in numerous international resolutions as having international legal personality. Many of these states, however, would refuse to allow that the same antigovernmental action should be either treason or legitimate military action depending upon who performed it.

The resolutions and conventions in which these newer and Communist states incorporate their views usually do not identify the targets of the armed conflicts: colonialist and white racist regimes. These resolutions are formulated in abstract, general terms but applied in practice only to such regimes. It is therefore impossible to predict how, should these views become customary law, they might in the future serve as excuses by all kinds of groups and factions for engaging in legitimate warlike behavior. It would appear, for instance, that many different kinds of groups could justify their use of force and claim "humane" treatment while possibly denying it to their adversaries on the basis of the 1974 U.N. General Assembly Resolution 3328 (XXIX). This resolution reaffirms the General Assembly's "recognition of the legitimacy of the struggle of the peoples under colonial and alien domination to exercise their right of self-determination and independence by all necessary means at their disposal." Yet in spite of Communist writings declaring liberation wars to be just as well as sacred, and despite the increasingly frank recognition by international society of the right to self-determination and insurgency to achieve independence, the combined efforts of the

Communists and newer states have as yet failed to legalize liberation wars under universal international law.

The whole treatment of forcible decolonization is yet another illustration of the reluctance of states to interfere with well-established principles and norms of international law (quite apart from the fact that the issue of decolonization, although not its consequences, as understood by the Third World is nearly passé). Rather than departing from traditional law and dealing with decolonization and its legacy as a discrete process requiring new and unique regulation under modern conditions, all states are straining to fit their politically determined positions on the issue into generally accepted categories of legal principles: aggression, self-defense, legitimacy of the use of force, and so on. Verbal emphasis upon human rights in this context might be considered an innovation were it not for the frequent practice of the very states agitating in the international arena most violently for human rights to use inhumane methods in their internal wars. It troubles states little that the patently expedient use of law produces inconsistencies, double standards, and eventual disrespect for the law. At least this attitude is a left-handed compliment to the value of and respect for international law!

27
REGULATION OF THE
APPLICATION OF FORCE

General Principles

Because war is the most extreme form of the application of force, the assumption must be made that any legal application of force going beyond that allowed in war is illegal. In situations less extreme than war, there may be limitations in the use of force according to general international law that do not apply to warfare.

It may appear paradoxical that war is illegal, yet rules of war continue in force, or, to put it differently, that there may be legal and illegal action within the overall illegal action. The reason for this paradox is that most rules of war, whether general or conventional, were created before war became illegal or that, recognizing reality, states felt it was better to regulate the conduct of war even if such conduct might be illegal. This consideration is, however, fairly irrelevant in view of the fact that the rules for the conduct of war are largely as ineffective as the rules forbidding war itself.

The rules of general international law regulating the use of force have rarely kept pace with developments in war technology. For this reason, many rules, while still technically valid, have been ignored in recent wars, and in future all rules are likely to be ignored. How, for instance, can women and children or historical buildings be protected during the use of atomic weapons?

Many widely accepted conventional rules have often been adopted as a result of experiences in past wars, experiences that turned out not to be repeated in subsequent wars. Because people are devoting greater effort and ingenuity to developing new weapons and methods than to controlling or not developing them, the regulation of the use of force in war has always lagged behind, which is to say, it has always been inadequate. The various attempts to limit the manufacture, proliferation, use, and location of atomic and other weapons are not likely to change the situation.

In the implementation of the ineffective norm that wars are now illegal, the most fundamental rule is that warfare should be humanized as much as the conduct of war permits. This prescription provides the rationale for almost all other rules, general or conventional. It is reinforced by the trend of making human rights binding law. But it remains true that humanitarianism is being given only the space left over by the conduct of war.

Several other rules emerge from this fundamental rule: Force should be used only against combatants (usually defined as individuals clearly recognizable by wearing a uniform and carrying weapons openly or by having other unmistakable signs); unnecessary suffering must be avoided; force should be applied chivalrously, not treacherously. These principles apply to all armed combat, regardless of who started it or who the parties are or on whose behalf the combatants are active. Details of these principles are much debated, but they appear well justified if humanitarianism is their rationale.

The large number of conventions concluded during the last hundred years or so are either based upon or specifically include these principles. Outstanding among them are the Hague Conventions of 1899 and 1907, the 1949 Geneva conventions, and two 1977 Protocols (the first relating to international armed conflict, the second to noninternational armed conflict). The Nuremberg Tribunal of war criminals stated explicitly that some of the conventions were declaratory only. But customary law remains effective. For instance, the preamble to the Regulations Respecting the Laws and Customs of War on Land adopted at the 1907 Hague conference states that all cases not covered by codified rules do not thereby become subject to the arbitrary will of the combatants. Rather, these cases are subject to general principles of international law derived from the usages of civilized nations—that is, customary law, the rules of humanitarianism, and the demands of public conscience. These principles apply to all kinds of warfare: on land, in the air, and on the sea. The increasing indistinctiveness of these kinds of warfare made this expansion mandatory. Changes in the conduct of warfare, combined with the erosion of sovereignty's content, have led to changes in the rules of the conduct of violent conflict and eventually to new major conventions.

Beginning in the middle of the last century, all conventions and recommendations relating to warfare completely respected sovereignty and therefore referred only to international (intrastate) conflicts. Beginning in 1949 with the four Geneva conventions, some limited attention was paid to intrastate violent conflict. In an article common to all the conventions, the parties to an "armed conflict not of an international character" are obliged to observe a minimum standard of conduct.

Since then, concern with the humanitarian aspects of all armed conflicts has grown parallel to the increasing frequency of intrastate wars (civil wars, wars of liberation). In 1977, a diplomatic conference, which had been meeting in Paris since 1974, adopted new regulations (the two Protocols) to supplement the 1949 Geneva conventions. They include humanitarian rules for conflicts hitherto considered internal wars: self-determination through wars against colonial domination, foreign occupation, and racist governments. The second Protocol devotes itself in detail to the humanization of intranational wars, hitherto neglected by all other conventions. This broadening of the regulations grants protection only to victims of those kinds of conflicts whose definition is clearly dependent upon the politics of the day. This change reflects the majority votes of the newer and Communist states, which are mainly concerned about the international recognition of wars of liberation as legitimate or "just" wars, while being anxious to preserve their sovereign right to conduct their own internal conflicts unhampered by constraints of international law.

In sum, the application of general rules about the use of force, about the conventional controls and limitation on the use of force, and about the differentiations between the types of war and types of force connected with them have become so quickly outdated that the discussion of most of them is mainly of historical interest. Generally, however, only those rules making reciprocity effective in inducing combatants to some restraint may still be obeyed—if their weapons allow them to do so. These rules relate much more to the treatment of individuals (prisoners, wounded, enemy nationals, civilians) than to the use of force during the conduct of hostilities when the aim is defeat of the enemy and the fate of the state is at stake. The underlying rationale of such rules—humanitarianism—has remained intact but has never overcome nationalism, greed, ambition, and all the other factors that cause wars.

Weapons and Methods

In regulating the use of force, international law has focused upon types of weapons (bullets, bombs, gas, poisons, bacteria, nuclear arms) and on the methods of their use (for example, advance warning of city bombardment). But, it seems, the more recent the developments in any of these weapons, the more inadequate or outright inapplicable becomes their regulation. One only needs to recall such methods as saturation or fire bombing, defoliation, and the mining of vast ocean areas to realize the futility of these regulations. Any control of nuclear warfare is nonexistent, unless one applies existing rules by analogy. Certain agreements about what not to do, such as placing nuclear weapons on the ocean floor, in the atmosphere, in outer space, on celestial bodies, or into certain geographic areas, have apparently been kept for a number of possible reasons, among which obedience to international norms can hardly be found. Aerial warfare or warfare on the seas is little better regulated, and these regulations are equally little obeyed. The more that weapons become instruments of mass destruction, the more useless become the fine distinctions (women versus men, historical monuments versus military installation or factories) that have survived from the days when the use of force was more "individualized" and less destructive.

In the struggle between the demands of civilization and the requirements of war, the latter have always been victorious. The nature of future war, with the importance of the elements of surprise and total destruction, will undoubtedly guarantee that victory again and thereby the virtually total defeat of legal controls. The neglect of legal considerations even in the "conventional wars" that have occurred since World War II (the use of gas in the Iraq-Iran war, the mining of territorial waters of Nicaragua by the United States, the wanton burning down of villages and mass killings of civilians in African wars) makes this prediction very reliable, almost a certainty.

Use of Force Short of War

To the extent that the individual use of force by a state remains legal, it must be kept within the limits of the permitted use of force during war as a minimum. The major additional limitation is that the use of force against an illegal act by another state must be in proportion to the action of the other state. In cases where the counteraction (retaliation) is approximately the same as the initial illegal action, proportionality can be established with reasonable reliability. But in other cases, no general rule can be established. How much material damage is allowable in retaliation for the killing of a citizen? The United States should have struggled with this problem in Vietnam, in Grenada, in Libya, and in Panama but apparently did not. Or if it did, the United States arrived at rather astonishing conclusions. The same goes for the Soviet Union in Eastern Europe, Afghanistan, and Armenia; for both sides in the western Asian war; and for the Irish in Northern Ireland.

Clearly, precedents are no guide. As long as sovereignty permits each state to make its own evaluation and judgment in this respect, individual political considerations will weigh heavily in the decision, and no regularities in the treatment of such cases can be developed. In fact, much of the time retaliation is simply a pretext for doing great damage, all out of proportion to the original injury, to the other state. The most that can be expected is that clearly undue retaliation will provoke the world's reaction to the behavior of the retaliating state and perhaps moderate its retaliation to reasonable proportions.

28
THE POSITION OF THIRD STATES UNINVOLVED IN THE USE OF FORCE

In Peacetime

The practice and opinion of most states today are that third states should not be affected by the unilateral or mutual application of force between other states during peacetime. This rule follows first from the fact that the use of force in peacetime is legitimate only against the illegal act of another state, if at all. As third states have not committed such acts, force cannot be used against them. This rule follows second from the fact that all measures of self-help are in response to situations created by a given state in which the third state played no part.

Before 1850 this legal position did not prevail; in cases of the pacific blockade of a state, the blockading state could legally prevent ships from all states reaching the blockaded port. But since then and, ironically, following the repeated insistence of the United States, the position has changed. It is now generally agreed, and confirmed in the *Oriental Navigation Co.* claim before the U.S.-Mexican General Claims Commission (1928) and in *China Mutual Trading Co. v. American President Lines* (1953) before the Hong Kong Supreme Court, that a peaceful blockade can be undertaken only against ships of the blockaded state, not against ships of third states.

President Kennedy broke this rule when he established in 1962 a "defensive quarantine" on the shipment of offensive arms to Cuba and declared—with the dutiful backing of the Organization of American States—that "all ships of any kind bound for Cuba from whatever nation or port will, if found to contain cargoes of offensive weapons, be turned back." The United States based the legality of this action not on any measure of forcible self-help but on the controversial grounds that the Cuban situation threatened the peace and security of the U.S. continent. The Soviet Union, whose ships were mostly concerned, could have considered this action an act of war under traditional international law had it chosen to do so.

Related to this situation is the question of whether in the name of self-defense or necessity a state may use force (such as occupation) against a third state in response to actions undertaken against it or threatened against it by another state. Germany claimed such a right when it invaded Belgium in 1914 and was generally condemned for it. The German invasion of Norway in World War II was justified by Germany as preventive self-defense to forestall an allied invasion and subsequent attack from Norway against Germany. The Nuremberg Tribunal admitted that under the conditions for anticipatory self-defense measures detailed in the *Caroline* case (1837), such a defense measure could be legal, but the tribunal found that in the case at bar these conditions were not fulfilled.

As long as forcible measures are taken by states against each other in peacetime, third states need not act as neutrals. They have neither obligations to act as neutrals nor a duty to grant the parties concerned their rights as belligerents. The rules of neutrality apply only in wartime.

For those states that are members of the United Nations or of regional organizations or are parties of certain defense arrangements, a legal necessity may exist for participating in collective forcible enforcement action against the illegal action not necessarily directed against them directly. One rationale for these arrangements is similar to that underlying the idea of collective security—and long since proven untenable—namely, that peace is indivisible.

Nevertheless, the International Court of Justice in the *Nicaragua (Merits, Judgment)* case, (1986, p. 1068) declared, "There is no rule in customary international law permitting another State to exercise the right of collective self-defense on the basis of its own assessment of the situation. Where collective self-defence is invoked, it is to be expected that the State for whose benefit this right is used will have declared itself to be the victim of an armed attack." An innovation in the claimed right to use force legitimately against a state that has not acted illegally was contained in President Kennedy's "quarantine" proclamation: "It shall be the policy of this nation to regard any nuclear missile launched from Cuba against any nation in the western hemisphere as an attack by the Soviet Union on the United States, requiring a full retaliatory response upon the Soviet Union." If the principle becomes established that the state supplying arms or that the state approving the supply of arms with which the receiving state attacks another state may itself be considered an aggressor, the United States and other major arms suppliers would soon find themselves at war all over the world. The favorable aspect of this principle might be an end to proxy wars, a result President Kennedy probably did not have in mind.

In Wartime

In a situation of war the position of third states in regard to the use of force, either by the belligerents or themselves, changes substantially.

316 THE POSITION OF THIRD STATES

As long as third states remain neutral or are permanently neutralized (such as Switzerland and Austria) or at least are nonbelligerents (do not participate in armed combat but are otherwise partial in the treatment of the belligerents), the belligerents as well as third states have rights and duties toward each other whose specific nature is far from clear in all cases. The reason for the obscurity is that the two sides have extremely opposite interests, and each demands fulfillment of alleged obligations while being reluctant to grant corresponding rights. Moreover, the entire complex status of neutrality as defining the relations between neutrals and belligerents is constantly changing because the conditions of war are changing and because the relations depend to some extent on the strength of the parties involved.

The question has been raised as to whether for neutrals membership in the United Nations destroys the feasibility of neutrality. Voting yes or no or abstaining is, in fact, taking sides. The obligation to participate in collective security action may make neutrality impossible. Switzerland has not joined the organization in the belief that it would be extremely difficult to remain totally impartial. Austria did not share that concern and joined. There are possibilities for neutral states under Article 48 of the charter to remain neutral even when collective action is taken, but Switzerland was not persuaded.

What the rules regarding forcible action by belligerents or neutrals against each other may be under traditional general international law, or even under more specific rules created in numerous conventions relating to neutrality, is largely a matter of controversy. The rules are often sufficiently broad, vague, or nonexistent to permit all concerned to find a legal justification for whatever action they choose. Moreover, because great inequality often exists between a belligerent and a neutral state, reciprocity scarcely exists, and the temptation is great for the belligerent to ignore the rules of neutrality if that serves its purpose.

In principle, no belligerent is permitted to perform acts of war from the territory of a neutral state. In turn, the neutral state must use all means at its disposal to prevent its territory from being used unlawfully by the belligerent state. This includes use of force by the neutral state (hence during 1989–1990 in a debate about whether to abolish the Swiss army, the argument was made that abolishing the army would make neutrality impossible). If the neutral state fails to prevent such misuse and one of the belligerents misuses the territory, the other belligerent is then permitted to do likewise in counteraction, and the neutral state's territory may become a battlefield. If a neutral state granted one of the belligerents a base on its territory before the war (an unlikely situation), the other belligerent may attack it—following the principle that one enemy may fight another where it can be found.

Most neutrality laws relate to naval warfare because most controversies between neutrals and belligerents developed in regard to ships, goods, and commerce across oceans. Under the impact of developments described earlier (the making of fine distinctions between ownership of goods), belligerents tend to consider all goods contraband and to assume that the ultimate destination of most goods is the enemy. This allows them to cut off all trade of the enemy and to use force, if necessary, against neutral ships. When to this right of belligerents is added their right of angary—that under certain conditions they may seize property, including ships and goods of neutrals, for their own use against proper compensation—it becomes clear that belligerents have relatively far-reaching rights to use force against neutrals during naval warfare. Indeed, under the impact of modern methods of warfare, the rules protecting neutral shipping and goods (and, for that matter, property located on land in enemy territory) had deteriorated to such a degree by the end of World War II that the existence of any rules protecting neutral interests outside the neutral state has become questionable.

Civil wars and wars of national liberation represent special problems for states wanting to remain neutral. Depending upon how, for instance, a war of liberation is interpreted, whether as an internal affair or as a war of the oppressing state against the oppressed state, a third state could legitimately (according to traditional international law) assist the government against the insurgents, or it could not. The scores of U.N. resolutions calling on all members to support liberation struggles could, if they become customary law, oblige member states to support the liberation forces and make it illegal for them to support colonial governments. Although it would be possible theoretically to argue these issues on legal grounds, the practice of states makes clear that they consider these to be fundamentally political issues and treat them as such.

REFERENCES AND READINGS FOR PART 9

Legality

Cassese, Antonio, ed. *Violence and Law in the Modern Age.* Princeton, NJ: Princeton University Press, 1988.

"Comment: The use of non-violent coercion." *University of Pennsylvania Law Review* 122 (April 1974): 983–1011.

Elegab, Omar Yousif. *The Legality of Non-Forcible Counter-Measures in International Law.* Oxford: Clarendon, 1988.

Green, L. C. *Essays on the Modern Law of War.* Dobbs Ferry, NY: Transnational, 1984.

Guelke, Adrian. "Force, intervention and internal conflict." In *The Use of Force in International Relations,* edited by F. S. Northedge, pp. 99–123. London: Faber & Faber, 1974.

Lillich, Richard B. *Economic Coercion and the New International Economic Order.* Charlottesville, VA: Michie, 1976.

Lupis, Ingrid Detter de. *The Law of War.* Cambridge: Cambridge University Press, 1987.

Paust, Jordan S., and Albert P. Blaustein. "The Arab oil weapon: A threat to international peace." *AJIL* 68 (July 1974):410–439.

Paust, Jordan S. et al., eds. *The Arab Oil Weapon.* Dobbs Ferry, NY: Oceana, 1977.

Röling, B.V.J. "Aspects on the ban on force." *Netherlands International Law Review* 24 (special issue 1977):242–259.

Shihata, Ibrahim F.I. "Destination embargo of Arab oil: Its legality under International Law." *AJIL* 68 (October 1974):591–627.

Wilson, Heather A. *International Law and the Use of Force.* Oxford: Clarendon, 1988.

Reprisal

Akehurst, Michael. "Reprisals by third states." *BYIL* 44 (1970):1–18.

Bowett, Derek. "Reprisals involving recourse to armed force." *AJIL* 66 (January 1972):1–36.

Elegab, Omer Yousif. *The Legality of Non-Forcible Counter-Measures in International Law.* Oxford: Clarendon, 1988.

Kalshoven, Frits. *Belligerent Reprisals.* Leiden: A. W. Sijthoff, 1971.

Renwick, Robin. *Economic Sanctions.* Cambridge, MA: Harvard University Center for International Affairs, 1982.

Tomuschat, Christian W. "Repressalie und Retorsion." Z 33 (1973 I):179–222.

Tucker, Robert W. "Reprisals and self-defense: The contemporary law." *AJIL* 66 (July 1972):586–596.

Zoller, Elisabeth. *Peacetime Unilateral Remedies: An Analysis of Countermeasures.* Dobbs Ferry, NY: Transnational, 1984.

Self-Defense

Delivanes, Jean. *La légitime défense en droit international public moderne.* Paris: Librairie Générale de Droit et de Jurisprudence, 1971.

Dugard, C.J.R. "The Organization of African Unity and colonialism: An inquiry into the plea of self-defense as a justification for the use of force in the eradication of colonialism." *Int. & Comp. L. Q.* 16 (January 1967):157–190.

Moore, John N. *Law and the Grenada Mission 1984.* Charlottesville: Center for Law and National Security, University of Virginia, 1984.

Schwebel, Stephen M. "Aggression, intervention and self-defense." *ADIRC* 136 (1972 II):411–497.

Zanardi, Parluigi L. *La legitima difesa nel dirrito internazionale.* Milan: A. Giuffré, 1972.

Aggression

Dinstein, Yoram. *War, Aggression and Self-Defence.* Cambridge: Grotius, 1988.

Doose, Jeffrey A. "The United Nations definition of aggression: A preliminary analysis." *Denver Journal of International Law and Policy* 5 (Spring 1975):171–199.

Ferencz, Benjamin B. *Defining International Aggression: The Search for World Peace,* 2 vols. Dobbs Ferry, NY: Oceana, 1975.

Garvey, Jack I. "The U.N. definition of aggression: Law and illusion in the context of collective security." *Virginia Journal of International Law* 17 (Winter 1977):177–199.

Meier, Gert. "Der Begriff des bewaffneten Angriffs." *AV* 16 (1975 IV):376–386.

Rubin, Alfred P. Book review of *Defining Aggression: The Search for Peace. Harvard International Law Journal* 17 (Spring 1976):435–439.

Stone, Julius. "Hopes and loopholes in the 1974 definition of aggression." *AJIL* 71 (April 1977):224–246.

Wilson, Heather A. *International Law and the Use of Force by National Liberation Movements.* New York: Oxford University Press, 1988.

War, Civil War, Liberation War

Bond, James E. *The Rules of Riot: Internal Conflict and the Law of War.* Princeton, NJ: Princeton University Press, 1974.

Dhokalia, R. P. "Civil wars in international law." *Indian Journal of International Law* 11 (April 1971):219–250.

El-Ayouty, Yassin. "Legitimization of national liberation: The United Nations and southern Africa." In *Africa and International Organization,* edited by Yassin El-Ayouty and Hugh C. Brooks, pp. 202–229. The Hague: Martinus Nijhoff, 1974.

Falk, Richard A., ed. *The International Law of Civil War,* Baltimore, MD: Johns Hopkins University Press, 1971.

Farer, Tom J. "The regulation of foreign intervention in civil armed conflict." *ADIRC* 142 (1974 II):291–406.

Forsythe, David P. "Who guards the guardians: Third parties and the law of armed conflict." *AJIL* 70 (January 1976):141–161.

Klein, Eckart. "Nationale Befreiungskämpfe und Dekolonisierungspolitik der Vereinten Nationen: Zu einigen völkerrechtlichen Tendenzen." *Z* 36 (1976 I–III):618–653.

Kutner, Luis. *Due Process of Rebellion.* Chicago: Bardian House, 1974.

Little, Richard. *Interventive External Involvement in Civil War.* Totowa, NJ: Rowman and Littlefield, 1975.

Luard, Evan, ed. *The International Regulation of Civil War.* New York: New York University Press, 1972.

Melzer, Yehuda. *Concepts of Just War.* Leiden: A. W. Sijthoff, 1975.

Moore, John N. *Law and Civil War in the Modern World.* Baltimore, MD: Johns Hopkins University Press, 1974.

Oglesby, Roscoe R. *Internal War and the Search for Normative Order.* The Hague: Martinus Nijhoff, 1971.

Roberts, Adam, and Richard Guelff. *Documents on the Laws of War.* Oxford: Clarendon, 1989.

Rosenau, James N., ed. *International Aspects of Civil Strife.* Princeton, NJ: Princeton University Press, 1964.

Schindler, Dietrich, and Jivi Toman. *The Laws of Armed Conflict.* Dordrecht: Martinus Nijhoff, 1988.

Snyder, Frederick E., and Surakiart Sathirathai, eds. *Third World Attitudes Toward International Law.* Dordrecht: Martinus Nijhoff, 1987, pp. 125–158.

Suter, Keith. *The International Law of Guerilla Warfare: The Global Politics of Law Making.* New York: St. Martin's, 1984.

Humanizing War

Abi-Saab, Rosemary. *Droit humanitaire et conflits internes: Origine et évolution de la réglementation internationale.* Paris: A. Pédone, 1986.

Baxter, Richard R. "Humanitarian law or humanitarian politics? The 1974 diplomatic conference on humanitarian law." *Harvard International Law Journal* 16 (Winter 1975):1–26.

Bothe, Michael, Karl Joseph Partsch, and Waldemar A. Solf. *New Rules for Victims of Armed Conflict.* The Hague: Martinus Nijhoff, 1982.

Cassese, Antonio. *The New Humanitarian Law of Armed Conflict,* 2 vols. Dobbs Ferry, NY: Oceana, 1979.

Dinstein, Yoram. "Another step in codifying the laws of war." *Yearbook of World Affairs* (1974):278–292.

Draper, G.I.A.D. "The status of combatants and the question of guerilla warfare." *BYIL* 45 (1971):173–218.

Freymond, Jacques. "Confronting total war: A global humanitarian policy." *AJIL* 67 (October 1973):672–692.

Fujita, Hisikayu. "La guerre de libération nationale et le droit international humanitaire." *Revue de Droit International de Sciences Diplomatiques et Politiques* 53 (April-June 1975):81–142.

Gilmore, William C. *The Grenada Intervention Analysis and Documentation.* New York: Monsall, 1984.

Kalshoven, Frits. "Reaffirmation and development of international humanitarian law applicable in armed conflicts: The diplomatic conference, Geneva, 1974–77." *Netherlands Yearbook of International Law* 8 (1977):107–138.

Lattmann, Eveline. *Schutz der Kulturgüter bei bewaffneten Konflikten.* Zurich: Schulthess Polygraphischer Verlag, 1974.

Levie, Howard S., ed. *The Law of Non-International Armed Conflict Protocol II to the 1949 Geneva Convention.* Dordrecht: Martinus Nijhoff, 1987.

Lillich, Richard B. *Humanitarian Intervention and the United Nations.* Charlottesville: University Press of Virginia, 1973.

Meron, Theodor. *Human Rights in International Strife: Their International Protection.* Cambridge: Grotius, 1987.

Pictet, Jean. *Humanitarian Law and the Protection of War Victims.* Leiden: A. W. Sijthoff, 1975.

————. *Development and Principle of International Humanitarian Law.* Dordrecht: Martinus Nijhoff, 1985.

————, ed. *Commentary on the Additional Protocols to the Geneva Convention.* Geneva: International Committee of the Red Cross, Martinus Nijhoff, 1987.

Rosas, Allan. *The Legal Status of Prisoners of War.* Helsinki: Suomalainen Tiedeakatemia, 1976.

Swinarski, Cristophe. *Etudes et essais sur le droit international humanitaire et sur les principes de la Croix-Rouge.* Geneva: International Committee of the Red Cross, Martinus Nijhoff, 1984.

Tiewul, Sylvanus A. "Law of war: Humanitarian law in armed conflict." *Harvard Journal of International Law* 14 (Summer 1973):573–595.

Wilhelm, René-Jean. "Problèmes relatifs à la protection de la personne humaine par le droit international dans les conflits armés ne présentant pas un caractère international." *ADIRC* 137 (1972 III):311–417.

322 REFERENCES AND READINGS FOR PART 9

New Weapons and Technology

Dewar, John et al., eds. *Nuclear Weapons, the Peace Movement and the Law.* Houndsmills, Basingstoke, NH: Manville, 1986.

Miller, Arthur Selwyn, and Martins Feinrider, eds. *Nuclear Weapons and Law.* Westport, CT: Greenwood, 1984.

Singh, Nagendra, and Edward McWhinney. *Nuclear Weapons and Contemporary International Law.* Dordrecht: Martinus Nijhoff, 1989.

Stein, Eric. "Impact of new weapons technology on international law." *ADIRC* 133 (1971 II):222–387.

Trooboff, Peter D., ed. *Law and Responsibility in Warfare: The Vietnam Experience.* Chapel Hill: University of North Carolina Press, 1975.

Weeramanty, C. G. *Nuclear Weapons and Scientific Responsibility.* Wolfboro, NH: Longwood Academic, 1987.

Neutrality

Blix, Hans. *Aggression, Neutrality and Sovereignty.* Stockholm: Almqvist & Wiksell, 1970.

Leonhard, Alan T., ed. *Neutrality: Changing Concepts and Practices.* Lanham, NY: University Press of America, 1988.

Mojoryan, L. A. "Neutrality in present-day international law." In *Contemporary International Law,* edited by Gregory Tunkin. Moscow: Progress Publishers, 1969.

Norton, Patrick M. "Between ideology and the reality: The Shadow of the law of neutrality." *Harvard International Law Journal* 17 (Spring 1976):249–311.

Ogley, Roderick. *The Theory and Practice of Neutrality in the Twentieth Century.* London: Routledge and Kegan Paul, 1970.

Papacosma, S. Victor, and Mark R. Rubin, eds. *Europe's Neutral and Nonaligned States Between NATO and the Warsaw Pact.* Wilmington, DE: Resources Imprint, 1989.

Thürer, Daniel. "Die Armeefrage unter völkerrechtlichem Blickwinkel: Sinn und Funktion der schweizerischen Neutralität." *Neue Zürcher Zeitung,* August 4, 1989.

PART 10
THE DYNAMIC
CHARACTER OF
INTERNATIONAL LAW

The old Roman adage *ubi societas ibi ius* has once more proven correct in the case of international society. The growth of humankind into a society has been paralleled by the growth of international law because the legal regulation of social behavior is the only possible foundation of coexistence. Retention of the institution of sovereignty symbolizes the reluctance of states to accept limitations upon their behavior. This often creates a dichotomy between the wish of states to be their own highest authority and social needs to impose restraints upon their behavior. Retention of sovereignty makes international law paradoxical by providing a legal foundation for sovereignty yet at the same time also telling states what they may or may not do. The result is a fundamental contradiction: International law often enables states to pick and choose the legal norm best suited to serve their interests. In the case of Panama in 1989, for instance, the United States could have let the Panamanian people deal with Noriega (as the Soviet Union let the Romanian people deal with Nicolae Ceauşescu) in the name of noninterference with domestic affairs. Or the United States could have invaded the country in the name of self-defense or of saving of U.S. lives. In this sometimes hypocritical manner, a state can save its reputation as law-abiding and circumvent the ultimate result of sovereignty: anarchy.

The irony of the situation is that the insistence of states on being the masters of their own behavior by existing in splendid, sovereign isolation has produced the very thing they were trying to avoid: international law (rules restraining that mastery). It could not have been otherwise. For without the law, anarchy would arise, which states desire even less than a modicum of social order. Therefore, they have limited the exercise and effectiveness of sovereignty to their own territories, granting the same exercise to all other states. They have thereby limited the validity of their own legal order to within their frontiers, thus making international law possible and necessary. They have granted some legal principles universality and a few norms even peremptory validity.

323

Unquestionably, states acknowledge the need for law as an important support for the stability, regularity, and continuity of the international social order.

The denser the interaction between states, the more voluminous becomes the law. However sovereignty may be interpreted, on balance its substance is thinning while the substance of international law is fattening. Although sovereignty would logically lead to social chaos by denying, for instance, the binding nature of international norms and therefore treaties, states have never admitted this conclusion. Instead, they have avoided doing so and have maintained international social order much of the time by declaring that obedience to law is not a denial but an expression of sovereignty, by actually obeying the law when expedient or cheaper than disobeying it, and by using political power.

The content of this order, however, has forever been an object of a contest whose core lies in the political arena. Roughly speaking, the most powerful states exploit their power to designate politics and hence to shape the legal order. The weaker states may try to adjust the social order by enhancing their influence through alliances, by playing balance of power games, or by propagating new legal norms based on the appeals of widely acknowledged moral values such as justice or equity. Of this last method, the proposal for the New International Economic Order and for the making of racism illegal are outstanding examples. In other words, the strong tend to rely upon their strength, the weak upon publicly supported morality, law, and legal means. But they all uphold sovereignty, which enables them to act in that manner, although each has reasons of its own for doing so.

Powerful states insist on sovereignty to bolster their privileged position. Weak states use sovereignty as a shield against powerful states. Sovereignty is thus the fundamental principle upon which the international legal and world political orders are founded. Because norms and principles are conditioned by it and are interpreted to accord with it, basic legal innovations are extremely limited, and if they are introduced, they have to fit into the existing framework based on sovereignty. The possible exception of a European Community by 1992 is not based upon a rejection of sovereignty so much as on the built-in pressures toward a community extant since the Treaty of Rome and on the need to compete with the economies of the United States, Japan, and others. Most European states see no alternative, and it is a good illustration of how under modern conditions limiting sovereignty is necessary to fulfill national interests. The breakdown of isolation of states under the impact of interaction and interdependence has led to the adjustment of the rules securing isolated national existence and to their implementation by new, additional legal norms regulating the new relationships while preserving national independence (unless these new norms cause the death of outdated norms).

As the preceding survey of international law demonstrates, new conditions, such as international terrorism, control of outer space, exploitation of marine resources, restraints upon multinational corporations, and protection of the environment, are once again not treated as discrete events requiring radically innovative legal regulation when they probably should be. But no society has ever acted in such manner to cope with new problems. Instead, international society, like other societies, conceives of these conditions as part of social dynamics to be integrated into the existing system and to be treated within the existing framework of established principles and norms. Yet sooner or later, international society has usually had to find some legal modus vivendi to deal with new conditions. This capacity is testimony to the flexibility of the international legal system and, to be Pollyannaish, to its stabilizing effect upon international society. This capacity is also testimony to the political adaptability of states, the result mostly of demands of national, rather than international, interests.

The consequent reduction in the substance of sovereignty is in principle not a new phenomenon. The present development is merely a continuation and expansion of the restraint upon sovereignty that states have always accepted as a necessary response to new needs originating in changes in international society. This development implies that the freedom of action of any state diminishes as contacts between states increase. The uneasiness of states about this situation was well expressed by a Burmese prime minister when he said he wished he had atomic scissors to cut his country off the Asian continent and ship it into some peaceful part of the Pacific Ocean!

The frequent talk about a "new international law" is justified only if it does not refer to basic principles of the legal order grounded on sovereignty. The reason for the widening scope of international law today is the same as it has always been: New circumstances in the life of humankind deriving from science, technology, changing values, and so on require international regulation when their effects cannot be contained within national borders.

Many new legal norms stemming from international politics and new conditions of human existence decrease the content of sovereignty but not its influence upon the integration of the innovations into the existing fundamental system. It is also true, however, that the widening scope of international law can increase the content of sovereignty. The "new" law of the sea subjects ever larger sections of the once free high seas to the sovereignty of states. The control of the environment remains, on the whole, under the sovereign authority of individual states. The same remains essentially true of the protection of human rights (with the apparent result that they are faring worse than ever before). The allocation of wavelengths for broadcasting from stationary satellites is dominated by the requirements of sovereign states. The NIEO aims at reordering the economic system to make sovereignty and independence of Third World states real, not to abolish them. In other respects—for instance, the Antarctic regime, the outer space regime, an international authority envisaged for the deep seabed, or moon exploitation—the "new" law amounts to a holding operation until activities can actually begin. In the meantime, the resources are the "common heritage of mankind," a concept that would exclude sovereignty but whose realization lies in the future. Enough has already been said, especially by those states most likely to be the exploiters of resources, to assume that the common heritage of mankind will fall victim to sovereign rights when the exploitation begins. In short, the "new" law refers to new subject matter needing regulation. But it renders obeisance to sovereignty, even while asking for cooperation in matters that can hardly be successfully handled in any other way.

Although changes in fundamentals are practically very rare, there are, as there have to be, reactions to new conditions going beyond limited subject matter. One change is a trend to increase or create responsibility of states—almost always by conventions—to the entire international society rather than only to particular states (for example, declaring certain crimes *erga omnes*, instituting liability for pollution affecting any part of the globe including pollution of the sea by oil, and making human rights an international concern). Another change is that restraints upon national behavior are positively desired—hence experienced as less onerous—for the satisfaction of national interests. That national interests require interaction adds a dimension to the significance and efficacy of international law. For in that case, national selfishness, mutuality of interests, and reciprocity become powerful motives for obedience to the law.

Obedience to law for selfish reasons, unsupported by any sense of loyalty to the society, probably does not replace the benefits of a sense of community among humankind. Such a sense would presumably help in the growth and maintenance of a universal legal system. But this sense is not indispensable for an adequately efficacious system. After all, the contemporary weakening within national communities resulting from the growing size and pluralism of states also tends to narrow a common value system—except nationalism—without necessarily destroying effective national legal systems. In turn, the argument could be made that the greater diversity in cultures and value systems in a growing international society with the simultaneous increasing volume of contacts enforces more rather than less obedience to international law as one means of survival.

At any rate, an alternative possibility for an effective international legal system exists. This possibility may lack the completeness and emotional support of a community base, yet it may be adequate for peaceful, orderly relationships among states. It must be remembered that states are in contact because their interests suggest, or even make it imperative, that they be (a situation increasingly replicated in large states where the interest, rather than the sentiment, nexus maintains the society). A multitude of transnational overlapping and crisscrossing interests could become a functional equivalent for a sentimental community. Law would be based upon the satisfaction derived from complementary behavior among states to satisfy interests and less upon the member states' loyalty to the international society or mutual trust.

The growing volume of international conventional and treaty law, especially in the areas of commerce, finance, communication, and environmental protection, is evidence that states relate on the basis of interests in which ideological and cultural differences play no greater role than when a customer buys a bottle of milk at the grocery store. This volume is, as even President Gorbachev recognized, also evidence that different national social systems are no barrier to utilitarian international relationships and their legal regulation. And this volume is evidence, finally, that states will obey legal norms if thereby the satisfaction of their interests is advanced. To quote Lenin: "There is a power bigger than the desire, will and decision of any of the hostile governments or classes; that power is the general world-wide interrelationship of economies which obliges them to take this [peaceful coexistence] path of intercourse with us."

The Communist states have learned that international law is a reality. Although ideology is a more prominent topic with them than elsewhere, they have on several occasions made exceptions to ideological requirements regarding international law in favor of "nonideological" concessions to the law in order to satisfy individual interests. Any formal infringement upon sovereignty, however, which they interpret very broadly, is adamantly rejected.

Most newer states have also abstained from translating their revolutionary fervor against international law into practice. On the contrary, they quickly became realists recognizing that contemporary states and their interrelations could not rest on ideologies, value systems, or religions peculiar to individual states. They were aware that the Western-produced legal system responded best to the goals and objectives that the new states took over from the older states, and so they accepted the bulk of the fundamental principles and norms of the international law they found at their birth.

But, like all states, the newer states are interpreting and using existing legal principles for the fulfillment of their political and economic purposes. They are insisting, therefore, that sovereign equality, independence, nonintervention, and other basic principles become realities in their case, too. For, they feel, the corruption of these principles made colonialism possible and permits some of its consequences to continue in some form even today. Rather than introducing "new" law, as they often claim, these states are accepting the bulk of existing principles but demanding that they are in fact applied. They are demanding, more especially, that the dichotomy between the norms and the reality be closed. If this is

done, they argue, as it has largely been in the area of political decolonization, it will also affect the economic sphere, in which traditional
law still hampers the development of the Third World states. Their
complaint is not so much about the legal systems' basic norms as it is
with some specific norms and the pro-Western interpretation and application of the entire system. The effort of newer states is therefore
directed toward the elimination of some specific rules enabling the older
states to exploit the newer states; toward the introduction of some, indeed
new, specific rules speeding their development (and expressed in the
NIEO); and, overall, toward a truly universal, just application of the
international legal system.

International law did not stand still until the Communist and Third
World states demanded "new" law. It has always reflected the changing
power structure and interests of states, primarily the dominating states.
The hardy survival of some major aspects of traditional customary law
(especially norms relating to sovereignty and its consequences) is due
mainly to the fact that its values are shared by all states, including the
newer and Communist states. The dynamism of the legal system has
always been expressed mainly by treaty law. The enormous rise in the
volume of such law now is due not to the arrival of new states but to
the rise of many new interests among states.

That international law is weak and inadequate is the result neither
of an unawareness of the need for it nor an unwillingness to obey it.
Nor is this weakness due to the variety of value systems among states.
The weakness of international law, like that of the international political
system on which the legal system depends, is primarily due to the
absence of the one interest that could almost by itself guarantee an
efficacious legal system: the interest among all states in maintaining the
welfare or at least the social order of international society as their
predominant social value. As such a value is growing, it will in all
likelihood serve the interest of individual states better than the almost
exclusive interest of these states in themselves.

The contemporary status of international law and especially the
direction of its future development show a general recognition that the
welfare of international society is important for the fulfillment of purely
national interests. For the time being, that recognition is reflected in
much rhetoric on the international scene and little practice. But rhetoric,
when forced by conditions, very often eventually turns into reality. When
states become convinced that support of one overarching interest in the
welfare of international society will facilitate fulfillment of interests now
leading states to interaction, states will be ready to create a political
and legal international system comparable to national systems in which
the efficacy of law is reliably assured.

CASES CITED

Full titles of books in which cases are found are given in the Selected Bibliography. Numbers in parentheses refer to pages in the text of this book. If a case is officially called "case concerning . . . " or something similar, the case is listed under the name of the parties. For cases called "United States v.," the name of the other party is listed first. When the page number of the case and the page of the volume in which the case appears differ, the volume page number is quoted. Citations from the Soviet press are taken from the *Current Digest of the Soviet Press.*

Abu Dhabi Award (Petroleum Development Ltd. v. Sheikh of Abu Dhabi), Int. & Comp. L. Q. 1 (April 1952):247–261 (123)

Access to or Anchorage in the Port of Danzig of Polish War Vessels, PCIJ Ser. A/ B 43 (1931):128–164 (210)

Acquisition of Polish Nationality, PCIJ Ser. B 7 (1923):1–26 (210)

Administrative Decision V, UN Reports 7, 119–155 (166)

Agency of Canadian Car and Foundry Co. United States v. Germany, Hackworth, *Digest of International Law* 5 (1943):833–837 (228)

Alabama Claims, United States–Great Britain Arbitration, Papers Relating to the Treaty of Washington 4 (1872):49–544 (225)

Aldona S. v. United Kingdom, Leech, *International Legal System,* 306–308 (71)

Al-Fin Corporation's Patent, In re, Leech, *International Legal System,* 756–761 (113)

Alfred Dunhill of London v. Republic of Cuba, 425 *US Reports* 682 (27)

Aluminum Company of American et al., United States v., 148 F. 2d. 416 (1945) (145)

Amoco International Finance Corp. v. Islamic Republic of Iran, U.S. Claims Tribunal, 27 *ILM* (1988):1314–1405 (227)

Anna, Dickinson, *A Selection,* 334–336 (129)

Antelope, 10 Wheaton *US Reports* 66 (19, 82, 239)

Application of the Convention of 1902 Governing the Guardianship of Infants (the Boll Case) Netherlands v. Sweden, Case Concerning the, ICJ (1958):55–73 (30, 32)

Arantzazu Mendi, ILR 41 (1970):18 (28)

Baker v. Carr, 369 *US Reports* 186 (28)

Baker, U.S. v., 609 F. 2d. 133 (1980) (121)

Banco Nacional de Cuba v. Chase Manhattan Bank, 658 F. 2d. 875 (1981) (27)
Banco Nacional de Cuba v. Sabbatino, 376 US Reports 398 (26, 27, 28, 175, 274, 279)
Bank of China v. Wells Fargo Bank and Union Trust Co., 104 F. Supp. 59 (1952) (29)
Barcelona Traction, Light, and Power Co. Ltd. (Judgment), ICJ (1970): 3–357 (40, 47, 170, 216, 222) (New Application) (1962) (72)
Boffolo, Jackson H. Ralston, *Venezuelan Arbitrations of 1903*, Senate Document 316, 58th Cong. 2nd sess. (Washington, DC: Government Printing Office, 1904), 696 (168)
Boll Case; see *Application of the Convention of 1902*
Brazilian Loans, Case of the; see *Payment in Gold of the Brazilian Federal Loans*
Broadbent v. Organization of American States, 628 F. 2d 27 (1980) (151)
Burthe v. Denis, 133 US Reports 514 (228)

Caccamese, ILR 22 (1955):338–240 (228)
Caire, Jean-Baptiste (France and Mexico), Ann. Dig. 5 (1929–1930):146–148 (224)
Canevaro, Case (Italy v. Peru) 1912, Scott, *Hague Court Reports* (1916):284–296 (228)
Cantero Herrera v. Canevaro & Co., Ann. Dig. 4 (1927–1928):219–222 (19)
Caroline, Moore, *Arbitrations* II (1906):409–414 (300, 304, 315)
Castioni In re, Dickinson, *Cases and Materials*, 488–494 (179)
Cayuga Indians Arbitration (Great Britain v. United States), Nielsen, *American and British Claims Arbitration* (40)
Certain Expenses of the United Nations, Article 17 Paragraph 2 of the Charter, ICJ (1962):151–308 (68, 211, 248, 285)
Certain Norwegian Loans (France v. Norway), Case of ICJ (1957):9–100 (229, 286)
Chamizal, AJIL 5 (July 1911):785–833 (131)
Chattin (United States) v. United Mexican States, AJIL 22 (July 1928):667–682 (171, 223)
China Mutual Trading Co. v. American President Lines, Hong Kong Supreme Court (1953), AJIL 47 (October 1953):721 (314)
Chorzów; see *Factory at Chorzów*
Church v. Hubbard, 2 Cranch 6 U.S. Reports 187 (121, 305)
Clipperton Island (France and Mexico), AJIL 26 (April 1932):390–394 (130)
Collision with Foreign Government-Owned Motor Car, ILR 40 (1970):73–98 (19)
Competence of the General Assembly for the Admission of a State to the United Nations ICJ (1950):4–57 (210)
Competence of the International Labor Organization to Regulate, Incidentally, the Personal Work of the Employer, PCIJ Ser. B. 13 (1926):7–26 (210)
Competence of the International Labor Organization with Respect to Agricultural Labor, PCIJ Ser. B 2/3 (1922):6–61 (210)
Conditions of Admission of a State to the United Nations, ICJ (1948):57–119 (210)
Continental Shelf (Libyan Arab Jamahiriya/Malta) (Judgment), Case Concerning 24 ILM (1985):1189–1276 (42, 137)

Continental Shelf (Tunisia/Libyan Arab Jamahiriya) Judgment, 21 ILM (1982): 225–
    317 (41)
Corfu Channel Case (Great Britain v. Albania), ICJ (1949):4–169 (39, 88, 195, 216,
    217, 218, 305)
Customs Regime Between Germany and Austria, PCIJ Ser. A/B 41 (1931):37–54
    (81)
Cutting Case, Dickinson, *Cases and Materials*, 404 (145)

*Delimitation of the Maritime Boundary Between Guinea and Guinea-Bissau, Dispute
    Concerning*, 25 ILM (1986):251–307 (42)
*Delimitation of the Maritime Boundary in the Gulf of Maine Area (Canada/United
    States of America), Case Concerning the*, ICJ (1984):245–352 (37, 42, 133)
Dickson Car Wheel Co. (U.S.) v. United Mexican States, UN Reports 4, 669–691
    (197)
Diggs v. Schultz, 470 F. 2d. 461 (1972) (24)
Diplomatic and Consular Staff in Teheran (U.S.A. v. Iran), ICJ (1980):33–34 (223)
Diversion of Water from the Meuse (Judgment), PCIJ Ser. B 5 (41)

Eastern Carelia, Status of, PCIJ Ser. B 5 (1923):1–29 (274, 285)
Eastern Greenland, Legal Status of, PCIJ Ser. A/B 53 (1933):22–75 (95, 130, 196)
Eck v. United Arab Airlines, 360 F. 2d. 804 (211)
Effects of Awards of Compensation Made by the U.N. Administrative Tribunal, ICJ
    (1954):47–63 (68)

Factory at Chorzów, Case Concerning (Jurisdiction), PCIJ Ser. A 9 (1927):5–34 (39,
    41, 209, 210, 216, 226)
Filartiga v. Peña-Irala, 630 F. 2d, 876 (1980) (16, 25, 48, 90, 147, 148)
Finnish Vessels in Great Britain During the War, Ann. Dig. 7 (1933–1934):231–241
    (229)
First National City Bank v. Banco Nacional de Cuba, 406 US Reports 759 (42B)
    (27)
Fisheries Case (United Kingdom v. Norway); see *Norwegian Fisheries*
Fisheries Jurisdiction Case (United Kingdom . . . v. Iceland) (Merits, Judgment), ICJ
    (1974):3–251 (32, 47, 122, 137, 204, 213)
Florida Bonds, Moore, *Arbitrations* 4 (1898):3594–3616 (224)
F. W. Stone Engineering Co. v. Petroleos Mexicanos, Leech, *International Legal
    System*, 389–390 (28)

Gelbtrunk, Rosa, AJIL 21 (April 1927):357–361 (225)
Gentini (Italy v. Venezuela), Jackson H. Ralston, *Venezuelan Arbitrations of 1903*,
    Senate Document 316, 58th Cong. 2d Sess. (Washington, D.C. Government
    Printing Office, 1904):720–730 (200)
German Interests in Polish Upper Silesia, Case Concerning Certain (Merits), PCIJ
    Ser. A 7 (1926):5–76 (25, 174)
German Settlers in Poland, PCIJ Ser. B 6 (1923):6–43 (278)
Goa Case; see *Right of Passage*

Legal Status of Eastern Greenland; see Eastern Greenland
Lehigh Valley Railroad Co., v. State of Russia, 21 F. 2d. 396 (1927) (67)
Letelier v. Republic of Chile, 488 F. Supp. 665 (1980); 748 F. 2d. 790 (1984) (27, 148, 151)
Lighthouses Case Between France and Greece, PCIJ Ser. A/B 62 (1934):4–29 (210)
Lighthouses in Crete and Samos, PCIJ Ser. A/B 71 (1937):94–106 (108)
Lola, the S.S., 175 US Reports 677 (35, 51)
Lotus, the S.S., PCIJ Ser. A 9 (1927):4–33 (22, 37, 118, 127, 143, 144, 145, 151, 153, 210, 211)

Mackin, United States v., 668 F. 2d. 122 (1981) (179)
Marino-Garcia, United States v., 679 F. 2d., 1373 (1982) (148, 152)
Mavrommatis Palestine Concession (Jurisdiction), PCIJ Ser. A 2 (1924):7–37 (73, 166, 275)
Mendaro v. The World Bank, 717 F. 2d 610 (1983) (151)
Military and Paramilitary Activities in and Against Nicaragua (Nicaragua v. United States of America) (Jurisdiction) (1984) and *(Merits, Judgment)* (1986); see *Nicaragua*
Minquiers and Ecréhous, ICJ (1953):47–109 (200)
Mortensen v. Peters, Dickinson, A Selection, 65–74 (23)

Namibia (South-West Africa) (Advisory Opinion); see Legal Consequences . . .
Nationality Decrees Issued in Tunis and Morocco, PCIJ Ser. B 4 (1923):6–32 (85, 140, 144)
Naulilaa Incident Arbitration, UN Reports 2, 1011–1033 (298)
Neer and Neer (United States) v. United Mexican States, Ann. Dig. 3 (1925–1926):213–214 (171)
New York & Cuba Mail v. Republic of Korea, 132 F. Supp. 684 (1955) (28)
Nicaragua (Jurisdiction) (1984), 24 ILM (1985):59–181 (286)
Nicaragua (Merits, Judgment) (1986), 25 ILM (1986):1023–1091 (37, 38, 85, 86, 87, 93, 184, 202, 216, 273, 286, 288, 295, 303, 315)
Nishimura Ekiu v. United States, 142 US Reports, 651–664 (167)
N. K. v. Austria, ILR 77 (1979):472 (223)
North Atlantic Coast Fisheries Arbitration, Scott, Hague Court Reports (1916):141 (17, 133)
North American Dredging Co. of Texas (United States) v. United Mexican States, AJIL 20 (October 1926):800–810 (221)
North Sea Continental Shelf Cases (Federal Republic of Germany/Denmark; Federal Republic of Germany/Netherlands), ICJ (1969):3–257 (34, 35, 123, 278)
Norwegian Claims, Scott, Hague Court Reports, 2d ser. (1932):39–82 (226)
Norwegian Fisheries (United Kingdom v. Norway), ICJ (1951):116–206 (36, 134, 135, 196, 200)
Nottebohm (Liechtenstein v. Guatemala) (Second Phase) (Judgment), ICJ (1955):4–65 (139, 140, 228)
Nuclear Test Cases (Australia v. France) (New Zealand v. France), ICJ (1974):253–274 (199, 286)

Strassheim v. Daily, 211 *US Reports* 280 (146)

Tel-Oren [Hanoch] v. Libyan Arab Republic, 726 F. 2d. 774 (1984) (26, 90, 148)
Temple of Preah Vihear (Cambodia v. Thailand), Case Concerning the (Merits), ICJ (1962):6–146 (131, 196)
Territorial Jurisdiction of the International Commission of the River Oder, Case Concerning, PCIJ Ser. A 23 (1929):5–32 (209)
Texaco v. Libyan Republic. 17 *ILM* (1978):1–37(71)
Tinoco Claims Arbitration, Ann. Dig. 2 (1923–1924):34–39 (112)
Trail Smelter Arbitration (United States–Canada), AJIL 35 (October 1941): 684–736 (217, 264, 265)
Trojanos v. Marcos, July 18, 1986, U.S. District Court, Hawaii (148)

Underhill v. Herandez,, 168 *US Reports* 250 (26)
United Kingdom and France (Merits) Arbitration on the Delimitation of the Continental Shelf (1977), 18 *ILM* (1979):397–494 (40)
United Kingdom v. Norway; see *Norwegian Fisheries*
United States v.; see names of parties
United States Diplomatic and Consular Staff; see *Diplomatic and Consular Staff*

Verlinden v. Central Bank of Nigeria, 20 *ILM* (1981):639–649; 22 *ILM* (1983):647–657 (151)
Victory Transport Inc. v. Comisaria General de Abastecimientos y Transportes, 336 F. 2d. 354 (1964) (71)

West Rand Central Gold Mining Co. v. the King, Dickinson, *Cases and Materials*, 298–303 (24)
Wildenhus's Case, 120 *US Reports* 1 (128)
William E. Chapman (United States) v. Mexico Claims, AJIL 25 (July 1931):544–553 (173)
Williams, United States v., 617 F. 2d. 1063 (1980) (152)
Wimbledon, the S.S., PCIJ Ser. A 1 (1923):6–47 (91,·216, 228)

Youman's Claim, AJIL 21 (July 1927):571–579 (224)

SELECTED BIBLIOGRAPHY

Decisions and Awards

Hambro, Edvard. *The Case Law of the International Court*, 7 vols. Leiden: A. W. Sijthoff, 1952–1972.

Hudson, Manley O. *World Court Reports, 1922–1944*, 4 vols. Washington, DC: Carnegie Endowment for International Peace, 1934–1943.

International Court of Justice. *Reports of Judgments, Advisory Opinions and Orders.* Annual (1947–   ).

Nielsen, Fred K., reporter. *American and British Claims Arbitration*, under Agreement of 18 August 1910. Washington, DC: GPO, 1926.

Permanent Court of International Justice. *Ser. A. Judgments and Orders* (1922–1930); *Ser. B. Advisory Opinions* (1922–1930); *Ser. A/B. Judgments, Orders, and Advisory Opinions* (1931–1940).

Scott, J. B. *The Hague Court Reports*, 2 vols. (1916); 2d ser. (1932). New York: Oxford University Press.

United Nations, *Reports of International Arbitral Awards* (1948–   ).

United States, Department of State, Claims Commission, United States and Mexico. *Opinions of Commissioners Under the Convention Concluded September 8, 1923*, 3 vols. (1927, 1929, 1931). Washington, DC: GPO.

Digest of Cases

Annual Digest of Public International Law Cases, vols. 1–6. *Annual Digest and Reports of Public International Law Cases*, vols. 7–16. *International Law Reports* vols. 17–   . Edited by Hersch Lauterpacht, E. Lauterpacht, Arnold D. McNair, et al. London: Longmans, Green, 1932–1937; Butterworth, 1938–   .

Boyd, John A. *Digest of United States Practice in International Law*. Washington, DC: GPO, 1977.

Deak, Francis, and Frank Ruddy, eds. *American International Law Cases*, 17 vols. (1971–1977). Dobbs Ferry, NY: Oceana.

Digest of International Law or *Digest of United States Practice in International Law*. See under names of authors in this section.

Hackworth, Green H. *Digest of International Law* (1940–1944). Washington, DC: GPO.

*International Law Reports, 1950–   *. See *Annual Digest*.

Kiss, Alexandre-Charles. *Répertoire de la pratique française en matière de droit international public* (1962–1972). Paris: Editions du Centre National de la Recherche Scientifique.

Leich, Marian N. *Digest of United States Practice in International Law* (1978–). Washington, DC: GPO.

McDowell, Eleanor C. *Digest of United States Practice in International Law.* Washington, DC: GPO, 1975–1976.

Moore, John B. *History and Digest of International Arbitration to Which the United States Has Been a Party,* 6 vols. Washington, DC: GPO, 1898.

———. *A Digest of International Law,* 8 vols. Washington, DC: GPO, 1906.

Parry, Clive E., ed. *A British Digest of International Law.* (1965–). London: Stevens.

Pradelle, A. de la, N. Politis, and André Salomon. *Recueil des arbitrages internationaux,* 2nd ed., 3 vols. (1954–1957). Paris: Editions Internationales.

Rovine, Arthur W. *Digest of United States Practice in International Law.* Washington, DC: GPO, 1973–1974.

Stuyt, A. M. *Survey of International Arbitrations, 1794–1970.* Dobbs Ferry, NY: Oceana, 1972.

Syatauw, J.J.G. *Decisions of the International Court of Justice.* Leiden: A. W. Sijthoff, 1969.

Whiteman, Marjorie M. *Digest of International Law.* Washington, DC: GPO, 1963–1970.

Collections of Cases and Materials

American Society of International Law. *International Legal Materials.* Washington, DC: American Society of International Law, quarterly.

Bishop, William W. Jr. *International Law Cases and Materials,* 3rd ed. Boston: Little, Brown, 1971.

Briggs, Herbert W. *The Law of Nations: Cases, Documents, and Notes,* 2nd ed. New York: Appleton-Century-Crofts, 1952.

Collins, Edward, Jr. *International Law in a Changing World: Cases, Documents and Readings.* New York: Random House, 1970.

Dickinson, E. D. *A Selection of Cases and Other Readings on the Law of Nations.* New York: McGraw-Hill, 1929.

———. *Cases and Materials on International Law.* Brooklyn: Foundation Press, 1950.

Friedmann, Wolfgang, O. Lissitzyn, and R. C. Pugh. *International Law Cases and Materials.* St. Paul: West, 1969.

Green, Leslie C. *International Law Through the Cases.* Dobbs Ferry, NY: Oceana, 1970.

Harris, D. J. *Cases and Materials on International Law,* 3rd ed. London: Sweet and Maxwell, 1983.

Henkin, Louis, R. C. Pugh, O. Schachter, and H. Smit. *International Law Cases and Materials,* 2nd ed. St. Paul: West, 1987.

Hudson, Manley O. *Cases and Other Materials on International Law*, 3rd ed. St. Paul: West, 1951.

Leech, Noyes E., C. T. Oliver, and J. M. Sweeney. *The International Legal System Cases and Materials*. Mineola, NY: Foundation Press, 1973.

Orfield, L. B., and E. D. Re. *Cases and Materials on International Law*, rev. ed. Indianapolis: Bobbs-Merrill, 1965.

Sohn, Louis B. *Cases and Other Materials on World Law*. Brooklyn: Foundation Press, 1950. *Supplement*, 1953.

Steiner, Henry J., and D. F. Vagts. *Transnational Legal Problems*, 3rd ed. Mineola, NY: Foundation Press, 1986.

Sweeney, Joseph M. et al. *The International Legal System: Cases and Materials*, 3rd ed. Westbury, NY: Foundation Press, 1988.

Weston, Burns H., Richard A. Falk, and A. A. D'Amato. *International Law and World Order*, 2nd ed. St. Paul: West, 1990.

Surveys of International Law

Academy of Sciences of the USSR, Institute of State and Law. *International Law*. Moscow: Foreign Languages Publishing House, n.d.

Akehurst, Michael. *A Modern Introduction to International Law*. 5th ed. London: Allen and Unwin, 1984.

American Law Institute. *The Restatement of the Law, Second, Foreign Relations Law of the United States, 1965*. St. Paul: American Law Institute Publishers, 1965.

———. *Restatement of the Law Third, The Foreign Relations Law of the United States, 1987*. St. Paul: American Law Institute Publishers, 1987.

Bledsoe, Robert L., and Boczek, Boledav A. *The International Law Dictionary*. Santa Barbara, CA: ABC-Clio, 1987.

Brierly, J. L. (Humphrey Waldock, ed.) *The Law of Nations*, 6th ed. New York: Oxford University Press, 1963.

Brownlie, Ian. *Principles of Public International Law*, 3rd ed. Oxford: Clarendon, 1979.

Buergenthal, Thomas, and Harold G. Maier. *Public International Law in a Nutshell*, 2nd ed. St. Paul: West, 1990.

Cassese, Antonio. *International Law in a Divided World*. Oxford: Clarendon, 1986.

Chandra, Prakash. *International Law*. Delhi: Vikas, 1985.

Chen, Lung-chu. *An Introduction to Contemporary International Law: A Policy Oriented Perspective*. New Haven, CT: Yale University Press, 1989.

Cheng, Bin, and F. D. Brown, eds. *Contemporary Problems of International Law*. London: Stevens, 1988.

Cohen, Jerome A., and Hungdah Chin. *People's China and International Law: A Documentary Study*. Princeton, NJ: Princeton University Press, 1974.

Dinstein, Yoram, ed. *International Law at a Time of Perplexity*. Dordrecht: Martinus Nijhoff, 1989.

Falk, Richard A., Friedrich Kratacheril, and Saul H. Mendlovitz. *International Law: A Contemporary Perspective*. Boulder, CO: Westview, 1985.

Giuliano, Mario. *Diritto internazionale.* Milano: A Giuffré, 1974.

Glahn, Gerhard von. *Law Among Nations,* 5th ed. New York: Macmillan, 1986.

Green, N. A. Maryan. *International Law.* London: Macdonald and Evans, 1973.

Hingoram, R. C. *Modern International Law,* 2nd ed. New York: Oceana, 1984.

Hsiung, James C. *Law and Policy in China's Foreign Relations.* New York: Columbia University Press. 1972.

Janis, Mark W. *An Introduction to International Law.* Boston: Little, Brown, 1987.

Jankovic, Branimir M. *Public International Law.* Dobbs Ferry, NY: Transnational, 1983.

Kaminski, Gerd. *Chinesische Positionen zum Völkerrecht.* Berlin: Duncker und Humblot, 1973.

Kaplan, Morton A., and Nicholas deB. Katzenbach. *The Political Foundations of International Law.* New York: Wiley, 1961.

Kelsen, Hans (Robert W. Tucker, ed.). *Principles of International Law,* 2nd ed. New York: Holt, Rinehart & Winston, 1966.

Kröger, Herbert, ed. *Völkerrecht,* 2 vols. Berlin: Staatsverlag der Deutschen Demokratischen Republik, 1973.

Macdonald, R. St. J, Gerald L. Morris, and Douglas M. Johnston. *Canadian Perspective on International Law and Organization.* Toronto: Toronto University Press, 1974.

Maris, Gary L. *International Law: An Introduction.* Lanham, NY: University Press of America, 1984.

Monaco, Ricardo. *Manuale di diritto internazionale publico,* 2nd ed. Torino: Unione Tipografica, 1971.

O'Connell, D. P. *International Law,* 2nd ed., 2 vols. Dobbs Ferry, NY: Oceana, 1970.

————, ed. *International Law in Australia.* Sydney: Law Book, 1965.

Oppenheim, Lassa F. L. (Hersch Lauterpacht, ed.) *International Law* (vol. 1, 8th ed., 1955; vol. 2, 7th ed., 1952). London: Longmans Green.

Parry, Clive, and John P. Grant, eds. *Parry and Grant Encyclopaedia of International Law.* New York: Oceana, 1986.

Rousseau, Charles. *Droit international public,* 11th ed. Paris: Dalloz, 1987.

Schwarzenberger, Georg, and E. D. Brown. *A Manual of International Law,* 6th ed. South Hackensack, NJ: Fred B. Rothman, 1976.

Seidl-Hohenveldern, Ignaz von. *Völkerrecht,* 6th ed. Cologne: Carl Heymann, 1987.

Sereni, Angelo P. *Diritto internazionale.* Milano: A. Giuffré, 1956–1965.

Shaw, Malcolm N. *International Law.* Cambridge: Grotius, 1986.

Slomanson, William R. *Fundamental Perspectives on International Law.* St. Paul: West, 1990.

Sørensen, Max, ed. *Manual of Public International Law,* 2 vols. New York: St. Martin's, 1968.

Starke, Joseph G. *An Introduction to International Law,* 9th ed. London: Butterworth, 1984.

Strupp-Schlochauer. *Wörterbuch des Völkerrechts,* 3 vols. (1960–1962). Berlin: Walter de Gruyter.

Tunkin, Grigory. *Theory of International Law.* Cambridge, MA: Harvard University Press, 1974.

———— . *International Law.* Moscow: Progress Publishers, 1986.

Verdross, Alfred, and Bruno Simma. *Universelles Völkerrecht,* 3rd ed. Vienna: Springer, 1984.

Visscher, Charles de. *Theory and Reality in International Public Law,* rev. ed. Princeton, NJ: Princeton University Press, 1968.

Wallace, Rebecca M.M. *International Law.* London: Sweet and Maxwell, 1986.

ABOUT THE BOOK
AND AUTHOR

The second edition of this classic text has been fully revised and updated to reflect the most recent developments in world affairs. A new chapter on environmental protection, updated coverage of the law of the sea, new views on outer space law, and expanded coverage of human rights and political and economic cooperation form the cornerstone of this revision.

The spectacular events in Eastern Europe and China over the past year highlight the dynamic and interdependent character of international law. Levi puts these events in context as he elucidates Gorbachev's pronouncements on political cooperation and the primacy of international law or examines the U.S. invasion of Panama in regard to the sovereign immunity of states. Examples of similar events of global legal concern—from Nelson Mandela's dramatic release to the war on international drug traffic—are liberally distributed throughout the revised edition.

Levi emphasizes the political dimension of international law over a legalistic, case law approach—but cases are not neglected, as over two hundred references to specific decisions are cited in the text. Other features directed to the political science student of international law include part-by-part bibliographies organized by subject, a complete appendix of cases cited, and a general bibliography including digests of cases, casebooks, and surveys of international law.

Werner Levi teaches as a professor emeritus of political science at the University of Hawaii at Manoa. His previous publications include *From Alms to Liberation: The Catholic Church, the Theologians, Poverty, and Politics* (1989); *The Coming End of War* (1981); *Law and Politics in the International Society* (1976); and *International Politics: Foundations of the System* (1974).

INDEX